HUMBOLDT REDWOODS STATE PARK

The Fight
to Save the Redwoods

The Avenue of the Giants near Dyerville ca. 1920. The use of light in this photograph makes it an excellent example of the early emphasis on the qualities of mystery and religious inspiration associated with the redwoods. This photographic style contrasts with modern interpretations of the redwoods. (See figure 5.) Photo by Gabriel Moulin. Courtesy of Moulin Studios.

The Fight
to Save the Redwoods

A History of Environmental
Reform
1917–1978

Susan R. Schrepfer

The University of Wisconsin Press

Published 1983

The University of Wisconsin Press
114 North Murray Street
Madison, Wisconsin 53715

The University of Wisconsin Press, Ltd.
1 Gower Street
London WC1E 6HA, England

First printing

Printed in the United States of America

For LC CIP information see the colophon

ISBN 0-299-08850-2

To John Tarter

CONTENTS

LIST OF ILLUSTRATIONS

LIST OF MAPS

PREFACE

PERHAPS SENSING an old vulnerability in the "forests of the night," twentieth-century man shivers in the misty recesses of the redwoods. These are ancient trees, some as much as two thousand years old and towering over 350 feet. The armies of trees that J. R. R. Tolkien marched across the hills of Middle-earth might well have been redwoods, for few sylvan families have traveled further or longer. They are descendants of species that once covered the world. How different Kansas and Alaska were when these moisture-laden, temperate forests grew there fifty million years ago, before the cooling of the earth and the shifting of the land forced them south. The last wave of glaciation pursued the European trees to extinction and spared only a few of the Asian Dawn Redwoods, or *Metasequoia*. On the continental margin of western North America, two slivers of redwood forests remained: the *Sequoia-dendron gigantea*, or Big Trees of the Sierra Nevada; and the *Sequoia sempervirens*, or coastal redwoods. The latter is the subject of this work.

When the first Europeans settled *Alta California* in the eighteenth century, the coastal redwoods grew—as they had during the twenty million years since the ice—in a bank that followed the Pacific Ocean from the Santa Lucia Mountains in Monterey County northward the length of California to a point a few miles within the Oregon border. Beneath the graceful trees of this rain forest grew flowering azaleas, scarlet rhododendrons, shadowed ferns, and carpets of sorrel. For all its beauty, this was a dark wilderness, the lushness of its understory difficult to penetrate. The Spanish left wild its two million acres.

The repose of the Hispanic frontier was finally broken in the 1840s, as enterprising Yankees swarmed west. Walt Whitman heard the ensuing decades as "a chorus of dryads, fading, departing" while the "mighty, dying" redwood bade "farewell." The trees built the San Francisco of the Forty-niners, propped the new state's vineyards, and bound it by rail to the rest of the nation. In the 1870s Asa Gray declared that the *Sequoia*, with its great longevity, proved the theory of evolution. Some thirty years later, naturalist John Muir pleaded for the preservation of these godly creations. Theodore Roosevelt added his voice to the cause. By that time the East Bay redwoods were gone, and only a few groves remained south of San Francisco. The woods of Humboldt and Del Norte counties were untouched, but the federal General Land Office had sold or granted them to lumbermen and speculators.

A sustained effort to buy back these redwoods for the public began in 1918 when the Save-the-Redwoods League held its first meeting in San Francisco's Palace Hotel. For the next sixty years, this organization and the Sierra Club pitted their vigor as fund raisers, negotiators, politicians, and publicists against the enterprise of the loggers in a race for the old trees. The race is now largely over. Its history is an interesting, often tragic story in its own right—and one that explains much about the present landscape of California's northern coast. The chapters that follow, however, are primarily an effort to describe the sixty-year redwood preservation campaign in the context of scientific change and American social reform— from the progressive years of the early twentieth century to the militant protest movements of the past quarter century.

Decade by decade, the old redwoods have fallen. Today few remain beyond that 4 or so percent of the original stand preserved in public parks. This is the history of the individuals who saved these trees.

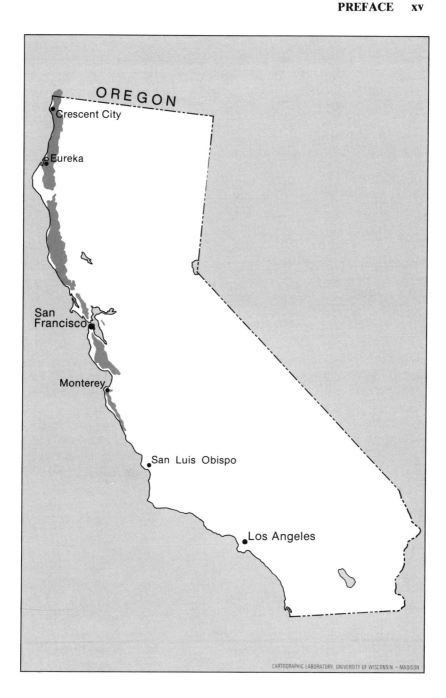

Map 1. Original belt of the *Sequoia sempervirens* redwoods

ACKNOWLEDGMENTS

DURING THE years spent working on this manuscript, both in California and the East, I accumulated debts requiring acknowledgment. Many of those active in environmental issues and the redwood controversy gave invaluable information, helped sharpen my analysis, and criticized the manuscript. I want to thank particularly David R. Brower, John B. Dewitt, Newton B. Drury, Richard M. Leonard, and Michael McCloskey. Had not the Save-the-Redwoods League and the Sierra Club freely opened their records, this study would not have been possible.

For guidance through various extensive collections, I am obliged to librarians at the Bancroft Library of the University of California, the University of Arizona, the Lyndon B. Johnson Presidential Library, Rutgers University, the Library of Congress, the National Archives, and the Sierra Club's Colby Library.

Among friends and colleagues whose encouragement and comments I gratefully received were Jim Chapin, Richard C. Davis, Lawrence McLaughlin, James Reed, Harold K. Steen, and Judith Steen. Parts of the book benefitted from critical reading by Ivan Doig, Robert V. Hine, and Donald Swain. As interviewers and chairmen of the Sierra's Club's History Committee, Ann and Ray Lage facilitated this work. The general support of Willa Baum and Amelia Fry Davis meant a great deal to me. With skill and forbearance June Johnson helped in the preparation of the manuscript. The Research Council of Rutgers University contributed financially. The editor of the *Journal of Forest History* kindly granted permission to use ideas and material that previously appeared in the April 1980 issue under the title, "Conflict in Preservation: The Sierra Club, Save-the-Redwoods League, and Redwood National Park."

I thank, too, my parents, Rita and Robert Schrepfer, and my brother

Steven whose moral and material support has sustained me in the long research effort. Above all, I am indebted to my husband, John Tarter, who contributed to every stage of this project, from the initial conceptualization and research to the final composition.

The Fight
to Save the Redwoods

1
Progressives and Scenic Preservation

ON AN August afternoon in 1917, three men drove north from San Francisco in search of "a forest wall reported to have mystery and charm unique among living works of creation." Madison Grant, Henry Fairfield Osborn, and John Campbell Merriam left from the Russian River in Sonoma County to camp in the northern redwoods, made accessible that year by a new highway. The trio had first swung west to the Pacific Ocean and followed the coastline to Fort Bragg. Below Shelter Cove they crossed inland over low coastal mountains and descended into the valley of the South Fork of the Eel River. They turned north on the dusty new highway as it followed the South Fork over hilly, wooded terrain. Merriam said of this stretch, "Dark masses of fir gave place now and then to redwood, or a patch of ripened grass-land rested like a golden brooch in the deep green velvet of the forest."[1]

Soon they were in dense forest. A few miles above the junction of the South Fork and the main Eel River, they turned south into the valley of Bull Creek. They left the highway and "dropped down a steep slope into primeval redwood timber," their car quietly rolling over the "leafy carpet." Merriam recalled how the three proceeded on foot, as the "shade deepened into twilight." Between close-set trunks, they looked as if "through windows framed in shadow, often darkening till all detail disappeared."[2]

Their dismay that none of the groves they would visit were in public ownership grew as sounds of logging filtered into their camp. They resolved to rescue Bull Creek.[3] Their decision can only be fully understood in the context of these scientists' lives, the trees' unique character, and the emergence of the preservation movement.

A distinguished-looking, middle-aged New York patrician of "strong impulse," Madison Grant was the product of eastern prep schools and colleges. Trained as a lawyer, he had inherited wealth that allowed him to be an amateur natural scientist and to help found the New York Zoological Society, the American Bison Society, and the Boone and Crockett Club. The second edition of his popular book *The Passing of the Great Race* had recently come off the press. In it he predicted the extinction of the Nordic race through interbreeding with what he saw as inferior stock.[4]

Figure 1. Redwoods in the Eel River area, the Devil's Elbow Curve, June, 1919. The recently graded Highway 101 as it wound through the redwoods near the Eel River. Photo by Edward Ayer. From the Edward Ayer Collection. Courtesy of the Save-the-Redwoods League.

Educated under Thomas Henry Huxley in London and Francis Balfour at Cambridge, Henry Fairfield Osborn had returned to teach at Columbia University in 1880 as a young comparative anatomist.

In 1917 he was sixty; by then, as curator and collector, he had made the New York Museum of Natural History a great repository of fossils and pioneered the use of lifelike fossil displays. His books and articles popularized Darwinian theories of evolution, from their paleontological evidences to their religious implications.[5]

John Campbell Merriam had attended a small Presbyterian college in his home state of Iowa, after which he took his doctorate in paleontology at the University of Munich. In the mid-1890s he began teaching at the Berkeley campus of the University of California and spent the next years uncovering traces of the Pacific Coast's prehistoric past.[6] By 1917 he had related western invertebrate and paleobotanical evidence to a stratified geologic column. This enabled him to place the natural history of the West Coast within the world pattern of evolution.[7] As he aged, however, Merriam thought increasingly about the philosophic import of Darwinian evolution.[8] He was a sober man who in 1917 was simultaneously involved in the defense work of World War I and in efforts to establish international understanding. This summer venture was a brief retreat from worldly cares into a forest of beauty and evolutionary significance.

Although in 1917 much remained to be learned about the redwoods, the United States Forest Service had confirmed the tree's longevity, now known to be as much as two thousand years. It was, however, the history of the species that interested scientists. Fifty million years earlier, redwoods had grown throughout the present United States. Twenty million years before, the tree had withdrawn to form its still-existing narrow belt along the Pacific Coast from Monterey Bay to the Oregon border.[9] Merriam later recalled his first moments in the redwoods that August: "In swift panorama the history of these trees . . . passed before me, stage after stage from the remote past."[10]

Cast in elusive light, these sylvan giants lent themselves to such imaginings. Older redwoods are 16 feet or more in diameter and 100 to over 360 feet tall. Grant correctly prophesied that the tallest known living things on earth would one day be found in either Bull Creek Flat or along nearby Redwood Creek. The tree is massive yet graceful. Its delicate foliage consists of narrow needles one-half to three-quarters of an inch long and arranged in a flat spray. Branches grow only on the upper reaches of the mature shaft, so that in an old forest the fluted, red-brown trunks are not softened by foliage. Osborn spoke of such a place as "consisting of long aisles between . . . giant columns of the trees." Above, the sky is screened by lacy branches. Below, smaller vegetation is "patterned with shifting mosaics of sun and shadow."[11]

The winter rains of northern California only partially fulfill the redwoods' need for abundant water, so the conifers now grow exclusively where summer fogs sweep in off the Pacific Ocean. An old woodsman explained this dependence to a visitor in 1901:

"Surely the fog is clearing away—lifting or dissipating under the influence of the rising sun," I ventured to say. . . .

"The trees is drinkin' it," shouts John, from his place at the head of the caravan. . . . "That's whut they live on mostly. When they git down breakfast you'll get warm enough."[12]

Grant later concurred: "in summer it is hard often times to tell whether it is raining or not, so saturated with moisture are the foliage and the trunks. . . ."[13]

Slope groves support a tangled understory of lush green shrubs—from dogwood, California huckleberry, and the dreaded poison oak to the vivid flowering azalea and rhododendron. The vegetation is more subdued in the rich bottom lands of the river basin, where the redwood reaches fullest fruition and blocks out sunshine. Here the flat, shadowy floor is covered with fallen needles and branches through which grow such small flowering plants as the white-blossomed sorrel and ferns in great variety. For millions of years, this understory has moved with the redwood across the North American continent.

A dim perception of this evolutionary past triggered the interest of the scientists in 1917. Their involvement was part of America's transition from a frontier society into an urban, bureaucratic nation in which scientists and professional land managers assumed an increasing role in land-use decisions.

One need only step back into the nineteenth century to perceive this shift. Those who suggested then that resources might not be limitless were an unheeded minority. A few prominent Californians did predict that redwoods might one day be exhausted. In 1880 Secretary of the Interior Carl Schurz recommended two townships—or 46,080 acres—be withdrawn from sale or disposition.[14] But most westerners placed their faith in the tree's "phoenix-like powers of reproduction"—the proliferation of sprouts in a logged or burned-over forest. Journalists noted that each giant was replaced by six to twenty "herculean infants" that would be ready for the saw in twenty years.[15]

Through the 1880s the United States ignored the romantic philosophers, landscape painters, or gentlemen sportsmen who advocated scenic protection. Implementing a national policy in effect since the time of Jefferson, the government sold or granted most of the public domain to private owners. The character of those few scenic areas that were saved proved nineteenth-century Americans rarely appreciated nature for itself.[16] Early preservation of the redwood's Sierra Nevada cousin—*Sequoiadendron gigantea*, or Big Tree—owed much to the mammoth trees' suitability as "earth monuments," consolations to a young nation jealous of Europe's relics. The Big Trees had also proved too brittle to be used for lumber.[17]

The coastal redwood is a distant cousin of the more massive yet shorter Sierra Nevada tree. Both have upon occasion been carved into tunnel trees or stripped, their bark shipped eastward for exhibition. Like the Big Tree, the redwood was deemed an oddity worthy of national esteem, but the fate of the two was to prove quite different. Redwood is too soft for indoor use, but natural resistance to insects and rot make it ideal for exterior use. Nineteenth-century San Franciscans believed redwood buildings were fire resistant. Repeated burnings of their city later dissuaded them. It's the tree's red bark, not its pink heartwood, that retards flame. However, the tall, straight, almost limbless shafts yield lumber that takes a beautiful finish.[18]

Except for a few groves in Santa Cruz, San Mateo, and Monterey counties, no unlogged stands remained south or east of San Francisco by 1880. The trees in Santa Clara County, the East Bay, and Santa Cruz County had been cut to accommodate the Gold Rush. They had been used to build Oakland, Berkeley, and the communities of Santa Clara County.[19]

It is not difficult to comprehend even wasteful logging when reading it described by an economist as the trade-off of large quantities of raw material "for the scarcer factors of capital and labor."[20] The pioneer's immunity to sylvan beauty was also the product of centuries of European aversion to wilderness, intensified by the need to survive in the hostile New World.[21] The reactions of those who visited the wild woods north of San Francisco in the 1870s and 1880s, however, show that nineteenth-century attitudes toward nature cannot be portrayed solely in such negative terms as trade-off, survival, fear, or cultural animosity.

Not until 1850 had a trail been blazed from the Russian River up across the Ridgewood Summit and down into Mendocino and Humboldt counties. Pursuing this route in 1874, Walt Whitman produced a poetic celebration of Mendocino that reeks of lusty, savage nationalism. Through his "Song of the Redwood-tree" sounded "the music of the choppers' axe" and the shriek of the falling redwood. But he called the chant of the dying monarch a joyful song of abdication to "them predicted long ago," "a race superior." He felt that freed from Asian fetishes and the bloody past of Europe, in this virgin land will a new race, "hardy, sweet, gigantic grow, here tower, proportionate to Nature."

In the 1880s and 1890s an occasional journalist endured the ungraded dirt paths, bumpy corduroy log roads, and lurching mud-wagons to intrude upon the little-known wilderness of Humboldt and Del Norte counties.[22] Although the frontier was rapidly becoming part of America's past, abundance and the romance of the woodsman precluded sorrow at the trees' demise. Writing for *Harper's Magazine* in 1883, Ernest Ingersoll proclaimed "no attitude more manly or motion more muscularly graceful than those of the chopper." In camp Ingersoll found the redwood loggers a nomadic lot prone to exchanging bear stories and reminiscing about dance houses, poker tables, and gun battles. A subsequent journalist described with pleasure the noisy, commercial air of the booming frontier logging towns. The chopper was a "serene, healthy, and home-loving" man in harmony with his environment. Neither writer extolled the redwoods' beauty, bemoaned their fate, or suggested their preservation.[23]

These logging scenes were isolated evidences of industry in a largely unsettled region. But the history of American lumbering was one of ceaseless migration—from the Atlantic seaboard, through the Great Lakes region, into the southern pine, and westward. As the forests of Michigan and Wisconsin showed signs in the 1880s of depletion, the timber barons began moving west their millions in timber-made capital. Turn-of-the-century settlement of treeless southern California and the disappearance of the Bay Area redwoods sparked demand for northern lumber. The price of acreage in Humboldt and Del Norte soared, and the redwoods passed out of the public domain.

Following depression in the 1890s, logging increased between 1899 and 1914.[24] Significant acceleration, however, awaited the close of World War I. In the 1910s Californians approved a bond issue for the construction of a highway from San Diego to the Oregon border. By 1917 the route from San Francisco Bay through Humboldt and Del Norte counties had been surveyed and graded. Although steep, windy, and impassable in winter, the new highway opened the redwood country. Also by 1917 the Panama Canal was moving bulk cargo to the Atlantic Coast, and a railroad ran from San Francisco to Eureka. The fate of the northern woods was in large part sealed by the new transportation, growing demand, and passage out of the public domain.

Unlike the eastern forests, however, the logging of these woods would not be completed in a frontier society. Americans were changing their attitudes toward resources and wilderness. Between the 1890s and World War I, leaders sounded the alarm of impending forest depletion. The seeds of this change had been taking root for two centuries throughout the western world, and their flowering was neither a response to a uniquely American situation nor solely a reaction to crises.

Reflecting in the 1860s upon his New England childhood, George Perkins Marsh commented that "every middle-aged man who revisits his birth place after a few years of absence looks upon another landscape than that which formed the theater of his youthful toils and pleasures." Industrialization increased the speed and therefore the perception of environmental change. Nevertheless, in his book *Man and Nature*, written during his travels as America's ambassador to Italy, Marsh also noted that preindustrial societies had for centuries wrought destruction as thoroughly, if not as rapidly, upon the lands of the Mediterranean littoral.[25]

From the sixteenth through the eighteenth centuries, Germany, France, and England experienced timber shortages that disturbed manufacturing and worried monarchs whose power rested upon wooden fleets. Yet peasant hostility, inadequate bureaucracies, and lack of scientific knowledge defeated efforts at conservation.[26] The nineteenth-century triumph of the bureaucratic state and of private property over the peasants' common rights in Germany, France, and to a lesser extent England provided the political and economic centralization necessary for forest management.

Western man's ability to perceive the principles behind human modification of the environment increased significantly in the eighteenth century. Such Americans as Thomas Jefferson and western Europeans as Comte de Buffon tried to explain the relationships between various parts of the observed world by natural, not theological, laws and laid the basis for the nineteenth-century advances exemplified by Marsh's work.[27]

From the 1860s through the century's close, Germany, France, and England developed forestry programs that owed their epistemological origins to the heritage of Jefferson and Buffon. These nations established state forests, schools of forestry, and such public regulation of private forestry as the prohibition of grazing and the requirement of reforestation. Central to these systems was the professional forester dedicated to "rational treatment of forests" and "the application of the principles embodied in the science of forestry."[28]

Despite stronger fidelity to laissez-faire, the United States also developed professional training, federal programs for private forestry, and public forests. In 1879 the nation established a small Division of Forestry. Directed by the German-born and -trained Bernhard Fernow, it advanced research. His successor, the French-trained American Gifford Pinchot, enlarged and popularized the division between 1898 and 1910. This outspoken patrician and friend of Theodore Roosevelt broadened its focus to promote private industrial forest management. In 1891 Congress had granted the president authority to create forest reserves, a power subsequently exercised by presidents Harrison, Cleveland, and Roosevelt. In 1905 Pinchot succeeded in having these reserves transferred from the Department of the Interior to the Department of Agriculture and Forest Service administration. With the Cornell and Yale schools of forestry and the Society of American Foresters in existence by 1900, the nation possessed the fundamentals for conservation.

As conservation, or wise use of natural resources, owed much to modern science, the movement to preserve wilderness bore a debt to the romanticism of the eighteenth and nineteenth centuries as well as to the growth of curiosity regarding the principles governing the natural world. Once feared, forests now delighted gentlemen naturalists and romantics seeking the exotic and mysterious. Although found among Europeans and patricians of America's eastern seaboard in the eighteenth and nineteenth centuries, love of nature was not widespread in the United States until urbanization and technology had produced a small but vocal national reaction. As a result in part of this growing appreciation of nature, Congress in 1862 transferred to the state of California Yosemite Valley to be administered as a public park and in 1872 established Yellowstone National Park.

What Pinchot was to early conservation, John Muir was to the wilderness movement. A romantic philosopher, natural scientist, and wayfarer, Muir had wandered from Wisconsin to the mountains of California. In the 1880s he promoted wilderness protection, working successfully to establish Sequoia and General Grant national parks out of public domain lands.[29] In 1892 he helped found the Sierra Club, a San Francisco-based citizens' group dedicated to fostering outdoor recreation and the defense of the Sierra Nevada. Muir believed that those who enjoyed the mountains would be their most avid defenders.

Almost one-third of the club's 182 charter members were academics —many in the natural sciences—from the new University of California, Stanford University, Mills College in Oakland, and the California Academy of Sciences in San Francisco. Four were with either the U.S. Coast and Geodetic Survey or the U.S. Geological Survey. Only five were women. The rest of them were almost all businessmen and lawyers working in San Francisco's financial district. In fact, it was there that the club established its headquarters. Most of the Sierra Nevada was still in public ownership, so that the club's defensive energies consisted largely of guarding against exploitive public management. Faced with the state of California's gross mismanagement of Yosemite Valley, Muir and the club, aided by the Southern Pacific Railroad, fought for and in 1906 won federal recession of the valley.

At first Pinchot and Muir had thought themselves allies, but Pinchot had little sympathy with wilderness; he believed forests and land were to be used. In contrast, Muir preferred some forests left uncut, with recreational, spiritual, and scientific values unimpaired. His gentle reverence for nature contrasted sharply with the robust, manipulative approach of the European-trained Pinchot. San Francisco's turn-of-the-century application to convert Yosemite National Park's Hetch Hetchy Valley into a reservoir severed the already strained friendship. Pinchot and his supporters favored this water conservation project. Against this threatened desecration, Muir waged the country's first nationwide publicity campaign in defense of wilderness. He battled for over a decade, only to lose in 1913.[30] The philosophical divide between Muir and Pinchot is reflected in the history of the word "conservation," which came into widespread use around 1908. Pinchot claimed to have originated the term and employed it deliberately to exclude those who advocated wilderness preservation. Although his claim to originality was erroneous, his application was historically justified.[31]

Despite the schism, both conservation and preservation prospered. By 1916 the Forest Service administered 155 million acres of national forest. That same year the National Park Service was created within the Department of the Interior to oversee lands the federal government had decided over the years to retain as parks—from Yellowstone to the Sierra Nevada preserves championed by Muir. President Woodrow Wilson's secretary of the Interior, Franklin K. Lane, appointed the former California industrialist Stephen Mather to head the new service.

Local as well as national appreciation of nature awaited establishment of cities, colleges, and inland transportation. Thus the first redwoods saved were in Big Basin, thirty-five miles south of San Francisco on a northwestern slope of the coast range. During a mid-May 1901 tour of the basin, twenty-six residents of cities in the central coastal counties, including men from local colleges and a significant representation of women, formed the Sempervirens Club. Arguing that a park would serve as a laboratory for the University of California's proposed forestry school, the club advanced state legislation to save the basin.[32]

In 1901 the legislature appropriated $250,000 to purchase the land and established a commission to manage the California Redwood State Park, later renamed Big Basin Redwood State Park.[33] The railroad's support had brought this quick success. The park added passengers to the lumber the powerful Southern Pacific Railroad already carried into the Santa Cruz area. Republican Governor Henry T. Gage—legal counsel to Southern Pacific before assuming office—had abandoned his usual fiscal conservatism to sign the park bill. The first California Redwood State Park commissioner was a railroad land agent, and one club enthusiast confided in 1902 that "within a short time a railroad will run into the park."[34]

Support for a redwood park appeared later in northern California, increasing with the region's accessibility and population. However, in keeping with the less urbanized character of Humboldt County, western boosterism motivated this park effort. Interest in redwoods expressed by such outsiders as Theodore Roosevelt and transportation advances spelled tourism. Between 1905 and 1911 Humboldt County's boards of trade, chambers of commerce, local women's groups, and schoolchildren petitioned Washington and campaigned locally for a park—either on the new line of the Northwestern Pacific Railroad or on one of the area's new motor roads.[35] Enthusiasm peaked in the heady fall days of the 1913 Three States Good Roads Rally sponsored by the Humboldt Promotion and Development Committee, yet it soon died, despite support from the region's congressmen and the State Highway Commission.[36]

Although the movement that began with Osborn, Grant, and Merriam's trip in 1917 occasionally allied with residents of Humboldt and Del Norte counties, it expanded out of a national and less commercial interest. Since the turn of the century, Muir, Roosevelt, Mather, and California's reform-minded congressman William Kent had been concerned about the redwoods.[37] Kent had purchased a grove on the northern peninsula of San Francisco Bay and in 1908 donated it to the federal government as Muir Woods National Monument. In 1913 he had sponsored a congressional resolution calling for a redwood national park.[38] Grant, Osborn, and Merriam were personal friends and fellow campaigners of these national leaders and knew of their enthusiasm for the redwoods.[39]

Impelled, then, by scientific curiosity and national interest in the trees, the three had made their visit to the redwoods in 1917. In 1918 they established the Save-the-Redwoods League and gathered sponsors. From the University of California, Merriam enlisted professors, administrators, and alumni, including Bay Area businessmen. In the East Grant contacted the monied as well as those associated with park and wildlife preservation, the good roads movement, and automobile associations.[40]

The shock that pulled the league into focus came in June, 1919. Postwar needs caused demand for lumber to soar.[41] Small logging operations sprang up along the new highway, threatening the groves of the South Fork of the Eel River. Motoring through the area, a retired Chicago philanthropist and friend of Grant, Edward Ayer, found scenes "worse than the devastated districts of France."[42]

Figure 2. Redwoods in the Eel River area, June, 1919. Logging along what would one day be the Redwood Highway. Photo by Edward Ayer. From the Edward Ayer Collection. Courtesy of the Save-the-Redwoods League.

In haste, Merriam and three other Berkeley professors; J. D. Grant, a California entrepreneur in petroleum and hydroelectric power; Mather of the Park Service; and the New York patrician Grant converged upon San Francisco's Palace Hotel. On August 2, 1919, inside the ornate, eight-story brick and terra cotta structure with its glass-domed garden court, the seven men elected officers and resolved to rescue outstanding redwood groves threatened by logging.[43]

On October 14, 1920, twenty-six men signed the bylaws making the league a nonprofit, California corporation. Between 1920 and 1939 the group was to have seventy-nine councilors. Analysis of the economic and social backgrounds of these individuals is useful in understanding the origins and nature of the scenic preservation movement. Ten were females. Except for one easterner, the women were wealthy residents of the Los Angeles or San Francisco Bay areas. All were active in such women's civic groups as the prestigious Garden Club of America and the California Federation of Women's Clubs—both league contributors.

Of the sixty-nine men, all but a Canadian and a German were at least second-generation Americans. Most were born in the 1870s and 1880s. One-third were native to either the northeastern United States or the Midwest and had moved to California. Another one-third were both native and resident to the state. Finally, somewhat over one-third never lived in California at all. A skewed geographical distribution persisted through the next half century. West Coast membership was heaviest, followed by that of New England and the Middle Atlantic seaboard. Little interest came from the more rural portions of the nation.

At least fifty-eight of the sixty-nine male councilors in the 1920s and 1930s graduated from a four-year college or university, generally in the 1890s and 1900s. Thirty-six had multiple degrees. Over twenty went to private eastern institutions, primarily Yale. Six attended European universities and five attended midwestern colleges. At least thirty were officially associated with the University of California at Berkeley, sixteen as alumni.

Known religious affiliations were all Protestant—Episcopalian, Presbyterian, and Congregationalist. The men were, however, generally of loose religious affiliation. They were Republicans and members of such select fraternal associations as the Commonwealth, Pacific Union, and Bohemian clubs of San Francisco, and the Union, and Boone and Crockett clubs of New York. Such memberships were far more common than affiliations with organized religion.

They were prominent professionals or businessmen listed in national and regional biographical publications. Over half had vocations that made involvement in preservation reasonable; they were landscape architects, preservationists or conservationists in government service, editors of publications that sponsored parks, and natural scientists. Of the thirty-three whose vocations were unrelated to parks, six were professionals: an engineer, four professors, and one practicing lawyer. The other twenty-seven were businessmen, from bankers to manufacturers. Most were independent entrepreneurs. Although fourteen had inherited substantial wealth, the majority depended upon earned income. The businessmen were prosperous pillars of the community—university regents, college controllers, and corporate directors.

Although the ties of this organization to national conservation are easily traced, less obvious is its relationship to other reforms of the progressive years. Historian George W. Mowry described the California progressive of the 1900s and 1910s as generally a Protestant, college-educated, urban male who "held a significant niche in the American economic structure"—attorney, journalist, independent businessman, real estate operator, doctor, banker. They were not affiliated with large corporations. Mowry concluded that progressivism was a protest by "some peculiarly individualistic social and economic groups against the rapid concentration of twentieth-century American life and its attending ethical, economic, and political manifestations." "Looking backward to an older America, it sought to recapture and reaffirm the older individualistic values. . . ."[44] Subsequent composite biographies of progressives throughout the United States reveal the same urban, educated, native-born pattern. The leadership of the redwoods league was even more likely to be educated, upper middle class, and urban; otherwise, the biographies correlate well.

More recent historians, however, have criticized Mowry's interpretation. Despite their rhetoric, progressives from Roosevelt to Wilson as well as those in the league were not fundamentally opposed to business consolidation. Moreover, Mowry's composite biography also describes the period's conservatives, precluding correlations between background and ideology.

The character of the league itself argues against facile generalizations. The group counted among its leaders both men such as William Kent—regarded as a leftist progressive—and Benjamin Ide Wheeler and Frederic A. Delano—deemed more moderate progressives. Almost all of the twenty-six incorporators considered themselves progressives, and about half were active in prewar reforms. Information is lacking on the prewar political sentiments of younger councilors who joined in the 1930s, but at least half of all the councilors who served between 1920 and 1939 had supported Roosevelt and Hiram Johnson, California's progressive governor, in the 1910s. Complicating categorization, however, the group also included the California banker and Johnson's arch opponent, William Crocker.

Some historians have suggested that the concept of progressivism be abandoned because of the ideological diversity of the participants and the inability of historians to identify common motivational factors.[45] Although Samuel P. Hays has more recently been among these, he himself had previously employed the concept with success by demonstrating that the essence of the progressive conservation movement lay in professionalism. He saw such reformers as Pinchot inspired less by any large political or grass-roots sympathy than by their professional loyalties as, for example, foresters or geologists. They sought efficient resource management. Although the park movement began in the progressive years, Hays excluded its participants from his interpretation, describing them as nonrational, romantic enthusiasts who embarrassed Pinchot's efforts to achieve comprehensive, rational resource planning.[46]

Certainly wilderness preservation differed from resource conservation. Such men as Muir and Merriam were part of the romantic tradition, but they were also heirs to the intellectual revolutions that produced the scientific forester. Some scientists took a bloodless, mechanistic approach to nature, but Merriam, Osborn, Muir, and their allies combined the empirical and the romantic. Moreover, many in the league were natural historians, professional preservationists, foresters, and landscape architects who fostered parks in the pursuit of career-related ideals. Inclusion of professional botanists, biologists, paleontologists, and geologists was vital to the establishment and expansion of the National Park Service and lay preservation groups.

But what of league councilors whose careers did not relate to parks? How does one account for that half of the group who were lawyers, industrialists, and businessmen? Were they members of an older, more individualistic society who had suffered a loss of status in the face of the large industrial corporation and organized labor? Were they involved due to pessimism about the drift of American society? Some have suggested that the park movement did in fact reflect such a generalized nostalgia—that in the fashion of the Country Life movement, park promoters idealized rural life and sought to restore nineteenth-century morality. Samuel Hays has argued that park advocates looked upon nature as an antidote to industrialization and urbanization.[47] It would be reasonable to assume their efforts in the 1910s did somewhat reflect a reactionary mood.

In fact, however, parks were as much a fulfillment of as a rebellion against modernization. The league's leaders were active in such other groups as the Sierra Club and in the Park Service, yet they were far from pessimistic about industrialization. Nor is there evidence of personal alienation. The diversity of backgrounds in the league forces a broader interpretation than that originally advanced by Hays in analyzing career conservationists, but it does not preclude generalizations identifying participants as fully within the mainstream of modernization.

There are characteristics within the league that do not distinguish it from the period's new trade associations—some of which opposed parks—but do demonstrate the forces that produced both the professionally motivated and the nonprofessionally motivated preservationist. These individuals were financially comfortable, free to look to interests beyond their immediate jobs. The growing class of career scientists supported by universities, foundations, and government looked toward associations with others in their professions. Editors, landscape architects, and career conservationists advanced causes relating to their work. Patricians joined the league, but so did business-men who now possessed the economic independence to pursue philanthropic activities previously restricted to the upper class. These businessmen were now free to associate in worthy causes with others throughout the nation—fellow alumni of Yale, Harvard, or the University of California.

Mobility, education, and social position gave the league's leaders a broad geographical perspective previously found only among a few eastern gentlemen. Only two league councilors in the 1920s and 1930s lived in the northern redwood counties. As previously stated, over one-third had never even lived in California. These men and women were members of what Robert H. Wiebe has called America's "new middle class," people who had the time, economic security, and facilities with which "to look beyond the day's work and try to locate themselves within a national system."[48]

Far from being dismayed by industrial society, these individuals found the new order offered them opportunities for civic involvement, professional advancement, and profit. They developed, as Wiebe suggests, a "consciousness of unique skills and functions" and were eager "to join others like themselves in a craft union, professional organization, trade association, or agricultural cooperative."[49] Although these arguments do not explain why some San Francisco lawyers or eastern editors did *not* support parks, they do explain why the group was so well endowed with prosperous professionals and businessmen. A college education, membership in certain clubs, and an urban residence on either coast were necessary without being sufficient to explain participation.

Lacking strong religious affiliations and educated at increasingly secular institutions of higher learning in Europe and America, these men and women enjoyed an organized civic and professional involve-ment and the pursuit of a faith combining scientific respectability and romantic intensity.

2
Citizen Reform:
California's State Park System

IN THE summer of 1919, in response to accelerated western logging and the concern of the Save-the-Redwoods League, Congress passed a resolution directing the secretary of the Interior to investigate the advisability of a redwood national park.[1] A year later the secretary recommended a park along Del Norte County's lower Klamath River, a broad waterway lined with sweeping green hills.[2] But neither the resolution nor the report led to federal financing—nor had anyone, including Stephen Mather, National Park Service director and author of the resolution, anticipated they would.[3] Existing national parks were areas that had never been removed from the public domain.

The redwoods of Del Norte and Humboldt counties had passed into private ownership, and there was no federal inclination to purchase them back. The resolution and the report could only express the hope that "public-spirited" individuals might donate the purchase price. Mather's annual report for 1920 also indicated that he expected the league—an organization similar to those he "god-fathered" in Oregon and Washington—to encourage the state of California to protect the trees lining the projected north-south Redwood Highway and rescue high quality groves there. The American motorist could then journey along California's scenic highway north from San Francisco, pause at various state parks, and eventually reach the federal reserve in Del Norte County.[4] But Mather's vision was only partially realized, and twenty years later the sweeping Klamath stands were logged. The House resolution of 1919 was significant only as a prelude to the search for alternate sources of funding.

The twenty-six men who signed the league's articles of incorporation in 1920 adopted the funding scheme outlined in the director's report.

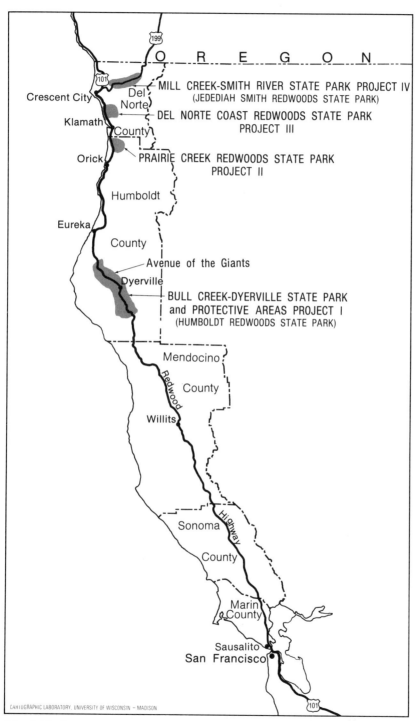

OREGON

199

101

Crescent City

Del
Norte
County

MILL CREEK-SMITH RIVER STATE PARK PROJECT IV
(JEDEDIAH SMITH REDWOODS STATE PARK)

DEL NORTE COAST REDWOODS STATE PARK
PROJECT III

Klamath

Orick

PRAIRIE CREEK REDWOODS STATE PARK
PROJECT II

Humboldt

Eureka

County

Avenue of the Giants

Dyerville

BULL CREEK-DYERVILLE STATE PARK
and PROTECTIVE AREAS PROJECT I
(HUMBOLDT REDWOODS STATE PARK)

Mendocino

County

Redwood

Willits

Sonoma

County

Highway

Marin
County

Sausalito

San Francisco

101

CARTOGRAPHIC LABORATORY, UNIVERSITY OF WISCONSIN — MADISON

Map 2. The four northern California redwoods state park projects, 1937. Project I, 21,150 acres, value $4,315,000; Project II, 7,750 acres, value $1,078,000; Project III, 2,800 acres, value $448,500; Project IV, 141 acres, value $36,500.

In the course of the next decade, the organization remained officially receptive to federal involvement but relied upon state and philanthropic support. The league replaced California's decentralized park administrative system with a bureaucratic structure that had a statewide perspective and a commitment to scientific land management. The league began as a spin-off of national progressivism, but it prospered during the 1920s within the cocoon of a faltering yet persistent progressive faction within the California Republican Party.[5]

In the late nineteenth and early twentieth centuries, many of America's new financial and industrial barons found a response to social incongruities in Andrew Carnegie's admonition that the rich volunteer their wealth for the public good. Between 1905 and 1915 the YMCA pioneered the high-pressure, professionally directed fund-raising campaign. There followed the successful war-related drives for liberty loans, Belgian relief, and the Red Cross.[6] Inspired by these efforts, private, nonprofit, corporate charities proliferated in the 1920s. The income tax law of 1917 encouraged the "business of benevolence" by allowing the deduction of charitable contributions up to 15 percent of taxable income.[7]

In the absence of congressional appropriations, Mather used his own fortune and the money of rich friends to establish the national parks. His was the achievement "of a wealthy man. The big gesture, the princely gift, that was the rich soil out of which the National Park Service grew."[8] In 1918 and 1919 the director brought the same charisma, philanthropy, and influence to the redwoods. He told Secretary of the Interior Franklin K. Lane of the trees' plight; Lane became league president at the organization's first meeting in August, 1919.[9]

Mather attended that initial gathering in San Francisco.[10] Afterward he drove north, where he found that the projected parkway was lined, as Edward Ayer had reported, with burned stumps and denuded lands as it wound along the South Fork of the Eel River.[11] Humboldt County had acquired the land but not the trees along the new highway's right-of-way.[12] This access had invited logging. The director and his companion, Madison Grant, were met by representatives of the local chambers of commerce who escorted them into Eureka, the county's largest community. At a rally in his honor, the tall descendent of Increase and Cotton Mather announced that he and progressive state congressman William Kent would each contribute $15,000 to acquire the trees. Filling its members' heads with visions of tourism, Mather persuaded the Humboldt County Board of Supervisors to match the gift.[13] Returning East, he prevailed upon George Lorimer of the *Saturday Evening Post* and Gilbert Grosvenor of the *National*

Geographic Magazine to become league officers and inform national readerships that in California one- to two-thousand-year-old trees were being felled for railroad ties and grape stakes—an act akin "to breaking up one's grandfather clock for kindling."[14]

The flamboyant director's influence within the redwood movement declined after 1920. He had many other commitments and was plagued by ill health. However, the league continued to reflect his style, expanding from the fortunes, position, and connections of its councilors. Among these were pioneer western industrial barons such as Joseph D. Grant, who became chairman of the league's board. Ayer had fought the Sioux and logged wild forests of the Southwest but now sponsored the preservation of the redwoods and funded museums gathering Indian artifacts. Other councilors were such eastern patricians as Madison Grant. Mrs. Thorne Oakleigh, an officer of the league as well as the prestigious Garden Club of America, was a New York society matron whose husband sat on the boards of diverse corporations. The league also drew upon the powerful William Crocker and James Moffitt—president and vice-president of the Crocker National Bank in San Francisco. The league mainstays, however, were the academics and independent businessmen and professionals who contributed time and expertise—such men as the successful Bay Area subdivider Duncan McDuffie.

In addition to personal contributions, these councilors quietly solicited donations in the exclusive haunts of New York's Sphinx Club; Washington, D.C.'s Cosmos Club; and California's Bohemian Club.[15] Although their attempt to include redwood lumbermen in the league failed, they did obtain donations from a number of timber companies whose officials they encountered in these watering holes.[16] Imitating Mather's use of the guided scenic tour to snare political and financial support, they escorted potential benefactors down the Redwood Highway in a black, open-top touring car, encouraging these prominent citizens to select and name a memorial grove for family or friend.[17] Dedication ceremonies provided occasions for publicity, with bronze plaques embedded in granite placed among the trees. Memorial groves accounted for one-third of funds raised in the 1920s.[18]

The organization's incorporators saw federal parsimony as an opportunity as well as a handicap. John Merriam, the league's first secretary and after 1921 its president, asserted that the federal government should not "move to purchase such a park area until state and county efforts and private subscription have gone very far to show the fundamental interest of thinking people in the project."[19] Henry Fairfield Osborn wrote, "We, each and all, shall purchase these forests as fast as we can, *for our own*, with money subscribed in small or large amounts; than, we shall present them to Uncle Sam. . . . a definite recognition of the unitedness of government and people in America. . . ." J. D. Grant believed federal taxation destroyed private enterprise.[20]

Figure 3. President Herbert Hoover in the Frank D. Stout Memorial Grove, Del Norte County, 1928. On this camping trip to the redwoods, President Hoover visited lumber company officials but refused to meet with the league, which sought his assistance in negotiations with the timbermen. Hoover did not believe federal money should be used to establish redwood parks, a position he shared, ironically, with the men of the league. Damage to the bark at the base of the Stout Tree was already evident in 1928. For a view of the same tree thirty to forty years later, see figure 16. Wide World Photos. Courtesy of the Save-the-Redwoods League.

Inherent in such charity is a tendency toward elitism. Mather advocated that prospective members be screened to admit only those whose status would lend strength to the cause.[21] But elitism vied with a democratic urge also present within this citizens' organization. Merriam argued that the movement begin with a small group of "influential men" and then be expanded by means of "a general public statement . . . indicating the method by which a great many people in this country . . . can attach themselves to the league."[22] A grass-roots base would lend political weight and also allow Americans to prove themselves worthy of parks and the beneficence of the titans of wealth. The association introduced a graduated, paid membership. Prospective members were not screened, but general-subscription membership remained separate from the governance. The group's twenty-six incorporators became the first council, self-perpetuating and responsible for electing the board of directors.[23]

Although they believed in voluntary initiative, the incorporators placed great faith in professionalism. Late in 1919 they hired Newton Drury of the Drury Brothers Advertising Company as executive secretary. As a 1912 graduate of the University of California and secretary to its president Benjamin Ide Wheeler, Drury was well known to the men of the league. All over the United States, the business of charity was developing fund-raising specialists, of which Drury became a proficient example. He was to engineer legislation, orchestrate public support, and woo donors. He admired the national park leaders' use of modern advertising in "selling the national parks" and set out to employ similar techniques, as well as those developed in the 1910s by his partner, Aubrey Drury, for the Southern Pacific Railroad.[24]

Armed with Drury's expertise, in the fall of 1919 the crusaders turned their attention northward. Using the $60,000 Mather had raised, league, state, and county officials purchased options on those highway tracts most immediately threatened.[25] Upon returning East, Mather and Madison Grant had persuaded the chief buyers of the railroad ties produced from South Fork lumber—the United States Railroad Administration and the Santa Fe Railroad—to boycott these items.[26] By the end of 1919, the owners of South Fork trees close to the highway had grudgingly promised to sell their lands as funds became available and to refrain from cutting in the interim.[27]

The men of the league felt uneasy. A moratorium based upon boycott and limited financial compensation seemed precarious and unprincipled. In the winter of 1920 and 1921, they resolved that if full purchase prices were not forthcoming shortly, they would sanction the resumption of logging. Humboldt County residents feared new operations would spring up to supply new markets, and they attempted a boycott on all wood products from the entire watershed of the South Fork of the Eel River. The San Francisco group condemned the move as an unjust inconvenience to owners whose "properties might not be of park caliber" or for which funding was not imminent.[28] Impelled by pressure from loggers on one side and overenthusiastic park advocates on the other, the league accelerated its fund-raising.

In the summer of 1921, the initial memorial grove was dedicated to the first officer of rank to fall in World War I. The slow pace of charity clearly made immediate state appropriations essential. Legislation was further needed to empower the California State Board of Forestry to accept and administer gifts of money and land and to raise the power of eminent domain over highway right-of-ways from the county to the state level. In early 1921 Humboldt County state legislators sponsored a bill framed by county residents. The measure was to appropriate $300,000 and allow the State Board of Forestry to condemn timberlands adjacent to the highway in Humboldt County.[29]

Figure 4. Bolling Grove dedication, August 6, 1921. The first memorial grove dedicated by the Save-the-Redwoods League was in honor of the first officer of rank to fall in World War I. Left to right: Irwin T. Quinn, Madison Grant, Lawrence Puter, William H. Crocker, J. D. Grant, John C. Merriam, E. C. Bradley, Hans Nelson, J. C. Sperry, Newton B. Drury. Courtesy of the Save-the-Redwoods League.

Almost immediately the Redwood Preservation Bill tested the new organization's politics. Some of its councilors doubted the propriety of the State Board of Forestry possessing the right of eminent domain over an entire county. Despite this concern, the league authorized Drury to campaign for the measure.[30] It capitulated, however, under fire from the timbermen's trade associations. In the center of this tempest was the Pacific Lumber Company, owner of the finest groves along the South Fork. The measure had the support of the state's organized and newly enfranchised women, of Humboldt County residents, and of the largest affected landowner—a corporate speculator. Nevertheless, the league elected to have the condemnation provision restricted to the southern portion of the county—the area most immediately threatened by the axe—thus excluding Pacific

Lumber's lands. The capitulation attests both to the league's moderation and to the power of organized interests within the state legislature.[31]

At the final 1921 hearing, organized women, local boosters, eastern and western urban gentlemen, state highway officials, and the now-appeased lumbermen all testified in behalf of the bill. Its senatorial sponsor announced, "Mr. Chairman, there is no opposition."[32] Drury escorted a number of state legislators on a tour of the Redwood Highway. The California Assembly and Senate unanimously passed the measure. The reformers' tactics had mirrored those of their opposition. From the league to the various chambers of commerce, nonprofit associations advanced preservation, while boards of trade and the corporate-sponsored California Taxpayers' Association fronted the opposition.[33]

The state faced a deficit for the biennium of $14,000,000, and the governor threatened a veto. Legislators debated increasing the tax on public service corporations. The park men disliked both unbalanced budgets and public levies. Following a bout of soul-searching, however, they barraged Governor William D. Stephens with photographs, publications, and telegrams supporting the measure.[34] Formerly a prosperous southern California businessman and president of the Los Angeles Chamber of Commerce, Stephens had in 1912 won a congressional seat as the candidate of the progressives' Lincoln-Roosevelt Republican League. In 1916 he had assumed the governorship as progressive successor to Hiram Johnson. His minimal government scruples now warred with his reformist inclinations, causing his old friend and fellow progressive William Kent to intercede with, "Oh hell, Bill, if you can't get the money any other way, why don't you fire a few policemen and close the schools for a few days? This is something that can't wait."[35] The governor signed the bill. Now $300,000 was available to buy threatened tracts along the highway.

But passage of the bill was only the finale of a weak first act. Between 1923 and 1927 the league was forced to thread a course between unyielding industrial interests to the right and park radicals to the left. By 1927 Drury was describing his organization as "the moderates," as opposed to "the extremists."[36]

These reformers rode such a fine line in part out of fear that benefactors might close their wallets and the lumbermen might refuse to negotiate.[37] Yet the league's inclination sprang more directly from the values of its councilors, most of whom were sons of the middle class who had improved their fortunes. They were, in short, typical of the true American "self-made" man.[38] John Merriam, who in 1921 became head of the Carnegie Institution of Washington, D.C., was the native son of an Iowa farm family. Industrialist J. D. Grant was the son of a prosperous downtown San Francisco merchant. Comprised of such men, the league found itself at odds with "extremists" who did not respect property and industry.

Indeed, the league's businessmen and professional men were more circumspect toward the status quo than were some of the independently wealthy. The force of such flamboyant, rich crusaders as William Randolph Hearst, or even the league's own Madison Grant and William Kent, brought the organization's majority position into sharp relief. A journalist for *Hearst's International* labeled the redwood lumbermen as "destroying, dollar chasing, selfish humanity" engaged in "ruthless slaughter."[39] Drury's campaigns betrayed no such antagonism toward the wielder of the axe and advocated industrial cooperation.[40] For every time Grant called the loggers "vandals and barbarians" or urged, "bite hard on the Taxpayers . . . someone should suffer for the reckless squander of public property in the past," there prevailed the sober voices of Merriam, Eureka banker Arthur Connick, or University of California president Robert Sproul.[41] Whether academics or businessmen, prewar progressives or conservatives, they believed in upward mobility and the need to protect individualism.

Almost all of the incorporators and over half of the male councilors in the 1920s and 1930s are known to have been strongly sympathetic toward or active in prewar progressive reforms. Roderick Nash has written that after World War I, "conservationists spent more time in action, less in rhetoric and scolding."[42] Donald Swain demonstrated that conservation made significant strides in the 1920s but that, in contrast to the earlier reformers, many leading proponents now favored "voluntarism," "organized cooperation," and "decentralization."[43] These generalizations describe the promoters of the California state parks system and place the course of the conservation movement within the framework of America's larger reform impulse as it receded in the immediate postwar years. William Kent noted, "The war and the radicals in Russia have set back the course of democratic progress at least twenty years."[44] Evidence from the league suggests the impact of the war itself was minimal but that the effect of postwar radicalism was significant. Most league progressives had favored the League of Nations, their faith in progress toward international peace unshaken. In contrast, although sympathetic to labor, they had not approved of the political radicalism or union "excesses" so evident in 1919.[45]

And yet there were continuities between the 1910s and 1920s. Most of those who joined the league had been inclined toward the moderate progressivism of a Benjamin Ide Wheeler or a Frederic Delano—league councilors who had been members of the National Civic Federation formed in 1900. The federation included representatives of the public, business, and labor who wanted "laissez-faire replaced by a new creed involving a collective responsibility for the common good within 'the industrial and commercial framework. . . .'" The organization was "imbued with the ideas of social engineering and efficiency so popular at the time. It favored conciliation, rationalization, and, to a degree, humanitarianism." The group campaigned for antitrust legislation, a minimum wage, compulsory mediation of labor disputes, and workmen's compensation, all in the hope of curtailing the anarchical practices of independent businessmen and forestalling incipient radicalism. For such men, the state and private reforms of the 1920s that blossomed out of social consensus—from the numerous private charities and company unions to state parks and state forestry laws—were less a defeat than a fulfillment. These businessmen and academics did not consider reform alliances with business unnatural nor corporations as innately evil. Rather, they sought to distinguish between bad and good corporate practices.[46]

Not all of the league men and women had been moderate reformers. Leftist progressives Madison Grant and William Kent were seduced into alliance by the calming effect of postwar radicalism, the political limitations of the 1920s, and the siren song of business support. William Crocker had been a corporate opponent of the progressives, but in the prewar years some businessmen had discovered that through cooperation they could affect the course of reform.[47] The league represented the type of coalition of left- and right-wing that had been both a product of the progressive years and an ideal of the moderate progressive.

In the early decades of the century, the business world began to develop methods of molding public policy and opinion. The goal was corporate efficiency through internal and external harmony.[48] Meanwhile American reform had undergone a similar transition. Reform had moved from the individualistic philanthropy of the nineteenth century to the elite morality of the progressive period's various reform leagues—and then in the 1920s to the reliance upon professional public relations and lobbying. The redwood league combined these traditions and harmonized public and private welfare. Industrial and nonprofit corporations had similar structures and methods. Years later the league's president would praise Drury by saying that the latter could have had a brilliant career in industry and describing the league as a successful business in terms of funds raised, legislation procured, and low overhead.[49]

Civic-minded businessmen and academic reformers found they spoke the same language and had similar backgrounds.[50] Those in the league had attended the same colleges, frequented the same clubs, and were Republican, native-born Protestants. They prized party loyalty, a position only heightened by their lapse in 1912 to vote for Theodore Roosevelt's progressive Bull Moose Party, and this loyalty ultimately allied many California reformers with the stand-patters of the state's Republicans. As long as businessmen were happy with the league's methods, they helped save the redwoods. An old agitator like Kent had little room for protest.

Although the league evidenced internal consensus, achieving a broader consensus was more difficult. The embarrassment generated by the 1921 legislation and Hearst press "extremism" was minor compared to the dilemmas posed in 1923 by three bills introduced in the Calfornia legislature. Some residents of Humboldt and Del Norte counties wanted the highway commission empowered to condemn redwoods along all state roads within their counties. Southern Californians tried to give that agency the right of eminent domain over lands along all California highways. The third bill proposed that once a private agent deposited in the treasury funds equalling the value of land that agent wished acquired as a park, condemnation proceedings would automatically follow an owner's refusal to sell. Drury understood that the latter measure was backed by an anonymous rich woman who wanted to buy Calaveras Grove for the public and by William Randolph Hearst, who wished to purchase a Santa Cruz grove. Neither benefactor had been able to obtain a price on these stands.[51]

The bills' sponsors requested league endorsement. Refusal would antagonize potential political allies and donors, imperil publicity from the Hearst press, and alienate Stephen Mather, who supported the legislation. But the "moderates" called the measures unnecessary and dangerous, noting that the California State Highway Commission could already condemn a three-hundred-foot right-of-way along both sides of all highways and a wider strip along those in southern Humboldt County.[52] They also indicated that they expected donations from and were negotiating land purchases with the timbermen. Supporting actions hostile to industry "did not appear to be good tactics or good faith."[53]

Merriam explained further that the legislation threatened to cause the "disorganization of industry." The league could not countenance a proposal giving "free reign to condemnation, largely on the whim of individuals who happen to be ready and willing to put up the money." "Protection of legitimate industry" necessitated a "large plan of park development" wherein the state could condemn only those lands that experts judged of park caliber. Thus conviction precluded endorsement of the measures, but discretion prevented public opposition. Merriam's organization declined support but thanked the legislators for their interest in the redwoods.[54]

In March, 1923, the lumbermen advanced upon Sacramento determined to abolish all park laws of eminent domain. The loss of these would cripple the league's program. The logging interests also sought a moratorium on park purchases pending a statewide park survey, which they hoped would limit acquisitions and enable owners to anticipate sales. The league supported the survey but opposed the moratorium. The timbermen also beseeched legislators to prohibit the condemnation of any portion of a logging unit, effectively barring acquisition of many stands along the South Fork.[55]

Drury hurried to Sacramento to talk with industry representatives. In May, 1923, a compromise bill was passed; Drury had triumphed. Condemnation would not be automatic, but the power could be used anywhere in California once a state board declared the land suitable for a park. A scenic survey was authorized, but no moratorium was placed upon land purchases. The timbermen had agreed to forgo the restriction against condemnation within a logging unit; however, the bill admonished the Board of Forestry to give the integrity of such units due consideration.[56]

Not content with emergency measures and pragmatic compromises, the league in 1925 promoted legislation for land planning in the redwood country through a statewide program. At its prompting, a bill was introduced into the Senate to authorize and fund a scenic survey of California and to permit acquisition and condemnation of areas designated of park caliber.[57] Although the survey had made its legislative debut at the will of industry, as early as 1919 the reformers had wanted to employ a landscape architect to select the most outstanding groves.[58] A master plan would raise land prices, but it would also minimize inconvenience to property owners, lessen political opposition, and permit the state to develop complementary park and highway systems. Above all, a long-range acquisition schedule would ensure protection of the most scenic and scientifically important areas.[59]

The cornerstone of this comprehensive system of resource management was to be a central park commission with jurisdiction over all present and future state parks.[60] To the league's discomfort, Humboldt Redwoods State Park had fallen under the jurisdiction of the California State Board of Forestry. The foresters had proved too friendly toward industry, and the scenic highway program floundered without occasional threats of condemnation. Moreover, some forestry practices—

such as the construction of fire barriers and roads—were anathema to wilderness management. The men of the league did not believe that the State Forestry Board had demonstrated an aptitude for park management. This task required specialized training in the subtleties of wilderness protection, as well as in the accommodation and instruction of the public.[61]

In behalf of its proposals, the league launched a six-month campaign in January, 1925, with a mass meeting sponsored jointly with the Sierra and the Sempervirens clubs.[62] Automobile clubs, patriotic groups, and the State Board of Forestry endorsed the bills, as did national preservation and conservation groups.[63] The Pacific Lumber Company led the opposition, arguing that designating an area for acquisition would automatically confuse the land's title. The lumbermen protested that a park commission would be less sympathetic toward them than was the State Board of Forestry.[64]

Several California newspapers and trade associations reflected this position.[65] The *San Francisco Chronicle* attacked the league, "from its title a sentimental organization," and the position that a park board deals with "preservation, recreation, education and scenic beauty" whereas the forestry board must be wise in the ways of "timber, live-stock, hay and grain." "The inference is," the editorial sneered, that "people who know about corn and pigs . . . cannot know anything about education or scenic beauty. . . ."[66] Three foresters on the league's council—George Pardee, ex-chairman of the California State Board of Forestry; Walter Mulford, professor at the University of California; and William Greeley, conservative chief of the Forest Service—similarly believed that one agency could "develop each tract for its highest purposes whether economic or recreational."[67]

The redwood group appeared to be reaping the bitter fruits of the rivalry that had begun with John Muir and Gifford Pinchot—a rift that the U.S. Forest Service and the National Park Service perpetuated. But in fact the league's legacy was less one of antagonism than an acute awareness of the disparity of function between forest conservation and park preservation. The league was a cooperative effort by those who had taken different sides in the battle over Hetch Hetchy Valley. Its leaders included Muir's two fighting allies, Henry Fairfield Osborn and William Colby, as well as proponents of the reservoir William Kent, Franklin K. Lane, and Pinchot's hand-picked successor as Forest Service chief, Henry Solon Graves.[68] Most foresters, from those on the California State Board of Forestry to the leaders of the American Forestry Association, endorsed California's park legislation of 1925.

Arthur H. Breed, Republican senator from Alameda and a founder of the Lincoln-Roosevelt Republican League in 1907, sponsored the bills. His efforts and Drury's lobbying resulted in the unanimous passage of the measures in April, 1925.[69] Since 1920, however, California's Republican progressives had been fighting the rising tide of right-wing influence within their party. This influence was spearheaded by the California Taxpayers' Association, funded by the state's largest corporations.[70] In 1925 Governor Friend Richardson, whose election three years earlier had been a victory for these forces, vetoed the park bills. The redwood men had assured him that a central commission would make parks an economic asset, but he remained skeptical about the state's ability to succeed in a business venture and feared the bills would eventually cost the taxpayers millions. His political philosophy relegated park development to the local community and decentralized park administration.[71]

In 1926 the league retained Frederick Law Olmsted, landscape architect from Massachusetts and son of the designer of New York's Central Park. He was to study California's state park problems and recommend "what legislation should be asked for the coming session of the Legislature."[72] Impressed by California's size, Olmsted advised that local park commissions were the most practical solution. The league and its allies in the Sierra Club did not take this advice. Drury assured the easterner, "Our constantly improving system of roads and the many facilities for transportation make the administration of State Parks from a central agency comparatively simple."[73]

The league did not want to postpone the creation of a rational, efficient bureaucracy. Agencies administering the state parks included the California Redwood State Park Commission; the Mount Diablo State Park Commission; the State Board of Control; the State Fish and Game Commission; the State Highway Commission, with its three-hundred-foot right-of-way; and the California State Board of Forestry, with authority over the Humboldt and Burney Falls parks.

The league opposed such decentralized management. Drury explained that local commissions attracted a "lesser calibre of men" and displayed "a provincial attitude." Such bodies placed "the self-interest of individual communities" over the "general interest." Moreover, a central commission would function as a repository for experience in park administration, as did the national park system. In addition, the league wanted trained park superintendents and hoped that a central, specialized agency run by professionals would sponsor scientific research. Lacking data on the redwoods and the mechanics of preservation, Drury's group had funded several botanical studies. In 1925 it had retained the California landscape architect Emerson Knight to frame a park protection plan.[74]

Samuel P. Hays has written that, unlike the utilitarian conservationists, park enthusiasts had little interest in "rational comprehensive planning."[75] But such planning was the primary goal of those who established the California state park system. In fact, throughout the twentieth century preservationists have fought local control, seeking instead scientific land management.

These mobile, urban-based reformers sought a political reorganization in which the level of decision-making was elevated. Eighteenth- and nineteenth-century American law relegated land-use decisions to the local and private sectors, denying cosmopolitans a voice in the fate of wild lands. Obviously, establishment of a permanent system of local commissions would not shift this balance of power. The effort of these land reformers was thus similar to prewar municipal reformers who found that the ward system and city legislatures did not adequately represent their city-wide political and economic interests. The park men were not pursuing self-interest but similarly strove to replace the political status quo with a businesslike administration that was rational, efficient, and more truly reflective of concerns that were "not bounded by geography."[76]

In 1926 Clement C. Young was elected governor of California— a victory for the state's progressive Republicans. The progressives had also won control of both houses of the legislature. The league launched a program of resource planning even more comprehensive than its earlier proposal. In contrast to the federal Forest and Park services housed in the departments of Agriculture and Interior respectively, the state's Division of Forestry and Division of Beaches and Parks were to be administrative subdivisions within a Department of Natural Resources. As in the 1925 bills, the park commission was to be equipped with condemnation powers and empowered to execute a scenic survey. Now the park advocates added legislation for a constitutional amendment authorizing a six-million-dollar bond issue for land purchases throughout California.[77]

For all their faith in professional expertise and rational bureaucracy, these reformers favored control by volunteers. The bond issue authorized the sale of bonds only as matching funds were made available by private funding. The fifty-fifty principle was designed to allow for expression of citizen initiative and to mollify taxpayers.[78] The idea was inspired as well by Andrew Carnegie's philanthropic adage, "To assist but rarely or never to do all."[79] This philosophy of self-help was also favored by Steve Mather and John D. Rockefeller, Jr. Nor was philanthropy to be the only role of laymen in state conservation. Paid employees were to serve within the Department of Natural Resources and the Division of Beaches and Parks; however, the policy-making California State Park Commission was to consist of nonsalaried appointees, men of "sufficient leisure and sufficient sympathy," disinterested, and public-spirited.[80]

To quiet suspicion that the bills would benefit the redwoods only, the league in 1926 established the State Parks Council to front the fight.[81] The council was directed from the league's San Francisco office but had an auxiliary headquarters with the Los Angeles Chamber of Commerce to deflect the sectional animosity of southern Californians.[82] Drury and the council's president, Duncan McDuffie, league director and Sierra Club president, organized what was at the time the largest publicity campaign in California's history.[83] A few lumbermen and foresters as well as the California Taxpayers' Association still offered some weak opposition.[84] But the state's increasingly urban-based, motorized public wanted parks. Automobile clubs as well as women's, teachers', sportsmen's, and fraternal organizations endorsed the proposed legislation. Chambers of commerce from Crescent City to San Diego and major newspapers from the "extremist" *San Francisco Chronicle* to the conservative *Los Angeles Times* supported the measures.[85] In April, 1927, the bills passed unanimously and were signed by Governor Young.[86]

The bond issue appeared on the November, 1928, ballot. The State Parks Council's campaign was massive and successful.[87] Nowhere in the state did the negative votes outweigh the positive. Fifteen counties favored the measures two to one; twenty-three voted three to one; and fifteen passed the bills by even higher margins. The more Democratic counties tended to deliver the lower pluralities.[88]

There is substantial evidence of the persistence of popular reform sentiments in California in the 1920s. The state legislature had passed a child labor law in 1927. Along with the park bond on the 1928 ballot, aid to the needy blind and the physically handicapped passed by large margins—with the distribution of these votes correlating with that for the park bonds. Yet the voting profile approving the California Olympiad Bond Act also correlates with that of the park bonds. These voting profiles and the character of press support show that enthusiasm for parks represented both a general reform impulse and love of the outdoors. Nevertheless, support also reflected interest in the economics of tourism; the strongest votes come from rural counties likely to provide park sites. The urbanized Los Angeles and San Francisco counties passed the measure by the relatively lower margin of two to one.[89]

In 1927 Frederick Law Olmsted had completed the park survey. He calculated that only about 3 percent of the forest in the northern counties could be saved. Such exceptional stands as those on Redwood

Figure 5. Humboldt Redwoods State Park. Photo by David Swanlund.

Creek and the Klamath River were excluded because of their size and inaccessibility. Instead, the preservation schedule focused on the densest and most accessible groves lining the river flats. The league would be hard-pressed to raise the money to buy even these trees. In addition, its officers were too eminently reasonable "to support a plan which would eliminate the redwood from commercial use."[90]

Figure 6. Prairie Creek Redwoods State Park, Fern Canyon, July, 1966. Photo by Howard King. Courtesy of the Save-the-Redwoods League.

Olmsted sanctioned four projects. He selected stands representative of the botanical zones within the northern redwood belt. Each project centered on a watershed chosen for its beauty and accessibility as well as the age and purity of the groves. The farthest south was Humboldt Redwoods State Park on Bull Creek and the South Fork of the Eel River. To its north yet still in Humboldt County was Prairie Creek Redwoods State Park. Its western boundary was Gold Bluffs

Figure 7. Del Norte Coast Redwoods State Park ca. 1920. Photo by Gabriel Moulin. Courtesy of Moulin Studios and the Save-the-Redwoods League.

Beach, and its eastern dense forests enclosed a green meadow on which grazed two herds of Roosevelt elk. Jedediah Smith Redwoods State Park encompassed the lush alluvial plains of Mill Creek and the Smith River in Del Norte County. The small Del Norte Coast Redwoods State Park contained the spectacular meeting of forest, cliff, and ocean.[91]

By 1928, the decade's peak year for American philanthropy, the league had raised over half a million dollars to acquire three thousand acres of redwood forest.[92] After 1928 every dollar raised was matched with public funds. Thriving upon donations from America's elite and enjoying broad political support, the organization had become a successful business. It built for California a rational structure of resource management and established four redwood parks to which in the next decades it would add lands bit by bit. The effort bridged the traditional charities of the nineteenth century and the public structures of the twentieth; it was both zealous in its privatism yet democratic in its spirit.

It has been said that progressivism died with World War I. In many ways this is a statement of the obvious; yet the obvious can often be deceiving. Among the men and women who tried to reform society in the years before the war, there were many for whom the state and private reforms of the 1920s were a triumph. This continuity between the 1910s and 1920s is evident whether the park movement is viewed as part of a process of modernization sparked by technological change or simply as a sequence of calculated political decisions. The league responded to the need for centralization and rationalization, but it did so with caution.

3
Ideology of Reform: A Natural Theology

IN DECIDING to save the redwoods, the league was building upon almost a century of western science. As early as the 1830s, imprints of leaves and cones very similar to California's redwoods had been found in prehistoric sedimentary rocks of Europe and North America.[1] Age determinations revealed the genus *Sequoia* and its immediate ancestors to be millions of years old. Charles Darwin's *The Origin of Species* (1859) gave such discoveries theoretical significance. Speaking before the American Association for the Advancement of Science in 1872, Asa Gray declared that the longevity of *Sequoia* refuted Genesis; here was proof of evolution.[2]

Even as Gray spoke, civilization was threatening America's fossils and California's forest of living relics. Over the next fifty years, the western wilderness vanished with unparalleled speed. Early twentieth-century efforts to save redwoods stemmed from a desire to preserve artifacts critical to the emerging disciplines of paleontology and paleobotany. Scientists such as John Merriam, Vernon Kellogg, Ralph Chaney, Henry Fairfield Osborn, and Willis Jepson envisioned parks as laboratories and classrooms. They also believed them temples to the universal design behind evolution, superlative examples of "the garment of God," Merriam's description of nature.[3] If most Americans never read Goethe, whose *Faust* inspired that phrase, the public was sympathetic to the ancient *Sequoia's* precarious last stand on the continental margin of North America.

When Merriam joined the faculty of the University of California in the 1890s, little was known of the Pacific Basin's remote past. By the time he departed for Washington, D.C., in 1919, he had pioneered the field.[4] His student Ralph Chaney carried forward the work over the next three decades. Berkeley professor, redwood league councilor and president after Merriam's resignation in 1944, Chaney reconstructed the trees' migrations and used them to unlock further the West Coast's geologic sequence. Collectors all over the world sent him finds. He theorized that one hundred million years ago much of England and western Europe as well as portions of present-day Russia, China, and Japan had been covered by a redwoodlike forest—thought at first to be *Sequoia* but identified in the 1940s as a related genus, *Metasequoia*.[5] Dinosaurs and flying reptiles had dwelled in these forests while small, fleet mammals clung to life there. As mammals gained ascendancy, the redwoods' ancestors began to migrate.

In 1927 Chaney told the Paleontological Society of America that field studies had shown a close association between the flora of Fushan, Manchuria, and the *Sequoia* flora of eastern Oregon, indicating the possible interchange of life between continents. The American Museum of Natural History sent an expedition to St. Lawrence Island, midway between North America and Asia.[6] In late 1930 Chaney cabled Merriam: "Sequoia flora of Middle Tertiary Age just received from St. Lawrence Island represents first actual record of land bridge between North America and Asia."[7] The press announced that the unearthing of this "missing link" indicated that the human race originated in central Asia and spread to America over a land connection.[8]

When the trees crossed this bridge approximately fifty million years ago, the Arctic was not frozen. Western America was warm and humid. Subtropical forests of fig, palm, avocado, and mahogany dominated what is now California, Oregon, and Washington. The *Metasequoia* remained in cooler Alaska and northern Canada. Some twenty million years later, the earth entered a period of uplift and glaciation. North America chilled, and the sea withdrew from the continental margins. The subtropical forest was impelled southward, and the more temperate *Metasequoia* forest, now joined by the *Sequoia*, moved into present British Columbia, Washington, Oregon, Idaho, Wyoming, and even more easterly portions of the continent. They carried with them ferns and flowers found under the redwoods today. Twenty-five million years ago volcanic lava and ash sealed the record of the two redwood species growing side-by-side in Oregon's John Day Basin, allowing Chaney to see this mixed forest as it stood on the eve of climatic and geologic upheavals.

Over the next several million years, formation of the Cascade Mountains modified the winds and rains. This change and the continued cooling rendered the North American *Metasequoia* extinct, a fate the genus also met on the European continent. Dogged by the spreading freezes of the Pleistocene, the *Sequoia* continued to move south and west, only to be driven to a precarious survival along the northern coast of present-day California. The climate created by the wall of the Cascade Mountains barred the species' reentry into the Pacific Northwest after the ice receded. For some twenty million years, the trees have grown only where bathed by the fogs that sweep off the Pacific from Monterey Bay to the Oregon border.[9]

In the 1930s and 1940s, Chaney used his reconstruction of these migrations as a guide to age determination for western America in the Cenozoic era, the era antedating and including the Land Bridge of the Miocene and extending through the Pleistocene to the present. At that time geologists and paleontologists normally used two keys in age determination: the vertical sequence of the beds and the level of development of the flora fossils within the beds. These approaches did not help the student of Cenozoic paleobotany in western America because the flora fossils of this period—flowering plants and conifers— had remained fairly constant. Moreover, the area covered by the sediment layers were limited and often unrelated to their underlying formations. Given the approximate ages of the climatic and geologic changes causing the redwoods' migrations, Chaney argued that the discovery of a *Sequoia* or *Metasequoia* fossil dated the sediment layer in which it was found. Knowing the *Sequoia*'s present environmental requirements also allowed him to reconstruct its remote environments.[10]

Merriam and Chaney believed the destruction of important natural phenomenon threatened the work of the natural sciences. From the 1910s through his death in 1945, Merriam urged preservation of many areas of evolutionary significance, from Darwin's Ecuadorian Galapagos Islands and San Francisco Bay area shell mounds to the John Day Basin of Oregon.[11] He cited the sad example of China, where the sole remnants of wilderness were the sacred forests surrounding ancient temples. Only in these areas could one "compare the original face of the land with the heavily eroded areas of today" or study the ancient maiden hair or ginkgo tree.[12]

Darwin's theories of evolution stimulated paleontological interest in nature, but wilderness had other laboratory uses as well. By studying a cross section of an ancient redwood, Emanuel Fritz, professor of forestry at the University of California and league councilor, identified the scars of fires dating from 1147, 1595, 1678, 1806, 1848, 1866, 1883, 1895, and 1920. Chaney used individual trees to reconstruct the climatic cycles of the northern counties and the flood history of their river basins. The botanist and league officer Willis Jepson studied the forest ecology.[13] Speaking during the depth of the Great Depression,

Merriam warned Americans that wilderness was not merely the "play-thing of the scientist." He predicted flora and fauna not in economic use might one day contribute to human survival and industrial progress.[14]

In addition to promoting redwood preservation, scientists supported the establishment of the first national parks.[15] Even before the National Park Service was created in 1916, educational institutions were con-ducting field courses in the wilderness. In 1918 the service created a National Park Educational Committee to advise the agency about the use of parks as field laboratories.[16]

These natural reserves were also to serve as classrooms for the instruction of the general public, reflecting a development peculiar to the early decades of the century. Technology had brought improved communications, increased literacy, and extended leisure time. Adult education flourished as a result. Such men as Raymond Fosdick, Robert Millikan, Francis Mason, Alfred Noyes, and Glenn Frank publicized the research of geologists, paleontologists, and astronomers. The statesman Elihu Root urged public dissemination of scientific knowledge.[17] The movement to save the redwoods included the following scientific popularizers: Madison Grant, director of the New York Zoological Park and Aquarium; Edward E. Ayer, head of the Chicago Museum of Indian History; Gilbert Grosvenor, founder of the National Geographic Society; and Henry Fairfield Osborn, father of the New York Museum of Natural History.

Merriam also participated in the adult education movement of the 1920s and 1930s.[18] In addition to authoring lectures, radio broad-casts, and newspaper articles and serving as the league's president for twenty-six years, Merriam wrote natural history essays—a post-Darwinian development in vogue at the turn of the century.[19] Each of his essays was a simplified dramatization of a fragment of past ages—a fossil footprint in the Grand Canyon, the jaw of a saber-toothed tiger from the La Brea tarpits, a living redwood—"the assured reality" of each opening a view "across the eons connecting past and present."[20]

Far better than museums, lectures, or essays, however, was nature itself. Park interpretive programs wed adult education and nature preservation. The Park Service launched its first such program in Yosemite Valley during the summer of 1919.[21] Advice and funds poured in from scientific and lay conservation groups.[22] In 1927 the service appointed an Advisory Board on Educational and Inspirational Use of the National Parks, of which Merriam was a member. A diversity of interpretive facilities appeared in other national parks and monu-ments, from guided tours and auto caravans to nature trails, exhibits, campfire talks, museums, and observation stations. The national park system was dubbed the "University of the Interior," and parks "Open-Air Schools."[23]

Merriam carried this effort over into the state parks.[24] Year after year he told the league to study the educational and inspirational values of the redwoods.[25] He and other league scientists did research on the trees and arranged for their findings to be conveyed to the public in pamphlets and articles as well as through fireside lectures, nature walks, and exhibits. Labels on the growth rings of a downed redwood over one thousand years old, for example, told visitors of the afflictions the living tree had suffered. There were scars from fire and disease as well as cracks from internal stress and a large buttress the giant tree had formed to compensate for an injury that had thrown it off balance.[26]

The league and the Park Service sponsored interpretive work and publicized research in part to increase financial and political support. For the league this effort was a success. The public was intrigued by the unearthing of redwood fossils from China to California and by the discovery of an Arctic Land Bridge. There was drama in the redwoods' southern migration impelled by shifts in the great land masses and dogged by the spreading freezes. Sir Arthur Conan Doyle's 1912 novel *The Lost World* told of scientists who discovered an isolated region in which prehistoric forms of life had survived into the present. Both Merriam and the California press noted the similarity between Doyle's "island in time" and the redwood forest.[27] Through the 1920s and 1930s, stories of cave men and vanished species were popular.[28] In 1927 Chaney noted that the "Lost World craze" had stimulated enrollment in his introductory paleontology course at the University of California.[29]

As late as 1948 there was great public interest when the *Metasequoia* or Dawn redwood, long thought extinct, was found alive in remote China. Every step of Chaney's journey—paid for by the league—into China to retrieve the tree was covered by a reporter from the *San Francisco Chronicle*. Californians saw weekly photographs of the paleobotanist's progress, on foot, by river sandpan, and in sedan chair. They read how armed retainers guided him safely through the mountains into the Valley of the Tiger, where the trees grew.[30] In response to the excitement, the *Saturday Evening Post* carried an article, "There Could be Dinosaurs," which asserted that there was no positive evidence that somewhere a few living giant flying reptiles or dinosaurs did not still exist.[31] This public enthusiasm increased the league's popularity, since the present *Sequoia sempervirens* woodlands are essentially a Miocene forest within which dinosaurs had once lived.

Expediency does not, however, fully explain the interest of either the league or the Park Service in the natural sciences. The motives of participants were genuine, if diverse, ranging from the practical consideration that researchers should not get too far ahead of the public to philosophical concerns. The symbols the redwoods represented reflected the period's preoccupation with evolution and its implications—scientific, religious, and racial.

Eugenics played a small but interesting role in motivating some preservationists. Defined by its founder, the Englishman Sir Francis Galton, as the science "which deals with all influences that improve the inborn qualities of a race," eugenics emphasized human improvement through selective breeding. The movement was widely accepted within scientific and government circles in the 1920s and reached its height with the passage of the immigration acts of 1921 and 1924.[32]

At least eleven of the leading men in the league subscribed to this science. Four were well-known, published eugenicists active in the late 1910s and 1920s: Madison Grant, Henry Fairfield Osborn, Charles M. Goethe, and Vernon Kellogg.[33] William Kent and George Lorimer of the *Saturday Evening Post* campaigned with Grant and Goethe to have Congress pass immigration restrictions that would effectively bar all but northern Europeans from entering the United States.[34] The adventurer Major Frederick Burnham, a close friend of Grant, helped propagate the faith.[35] Harold Bryant of the National Park Service was associated with the Northern California Eugenical Society.[36] Benjamin Ide Wheeler, University of California president, betrayed a belief in eugenics in his interpretation of Greek history.[37] As late as the 1940s, Chaney explained to the students in his introductory paleontology course that by "carefully selecting the best to be found in physical, intellectual, and social spheres, rejecting the faults, the deficiencies and maladaptations that beset individual and national life, the individual may aid in the improvement of the group."[38] Newton Drury sympathized with the principles of eugenics, as did four of the six members of the Park Service's Educational Advisory Board as late as 1930.[39]

Of these men, however, Charles Goethe best articulated the relationship between preservation and eugenics. A wealthy resident of California's Sacramento Valley, Goethe was a philanthropist who contributed heavily to the redwoods and to the national parks. He saw a parallel between the "conservation of humans" and "conservation of other members of the environment."[40] At the heart of eugenics was the theory of the superior individual, generally defined in terms of race—the Nordic and pioneer American stock—and the theory of the mutant, translated into the unusually bright or "Gifted Child." The superior race and mutant must be made to survive, according to Goethe. Natural selection had to be replaced by artificial selection because the former was too slow, and often the superior man's breeding habits caused his extinction.[41]

Goethe wanted these natural laws of evolution taught to the public. He was one of the first to sponsor park naturalist programs and subsequently financed the early interpretive work of the National Park Service. He also contributed to the league's educational and junior membership projects. Although neither organization demonstrated official interest in eugenics, Gothe hoped such programs would make the electorate "biologic-minded." He felt knowledge of the laws of evolution demanded glimpses of the vistas of centuries, with their examples of extinct species and species that had survived according to the slow and not always beneficial laws of natural selection. He believed that increasing the public's biological awareness would ease passage of immigration laws and promote selective breeding.[42]

The popularity of eugenics in America in the 1920s reflected in part a fear of social and racial change, yet its advocates in the park movement were not pessimists. Indeed, in spite of its basic conservatism, eugenics can be seen as a reform effort.[43] As a program of social engineering, it reinforced, as did the park movement itself, its adherents' optimism as to the future of the human species in general and of American society in particular. Chaney described evolution as a "cheerful and inspiring view of life." He believed evolution to be the divine creative force, or what Charles Goethe called simply "God-in-Nature."[44] Osborn declared that eugenics taught that the twentieth century must now read the Biblical passage, "From plague, pestilence, and famine, good Lord, deliver us" as: "From ignorance of Thy Laws and disobedience of Thy Command, good Lord, deliver us."[45]

Nevertheless, the exact laws eugenicists divined from the redwoods were vague. The trees were frequently referred to as survivors of a master race, the fittest that had survived the tooth-and-claw struggle.[46] Madison Grant found in Hermann Keyserling's *The Travel Diary of a Philosopher* an eloquent expression of the eugenical lesson of the redwoods. The author declared the *Sequoias* had reassured him that the creative power of our planet was not dying out. Now we see, he proclaimed, that the youngest of the continents still possesses the primordial power of primitive days. *Sequoias* symbolized both the role Americans were to play in completing evolution and the power still within its borders, a power gone from a Europe fettered by traditions. These trees also proved that free struggle in evolution— or in social terms, freedom of opportunity—did not lead to equality. Orientals, according to Keyserling and Grant, know this; they do not ask for equality any more than do those plants under the *Sequoias*.[47]

Although many in the park movement subscribed to eugenics, neither the league nor the Park Service incorporated eugenics into interpretive programs or offically recognized the science. The league adopted the philosophy of Merriam, not Goethe. Although Merriam approved of pure eugenical research, he thought the eugenicists' emphases on race over individualism and heredity over environment wrong, and he feared that these tendencies could lead to the destruction of some classes of people.[48] As were those of the eugenists, however, his writings were shaped by interest in the social and religious implications of Darwin's theory of evolution. For over five decades the league mailed prospective members his messages.[49]

Indeed, he might be called the "philosopher of the redwoods." Merriam was born in 1875, died in 1945, and reached his full intellectual stride between the world wars. As head of the Carnegie Institution of Washington, D.C., for a quarter of a century he interpreted the state of the sciences. As advisor to the Park Service and league president, he interpreted the rationale of preservation. He saw nature— be it a petrified woodland, a living redwood, or the Grand Canyon— as more than a series of scientific technicalities.

> Tis thus at the roaring loom of time I ply and weave
> for God the garment thou see'st Him by.[50]

> How glorious art thou earth, And if thou be the shadow of
> some spirit lovelier still.[51]

Borrowing these lines from Goethe and Shelley, Merriam argued that the forces of nature held philosophical and religious truths. A paleontologist by training, he died a poet.

As with many of his contemporaries, Merriam's intellectual heritage was that of the nineteenth century: Charles Darwin's *Descent of Man* and *Voyage of the Beagle*, Sir Charles Lyell's *Antiquity of Man*, and Thomas Henry Huxley's *Man's Place in Nature*. He was profoundly affected by the poetry of Wordsworth, Shelley, Tennyson, and Bryant as well as by Goethe's *Faust*. Romanticism had paved the way for a positive reappraisal of nature by emphasizing the distant, the natural, and the sublime. Heir to the Enlightenment, nineteenth-century European romantics generally held that man's life on earth could be improved;[52] yet some Victorians felt their faith in a moral universe threatened by the idea of Darwinian evolution and the new theories of time and space. They saw the emergence of a tension between the artist and the scientist.

Merriam strove to synthesize the two. He did not agree with Wordsworth that the scientist's "poring and prying," "dividing and dividing still" destroyed nature's grandeur.[53] Like Tennyson, Merriam wanted to see morality in nature. His success was greater than Tennyson's, however, because he considered it more than a leap of faith, more than a "believing where we cannot prove."[54] California's forests showed that the cosmos was neither meaningless nor immoral. Science was proving that the universe was essentially progressive and that man could control his destiny.

Merriam was raised a Protestant;[55] however, as a graduate student at the University of Munich in 1890, he studied the romantics and the scientific method. These three influences shaped his non-Biblical, nonecclesiastical faith.[56] He was not deterred by those who saw evolution as contradicting Christianity and debasing man. Instead of "elaborately developed inherited doctrines" as to the origins of man, he advised scientific study. Research, he believed, was an act of reverence. Scientific technicalities were divine truths, so there was no reasonable basis for conflict.[57]

To those who saw evolution as demeaning, he replied that man's place in a "universe marked by unity and continuity in meaning" gave man a greater dignity.[58] He quoted Longfellow's "Psalm of Life," in which a footprint in the sandstone symbolized the idea that the influence of each life "may reach out undreamed of distance through time and space."[59] Since Merriam loved the Bible and argued that "science and religion both represent the truth regarding man and the universe," the Association for the Advancement of Science saw him as a man who could lecture on evolution, "possibly getting some people to see the reason in the theory without irritating their religious feelings."[60]

The league's president believed no one better expressed the wedding of divine and natural than the romantic poet William Cullen Bryant, whose "Forest Hymn" declared:

> My heart is awed within me when I think
>   Of the great miracle that still goes on
> In silence round me—the perpetual work
>   Of thy creation, finished, yet renewed
> Forever.[61]

In Merriam romanticism and Christianity merged with the rationalism of the scientist.

He dedicated himself to telling others of the magnitude, power, and laws of the universe, a task for which America's parks were well suited. In this the discoveries of the scientist joined the romantics' love of the sublime. To approach the Grand Canyon, "hidden in a great stretch of . . . level land," was a shock that "opens the windows of our soul so effectively, that they never again close completely against the wonders and beauties of the world."[62] To step into a redwood forest was to enter an "island of time." To look up from the trees' trunks and the shadows of other ages into the "living present" of the leaves and birds gave "a vision through the avenues of time from past to future." The parks force the visitor to think about creation, Merriam felt. Knowledge of the geologic processes behind the Grand Canyon, the biologic cycles inherent in the seasons, and the evolutionary forces represented by the redwoods stimulated spiritual inquiry.[63]

Figure 8. Mystery of the Forest ca. 1920. Redwoods near Dyerville Flat on the Eel River. These trees were logged many years ago. Photo by H. E. Tibbits. Courtesy of the Save-the-Redwoods League.

To Merriam preservation was a religious mission. Parks were "holy places," where "the visitor will worship and act in accordance with the request 'be still and know that I am God.'"[64] Redwoods were "temples, because through them we have turned toward contemplation of undefined sources of being and power. . . ."[65]

Given his sensibility, what truth did Merriam see in the forces of the earth? Of nature, Tennyson queried and Merriam read:

> And shall I take a thing so blind,
>   Embrace her as my natural good;
>   Or crush her, like a vice of blood,
> Upon the threshold of the mind?[66]

By the early twentieth century, some of America's great liberal philosophers had embraced blind nature. Influenced by Darwin's theories of evolution, such men as John Dewey, Oliver Wendell Holmes, and Thorstein Veblen had placed all faith in immutable moral values, all forms of idealism, on the defensive.[67] In 1908 Merriam had heard Veblen lecture on the demise of the absolute in science and economics. Nonetheless, even into the 1920s and 1930s, most scientists still thought the universe directional and orderly. There were many men in the league who agreed, from Henry Fairfield Osborn and Madison Grant to William Badé, Ralph Chaney, Vernon Kellogg, and Merriam.[68]

In the earth's biologic and geologic patterns, Merriam saw natural laws. One might expect, he reasoned, that somewhere some "spiral nebulae" floating in remote space would fail to follow the movement characteristic of elements in our solar system. But no, he added, there is unbelievably rigid adherence to these laws in all known regions of time and space. This consistency indicates a divine wisdom. Evolution attests to a central scheme. The Grand Canyon, with its "clear evidence of the interrelation among the major features," offered a refined view of one God.[69]

The most important strides of the past century had been made in biology, but Merriam predicted that other sciences would make discoveries of even greater religious significance. Physicists were exploring the "intimate structure of basic materials from which chemical compounds are formed." With knowledge of the atom, the known material world vanished and in its place appeared interlocking "energy complexes." The atom suggested that "the universe is only a varying expression, in a vast multitude of forms, of a fundamental something which we have yet to define." Physics for Merriam had confirmed the unity of the universe.[70]

Philosophers at least as far back as Locke had "wrestled with the possibility that man is a part of the universe," Merriam noted, but now evolution had proved man was "the outgrowth of natural processes."[71] "Out of this vastness," we have been born, so that elements in human nature exist in other organisms. Merriam anticipated that knowledge of human behavior would be gotten from animal behavior studies. The environment extended itself "into the very fiber of man's being" through his nervous system, digestive tract, and the secretions of his glands.[72]

Science had confirmed that sense of companionship with nature Merriam found attractive in the romantics. Twice he visited Wordsworth's Lake District, the mountains of which he saw as "sublime masses"; their "abrupt scarps and bold strong steeps" revealed the earth's power and motion.[73] He did not go so far as to bind himself, as had John Muir, to a tall conifer to experience fully a Sierra Nevada thunderstorm, yet Merriam enjoyed winter tempests in Washington, D.C.'s Rock Creek Park.[74]

Unlike Muir, however, Merriam was not a mystic, and his intellectual debt to the transcendentalists was less than Muir's. Merriam believed man was one with the natural world but never spoke, as had Muir, of losing consciousness of one's separate identity and blending with the natural world. Though assured of the religious truths in nature, he did not believe that the divine and the material were separate planes, as had the transcendentalists. Nature was "the garment of God"; changes in the universe were outgrowths of the nature of the universe itself.

The Social Darwinists of Merriam's day maintained that the natural laws of Merriam's orderly world were bloody, ruthless ones that demanded for progress natural selection and survival of the fittest. They maintained man would control nature to secure that which was agreeable to the individual rather than that which would benefit the race.[75] The anthropologists A. E. Wiggan and Charles Davenport told Merriam that the brain of man was not growing, that man as a breed was declining, and that evolution had stopped and man was plunging downward.[76]

Merriam asked how anyone could expect him to believe that the progress of the last thousand million years had ended, since within the "narrow space of a few centuries preceding us there has not as yet been seen such definite evidence of man's physical progress as characterized the separation of Neanderthal from Cro-Magnon man?"[77] He rejected arguments that evolution had ceased or past improvements had stemmed from random chance. To Merriam a fossil footprint was the "imprint of living feet that have never ceased to advance . . . upward through the ages." Evolution confirmed that life "developed continuously toward more complicated, more broadly comprehending and more intelligent forms."[78]

Tomorrow was secure, he believed. Geologists assured man the flexible crust of the earth would continue to change the mountains and continents so as to allow for the "alternating isolation and mixing of species" that develop new life forms. The "days of creation" had not ended.[79] Physicists and astronomers estimated that a stellar universe was as much as twenty thousand million years old. Merriam declared that the resurrection of Christ at Easter, which had for so long quieted the fears of many, symbolized the annual rebirth of the world. Spring proved that "in spite of minor fluctuations," the universe is "essentially progressive."[80]

Merriam did not agree with the prophets of doom who said heredity was the "maker of man." He preferred environmental explanations of evil. In a vein similar to such reform Darwinists as economist Thorstein Veblen, who argued for government reform instead of laissez-faire, Merriam felt that morals, education, art, and religion bettered humanity. Evolutionary progress need no longer come solely from the "bloody, brutal but beneficent hand of natural selection." He stressed social cooperation over natural selection.[81]

With science, man could shape his destiny. The uncivilized was not necessarily superior, Merriam felt. He maintained that those "natural elements that interfere with the highest development of man . . . should be eliminated" and those that "have human significance" should be used to further evolution. Such manipulation constituted a "constructive world movement" and included wilderness preservation.[82] Science had emancipated man from superstition. Earthquakes were no longer inexplicable acts of God, and one day man would protect himself against them. In 1927 Merriam declared that within a few centuries "the human race will have almost complete control of the biological world."[83]

He credited neither the idea that efforts to improve man's lot hastened his destruction nor that industrial progress was a disease. Unlike the transcendentalists, he did not reject the machine as the destroyer of the garden. He assured a colleague, "the machine contributes to our opportunity."[84]

Merriam respected and was close in temperament to the forester Aldo Leopold, whose thought Roderick Nash described as the "synthesis of the logic of a scientist with the ethical and aesthetic sensitivity of a Romantic. . . ." These contemporaries believed the unity of man and environment made wilderness preservation a necessity as well as a labor of love.[85] Merriam's wildernesses included, however, the unknown territories behind the microscope and telescope as well as the biological past. He remarked that the student of evolution encounters "a long sequence of wilderness. . . . Each he may explore with a sense of thrill in conquest experienced in the wild and unknown places of the earth today."[86]

Fascinated by the sublime, Merriam portrayed:

Worlds in the process of creation in the lightless spaces of the sky where no star ever shines; worlds that are as yet but cosmic dust, pushed about by tides of light. . . . micro-organisms drifting about dormant in the awful cold of the space between the stars, waiting for a world on which they can settle.[87]

The quote is reminiscent of Tennyson's stars that "blindly run" and his fears of a world of "changeless change," yet Merriam held firmly to his faith in an orderly universe.

Rarely is there evidence to establish cultural diffusion of basic themes. But many people—from authors of note to those unknown for their literary prowess—expressed appreciation of the redwoods. Romantic images flooded popular literature from the 1910s and 1920s. The trees told "mysterious tales of immemorial lore."[88] After a night spent "in a magic circle of the giants," one journalist related: "An uneasy ghostlike mist moved among the trunks . . . . Sometimes the moon peered down . . . sometimes it veiled its weary face"; the gods walked amid mortals that night.[89] During an evening passed in the redwoods, Bret Harte sensed "a weird twilight that did not come from the outer world, but seemed born of the wood itself." "A strange breath that filled these mysterious vaults had neither coldness nor moisture . . . the aisles might have been tombs, the fallen trees enormous mummies; the silence the solitude of a forgotten past."[90] Romantic love of the classical inspired pagan symbolism in the arts. A 1919 Sempervirens Club's play *The Soul of Sequoia* opened with the first awakening of life, "the mysticism of the Pipes of Pan," and the "frolicsome dances of nymphs."[91]

There was widespread awareness of the scientific value of the redwood as a "living link" with ages past. Under these "great god-trees," people imagined "prehistoric monsters."[92] Such people appreciated the sublime and felt a sense of oneness with the universe. In his *Sequoia Sonnets*, Charles Keeler included a poem entitled "Evolution":

> My spirit through the aeons patiently
>   Has labored out of star-dust, age on age,
>   From protoplasmic spawn amid the sea
>   In slow unfolding forms—a heritage
> Of thrilling wonder and sublimity.[93]

Echoing an almost universal imagery, Duncan McDuffie of the redwood league proclaimed that stepping onto Bull Creek was like entering "the portals of a cathedral dim, lofty, pillared, peaceful."[94] Into this "cathedral of trees" with their "living-columned aisles," men went to pray and praise. No temple could compare with this evidence of "earth's elemental powers."[95] Walking in these vaulted temples, most were smitten with humility. One man proclaimed, "If there is beauty like this, then perhaps it is true there is God."[96] This almost religious perception of the redwood's significance would bring the league into conflict with other park advocates.

4
Parks: Recreation
or Enlightenment?

IN MARCH, 1938, the Save-the-Redwoods League rejected a National Park Service proposal for a redwood national park. The superlative Mill Creek trees targeted by the service were threatened with logging, and the league was searching for funds to save them. Yet the directors asked the federal government to defer to the state's efforts to acquire the stand.[1] Thus the league formalized a long-maturing schism in the nation's preservationist ranks, the issue of which was the function of America's national parks. One summer three years earlier, John Merriam had made one of his many trips to Grand Canyon National Park. Standing on the rim, he listened to visitors' reactions, which reaffirmed his belief that Americans came to such areas to learn, not to play. He felt interpretive facilities should lead them further into a personal exploration of nature. Instead, the Park Service built museums that in his view pandered to the public and diverted attention from the natural phenomenon itself. Above the visitors' heads he could see an obtrusive and inauthentic seventy-foot Indian watchtower the service had constructed on the precipice over the Grand Canyon of the Colorado, and it saddened him.[2]

Merriam's reaction was shared by most of the league's councilors. This was a logical extension of their belief in the scientific and educational potential of parks and their faith in the wedding of the natural and the divine. Although in the early 1920s they had been receptive to federal involvement, they had soon begun to feel that the National Park Service was degrading the inspirational value of national parks and destroying their primitive character. The redwoods, they believed, deserved better. The league's aversion to the Park Service helps explain why no redwood national park was established by donation in the late 1920s, in the manner of a Shenandoah or a Great Smoky Mountains national park. It also explains in part why despite the massive expansion of the national park system during the New Deal, the 1930s brought two redwood national forest purchase units but no redwood national park. The league disagreed with the federal park administrators' conception of the intellectual capacity of average citizens and the function of a national park.

Disagreement and confusion among preservationists as to the purpose of national parks was not unique to the 1930s. It was evident as early as 1916 when the National Park Service was established and stemmed in part from a lack of legal definition. Robert Sterling Yard, retained by Stephen Mather to advertise the parks through the National Parks Association, later recalled, "At the very beginning arose among us the question: What are national parks anyway? Everyone knew generally and no one knew specifically." Horace Albright, Mather's successor as Park Service director, "searched law books and records in vain for a definition. Mather and I asked officials, members of Congress, mark-makers in the west . . . ," only, he added, to get radically different answers.[3] The system had emerged spontaneously; the first parks—as diverse as the vast wilderness of Yellowstone and the small resort of Arkansas's Hot Springs—had been carved out of the public domain for reasons not clearly articulated and an administration superimposed over them.

Yellowstone was set aside by Congress in 1872 "as a public park or pleasuring ground . . . for the benefit and enjoyment of the people." The act stipulated only that all timber, mineral deposits, natural curiosities, or wonders within the reserve be protected from spoliation and retained in their natural condition. The function of subsequent parks was similarly ill-defined. The act creating the National Park Service merely stated that the system was "to conserve the scenery and the natural and historic objects and the wild life therein and to provide for the enjoyment of the same in such manner and by such means as will leave them unimpaired for the enjoyment of future generations."[4] In 1924 Secretary of the Interior Hubert Work issued a statement meant to clarify policy; the parks must "be conserved in their natural state so that coming generations, as well as the people of our own time, may be assured their use for the purposes of recreation, education, and scientific research."[5]

Such declarations were inexplicit enough to allow for the development of two major factions within the preservation movement. The "purists" came to believe that recreation—fishing, skiing, and automotive tourism—should be minimal in national parks. They felt outdoor sports belonged in state and municipal parks and in national forests. Within an ordered, hierarchical public land structure, the national parks were, on the other hand, to fulfill a unique and crowning function. The Park Service was to permit only minimal conveniences and such mild outdoor activities as hiking and camping, so that the parks could serve educational, scientific, and even spiritual purposes.[6] "In addition to the human aspects of religion there must always be an idea of the vastness of the universe," Merriam wrote, and in this vastness we see "a tendency to uniformity that points to the existence of a Supreme Intelligence."[7]

Robert Sterling Yard, Newton Drury, William Colby, Duncan McDuffie, and others from the Sierra Club and the redwoods league shared this vision in the 1920s. Indeed, the purist position was most clearly represented among lay conservationists and those scientists and educators who served under Merriam's chairmanship on the Park Service's advisory committee for park interpretive programs.[8]

In contrast, most of the Park Service's formal leadership was comprised of the other faction of preservationists—"boosters" who promoted the parks, emphasizing good roads and comfortable accommodations. They did not, of course, deny God or higher values. Yet they were above all businessmen. They thought it "unwise and unreasonable" not to boost tourism or facilitate use. The "politics of the situation demanded" it. Mather and Horace Albright believed the parks needed to be "sold," promoted in exchange for congressional appropriations and popular support.[9] With this emphasis upon numbers, park administrators minimized questions of proper use. However, disagreement between the two factions was not total. Merriam was not averse to comforts; indeed he rarely camped, preferring park hotels. Moreover, the purists generally agreed with the Park Service's 1918 decision to permit automobiles in all parks but found discomforting the statement that "every opportunity should be afforded the public, whenever possible, to enjoy the national parks in the manner that best satisfies individual taste."[10] As much as Albright and Mather sought to protect the parks' natural features and called them the "outdoor universities," they could not resist the label "national playgrounds."[11]

The nineteenth-century pioneer booster had believed the iron horse promised economic growth; so too had Mather and Albright seen "every park visitor" as "a potential seller and investor" and every park as a step in the final conquest of the West. The service's annual report for 1925 opened with that theme: "The march of the huge trains along the scarcely discernible trails in the fifties marked the beginning of the settlement of the West. The new people were the settlers and the builders." Now the "new West" was being built up by the "hundreds of thousands in the past few years who have pulled up stakes . . . and invested in western ranches and fruit farms, in mines, and other industrial enterprises." The report added, "in all this the national parks, as the scenic lodestones, through their attractions draw these future settlers and investors for their first trip. . . ."[12]

The service's director and arch-booster, Albright, was convinced that tourists preferred outdoor recreation and entertainment to serious educational experiences. Shortly after Merriam's death in 1945, Albright wrote that he had "never felt" that the league's long-time president "had understood the ordinary American, let us say the common man, as Secretary Wallace calls him. Certainly I felt he had no understanding whatever of the outlook of the average American traveler."[13] And in Albright's view the common man was to be allowed his preferences. "The greatest good for the greatest number," the director declared, "has to have a small place even in the national park administration."[14]

In contrast, Merriam had spoken in 1926 of formulating studies that would present through the parks "the most interesting results in geology and paleontology" and hence greatly advance education in America. "The great number of intelligent people visiting the parks offers opportunities such as are difficult to secure elsewhere," he averred. Albright distorted the will of the majority and the responsibilities of leadership, Merriam wrote a friend.[15]

Despite the leadership's less idealistic view of human nature, the Park Service did expand its educational program, moving from a handful of nature guides for Yosemite in 1919 to the campfire lectures, displays, and literature available in all the parks by 1930. Purists and boosters alike participated but were soon arguing over the character of the programs. Those among the service's educational advisors who favored the approach strenuously advanced by Merriam included W. W. Campbell, astronomer and University of California president; Duncan McDuffie of the Sierra Club; and W. W. Atwood, geologist and president of Clark University—league councilors all. Agreeing with Albright were Hermon Bumpus and, to a lesser extent, redwood councilor Harold Bryant—both Park Service employees active in interpretive work.[16]

Albright and Bumpus sponsored park museums to spell out the significance of the preserved natural features. But the purists disapproved of educational facilities that spread "the whole picture before the visitor," so that he "deceives himself into thinking that everything has been seen at a single glance." They believed tourists must be encouraged to glean the benefits of "personal discovery." Merriam feared that if park education were overdeveloped, the learning process would be transferred away from the natural phe-nomena to museums all too similar to "stereotyped modes of instruction which have developed in the more formal and less effective types of schools."[17] He favored small, outdoor displays that prompted the visitor to open his own eyes. At Yavapai Station on the brink of the Grand Canyon, Merriam's geologic column explained how the visitor could read directly the geologic messages of the "abyss in time" that lay before him. At his Sinnott Memorial the significance and blue beauty of Crater Lake were explained from a vantage point selected to encourage the beholder to look for himself.[18]

Harold Bryant, elaborating in the *Journal of Adult Education* upon an idea popular within the Park Service in the 1920s, said that with proper improvements the parks would become the "great outdoor universities for which their superlative exhibits so finely equip them." Merriam's quick retort was that the parks already "were in their own right the great outdoor universities. This is due to the qualities they possess and not according to what the Park Service may do with them."[19]

In his biography of Horace Albright, Donald Swain wrote that during the 1930s "a growing number of old-line Park Service supporters, such as Yard and the leaders of the Sierra Club, had swerved sharply toward the 'purist' philosophy."[20] In the 1920s purists and boosters had in fact functioned side-by-side within the Park Service with a tolerable level of friction. The league had argued with the federal administrators, but it had funded the 1920 study by the Department of the Interior recommending a redwood national park on the Klamath River. As late as 1928 the San Francisco group had listed as its second, official goal the establishment of a "national redwood park." In August, 1930, however, the league amended its bylaws to delete this second objective.[21] The estrangement had come not, as Swain maintained, because the men had changed but because the situation was altered—by the swelling number of people and automobiles in the parks and the dramatic increase in funds available for park improve-ments and expansion.[22] By the mid-Depression years, Drury was bitterly complaining that the Park Service had an "itch to become a Super-Department of Recreation" or "a glorified playground com-mission." He was alarmed not only by the construction of tramways, toboggan runs, and ski lifts but also by "the almost hopeless lack of imagination, and the cheap showmanship" evident in the agency's programs.[23]

In the 1920s while president of the Carnegie Institution, Merriam had found a quiet haven—Rock Creek Park—only blocks from the automobiles, flashing lights, and streetcar lines of the nation's capital city. There he enjoyed the sound of the creek rapids, "rocks of enormous age, a relic of another world in time," and the seasonal rhythm of the beech trees. He chaired a committee on the city parks of Washington, D.C., and initiated a movement to plant dogwood along Rock Creek. In the 1930s the National Park Service defiled his sanctuary with a celebration of "Dogwood Day," consisting of "activities such as horse-shoe pitching" and "baseball games." To his further dismay, the service undertook the training of a chorus "to render high-class music at sunrise on Easter morning."[24]

By the mid-1930s Merriam was also protesting the service's desecration of the Grand Canyon. The seventy-foot "Indian Watchtower"— an "imitation, not even an authentic reproduction of aboriginal American architecture"—he felt was a needless invasion of the primitive and a threat to the integrity of the education program. It would, he feared, be mistakenly looked upon by visitors as "an original American building" and should be removed.[25] (The next year the *San Francisco Call-Bulletin* did indeed picture the tower with a caption calling it an "ancient monument.")[26] The service retorted that the structure had been planned by its landscape architects and had no relation to the educational program.[27]

Drury and Merriam came to have less and less faith in the service's landscape architects. Drury noted that while the Misíon La Purisíma Concepción in Santa Barbara County, California, might be "an excellent piece of work in type of restoration . . . (once you accept as desirable that sort of thing), the landscape men were all for utilizing a portion of the state holdings for an automobile trailer camp," on the premise that "open space should not be wasted."[28] Other structures resented by the purists included the Hope House at El Tovar at the Grand Canyon; the Pueblo-style building at Mesa Verde, Colorado; and the inauthentic house at Washington's birthplace and the restoration at Williamsburg, both in Virginia.[29] Attention to so many diverse undertakings crippled the naturalist program. The ranger naturalists often lacked expertise, the purists complained, and "jazzed up" their talks with "silly comments," delivered in the style of a "vaudeville show."[30]

The increasing flood of visitors was itself a formidable matter. "I like to sit at my hotel," Merriam wrote of Yosemite, "and enjoy the view. There are a good many hundred other people enjoying the view also. I would like to discover some means by which human beings could be made invisible in the national parks." He believed that through proper planning such areas could absorb large numbers and remain primitive. Instead, the Park Service exaggerated the problem with excessive and careless construction of buildings, roads, and other facilities.[31] Citing the "City of Yosemite," Merriam said it had to be resolved whether a national park was "an outing region, a resting place, a health resort, a place for general educational work, or a region in which certain exceptional natural features have an inspirational value." He believed the service's folly made for a paradox: "regions set aside for protection have been subject to much heavier use and wear than would be the case had the areas not been set aside. . . ."[32]

Afraid that all vestiges of primitive flora and fauna in the parks would be lost, in the 1920s Merriam had initiated a movement to have reserves created within them. These wilderness reserves were to be barred to all but emergency entrances for a period of years. Inspiration for the plan had come through Merriam's familiarity with the Belgian Congo's Parc National Albert, where such reserves afforded primitive isolation. In 1930 his proposal resulted in the establishment of a wilderness reserve of seven square miles in Yosemite. A year later the service adopted in theory the proposal for other parks—although contrary to Merriam's plan, entrance was to be permitted into the areas for scientific research.[33] The innovation was not widely adopted by the service, however, and did little to alleviate overdevelopment.

Contemplating mismanagement of the federal parks, the men of the league saw their own painstaking protection and educational programs as infinitely superior. If Yosemite could ill afford poor administration, the redwoods with their shallow, vulnerable root systems and lush undergrowth could withstand careless use even less.

Although preservation matured during the 1920s, the federal parks did not expand during that decade at nearly the rate they did in the 1930s. The purists believed that quality and primitiveness were the only justified criteria for national park status. Diluted standards, they felt, weakened the moral rectitude of the service and hence its ability to defend its domain against commercial exploitation or demands for development occasioned by such national emergencies as war.[34] Among the added or proposed national parks of the 1920s and 1930s, ones such as Ouachita in Arkansas and Mammoth Cave in Kentucky were seen by these men as simply inferior; others, such as Shenandoah in Virginia and Acadia in Maine, seemed neither outstanding nor primitive.[35] Both secretaries of the Interior in this period, Hubert Work and Ray Lyman Wilbur, explained that the parks had been established primarily because of their recreational value and their proximity to the eastern centers of population.[36] Both boosters and purists claimed to find in the early history of the system verification of their standards, with the latter claiming that the service had distorted its original purpose by deliberately emphasizing "the playground aspect of National Parks in order to secure support of the movement in Congress."

Merriam also charged that park attendance had "in large measure been stimulated by railroad companies and concessionaires whose interest" lay only in the "profit-producing aspect of park travel" without reference to the parks' use as "intended originally."[37] Park officials agreed that recreational emphasis and eastern parks were politically expedient but not that they violated standards.

The purists were further offended as they watched the Park Service acquire the Everglades without first considering how the delicate biota would withstand increased visitor traffic resulting from park status. A Park Service employee admitted that public acquisition was the agency's main concern, with the method of administration "of secondary importance."[38] The service ignored Merriam's suggestion that the Everglades—and the redwoods if federally acquired—be designated biological monuments rather than parks to avoid heavy recreational use. Since the Park Service failed to concern itself with proper protection for the Everglades, the league believed the redwoods would be accorded the same treatment should they fall into the government's hands.[39] And when the federal landscape architects finally did make a use and protection study for the redwoods, Drury pronounced the analysis oversimplified, unsubstantiated, and belated.[40]

Everglades National Park was established with the provision that no federal money be used to purchase the land. Similar clauses providing for acquisition "only by public or private donation" appeared in the acts for Shenandoah and the Great Smoky Mountains national parks.[41] The purists objected to this. They believed total reliance on private subscription seduced the government into accepting low-quality areas and invited local promotion.[42] Especially in times of depression, they felt that local boosters saw parks not as inspirational meccas but as tourist attractions. According to Merriam, one of the most flagrant cases of such promotion was that pursued in behalf of the Everglades by the Coe Committee of Florida. In 1929 Merriam had given his "unqualified support to this project in public speeches in Jacksonville." To his horror, he later learned that those on the Coe Committee "whom he supported were the owners of the worthless land which they expected to sell to the nation."[43] Throughout the Depression decade, the league watched with increasing discomfort as the Ward family, owners of certain low-quality redwood lands along the Klamath River, similarly lobbied vigorously for federal acquisition of their property. The family's efforts proved successful.[44] The Coe Committee—with the aid of the state legislature, Florida commercial bodies, and the National Park Service—also succeeded.

Examples of the Park Service's determination to grow abounded. The agency had assumed administration of Washington, D.C.'s city parks and grabbed every possible historical remain in the nation—shrine, site, cemetery—for its system of national monuments.[45] Drury was dumbfounded when he heard of the service's efforts to acquire Presidio Hill in San Diego, California, a complete restoration with an exotic garden, and the "Old Spanish Light-house," neither old nor Spanish. Nor were the league men pleased with the service's attempts to obtain the privately owned Redwood Petrified Forest in California's Sonoma County. This forest was already well administered and was considered of only state park quality.[46] Merriam noted that "Mr. Albright has stated before the Advisory Board openly on several occasions that the Park Service should . . . have more power, high salaries, and good positions. . . ."[47] Drury commented dryly that it all went to prove "Almost anything can be accomplished by those who have mastered the principles of Dale Carnegie's 'How to Make Friends and Influence People.'"[48] The league did not want the redwoods to fall prey to base expediency.

A large share of the service's growth came at the expense of the Forest Service, and the 1920s and 1930s witnessed constant friction between the federal agencies. Although the feud had begun with the split between Gifford Pinchot and John Muir, the flames of subsequent controversy were fed less by theoretical issues than territorial ones. According to Henry Graves, who became dean of forestry at Yale in 1920 after serving as chief of the Forest Service, conflict was inevitable since parks were often contiguous to national forests and the line between them "wholly arbitrary." Moreover, many parks contained "valuable material resources," while forests held features of "great scenic interest" and recreational value.[49] These territorial ambiguities and the periodic creation of national parks from national forestlands generated tension, one expression of which was the comment by Albright's successor as Park Service director, Arno Cammerer, that the Forest Service men were "jealous of and antagonistic toward the great success in the expansion of the National Park Service" and "constantly striving to block us. . . ."[50]

This bureaucratic rivalry centered on the disposition of forestlands whose value as recreational or wilderness areas surpassed their economic potential. Both services thus came to see recreation as a valuable pawn in the race for territory and congressional appropriations.[51] In the 1920s the purists had sided with the foresters in several skirmishes because they agreed on one policy, that national parks should be restricted to the scenically superior parts of the nation and not be subject to full recreational development.[52] In the 1930s this alliance grew stronger as the purists became convinced that the Forest Service preserved its wilderness areas more completely than the Park Service protected its parks. The foresters seemed less prone to improvements and were evolving a well-defined wilderness program.[53] Yard believed that preservation of the primitive had been simply an accident in national park policy, resulting from the fact that the first parks happened to be underdeveloped. He felt they were preserved only because they were great scenery, making the concept of the primitive no older within the Park Service than within the Forest Service.[54]

Believing that wilderness was safer with the federal foresters than with the Park Service, citizen groups from the Sierra Club to The Wilderness Society and the National Parks Association had for years opposed efforts to have Kings Canyon in Sequoia National Forest transferred to Park Service jurisdiction. In the late 1930s the service sponsored the Gearhart bill, which provided for the transfer of Kings Canyon and for national park acquisition of Redwood Canyon, a privately owned area in the Sierra Nevada. In a bid to break the club's opposition, Franklin D. Roosevelt's secretary of the Interior, Harold Ickes, asked to meet with its directors, who subsequently hosted him at the Bohemian Club in San Francisco. Ickes listened to their objections and agreed to have the bill amended to ensure that Kings Canyon would be kept as a wilderness park. The club endorsed the amended bill, although neither The Wilderness Society nor the National Parks Association did.[55]

Albright asked the league to support the bill with the provision guaranteeing the wilderness character of Kings Canyon.[56] The organization hesitated. Drury told Merriam that he thought Ickes well versed in the use of both "a pistol to the head" and the "siren's song"; with the former Ickes got the Forest Service to approve the transfer, and now the siren's song was "lip service to high park principles."[57]

Drury was not the only one in the league who doubted the words of the song. But the group's leaders did want Redwood Canyon saved. They tentatively decided that in view of the Forest Service's acquiescence and the bill's safeguards for the park's wilderness character, they might support the measure. They asked Merriam if the service could be forced to live up to its promises. He replied that pledges made for political purposes cannot be considered "honest statements."[58] Henry Graves; Frank Wentworth, Bay Area civic leader and industrialist; and other league councilors wrote to Drury protesting league approval of the transfer of Kings Canyon. Long-time councilor J. C. Sperry expressed the common opinion in declaring that Redwood Canyon ought to be a park but that Kings Canyon should remain a national forest, since it should be kept as primitive as possible, "and such would not be the case if it were a national park."[59] The council met again and passed a resolution favoring park status for Redwood Canyon only.[60] Congress passed the Gearhart bill in 1940.

Even the federal foresters, however, were not immune to criticisms from purists. In March, 1934, the National Forest Reservation Commission announced it intended to employ some of President Roosevelt's alotted $20,000,000—originally intended for the expansion of existing national forests east of the Great Plains—to establish new national forest purchase units in the West. The commission commented upon the desirability of having a redwood national forest and indicated that if the Forest Service could find a suitable area, the commission would be willing to consider the purchase.[61] The Forest Service approached the league. The latter's reaction was friendly but cautious; its directors wondered how much land the service proposed to acquire and what was to be the primary function of the reservation. The service replied that it hoped to acquire a large, multiple-use redwood national forest, the main purpose of which would be the production of timber. The trees were to be logged in a selective manner and the area replanted, the methods used designed for the edification of local lumbermen. President Roosevelt's original intention had been that these land acquisition projects be both conservation and relief measures. In accord with this, the service further explained to the league that the redwood national forest would serve two secondary purposes: recreational use and the stabilization of the local economy.[62]

The league charged that the service was taking advantage of an emergency to impinge upon private enterprise. Henry Graves pointed out that the American public would be very critical should the service acquire these very old trees and then proceed to cut them down. He suggested that instead the money be used either to demonstrate good silviculture on private lands, through cooperation with private owners, or to purchase and reforest cutover lands.[63] Some in the league were inclined toward Graves's position; others favored the Forest Service's proposal. But the majority believed that the best solution would be the establishment of a small, experimental tract designed to allow the federal foresters to develop and demonstrate good forestry practices to private timbermen. In the end, despite their aversion to the Forest Service's plan for a large and multiple-use redwood national forest, the league councilors gave their support.[64] Local residents of the northern counties voiced enthusiasm.[65] Federal foresters surveyed the region, and in August, 1935, the National Forest Reservation Commission approved but did not totally fund two redwood purchase units—the first in the very southern portion of the belt, Sonoma and Mendocino counties, and the second in the north, Humboldt and Del Norte counties. The following year the Southern

Redwood Purchase Unit was laid out; it was to comprise an area of 600,000 acres on three coastal watersheds.[66]

Although the league had backed the Forest Service, it was less charitable with the Park Service. At issue was the watershed of Mill Creek, a Del Norte County tributary of the Smith River. In 1925 and again in 1927, landscape architects had recommended state acquisition of 4,000 acres on Mill Creek, making it the league's fourth park project: Jedediah Smith Redwoods State Park.[67] The heart of the park was to be Mill Creek Flat, the trees of which were said to rival the beauty and magnificence of the alluvial stands along Bull Creek.[68] A depressed lumber market and business failures had long since caused the principal owner of the tract, the Del Norte Lumber Company, to take up its railroad and dismantle its mills. Since 1927 the preservationists had known the company wanted to sell.[69] In 1930, having acquired 134 acres of the flat, the league was told it could have the entire 18,380 acres for $2,750,000. By 1932 the price was down to $1,000,000. Nevertheless, as late as 1937 the group had acquired only seven additional acres.[70]

The following year National Park Service investigators recommended that the federal government purchase 18,000 acres on Mill Creek as a redwood national park. The league had known the Park Service might intervene and had previously decided not to endorse such a move.[71] Ironically, the Forest Service was concurrently considering the same Mill Creek area as a location for its Northern Redwood Purchase Unit.[72] The league's directors were less hostile toward the foresters than toward the Park Service, but the purchase unit was slated to be logged, a fate they felt unworthy of Mill Creek. So before either service could act, they passed a resolution asking "that full opportunity . . . be given the state to include the Mill Creek Redwoods in the system of State Redwood parks, and . . . that meanwhile consideration of the acquisition of these lands for either a National Forest or a National Park be deferred; and that the governmental agencies concerned be informed of this action."[73] This request was forwarded to Washington, D.C.[74]

The directors realized their decision was risky; they stood a chance of losing the tract entirely.[75] The Del Norte Lumber Company had recently sold 6,000 acres to a logging firm and was preparing to deed the rest to the state for taxes; the land would then be sold in parcels to the highest bidders. If the acreage were disposed of in this manner, the league would probably not have the funds to bid on it.[76] It was questionable that the group could obtain private money to purchase the land. The only source of state funding was the bill drafted by oil interests and designed to allow drilling on state-owned lands, 50 percent of the royalties to go to state parks. Most of these funds would be used for beach acquisitions, and the men of the league were not pleased with relying upon the oil industry for financing.[77] Yet they were even less pleased about having the Park Service in the redwoods.

The California legislature did pass the oil bill. And by mid-1939 the league had raised twenty-five hundred dollars in private, matching funds, enabling the state to purchase seven thousand acres in the heart of Mill Creek Flat. Several stockholders in the Del Norte Lumber Company had aided the process by holding the land and donating to the project; in the center of the flat today is a memorial grove dedicated to one of these individuals.[78]

Mill Creek Flat was saved, but the league would spend the next forty years trying to purchase the surrounding watershed, and much of the land acquired later would be logged. The league's 1938 vote dramatized basic issues in park administration and the politics of reform. The episode also explains in part why a redwood national forest was established during the New Deal but not a redwood national park. In the early 1940s the Forest Service began land acquisitions in its Northern Redwood Purchase Unit, having decided to locate it along the Klamath River in Del Norte County. Despite aversion to seeing the Ward family succeed in its lobbying, the league voted not to oppose the plan. Funds available to the Forest Reservation Commission had long since been expended, however, so the actual land bought within the two forest units was small and would remain so.[79] The Forest Service had moved into the redwoods. Park Service presence would wait another thirty years.

5
Progressive Opposition to the New Deal: 1930–1949

THERE ARE obvious continuities between the reforms of the progressive period and the New Deal, yet most of those who had considered themselves progressives and who lived into the 1930s opposed Franklin Delano Roosevelt.[1] The men of the league were no exception. Their 1938 vote against a redwood national park reflected differences over park administration, but it also indicated alienation from the New Deal. They repeatedly complained that the New Dealers ignored their years of experience as preservationists. This sense of political isolation was partly a result of party differences, but the rapid centralization of public power also threatened traditional elites. For the monied and the independent businessmen, philanthropy had long provided a voice in public policy, which federal initiative now appeared to be choking off. Similarly, the growth of public expertise promised independent professionals a decreasing role as government consultants.

The influence of these early reformers had been rooted in geographic communities or in professional contacts across the nation. Their anti-New Deal rhetoric expressed a search for community, as they looked from private city clubs to the state to defend their power against federal bureaucratization. It is a credit to the political sagacity of Secretary of the Interior Harold Ickes that to achieve goals he crossed party lines into the power base of nonbureaucratic elites—for instance, personally asking the Sierra Club to support Kings Canyon National Park and twice offering Newton Drury the directorship of the Park Service.

Drury's appointment also showed that the isolation of which these progressives complained was somewhat exaggerated and self-imposed. Their disagreements with the New Deal were partly ideological and were consistent with their earlier positions. Their opposition indicates the entrepreneurial character of their reform efforts. Their paternalistic assumptions that people must earn social amenities warred with the New Deal premise that social services were the public's right. They had pioneered public land management, but many never fully accepted bureaucracies. They preferred administrative expertise balanced by advisory boards or appointive committees. The tragedy of the Depression left them remarkably unaffected; they thought reform amid social unrest dangerous. The pragmatism of the New Deal shocked them. Their determination to make state reform work despite the evils of California politics in the 1930s indicates their distaste for Washington. Year after year Drury and Merriam exchanged bitter reflections on local and national politics.

Shortly after Frank Merriam's gubernatorial victory over Upton Sinclair in late 1934, Drury wrote Merriam that members of the California State Park Commission had been "summoned to Sacramento and presented with the implied alternative of their resignation and dismemberment of the park organization or the resignation of Colonel Wing," chief of the State Division of Beaches and Parks. Wing was in fact sacrificed and replaced with a former commissary contractor, James Snook of Oakland. In rapid succession, the assistant chief, commission secretary, and one of the commissioners also received dismissal notices. The governor then fired the long-time superintendent of the northern redwood park district, Enoch French, and replaced him with, in Drury's words, "a cheap politician with no park training."[2] The league's executive secretary hurried to meet with the new appointee, whom he found playing poker with "three cronies," giving the fellow, Drury later commented, "all the advantage of being 'warmed up.'" After the cronies had departed, the two "sparred verbally for some time." According to the executive secretary, the appointee was "far too smart to say that he would not take the position, as he obviously saw its 'trading' possibilities. . . . Sure enough . . . he was a road contractor" and wanted "to furnish gravel to the highways." French's position was saved through this intervention. "Politicians of the cheapest sort" and a desperate lack of funds, however, would dog the state park effort throughout the rest of the Depression.[3]

In the 1920s the league had established the California state park system and arranged $380,932 in state funding, which together with private monies had saved 6,514 acres of redwoods.[4] In the following decade Drury's group discovered that the administrative structure it had championed concentrated power in the state's chief executive.

Unable to prevent appointment of Chief Snook, Drury at first consoled himself with the fact that the chief's authority was small in relation to that of the commission. However, the legislation of 1927 had given the governor the right to appoint and dismiss commissioners at will. Without his support, the commission was powerless.

Snook and Drury soon clashed over park administration, the latter acting in his capacity as investigating officer for the commission. In the course of an early skirmish, Snook boasted that the governor had told him, "Jim, you go ahead and run the parks, and if the Commission make [sic] you any trouble, I'll run over them." But when the showdown came a year later, Frank Merriam dismissed his spoilsman. Taking advantage of the victory, Drury convinced the commission to establish an administrative committee—to consist of himself and a landscape engineer—that would decide on all questions of policy.[5]

The ineptitude of Snook's administration had, however, taken its toll. In 1936 the commission had proposed that a highway be built around the parks, with the original road left as a scenic parkway. Chief Snook and the Humboldt County Board of Supervisors had defeated the plan. Local boosters argued that an alternate route would "destroy the scenic value of the groves to travelers."[6] That same year a series of damaging park fires broke out, a result of the "total lack of organization" in the Division of Parks "during the ill-fated Snook regime."[7]

To make matters worse, the governor replaced Chief Snook with another political appointee. Drury urged the commissioners to stand firm and test the courage "in high places" to oust the entire body. But they "caved in" and in March, 1937, appointed "sight-unseen, Mr. 'Check' Henning, former Los Angeles city councilman and political wheelhorse, as chief of the division of parks."[8]

Nor was Frank Merriam's administration the worst of that decade in California. William Colby—redwood councilor, Sierra Club leader, and chairman of the State Park Commission in the mid-1930s—later recalled that the preservationists had some trouble with Governor James Rolph, more with Governor Frank Merriam, but that Governor Culbert Olsen was "worst of all."[9]

To obtain state funding during the Depression, the preservationists allied with the oil industry in support of drilling on state-owned tidelands, half of the royalties to go to parks. They received the measure's passage with mixed emotions. What the league, Sierra Club, and State Park Commission wanted but failed to get in the 1930s was a recurrent appropriation that did not have potential for political bargaining, as did the oil money. To control state park policy, the league's directors considered establishing a nonprofit trust similar to that supporting the Smithsonian Institute. Instead, however, they asked Drury to continue as advisor to the park commission and hold the political forces at bay.[10]

The league leaders contented themselves with the existing system because they considered the alternative, federal involvement, a greater evil. In 1937, discouraged with the ongoing battle, Drury wrote Merriam: "As I told you several years ago I am afraid that we made a mistake in providing that the state should be the custodial agency for the redwood parks. Were it not for the general breakdown of national park standards, I surely would advocate incorporation of the main redwood parks and Point Lobos in the national park system." On another occasion he confided that the "political quackery at the federal level" was "because of its plausibility . . . far more poisonous to the nation than the cheap and tawdry, though robust and frank, spoils system such as we have now in California."[11]

The league's officers flirted with the theories advanced by Merriam's brother Charles, a political scientist, on the potential of the "city state," but they concluded that states' rights had the greatest potential to stay "the spirit of dictatorship . . . abroad in the world."[12] By the early 1930s those who had once considered themselves progressives were in agreement with the group's right-wing advocates of states' rights. League leaders such as Vernon Kellogg, forester Walter Mulford, George Grinnell, and Hubert Work believed state sovereignty protected "local pride of possession" and individualism.[13] Councilors Albert W. Atwood of the *Saturday Evening Post* and W. W. Campbell, astronomer and president of the University of California, argued that local governments were fertile political proving grounds, the failures of which would not take a toll upon the entire nation. The men conceded that some functions demanded national uniformity but insisted that in general standardization was an unnecessary evil.[14]

When federal relief monies became available for state park work in 1932, the men of the league called the funding "another of these power organization movements taking advantage" of the Depression and threatening the redwoods.[15] Seeing the Civilian Conservation Corps damage the national parks, they feared the relief camps in the redwoods would similarly be staffed by political appointees untrained in the protection of the primitive.[16] To prevent this, they marshalled their forces. When representatives from California were called in 1932 to confer with the advisory council for the emergency conservation work, they presented the league's park use and protection studies as the bases for relief work.[17]

Once the camps were opened, the league remained vigilant. Drury reported that there had been some "gilding of the lily"—for example, relief crews raking the forest floor—but that the program had brought benefits. Men from the state unemployment camp and the Civilian Conservation Corps cleared campgrounds, opened roads, constructed sanitary systems, and reduced hazards. An "army of unemployed artists [and] draftsmen" from the States Emergency Relief Administration turned out park displays.[18] "It is an ill wind that blows no good," conceded the oil baron and archenemy of the New Deal J. D. Grant.[19]

In 1930 and 1933 bills were introduced into Congress to provide $5 million in federal funding, to be apportioned among the states on a fifty-fifty matching basis, for the purchase of state parks.[20] A few league councilors supported the legislation—Madison Grant, Duncan McDuffie, and George Cornwall, editor of the Portland *Timberman*.[21] But a majority voted against such aid. The California State Park Commission, the National Parks Association, the American Forestry Association, and leading members of the Sierra Club concurred, viewing federal aid as wrong and self-defeating.[22] They argued that if government must trigger park development, people did not want parks. Thrusting gifts upon a state destroyed initiative. And they claimed an unwilling population would not support a project once it was launched. If there was local desire but no money, Washington would lead the state into debt. To the satisfaction of these critics, Congress did not pass the federal aid bills.[23]

In 1936 federal legislation authorized the National Park Service to survey all park, parkway, and recreational facilities—including those of the states—and to transfer with the president's approval appropriate lands from the federal domain to any state or political subdivision thereof.[24] The league and its allies were receptive to appropriate transfers but not to the survey. Drury declared the act "an attempt to crystallize in a permanent government bureau the work undertaken as an emergency measure."[25] The league, National Parks Association, Sierra Club, and American Forestry Association found common cause in opposition. They felt that, unable to administer its own domain, the Park Service was posing as the savior of the states when it should instead pattern itself after California. The California landscape architect Emerson Knight accused the Park Service of "paternalism" and a "hard, ungracious and dictatorial manner" in carrying out the survey. He complained that the presumptuous tone of the service suggested "minds young and inexperienced."[26] The machinery set in motion for the survey was "too cumbersome and unwieldy" and the Park Service too remote and distended. Francis Farquhar of the Sierra Club asked, "What does Washington—and especially, Honorable Harold L. Ickes . . . know of 'the gray fog sweeping softly through the cypresses of Point Lobos?'" Knight charged that national control would create "uniformity of approach, attack and solution. . . . So precious is each state's atmosphere, charm and flora that we should do our utmost to safeguard these qualities for posterity." "Are we not," he asked, "already too much cursed with deadly, monotonous standardization?"[27]

The final blow came in the last year of the decade. In 1938 the league had thwarted Washington's redwood national park proposal by obtaining passage of legislation allowing slant oil drilling on California's beaches. Months later Secretary Ickes announced that he intended to have this source of state revenue diverted to the federal government for national defense. The redwood activists fumed at this. California had the "moral courage and financial courage to build its own parks," and now Ickes was trying to cripple the program. The secretary's attempt failed, but the redwood men's states' rightism did not abate.[28]

In the 1910s and 1920s, they had promoted centralized public administration but had never shaken a suspicion that bureaucracy deadened self-reliance. The New Deal bureaucracy was so large— argued J. D. Grant, Merriam, and Albert Atwood—that one individual could not grasp the workings of even a single agency. Responsibility became too diffuse to identify. The heads of federal bureaus had "extremely large powers compared with most leaders in human affairs."[29] Drury quoted Herbert Hoover on the implacable spirits of bureaucracies: "self-perpetuation, expansion, and an insistent demand for more power."[30]

The league leaders contended that salaried government administrators were not free men and should not make policy. Merriam advised an unheeding Ickes to rely upon a park director adept at business but urged that nonsalaried appointees should do the planning. The league president bemoaned the fact that all decisions were made by the secretary and the service's director rather than by the lay consultants on the Educational or the Science advisory boards.[31] The league was proud of its California system, which separated policy-making from administration. The state director of natural resources and the chief of the division of parks were salaried administrators; nonsalaried, private citizens appointed by the governor to the State Park Commission set policy. Drury was not convinced that civil service laws, the great progressive reform, should govern appointees for policy-making positions.[32]

League supporters believed in the nation's nonpartisan civic clubs. Merriam called them "modern town meetings." Such great city clubs as the Commonwealth Club of San Francisco and the City Club of

Chicago were the hope of democracy; filtering through them, having a "great influence in determining the policies of the nation," was the "best thought in the country." Drury maintained that some of the most effective planning in the nation was that being done by the Forestry and Wild Life Section of the Commonwealth Club.[33] Similarly, many leaders in the Society of American Foresters, American Forestry Association, Sierra Club, and league believed that specialized, lay conservation groups allowed for broadly based, nonpartisan decision-making without bureaucracy.[34]

In addition to upsetting the balance of power, these men believed Roosevelt's administrations were too pragmatic and lacked restraint. Within their own ordered cosmos, Merriam and his allies pursued what they called "constructive idealism," meaning they implemented basic ideals with restraint and simplicity. Merriam regretted that social scientists had not yet formulated rigid principles for society similar to the laws of gravitation and evolution. Showing a conservative attention to means, the league's leaders pursued a well-balanced, specialized program in which every step was fully understood before it was undertaken.[35] They expected as much from the federal government. Instead, they watched the growth of pragmatism in federal agencies, the destruction of states' rights, and the increasing power and ambition of men such as Secretary Ickes. Deriding the New Dealers as opportunists, one redwood director stated, "In an idealistic program, temporary financial advantage should not be the determining factor."[36]

They did not believe the Depression had discredited existing institutions. It had been the result of bad judgment and disorganization in business, of New York's "moral failure." Merriam advised the Park Service to acquire a Florida boom town, "with its macadam streets, cement sidewalks, ornate street lights and flimsy houses," as an instructive monument to the "gambling binges" of the 1920s. Restraint and individual control were the only cures for social evils.[37] "In a democracy the people must be greater than the government and . . . control it," Merriam said.[38] From the pages of the *Saturday Evening Post*, Atwood admonished reformers to learn patience; it was far easier to convince a bureaucrat than to sway a citizenry.[39] It was the duty of thinking men to formulate principles and effect social regeneration. Since the 1910s these reformers had distrusted what they felt was undiscerning popular support.[40]

Opposition to the New Deal and purism were complementary stances. As with the National Parks Association, the league, the American Forestry Association, and to a lesser extent the Sierra Club, the purist philosophy was generally accompanied by an anti-New Deal position, both philosophies emphasizing restraint, frugality, and idealism.[41] The league's officers found it easy to move from cosmic law to social principle, and they hoped parks would help the public make that leap.

A fear of being ignored reinforced the philosophical discontinuity between these reformers and the New Deal. In 1937 the organization received the Park Service's report recommending Mill Creek as a national park. Drury complained that it was inaccurate and that the league had not been consulted. Merriam replied that it was inconceivable that "any Regional Office should make a report first as to what should be done and indicate later it would attempt to find out" the intentions of other parties involved. Anticipating the Park Service's move, he had previously told Drury there was "grave danger in attempting to force a program of land purchase for national parks . . . without taking into consideration the long and careful study . . . by the Save the Redwoods League." He complained, "Frankly, I am sometimes a little irritated that the people with whom we have common interests come to Washington, proceed with their business . . . as if the long-extended experience of some of us . . . had no bearing on their programs."[42]

As an offshoot of the national preservation movement, the league had been nurtured in the 1910s and 1920s by the federal bureaus. The association's first Committee on a Redwood National Park had included Franklin K. Lane, secretary of the Interior; E. C. Bradley, assistant secretary of the Interior; Henry Graves, then of the Forest Service; Gilbert Grosvenor of the National Geographic Society; William Kent, sponsor of the 1916 National Park Service Act; and Stephen Mather of the Park Service.[43] Throughout the 1920s the league had communicated regularly with directors Mather and Albright about a redwood national park.[44] The service had volunteered that federal action would be "governed by the recommendations" of the league. Henry Graves and his successor as chief, William Greeley, also backed the redwood group. In 1925 Drury escorted Secretary of the Interior Hubert Work through the northern woods, and four years later Ray Lyman Wilbur, long-time league councilor, became secretary of the Interior.[45]

John Merriam had been a leader in the National Parks Association, American Forestry Association, American Association for the Advancement of Science, and National Conference on Outdoor Recreation. In mid-decade he had organized the Committee on the National Relations of the Redwoods, consisting of representatives from such groups.[46] Failure to establish a redwood national park in the 1920s was due to opposition from western resource users and states with no national parks, not to the league's lack of influence. It stemmed also from federal laissez-faire policies and ultimately from the league's own satisfaction with the California state park system.[47]

During the 1920s and early 1930s, Merriam had been active on the Advisory Board of the National Park Service and chairman of its Committee on Educational Problems in the National Parks. Two years after assuming office, Ickes replaced this committee with the Advisory Board on National Parks, Historic Sites, Buildings, and Monuments.[48] The old committee had consisted of men recommended by Merriam: four biologists, a paleontologist, an archaeologist, and a geologist.[49] Of the eleven on the new committee, only three had Merriam's approval. The other eight were historians. The new board displaced Merriam and his philosophy, diminishing his admiration for the service.[50] In contrast to the Park Service, federal foresters continued to consult the league in the 1930s, which partially accounts for the latter's receptivity to the Forest Service.[51]

These opponents of the New Deal perceived that the growth of the public sector threatened the private reformer. In this the league found kindred spirits among the leaders of the American Forestry Association, National Parks Association, and Sierra Club. The 1930s heightened these reformers' proclivity toward privatism. Merriam complained of "scientific politics," the government's increasing inclination to hire its own researchers rather than using university and foundation consultants.[52]

Insofar as these ex-progressives were in exile, however, it was partly self-imposed. Despite their Republicanism, the organization's national influence did not disappear under the New Deal. The chiefs of the Forest Service, Robert Stuart and Ferdinand Silcox, were league officers, and the Park Service directors, Albright and Arno Cammerer —old friends of Drury—became league councilors in the 1930s. Frank Kittredge, a regional director of the service, had long been acquainted with the league and professed great respect for its executive secretary.[53] John Merriam's son Lawrence worked for the New Deal Park Service and consulted with his father's allies. If Ickes never became a league councilor, it was because he was never asked.

Secretary Ickes ignored Merriam's protest against the new advisory board but arranged a meeting with him through his brother Charles. Afterwards John Merriam declared he was impressed with Ickes's "desire to do important work" and sympathized with "the tremendous handicap of anyone coming into a task as Secretaryship of the Interior without long experience" in the field. Merriam gave Ickes "as definitely as possible" his views on park administration. He reiterated the importance of having the Park Service director handle administrative business and having boards do the planning.[54]

Merriam held a formal dinner for the secretary, attended by those with whom the league president had worked in the educational program. The purpose of the gathering was to discuss selection of the next Park Service director. According to Merriam, the diners placed Drury "No. 1 on the list" of those they recommended for the position. Shortly thereafter Ickes offered the directorship to Drury, who declined out of principle and because federal salaries were too low.[55] Ickes's offer, ignoring as it did Drury's Republicanism, attests to the league's continued influence.

Insofar as these older reformers did lose influence in the 1930s, the responsibility was to some extent theirs. The league's ideological opposition to the New Deal resulted in part from its financial base. By 1940 public funding accounted for over half of the redwoods saved, but the organization had to raise matching private subscriptions. Such of its memorials as the Children's Forest, originally dedicated to deceased children, accommodated small donations, but its funding success depended upon large gifts. In 1939, for example, 189 persons gave 13 percent of the funding for the Avenue of the Giants; the remainder came from only five individuals.[56] Inclusion of John D. Rockefeller, Jr.'s two million dollar donation in the 1930s for Bull Creek Flat in Humboldt Redwoods State Park further diminishes the significance of the small gift. Since the early 1920s J. D. Grant, long-time chairman of the league's board of directors, had claimed that taxes were destroying America's entrepreneurs and thus the league.[57] (In fact, because of the charitable deduction, the income tax improved the group's fortunes.) But dependence upon the rich and well-born and believers in rugged individualism such as Grant contributed to the league's anti–New Deal stance.

Nevertheless, the organization's dominant tone was supplied by those who considered themselves progressives.[58] The broad spectrum of political inclinations among early twentieth-century reformers makes judgments as to the continuity of New Deal and progressive period reforms hazardous. The difference between such progressives as Harold Ickes and Herbert Hoover proved wide when both faced the Depression decade. Yet Otis L. Graham, Jr., has demonstrated that most progressives who lived into the 1930s did not support Roosevelt. He lists what bothered them about the New Deal: its spending, its encouragement of such special interests as labor, its seeming confusion and flexibility, and the hint of federal paternalism. In a passage that rings particularly true for the league men, he notes that many progressives believed "Power must be accepted with reluctance, borne with dignity, employed in a disciplined way through a clear program, aimed at achieving certain clearly stated ends."[59]

The antagonism league men felt toward the federal reformers in the 1930s involved little discontinuity. Even in the 1910s and 1920s, they demonstrated a philosophy that blended elitism and a democratic spirit, a predilection toward political morality, and a distrust of power. These traits, plus their idealism, set them apart from most New Dealers. The league's leaders harped on the importance and correctness of their programs during the 1930s in part because of their relative loss of influence as Republicans and purists—as well as the fear that bureaucracies threatened their role as independent scientists, educators, and conservationists. But it was also an insecurity of reformers who found themselves swimming against the liberal tide. The stridency registered, too, a budding fear that man was not as much in control of his world as they had thought.

In 1939 Secretary Ickes again faced the necessity of appointing a director for the National Park Service. Having personally solicited Sierra Club support for the establishment of Kings Canyon National Park, Ickes was acquainted with club leaders. He approached Joel Hildebrand, club president, saying that he wanted a westerner to head the service and asking for a suggestion. In the mid-1930s the club had lobbied unsuccessfully to get Drury appointed chief of California's Division of Parks. Not surprisingly, Hildebrand now promoted Drury's candidacy as director.[60] In 1939 Ickes once more offered the league's executive secretary the position. This time Drury accepted.

Samuel P. Hays has suggested that twentieth-century American reform has been a grand scheme of centralization induced by technology and scientific change.[61] This establishes a connection between the processes of adjustment to modernization attempted by the progressives and those made by the New Dealers, a connection that transcends the politics of individual participants. Drury's assumption of the directorship confirms this thesis. After having declined the position in 1934, he had told Merriam that he despised the overdevelopment of the national parks, the "cheap showmanship" of the service, and the sapping of the independence of states. But he had prophesied that "it seems inevitable that present tendencies will in the next generation focus most of the power for good or evil in this country increasingly in the central government." In all fields and especially preservation, he concluded, "The motive force is in Washington—there is no mistaking that. . . . From there the plans (if there are plans) will be made."[62]

Despite the seeming inevitability of standardization, reformers have maintained strong, ideological differences, the interplay of which affected the course of American politics. During the New Deal the league and its officers exerted a moderating influence within national preservation. Drury entered office determined to limit boosterism and centralization. As Park Service director from 1940 to 1951, he pursued a course of moderation and purism. He fought to end the park concessionaire's practice of throwing a ball of flaming brush over Yosemite Valley's Glacier Point for the entertainment of nightly visitors because the "fire fall" damaged the terrain and was inappropriate. He discouraged the service's scheduled feedings of garbage to the Yellowstone bears, a practice conceived to ensure tourists a glimpse of wildlife. Somewhat disgruntled, Albright is reputed to have commented facetiously to a friend that "Drury wants things so natural in the national parks that he would like people to check their contraceptives at the entrance station."[63] Drury spent his twelve years as director staving off industrial inroads into the parks, although Ickes eventually concluded Drury was "not a fighter" and too ready to compromise.[64] When lecturing in the early 1940s to a southern audience, the one-time campus progressive found, to his mild surprise, the crowd cheering his states' rights stance.[65]

If his new position had not changed Drury, neither did his departure for Washington alter the league. Aubrey Drury, his partner in Drury Brothers Advertising, assumed the league's management. Due to Aubrey's success as a fund-raiser, the memorial grove system occasionally outstripped state appropriations. However, the state cooperated through the 1940s, so the parks grew. The league worked to realize Mather's vision—a scenic parkway along the South Fork of the Eel River called the Avenue of the Giants. Since demand for timber was low, the Pacific Lumber Company deferred logging along the Avenue of the Giants and allowed the park men to place a sign soliciting funds on company lands. Other companies were similarly accommodating.[66] Neither the league nor Newton Drury encouraged federal involvement in the redwoods and were defensive when others raised the issue.

In 1945 and 1946 California's congressional representative Helen Gahagan Douglas sponsored a bill, inspired by Gifford Pinchot, to create a Franklin Delano Roosevelt Memorial National Forest. For $100,000,000 the federal government was to acquire 2,815,360 acres in northern California. The reserve was to encompass the northern habitat of the redwood, from Sonoma County to the Oregon border. The land was to be acquired in installments and administered by the Forest Service under the principles of sustained yield and selective cutting, which Pinchot recommended for the redwoods.[67] The press and chambers of commerce of Humboldt and Del Norte counties were outraged at the prospect of a "government grab" of 90 percent of their counties' lands.[68] Although the Forest Service was more receptive to the plan than was the Park Service, neither the Department of Agriculture nor the Department of the Interior sanctioned the bill. It was, however, strongly backed by Anthony Smith, assistant director of the Industrial Union Councils of the CIO, and endorsed by the membership of the CIO proper, the Farmers' Union, and the Union for Democratic Action.[69]

From the Park Service's wartime headquarters in Chicago, Drury denounced the bill as infeasible and pointed out that the state was already saving the redwoods. He could not, however, ignore the legislation. Should it pass, the league's projects would be threatened with federally directed logging. Drury contacted Frederick Law Olmsted, who had designed the California park system. The two studied a map of the redwood region. In November, 1946, they proposed that Representative Douglas amend her bill to direct that the watersheds above each of the four state parks, about 10 percent of the land, be managed as parks—that is, preserved, not logged.[70] Drury believed such a plan would give the parks appropriate settings and good watershed protection. He and Olmsted also proposed that the California State Park Commission administer these watersheds.[71] Representative Douglas incorporated the amendments into her proposal, yet neither Drury nor the Department of the Interior supported the revised bill she introduced in 1949.[72]

The league also refused endorsement. Denying their position was either political or ideological, the councilors explained that because of their relations with the state and the residents of Del Norte and Humboldt counties, they could not "approve or advocate the bill in question . . . even though it held out a glittering prospect of obtaining many of the league's objectives with ease." By publicly denying endorsement, they hoped that "should the bill fail we shall not have lost our friends in the redwood counties."[73]

Despite such disclaimers, the councilors were both ideologically opposed to the Douglas bill and personally interested in maintaining the status quo. Unlike the 1937 proposal, however, the chances that this bill would have passed were slim. Moreover, advocacy might have cost support from the state, which was sensitive to the northern counties' growing economic hostility to land acquisitions. Association with either New Deal legislation or Helen Gahagan Douglas's legislation might also have alienated donors drawn to the organization because it was a moderate, state and privately backed agent of reform.

The failure to establish a redwood national park in the 1930s or

1940s was tragic. The interwar decades were the last in which large, totally unlogged watersheds still existed. This was the last period in which a sizable public purchase might have been accomplished with ease. The league's leaders failed to realize the speed with which the postwar world was to accomplish that which the 1930s had failed to do—undermine the principles upon which their organization had been founded. They could not have foreseen that dramatic cultural, environmental, and social changes would soon produce from an old ally, the Sierra Club, an enemy that would usurp their leadership in the movement to save the redwoods.

6
Evolution and Ecology

PRIOR TO World War II, the Save-the-Redwoods League and the Sierra Club were allies. They shared common goals and a common philosophy, based in part upon the influence of evolutionary assumptions. During the 1930s and 1940s, the natural sciences made dramatic advances. The club was deeply influenced by the resulting modern ecological perspective. The league continued to reflect the thought of the earlier period.

Generalizations about the history of the twentieth-century biological sciences are hazardous, yet it is possible to suggest three periods in their development. During the progressive years from the 1890s through the 1920s, most scientists and probably most college-educated Americans subscribed to some directional interpretation of evolution. Either they simply believed, as did John Merriam, that natural history was progressive or else they advocated, as did Henry Fairfield Osborn, some specific theory of orthogenesis. Such assumptions had scientific as well as philosophical and religious origins. The evolutionary sciences not only allowed but encouraged many Americans to hold to their previously conceived view that the universe was ordered, thereby contributing to the intellectual climate of these years.

Like most reformers of the progressive years, early wilderness advocates were generally moderate reformers. Aside from an exceptional individual such as John Muir, club founder and its first president, they did not seriously challenge industrial or technological progress. Their faith in progressive evolution limited their advocacy of reform and prevented them from denying a belief in human control over the natural world. Theories of directed evolution presumed that nature produces ever more complicated, powerful, and adaptive creatures and that man's brain was the summit of this process. Technology, then, was the fulfillment of natural history.

The 1930s and 1940s witnessed significant advances in the biological sciences, especially in population genetics. Directional theories were discredited, and a consensus reached by 1950 within the scientific community that evolution was the product of random genetic change and the opportunistic process of natural selection. This view of natural history was absorbed into the consciousness of educated Americans in the late 1940s and 1950s. The new synthesis of genetics and selection underlay the ecological perspective and environmental militancy of much citizen activism of the past quarter century. This evolutionary synthesis proved just as conducive to the questioning of human dominance and material progress as did awareness of environmental deterioration. The synthesis underscored the chance course of natural history and the equality of species. The Sierra Club was caught up in this philosophical shift that coincided with, indeed helped cause, its entry into the redwoods' fate.

In the late nineteenth century, Charles Darwin's theory of natural selection had been well accepted, at least by younger naturalists of the period. Indeed, by the 1880s his followers had become highly theoretical and were attempting to explain all biological change by adaptation. Not surprisingly, about 1890 scientists began to question whether natural selection was in fact the controlling force in evolution, and by 1910 some were proclaiming the death of Darwinism. They did not doubt the fact of evolution but Darwin's explanation of its causes.[1]

Taking their cue from the Dutch botanist Hugo de Vries, some antiselectionists attacked Darwin's theory at its most vulnerable point—the lack of a sound theory of genetics. When de Vries rediscovered Mendel's work in 1900, this weakness was not rectified because the Dutch botanist disagreed with Darwin's position that small adaptive changes were the controlling factor in evolution. From the turn of the century through the 1920s, geologists estimated the age of the earth to be only about 100 million years. Given this estimate, early geneticists concluded that only dramatic leaps, or mutations, could explain the formation of new species. On the basis of experiments showing that artificial selection had no effect on certain plant species, they concluded that selection would not generate the genetic raw materials necessary for evolution. Thus the rediscovery of Mendel's experiments further undermined Darwinism.[2]

De Vries, however, projected random mutations, and many scientists soon concluded that his theory was no more adequate to explain evolution than was Darwin's. They pointed to the lack of fossil evidence of dramatic, adaptive genetic leaps. They argued that random mutations could not explain the substantial progress of natural history. Wrote one such opponent of discontinuous evolution, "You might as well argue about the random aberrations of a canal boat swinging on its tow rope as compared with the course of a ship on the open sea, as to conclude that the random mutations of *Drosophila* tell us much about the evolution of insects."[3]

Meanwhile botanists and paleontologists were also questioning the adequacy of natural selection to explain evolution. Among other issues, they found changes in organisms that appeared nonadaptive or actually disadvantageous to survival.[4] Darwin, Lyell, and Lamarck had pondered these problems. But the most serious doubt that now arose was the result of the weaknesses in early genetics and the unfortunate expression "survival of the fittest," which Herbert Spencer coined and Darwin accepted. It became clear to early twentieth-century scientists that survival was not the issue. The question was the multiplication of variants, or intraspecific diversity. Darwinian adaptation made for equilibrium. Early scientists such as Stanford's Vernon Kellogg and Henry Fairfield Osborn—both league officers— studied large populations and confirmed the statistical drift toward stability and specialization. How, then, could a species retain the genetic information to respond to environmental change? Critics noted, "Natural selection tends to preserve the type rather than the variants and hence opposes change."[5] One biologist wrote that natural selection was "an improbable assumption."[6] Almost all early twentieth-century scientists believed natural selection to be a factor in progressive evolution, but most doubted it was the primary cause.[7]

The result of these reservations as well as the rivalry between the geneticists and the selectionists was theoretical chaos among evolutionists during the decades between 1890 and 1930. In the vacuum that resulted, many scientists fell back upon theories of directed evolution. One of the most popular of these was orthogenesis—used here as an umbrella term referring to variant theories from the Russian zoologist Leo Berg's nomogenesis to Osborn's aristogenesis and Edward Sinnott's telism. First advanced in the 1880s and 1890s by, among others, Thomas Eimer and E. D. Cope, orthogenesis meant literally "straight origins," or "straight-line evolution."[8] The term varied in meaning from the overtly vitalistic and theological to the mechanical. It ranged from theories of mystical forces to mere descriptions of a general trend in development due to natural limitations of either the germinal material or the environment. Some late nineteenth- and early twentieth-century scientists such as Joseph LeConte, a University of California professor of geology, botany, and natural science, were dualists who saw evolution as the hand of God in nature. By 1910, however, most who subscribed to orthogenesis hypothesized some physical rather than metaphysical determinant of orderly change.

The first proponents had argued that directed evolution was caused by external circumstances such as climate or nutrition. This theory continued to be accepted by some paleontologists and biologists in the twentieth century but became known as orthoselection. By 1910 orthogenesis referred almost exclusively to momentum generated by a force within the organism itself.

Not all advocates of directed change specifically advocated orthogenesis. Such leading geneticists as Kellogg and David Starr Jordan— a founder of the Sierra Club and president of Stanford University— were not exponents of orthogenesis, yet they wrote of "orderly mutants," "homologous variation," and "determinate variation." They theorized that progressive genetic leaps were necessary to explain evolution and noted studies that indicated species mutate in a certain direction generation after generation. In 1934 scientists from the University of Michigan told the American Society of Naturalists that the repeated occurrence of white eye in *Drosophila* indicated that some "paths are closed."[9]

Nevertheless, it was paleontologists like John Merriam who most readily viewed evolution as progressive. In fact, a large factor in the acceptance of orthogenesis was their tendency to place fossils in a pattern with what they considered the most primitive at the bottom and the most modern at the top. They presumed, for example, that since cartilage and gills predated bones and lungs, they had somehow caused them. Possessing only a few fossils in a phylogenetic line, paleontologists drew the most economical line between them. In the 1910s the New York Museum of Natural History developed, under Osborn's direction, a display showing the horse evolving upward in a straight line from a small doglike mammal to the modern horse. Phylogenetic lines progressed in a manner seeming to early paleontologists so fixed as to be predestined.[10]

Biologists also used orthogenesis and orthoselection to explain both the extinction of species and the emergence of biological structures that were presumed to have been useless before fully developed, like the snake's rattle or the human ear. The most popular proof of orthogenesis was "parallelism," meaning the independent appearance of similar structures—such as the flower—in unrelated organisms or groups of organisms within different environments.[11]

Even staunch supporters of orthogenesis admitted that natural selection played a role in evolution, but they argued that the environment acted as a mere referee, eliminating only the grossly inadaptive variations. Many forms could survive within any given environment;

selection was not creative. There must be, they believed, some other force that accounted for the transition from single cell to complex organisms.[12]

The reasons for the acceptance of theories of orderly mutation, orthoselection, and orthogenesis are complex. Darwin had considered past evolution perfectionist, but he had tried to see selection as no more than a process. Yet under the influence of nineteenth-century notions of progress and religious sensibilities, many of his followers had transformed natural selection and mutation into theories of directed evolution, promoting popular acceptance of evolution. Thomas Huxley, Osborn's English mentor, was one such individual. The fusion of Christianity and evolution also accounted for some of the prevalence of explanations from design popular around the turn of the century.[13] By the 1910s, however, most American scientists had moved away from such overtly metaphysical explanations, and scientific reasons accounted in significant part for the prevalence of directional explanations.

Orthogenesis and related theories were popular in a period when biologists were searching for laws like those physicists and chemists were finding, and some naturalists were persuaded of the validity of orthogenesis by its corollary, the law of the "irreversibility" of evolution. In 1934 Harold Blum of the University of California argued before the American Association for the Advancement of Science that if chance variation were the rule in evolution, unfit mutations would continue to occur at a statistically constant rate despite their nonadaptive character. Instead, he noted that evolution had progressed and certain forms had long since ceased to appear. How does the prevailing close fit between the environment and the organism occur? Blum postulated a directive factor and found it in the second law of thermodynamics. Evolutionary changes are accompanied by an increase in entropy and are therefore irreversible. The loss of free energy is orthogenetic. Other exponents of orthogenesis simply argued that there was no paleontological evidence that phylogenetic lines ever retrogressed (the horse, for example, never reacquired the four toes characteristic of its ancestors) or of species abandoning advantages like the flowered structure once achieved. These they took as evidence that genetic change was not random.[14]

Above all, the state of biological research contributed to acceptance of directional theories. Few phylogenetic lines had been fully traced; the range of geological time was thought to be a mere 100 million years. Also little data was available on natural populations, and genetic theories were primitive. Introductory college texts as late as the mid-1930s told students, "It must be admitted that as yet biologists do not fully understand the manner in which evolution has taken place and the factors which have been responsible for it."[15] Scientists had only enough evidence to question natural selection. Their observations seemed to indicate evolution was directional, and many could not reconcile this order with random processes of natural selection or mutation.

Perhaps the greatest irony of this uncertainty was that fundamentals of what would become the accepted theory were known: Darwin's theory of natural selection, Mendel's work on inheritance, and the Hardy-Weinberg theory. But exponents of Mendelian heredity continued to ally through the 1920s with mutational theories—random or directed—and to fight the selectionists. These geneticists argued that the environment may be a selective agent but not a causal or creative one. Conversely, most proponents of natural selection rejected Mendelian heredity; without a good theory of genetic change, selection was not convincing. The controversy between geneticists and Darwinians, together with the primitive state of genetics, significantly delayed consensus as to the mechanism of evolution.[16] In the turmoil rival and generally directional theories were popular.

Although orthogenesis seemed to account for the facts and was popular from the 1890s through the 1920s, neither paleontologists nor geneticists could identify the force behind it. Participants at a 1921 Symposium on Orthogenesis before the American Society of Zoologists argued for a physio-chemical determinant—possibly hormonal—which was the most popular explanation.[17] After all, as one evolutionist wrote, "no chemical substance is capable of reacting in every conceivable way."[18] Another adherent argued that orthogenesis in fish was determined by egg-cases; yet another suggested a substance in the germ plasm accounted for evolution's perfecting tendency. One geneticist postulated that the genes that produce selectively neutral or detrimental characteristics may have a selective advantage in the embryo.[19] One exasperated biologist commented in 1935, "What the world needs, then, is not a good five-cent cigar, but a workable—and correct—theory of orthogenesis."[20] Failing to find a physical explanation, some proponents slipped into the overtly metaphysical realm or a vitalism similar to that of Henri Bergson, a tendency that other exponents found embarrassing and loudly disclaimed.[21] However, certainly all versions of the theory—mechanical or nonmechanical—were deterministic. In 1928 a botanist wrote, "Evolution is intrinsic, kinetic, progressive, orthogenetic, perfective and determinative."[22]

It is difficult to assess exactly how many scientists accepted orthogenesis, orthoselection, and related theories during their heyday from the 1880s through the 1920s. Textbooks suggested three explanations of evolution: Darwinian natural selection, de Vries random mutation, and orthogenesis. Some noted that the first two failed to explain the progressive appearance of new biological forms.[23] There were of course strident critics, especially among geneticists. Wrote one, "The theory of orthogenesis depends for its acceptance not so much upon our knowledge of certain facts as it does on our ignorance of them."[24] Despite such attacks, perhaps half of the geneticists, biologists, and paleontologists of the 1900s and 1910s advocated some measure of the theory and vied into the 1920s with the demoralized exponents of natural selection,[25] at the "lowest ebb" of its general acceptance during those years.[26] Indeed, the historian Edward Radl wrote in 1930 that Hans Driesch's work in the 1890s marked the "end of Darwinism."[27]

It would be most accurate to suggest that even into the 1930s many biologists, geneticists, and paleontologists fell back upon preadaptive or finalistic theories at some point in their careers, even if they did not overtly espouse orthogenesis. Through the 1920s and 1930s, the French geneticist Cuénot tried to reconcile random mutations with the nonrandom nature of adaptation. Failing, in 1942 he postulated a finalistic solution. Then in 1951 he reversed himself. In the 1940s Julian Huxley wrote that orthogenesis was not the prime cause of evolution. Pages later he stated that orthogenesis may sometimes be at work in evolution.[28]

Certainly through the 1920s, if not the 1930s, most geneticists and paleontologists assumed that evolution was directional even while they criticized orthogenesis. In the 1920s Huxley denounced all forms of vitalism yet maintained that evolution was progressive, meaning that organisms increased in size, in their capacity for self-regulation, and in the character of their psychical faculties.[29] Attacking the theory of orthogenesis, in 1928 the University of Chicago geneticist H. H. Newman wrote, "It should be said that definitely directed evolution is now believed to be one of the laws of organic evolution but we have no clear ideas as yet as to what are its causes. Therefore, orthogenesis is not a causo-mechanical theory of evolution at all."[30] As late as the 1940s, selectionists countered orthogenesis with their own theory of orthoselection.[31]

There were, of course, early twentieth-century intellectuals such as Thorstein Veblen and John Dewey who rejected teleological assumptions, and philosophers in the 1920s like Bertrand Russell who, influenced by Darwin's theories and World War I, saw an "indifferent universe" in which man was not in control of his fate.[32] Nevertheless, widely used college texts in the 1920s and 1930s indicate that Veblen and Russell's philosophical naturalism were not characteristic of at least the academic scientific community. Edited by H. H. Newman, the University of Chicago's undergraduate introduction to the sciences included essays from leaders in each major field from astronomy to physics. These denied the compatibility of the supernatural and empirical, but their assumptions were often teleological. They informed undergraduates that researchers were confirming the orderliness and hierarchical progression of natural history. We now know, they claimed, "order is universal," and the "old saying" that "an irreverent astronomer is mad" applies to the physicist and biologist as well. The texts announced that through science man learns "something of his own colossal stature." He sees that his own intelligence, "which enables him to make such sublime discoveries, is the supreme achievement of evolution."[33] A popular 1924 botany text opened with a photograph of the redwoods. The book concluded with a description of Ralph Chaney's research on the trees' migration across the Bering Sea and a statement assuring students of continued material progress within an ordered universe.[34]

Certainly the scientists who led the wilderness movement from the 1890s through the 1930s believed evolution directional. Natural scientist Joseph LeConte was one of the club's founders, the man to whom it dedicated its Yosemite Valley headquarters in 1902. Before his death the previous year, he had written extensively, outlining for fellow Americans a synthesis of direct agency and natural law. His was a rational, scientific theology in which God had both a real, independent existence and an immanence in nature—and in which man possessed two natures, the animal and the spiritual. With these dualities, LeConte perceived design in nature. Evolution was creation, "the conception of the one infinite, all-embracing design, stretching across infinite space." He believed the very existence of man proved that evolution moves toward "greater physical and spiritual development."[35] John Muir similarly combined an absorbing interest in geological and biological forces with faith in a universe of "law, order, creative intelligence, loving design." Such 1920s and 1930s club leaders as the professor of theology William F. Badé and the subdivider Duncan McDuffie also reached philosophical solutions allowing for both the inspiration of universal purpose and the evidence of science.[36] Club leader David Starr Jordan claimed to reject the metaphysical, but in addition to arguing for the "orderly mutant," he concluded his 1908 text on *Evolution and Animal Life* by saying, "We see the hand of the Almighty in nature everywhere. . . . We have found . . . that all we have ever known to be done on earth has been done in accordance with law."[37]

The thought of LeConte, Muir, Badé, and Jordan closely resembled that of the league's officers; in fact, the two organizations' leaderships overlapped. Vernon Kellogg co-authored *Evolution and Animal Life* with Jordan and wrote extensively in the first decades of the century on "determinant variation" in evolution.[38] Osborn's aristogenesis was a variant of orthogenesis. Merriam never discussed the precise mechanism behind progressive evolution but was convinced it existed. He retained his faith in cosmic design until his death in 1945. So did league director Willis Jepson. Ralph Chaney, the league's president from 1945 through the 1960s, advocated orthoselection.[39]

These men projected their teleological world view into the wilderness and park movement. To Muir, Badé, McDuffie, LeConte, Merriam, Osborn, and the others, wilderness parks were classrooms, museums, and temples within which one worshipped and studied a universe of continuity and design.[40] This explains their affinity for the "monumental" in nature[41]—such arresting sights of perfectionist geological and biological forces at work as a Yosemite or the redwoods.

If these scientists were unlike Veblen in their teleological world view, they did share with him what became known as reform Darwinism. They actively propagated the idea that man's reason liberated him from the laws of organic evolution and gave him the power of "self determined evolution."[42] They believed more human progress could be realized though social cooperation than through the survival of the fittest or laissez-faire. They fought to save wilderness and established centralized systems of professional, public land management.

Orthogenesis and related assumptions of directional evolution also limited, however, their advocacy of reform. Much has been written about the progressives' rejection of the formalism of Social Darwinism.[43] But widespread faith in progressive evolution indicates that even liberally inclined scientists had not freed themselves from an essentially deterministic perspective as had Veblen. The assumption behind orthogenesis and related theories was that nature produces ever more complicated, powerful, and adaptive creatures and that man is the summit of this process. Biologists were convinced that evolution proved man was part of the natural world and that his brain was the highest product of its directional momentum. Thus technology was not a violation of nature but a fulfillment of natural history. The combination of reform Darwinism and orthogenesis or related theories, therefore, inclined them at once toward collective responsibility for the human state and against serious questioning of industrial progress.

Not surprisingly, they balanced their desire to save wilderness against a fundamental optimism regarding progress in science and technology. Although romantics, the league's leaders did not reject civilization. The need to escape into the wilds was satisfied by a vacation outdoors and did not necessitate abandonment of urban life.[44] League councilor Albert Atwood of the *Saturday Evening Post* stated it was fitting that the automobile, "this highly mechanized product of an industrial civilization," should offer the means to offset any "evil effects that may flow from industrialization." Wilderness parks balanced a largely urban, mechanized society. Protected by the government, remnants of the primordial past would be museums for popular instruction in nature and laboratories for the scientist. For "surely the swift pace of material progress could not be maintained," Atwood wrote, "unless the primitive and indispensable instinct for outdoor life were satisfied."[45]

Many in the club shared this faith in material progress. John Muir fled cities and denounced America's materialism. In the years before World War I, he and the club fought the first national battle to preserve nature. Yet it was only with difficulty that he had marshalled the club behind his battle to save Hetch Hetchy Valley. The early club was a "highly imperfect instrumentality for propagating" the wilderness idea— "for by no means all the club's members were singlemindedly committed to wilderness values."[46] Most of the club's members were not refugees from civilization, and except for Hetch Hetchy they rarely challenged the nation's economic interests. They were satisfied through the 1940s to protect the lands already in public ownership, and most of these lands were economically "worthless."[47] Nor was the club averse in the 1890s to cooperating with the Southern Pacific Railroad to get Yosemite transferred from state to federal jurisdiction.[48]

Probably nothing, however, more clearly reveals these preservationists' lack of anxiety that technology and parks could be compatible than their attitude toward the automobile. The club's 1892 bylaws announced the following among its purposes: "to explore, enjoy and render accessible the mountain regions of the Pacific Coast," and to that purpose through the 1940s the organization "proposed roads up Tenaya Canyon, into Little Yosemite, and across Kearsarge Pass and all the highest passes of the Sierra Nevada. . . ."[49] Initially automobiles were barred from the national parks. Club leaders William Colby and John Muir were among the first to advocate that the "horseless carriage" be admitted into Yosemite National Park. Franklin K. Lane, Woodrow Wilson's secretary of the Interior and the league's first president, granted the automobile entrance into most of the national parks in 1912.[50] "At length," in the words of club leader Francis Farquhar, in the parks "as elsewhere, the automobile became an accepted way of life."[51]

The automobile similarly marked the league's program. The organization poured millions into acquiring the magnificent stands lining the Redwood Highway. The criterion of accessibility in part dictated the location of the redwood state parks. It also was a factor in the Department of the Interior's 1920 recommendation that the Klamath River was the best site for a redwood national park. Wanting people to visit the parks, purists from Muir to Merriam cultivated ease of access.[52]

The boosters of the National Park Service fostered usage much more than did the purists of the club and the league. Parkways, hotels, restaurants, stores, campgrounds, and roads civilized the national parks. The service shared the spirit of the federated National Conference on Outdoor Recreation, which found common cause in the 1920s with the National Highways Association, dedicated to achieving a "Paved United States in Our Day."[53] Between 1919 and 1929 visitation to the national parks quadrupled. Park Service boosters assumed that without this increased use made possible by the automobile, a large-scale preservation movement would have been impossible.[54] The establishment of the parks was a final conquest of the West.[55] Bordered, improved, well-traveled, the nation's playgrounds would complement a rapidly industrializing civilization that tended toward the good.

Most leaders in the club and the early Park Service were—like the league's councilors—men fully within the mainstream of the American business and industrial establishment. Stephen Mather had been an industrial developer of California borax before becoming the first director of the Park Service, and his successor, Horace Albright, entered the business world after his years with the parks. Many of the club's incorporators were San Francisco businessmen. The group's presidents included subdivider Duncan McDuffie, mining lawyer William Colby, petroleum engineer Alex Hildebrand, civil engineer and President Eisenhower's advisor on dams Walter Huber, and Walter Starr of the Sound Pulp and Paper Company. Through the 1940s club leaders acknowledged neither polarization between preservationists and entrepreneurs nor inherent evil in the industrial corporation. They believed cooperation with industry produced sound change and that not all wilderness could or should be saved.[56]

John Merriam had written in the 1930s and 1940s that those "natural elements that interfere with the highest development of man . . . should be eliminated," and those that "have human significance should be utilized in the furthering . . . of evolution." He had earlier predicted that within a few centuries man would control the biological world.[57]

Despite Muir's admonitions that the earth had not been created solely for men,[58] the Sierra Club similarly emphasized human needs during the interwar years. It found this priority compatible with the progressive notion of evolution. Bestor Robinson, club president in the 1930s and 1940s and director until 1966, advised preservationists not to let their love of nature overshadow concern for human needs. Mountains are to be used. "I want," he stated, "wilderness to contribute to the American way of life."[59] Hence in 1948 the club approved a well-planned ski resort in the Mineral King Basin of the Sierra Nevada as a means of offering the public an opportunity to enjoy the mountains. The club also hoped that development of the basin would deflect the establishment of ski resorts in scenically superior areas within the Sierra Nevada.[60] In the 1930s even the club's future executive director David R. Brower—who, in his own words, had not yet been "saved"—believed a tramway should be built up the wall of Yosemite Valley to enhance visitor enjoyment.[61]

Between 1960 and 1963 the redwood national park exploded into national politics with the club as a catalyst. But the group had changed since World War II. For many of its members the teleological world view had been replaced by a pervading naturalism, to which Loren Eiseley gave poetic voice. Archaeologist, paleontologist, and philosopher with the University of Pennsylvania, Eiseley authored the foreword for the club's book *Not Man Apart*. In the 1960s club publications quoted extensively from such of Eiseley's books as *The Immense Journey* and *Darwin's Century*. Eiseley also wrote portions of the club's literature on the redwoods and its volume on Darwin's Galapagos Islands, the latter designed to initiate a campaign for an Earth National Park—the logical extension of a web-of-life theory. Speaking for the club in 1965, Brower said of Eiseley, "we like his mind."[62]

Central to Eiseley's naturalism was the notion that man is inescapably part of nature. He expressed the obvious affinity between this perspective and ecology as follows: "If I remember the sunflower forest, it is because from its hidden reaches man arose. The green world is his sacred center."[63] These words implied more than man's physical dependence upon the chain of life; they suggested the universe is not only man's physical prison but his spiritual prison. The new environmentalism represented rejection of a universe of spiritual infinity and expanding material possibilities.[64] The teleological world view had demanded transcendence in order to grasp greater intelligence and purpose. That vision had since been lost. In its absence empirical evidence supported only the belief that randomness characterized the universe. Biology revealed interdependence, specialization, and adaptation, but it allowed no judgment as to superiority of species. Man was the accident of the chance-filled course of human genetics.

Thus the club moved from the philosophy of Muir, with his faith in a universe of "law, order, creative intelligence, and loving design," toward that of Eiseley, whose deepest thoughts were, in spite of his love for nature, "all of night, of outer cold and inner darkness."[65] The change was the result in significant part of a mid-century shift in American science.

The demise of directional theories and assumptions about evolution was gradual. Popular in the 1910s and 1920s, they were on the defensive by the 1930s, although still respectable. By 1950 they had been discredited.[66] The American Philosophical Association devoted its 1949 meeting to orthogenesis. The evolutionists present noted that some scientists still supported the theory, and two participating geneticists advocated orthoselection.[67] Indeed, even the most advanced geneticists continued to use the two terms into the late 1940s—however, not to denote explanations but rather to indicate continuous evolutionary change. By the 1950s even such vaguely directional theories were absent from scientific literature. As was noted at the 1949 meeting of the American Philosophical Society, evidence had been piling up against directional theories for some years.

As more fossils were classified, each case of what had been considered a straight line of phylogenetic development sprouted more complex patterns. Paleontologists now urged the Museum of Natural History to redraw its horse diagram. However, the old chart was reproduced in textbooks through the 1940s, leading scientists to joke, "There is a tendency to put the chart before the horse."[68] Although proponents of orthogenesis had touted examples of repeated occurrences of the same mutation in certain species, studies increasingly verified that, as de Vries had argued, mutations were random—meaning independent of the environment and tending to occur in all directions, within obvious limits. By 1949 the majority of geneticists were certain that mutations "have their basis in ultramicroscopic accidents occurring on a molecular and submolecular level . . ." and that only the small minority were adaptive, as would be expected in a chance system.[69] But as the known range of geologic time was pushed backward—in 1930 from 100 to 2,000 million years, and again in the 1950s to 4,500 million—their meandering nature seemed less of an argument against natural selection and random genetic change.[70] In reply to skeptics who could not believe such complicated organisms as ourselves could emerge by chance, the geneticist Muller could confidently answer in 1949, "An indefinitely continued and quite unrestricted multiplication of variations, then, could in the end, through sheer numbers attained, give opportunity for the most improbable of all arrangements, namely, complexly working adaptive organisms like ourselves, to come into existence without design."[71]

By World War II paleontologists also reached the point where they could explain, without resorting to orthogenesis, the existence of characteristics that appeared without advantage to the organisms before fully developed. For example, they had the evidence to show that even the ear's development was a slow process, every intermediate step of which had been advantageous to the species. Begun as a gill hole near jaw bones that touched a sensitive part of the brain, the ear evolved in random, empirically explainable steps.[72] Nor did the questions of neutral or disadvantageous characteristics convince evolutionists of the 1940s and 1950s of orthogenesis, as they had Osborn. Biologists increasingly found that even very small differences had selective value, if not always apparent to human observers.[73]

The demise of directional assumptions, however, was more than a matter of the specific disproof of their proponents' arguments. Orthogenesis was in the end swept out with a much broader brush, or what Julian Huxley called in 1942 the "evolutionary synthesis."[74] By 1950 evolutionists agreed that Mendelian genetics and natural selection were sufficient to explain evolution.

Much of the theoretical foundation for the advances of the 1930s and 1940s had of course been laid earlier. But if a great deal had been learned about the actual materials and mechanisms of heredity, the conflict between geneticists and selectionists had delayed understanding of the larger process of evolution. Some geneticists and naturalists before 1920 agreed that small adaptive changes were effective and that Mendelian heredity and Darwinian selection were compatible. Many others, however, continued to point out that Darwinism rested on the shaky theoretical basis that nature acted upon small genetic differences.[75] Between 1930 and 1950 this objection was fully overcome, the synthesis of Mendelian genetics and Darwinian selection consummated, and a view of evolutionary process arrived at that most scientists found convincing.

Most historians and scientists agree that major advances in the 1930s and 1940s paved the way for this consensus, but they are in less agreement as to the respective weight to assign breakthroughs in the various fields. Ernst Mayr sees the synthesis as the work in large part of three "bridge builders" in zoology and geology—Julian Huxley, G. G. Simpson, and Bernhard Rensch—who overcame the lack of communication and the mutual hostility between geneticists and naturalists. Mayr also claims the synthesis occurred only after scientists, primarily naturalists, had disproved such basic misconceptions as the lingering theory of the inheritance of acquired characteristics, the de Vriesian theory of discontinuous evolution or mutational leaps, and the associated tendency to see species as ideal or distinct types rather than populations.[76]

Indeed, the evolutionary synthesis necessitated a revolution in typology. Early twentieth-century taxonomists had classified specimens according to an ideal type, which presumed directional evolution. During the interwar years they switched from this philosophically idealistic systematics to naturalistic systematics. They increasingly described species by the range of their characteristics. Not until naturalists and then geneticists ceased to think of species as types and saw them as interbreeding populations only reproductively isolated from other groups could they see speciation as the product of small random changes occurring over thousands of years or more. As Mayr has pointed out, this revision of the definition and conceptualization of species was a vital part of the evolutionary synthesis.[77]

In contrast to Mayr, the historian William Provine emphasizes the role of population genetics in the synthesis. Provine argues, "the idea of natural selection involved difficulties . . . which were not satisfactorily solved until the rise of population genetics." Perhaps the most crucial contributions to population genetics were made by the Englishmen R. A. Fisher and J. B. S. Haldane and the American Sewall Wright. All three men had actually formulated their basic understanding of evolution in the 1920s but did not begin their seminal publications until 1920 to 1932. Sewall Wright described his own work as the development of a mathematical model to express the synthesis of all factors in evolution simultaneously, including the determinate factors of recurrent mutation, immigration, and selection—plus the cumulative effect of random fluctuations of gene frequencies. The work of Fisher and Haldane might be described in similar terms, although it will not be discussed here.[78]

During the 1930s and 1940s these geneticists constructed mathematical models indicating the significance of population size and structure. Early researchers such as Osborn, Merriam, and Kellogg studied large populations. Their work confirmed that such populations drift toward the statistical means of adaptability. Without resorting to orthogenetic or mutational theories, it was not at all clear how variations were preserved sufficiently to account for evolutionary change.

De Vries's rediscovery of Mendel's work in 1900 had been the first step in the understanding of the role of chromosomes and diploidy in preserving genetic variability. The earth's higher plants and animals are diploid species; that is, they have two sets of chromosomes, one from the mother and one from the father. As a result of this structure, G. H. Hardy wrote in 1908, "there is not the slightest foundation for the idea that a dominant character should show a tendency to spread over a whole population, or that a recessive should tend to die out."[79] Even such inadaptive genes as those for hemophilia can hide in a diploid species, so that the organism is able at some time in the future to draw upon hemophilia in a genetic combination that might increase its adaptability in the same or another environment. Through the 1910s and 1920s, researchers continued to verify the signifiance and prevalence of diploidy.[80] Scientists such as the University of California's Garrett Hardin concluded that evolution is not a perfect cybernetic system; it is far less efficient than the term "survival of the fittest" had implied. One major argument in favor of both mutations and orthogenesis was gradually removed. Dual chromosomes could not be construed as an orthogenetic force. Geneticists demonstrated that diploidy has a short-range selective advantage over the haploidy— species with one set of chromosomes. Lethal genes are fatal to haploid species.[81]

The Hardy principle, later known as the Hardy-Weinberg equilibrium, showed how variation was preserved in a random breeding population, but geneticists still needed to advance a convincing explanation of speciation. Sewall Wright set out to determine under what situations a species would be most likely to draw upon this genetic potential. He wanted to know what circumstances made selection most effective. In the 1930s he demonstrated what came to be known as the "Wright effect." He said that with small populations there was a greater probability that the statistically unexpected would happen. Large populations showed a drift toward the mean of adaptability. As with any purely chance model, the smaller the population, the less effective natural selection was in controlling the spread of gene frequencies—and genetic drifts often drive organisms into extinction. Yet in their statistical wanderings, some members find their way into new adaptive genetic combinations.[82]

Wright described his findings by picturing peaks on a landscape. Each peak was an adaptive genetic combination. He asked how a species that drifted to the top of one peak of specialization could move onto another. How could it escape if the water level between the peaks began rising—meaning, if the environment became harsher? Wright postulated that small populations held the answer. First, they provide greater stores of potential variability; second, their greater statistical drift might bring species across the trough into the proximity of a new adaptive genetic peak. He concluded that selection is most effective when there are many separate peaks in "the surface of selective values" and when populations are small enough and sufficiently isolated to permit more or less random differentiation.[83] Wright provided a mathematical model that demonstrated how genetic variability was maintained and how selection acted upon this variability. His model was compatible with de Vries's position that mutations were random, but it also confirmed Darwin's emphasis upon small adaptive changes. In 1949 Wright explained the process of speciation—the seemingly abrupt appearance of higher categories that mutationists had argued could only be accounted for by the process of discontinuous genetic leaps. He said that during a period of strong ecological pressure, a species underwent only gradual change. During these periods of equilibrium, the species gathers potential variables that permit dramatic change when a major ecological opportunity presents itself. "The result is the observed evolutionary cycle of occasional emergence of a new higher category, adaptive radiation, selective elimination of rival higher categories and return . . ." to equilibrium as the environment again restricts the species "to a single channel."[84] What had appeared to be a major mutational discontinuity was now understood as the result of a long accumulation of small variations.

Although Wright, Fisher, and Haldane presented their mathematical models during the 1930s, acceptance was far from automatic. As Wright himself noted, "Even as late as 1934 Henry Fairfield Osborn, the leading paleontologist, probably spoke for most naturalists in holding that natural selection was inadequate."[85] Many of the biologists and paleontologists failed to realize the significance of population genetics. For one thing, differences among the population geneticists themselves obscured their work and caused some biologists to dismiss it. It was not until 1942 that Fisher conceded the correctness of Wright's emphasis upon small populations. Moreover, the mathematical models were developed before the data on natural populations was available against which to test them.[86]

It was, for example, difficult to establish population size from fossils, so paleontologists had traditionally considered populations to have been large. Biologists were not convinced of the significance of Wright's model for small populations until it was demonstrated that breeding populations are generally specific despite continuous environments. Studying natural populations in the 1930s and 1940s, paleontologists and biologists concluded that reproductive cycles, limited mobility, migrations, and physical barriers make small populations the rule.[87]

The real advance of the 1940s, then, was the merger of the mathematical models of population genetics with the conclusions developed by geneticists and paleontologists studying natural populations. For example, in 1942 Mather and Wigan did an experiment on genetic change in fruit flies, the results of which were difficult to explain on the basis of the occurrence of a few mutations with conspicuous effects. Their results were in fact explainable in terms of a hypothesis very similar to Wright's theory: genetic variability accumulated that did not have a significant effect upon the phenotype but which was available for dramatic change when a new ecological situation occurred.[88] The most influential geneticist in the field of real populations between 1940 and 1960 was Theodosius Dobzhansky, whose work on natural populations was done in close collaboration with Wright. Studies by Dobzhansky and his colleagues published between 1938 and 1959 did much to convince evolutionary biologists of the validity of population genetics.[89] Harvard zoologist G. G. Simpson also contributed greatly to the synthesis by showing the compatibility of geneticists' mathematical models and paleontologists' fossil evidences.[90]

In 1949 Sewall Wright wrote, "It is the contention that the statistical consequences of the varying degrees of success of individual organisms in their efforts to live and reproduce give an adequate explanation for all known major phenomena of evolution when account is taken of the statistical effects of the known processes of heredity in populations of diverse structure."[91] As a result of the reconciliation of mathematical genetics with findings on natural populations, almost all evolutionary scientists could share Wright's confidence.[92]

It is often overlooked but significant that, as the French biologist Jacques Monod wrote in 1971, "the theory of evolution did not take on its full significance, precision, and certainty until less than twenty years ago."[93] The philosophical naturalism that underlies postwar biology was a result of two related aspects of the new synthesis. First, it established a chance model of natural history—the merger of random genetic drift and opportunistic natural selection.[94] Second, by 1950 it had discredited rival theories of directed evolution, from the orderly mutant to orthoselection and all forms of orthogenesis.[95] In the 1950s G. G. Simpson attacked such theories on methodological grounds. He pointed out that to discuss directional change, one must know the goal, and such can only be known metaphysically. Simpson wrote that orthogenesis proved only "that scientists' minds move in straight lines not that evolution does." He argued that metaphysical explanations could not be accepted as working hypotheses because they could not be tested and were not conducive to further research.[96]

In the 1940s and 1950s scientific philosophers—from Julian Huxley to microbiologist René Dubos and Loren Eiseley—popularized the new evolutionary synthesis. They pronounced evolution "opportunistic," "random," "unconscious," "disorderly," and "lacking in design."[97] In 1959 Garrett Hardin asked rhetorically if the concept of progress was in any way relevant to geology. No, he said; the evolutionary process consists of the small steps in the shift from one inefficient cybernetic system to another and cannot "be said to involve direction at all." Nor can the fitness of a species be judged superior in any absolute sense. A new form is better only in terms of its external and internal environment.[98] Huxley wrote in the 1963 revision of his *Evolution* that natural selection "does not ensure progress, or maximum advantage, or any other ideal state of affairs."[99] In the 1951 and 1957 editions of their famous introductory college text on zoology, Tracy Storer and Robert Usinger carefully avoided any implications of cosmic design and placed the phrase "higher animals" in quotes to assure readers that no value judgment was intended.[100]

In short, biologists, geneticists, and paleontologists had become suspicious of all absolutes. They no longer searched for ideal types or natural laws. They were content to find an occasional "sensible pattern."[101] They searched for the *hows* not the *whys*, or causes. Geneticists in the 1950s calculated the number of genetic combinations to be at least 10^{3000}. Rather than unlocking some ultimate program for progress, the environment could be said to do no more than eliminate the most inadaptive genetic variations. Evolution was opportunistic. "Natural selection seizes," Hardin concluded, "upon the best variations available at the moment" regardless of the species' ultimate potential.[102]

One might ask if the rejection of absolutes and directional theories was purely scientific—or whether it was produced by larger postwar forces pushing modern thought into skepticism. After all, many American philosophers had rejected teleological assumptions long before the scientists had, and the scientists' shift corresponds with World War II and the atomic bomb. Early biologists assumed that the rattlesnake's rattles were designed to warn men and wondered what selective advantage these had before they made noise. Today biologists say the rattles were not made for man's benefit; they are a lure that began as a difference in color and texture.[103] And yet neither conclusion can be proven. It seems that facts do not speak for themselves.

Or do they? In the 1950s scientists denounced orthogenesis as a methodological sin. They called natural selection and genetic changes unconscious, random, inefficient, and opportunistic. But their conclusions were based upon decades of research, during the course of which one phylogenetic line after another had changed into a complex system with dead ends, backtracks, and links to adjoining systems. Research into chromosomes and population genetics produced a new evolutionary synthesis, according to which opportunistic selection and random genetic change do in fact effectively explain evolution.

For some scientists in the 1950s the rejection of cosmic order reinforced fears about human progress. Shortly after America's deployment of the atomic bomb, G. G. Simpson wrote, "There is reason to believe that the trend of evolution by which man arose has now stopped. . . . Man's future biological evolution is more likely to be degenerative than progressive and there is no assurance that man can modify his destiny."[104] In the 1950s Hardin lectured on genetic damage to humans from atomic radiation.[105] For most scientists, however, overpopulation was what Huxley called "the problem of our age."[106] At the 1954 United Nation's Conference on World Population in Rome, scientists discussed the implications of resource shortages and expressed fear that mankind had, in Marston Bates's words, "run wild, like a weed escaped on a new continent."[107] The hordes of India loomed "frightening and . . . uncontrollable."[108]

Still, there were those like Huxley who finally denounced orthogenesis but continued to believe in human progress. In fact, the biological community of the 1950s, which so unanimously embraced philosophical naturalism, was generally optimistic about the potential of science to improve the condition of mankind.[109] If biologists reached the position of philosophical naturalism mostly as a result of their evidences, it can be asked if their position had a causal impact on the rest of society.

In specific terms, did the mid-century shift in science contribute to the militancy and popularity of the environmental movement of the past quarter century? If science acted as an independent variable in generating philosophical naturalism, did this naturalism contribute to subsequent environmental fears? The shift in the biological sciences cannot alone be said to have caused the ecology movement's skepticism. Without the atomic bomb, population bomb, DDT, and accelerated resource consumption, the movement would not have developed the militancy it did. This depended further upon a congenial political environment and long-range changes in the position of the professional classes traditionally drawn to the movement. Yet an idea can govern perspective, especially one sanctioned by science.

Scientists from Hardin to Dubos, University of Michigan biologist Marston Bates, one-time president of the American Association for the Advancement of Science Paul Sears, and University of Wisconsin botanist Hugh H. Iltis participated in the environmental movement of the 1950s and 1960s.[110] Many preservationists developed an interest in the biological sciences that complemented their enthusiasm for mountaineering. As early as the 1930s, Brower studied genetics, particularly the writings of population geneticist J. B. S. Haldane. Brower recalled some forty years later, "I dug through library shelves to find out all I could about what happened in the evolutionary course of things. I don't remember anything except Haldane." Brower was also affected in the 1950s by Sears, who emphasized technology's threat to the web of nature and by "Garrett Hardin's ecological law that efficiency and stability are incompatible."[111] Certainly most of those who were members of the club in the 1960s, a heyday of its militancy, were middle- and upper-middle-class professionals who had been educated after World War II and at least vaguely understood what Hardin or Dubos meant when they called evolution "unconscious." The frequency of images of a closed universe—spaceship earth and "cosmic prison"—verify the influence of philosophical naturalism.[112]

As a result, club activists no longer saw man as the summit of directional evolution. Indeed, in the face of the baby boom, they translated the random mutant into the vision of man as a "spore," "weed," "disease," or "cancer."[113] Changes in science encouraged environmentalists to emphasize the importance of genetic diversity and the value of all species, not just the most useful or spectacular. In the late 1960s club lawyers would seek legal denial of common law teleological assumptions by asking for standing to sue in behalf of nature's rights. They made a bid to establish the principle that the right to legal protection should not hinge solely upon the vested interests of human claimants. The Supreme Court ruled against the club, but in a dissenting opinion William O. Douglas, one-time club director, wrote that wild land, plants, and animals should have the right to stand before the courts in their own behalf.[114] The club became in the 1950s and 1960s increasingly intolerant of industrial progress and technology, denouncing roads, lumbermen, and the government.[115]

Philosophical naturalism need not have generated a loss of faith in human progress, as Julian Huxley indicated in the 1940s and 1950s, yet Huxley's own arguments show why such a disposition was conducive to pessimism. He called "totally false" natural religions that search for guidance in external powers. He maintained, "The purpose manifested in evolution, whether adaptation, specialization, or biological progress, is only an apparent purpose. It is as much a product of blind forces as is the . . . ebb and flow of the tides. It is we who have read purpose into evolution, as earlier man projected will and emotion into inorganic phenomenon like storm or earthquake." Huxley believed, however, in the likelihood of human progress—material, biological, and social. But he warned, "if we wish to work towards a purpose for the future of man, we must formulate that purpose ourselves. Purposes in life are made, not found." It is for man alone to determine whether future evolution will bring progress, stagnation, or degeneration.[116] He argued that full responsibility for the world rested with man, and the weight of judgment as to how purpose should be defined rested with the human mind. Marston Bates defined the purpose as simply "survival."[117] Evolution offered no assurances, leaving man alone to shape his fate.

For some, science filled the uncertainty. However, for the most part, having denied teleological assurances, by the 1960s it was clear that scientists had failed to establish their own moral authority, despite their importance in the environmental movement. Although the club relied increasingly upon ecology in its battles, its supporters denounced scientists as historically arrogant and reductionist. Sigurd Olson condemned them for their "mechanistic attitude" and noted that modern man was plagued with a "gnawing unrest that somehow the age of gadgetry and science could not still." William O. Douglas stated, "we should not take science, and its child Technology, as our savior."[118] Environmentalists of the 1960s idealized the pagan animism and arcadian pastoralism of the European barbarian and the American Indian.[119] They viewed the natural world as a mysterious, holistic if beautiful prison in which man possessed little freedom and of which he had but a dim perception.

With no little irony, environmentalists in that decade denounced science for its historical association with teleological assumptions. "Western science was," Lynn White, Jr., maintained, "cast in the matrix of Christian theology"—the latter remarkable for its non-repetitive, linear conception of time and its story of God's creation of the world for man's benefit and domination. Created in the image of the Almighty, man shared God's transcendence; nature had "no reason for existence save to serve man." White felt western man lacked a sense of the sacred in nature and was imbued with a Judeo-Christian aversion to wilderness. Americans lived in a "post-Christian age," perpetuating these destructive values.[120] Finding traditional religions "too anthropocentric," Brower made ecology, with its spirit of humility and stewardship, his religion.[121]

In a similar vein, the club parodied the Bureau of Reclamation's evocation of God's help in constructing Glen Canyon Dam and criticized the bureau for maintaining, "There is a natural world in our universe. God created both Man and Nature. And Man serves God. But Nature serves Man."[122] In the end, however, modern science failed to establish its own moral authority less because of its bedfellows than because of its own self-defined epistemological limits.

Few men captured more eloquently the merger of philosophical naturalism and fear of human action than did Eiseley, whose writings graced club literature of the 1960s, including that on the redwoods. Inherent in Eiseley's vision of a closed universe was the conviction that man can neither escape the cosmos nor master it. He chided that to speak of man, trapped in his body and the limits of time and space, as mastering the mysteries of the universe was "the equivalent of installing a grasshopper as Secretary General of the United States."[123] To the club, wilderness held answers to more questions than man yet knew how to ask. Its leaders saw the earth as "unmanageable" and felt scientists should seek to understand, not conquer.[124] Randomness denied man world priority. Science was a tool but one of limited moral authority. Humanity was, after all, only a temporary adaptation to a specific environment, and not an innately superior species.

The historian Donald Fleming correctly pointed out that the work of Alister Hardy, Aldo Leopold, and Rachel Carson on food chains did much to generate the modern ecological perspective. I would add, however, that the mid-century synthesis of opportunistic selection and random heredity was also at the base of the new ecology. The rejection of directed theories of evolution undercut the hierarchical ecology that had placed man and his technology confidently at the apex of natural history. Fleming wrote that Darwin "stood for something better than he realized." Lewis Mumford called it "a fresh vision of the entire cosmic process"; however, as Fleming complained, this vision went unappreciated until recently.[125] This was because

Figure 9. Ralph Chaney and Newton Drury, June 20, 1968. The two men are shown in Jedediah Smith Redwoods State Park on the National Parks Advisory Board Tour of the Redwoods. Courtesy of the National Park Service.

western scientists failed to embrace this chance model of evolution until the mid-twentieth century.

The club's politics during the 1960s had its roots in the mid-century Darwinian synthesis. The league's politics did not. By 1960 the club and the league had been headquartered across the street from each other for forty years. These had been decades of mutual support. The club guarded the Sierra Nevada, while "its California sister" purchased redwoods.[126] Club leaders from William Colby to William Badé, Willis Jepson, and Duncan McDuffie were also pillars of the league; Merriam and Newton Drury were honorary vice-presidents of the club. The mutuality had been reinforced by a common scientific heritage, but by 1960 this commonality was gone. Although Merriam had resigned as president in 1944, the league continued through the 1950s and 1960s to distribute his optimistic, teleological writings. The group's president in the 1960s was Ralph Chaney, whose faith in orthoselection and human progress was reminiscent of his predecessor and mentor.[127] The club absorbed the influence of young scientists in the 1950s and 1960s, while the league attracted few new academics. This divergence between the old allies would have serious ramifications for the redwoods. The club would demand massive federal action to save the last of the trees in a large wilderness park of ecological diversity. The league would defend its traditional program, including industrial cooperation and small, museumlike parks.

Between 1930 and 1950 scientists had disproved all directional theories of evolution, freeing wilderness advocates from the inherent determinism that had prevented earlier preservationists from challenging industrial progress and human mastery of the natural world. In the 1950s and 1960s, the realities of environmental deterioration interacted with this prevalent philosophical naturalism to produce anger and fear.

7
The Roots of Militancy:
1950–1964

IN A 1959 letter attacking a proposed freeway, David R. Brower, appointed executive director of the Sierra Club seven years earlier, quoted physicist J. A. Rush: "When man obliterates wilderness, he repudiates the evolutionary force that put him on his planet. In a deeply terrifying sense, man is on his own."[1] The statement typifies the union of philosophical naturalism and citizen activism that emerged out of the 1950s.

Man's new explosive powers made cosmic independence frightening. In addition to the atomic bomb, the postwar world brought, in social philosopher Lewis Mumford's words, "the population explosion, the freeway explosion, the recreation explosion, the suburban explosion."[2] The technology of resource exploitation that fed the consumer economy changed America's landscapes. Inroads into the wildernesses of the Far West were so dramatic in the 1950s as to constitute the closing of a latter-day frontier. The early pioneer had passed quickly over the mountains and forests of the West, but the extractive industries of the 1950s spared little, from Oregon's Cascades to California's Sierra Nevada. It was, however, the coastal redwoods that were hit the hardest.

Many in the Sierra Club responded to this transformation of the West that occurred between their youth and adulthood with an increased sensitivity to the relationship of man and the land and a growing determination to defend the environment. That a militant liberalism had infected the club by 1960 was evident in its strident demands for federal purchase of a large redwood park. While the club's organizational structure had incorporated currents of political militancy as well as of philosophical naturalism, the Save-the-Redwoods

League's closed and aging governance held to the efficacy and rectitude of moderation. This divergence began with the two organizations' responses to the 1950s.

In 1950 Secretary of the Interior Oscar Chapman approved inclusion of Dinosaur National Monument in the Upper Colorado River Project. The move shocked the club out of the relative lethargy that had characterized it during the interwar years. The Bureau of Reclamation planned to convert the red sandstone crevices formed by the Green and the Yampa rivers into a reservoir. Brower and Howard Zahniser of The Wilderness Society launched a campaign of opposition. Historians have since recognized the importance of the Dinosaur battle. Elmo Richardson documented its course, and Roderick Nash called the successful defense of Dinosaur a national "Decision for Permanence" in wilderness preservation, contrasting it with the loss of Hetch Hetchy in 1913.[3]

In defending Dinosaur, Brower and Zahniser posited the sanctity of the national park and monument system. Brower also told a congressional committee that the Bureau of Reclamation's calculations were in error. He demonstrated that if all the reservoirs the dam builders had planned for the Colorado River were built and filled, surface evaporation would lose more water than the dams would save. This testimony was based upon the evidence that Walter Huber, special adviser to President Eisenhower on dams and president of the American Society of Civil Engineers, had secretly verified for the club.[4] With these arguments, the club and The Wilderness Society held up the entire $5 billion Upper Colorado Basin Project for six years. A week after the bureau agreed to drop Dinosaur in 1956, Congress passed the enabling legislation for the Colorado River Project.

The Dinosaur battle proved a political maturity and popular support that the wilderness movement had previously lacked, yet the campaign differed in several ways from the battles that would come in the following decade. First, it had the united support of the nation's preservationists, from the activist Brower to more moderate club leaders and ex-directors of the National Park Service Horace Albright and Newton Drury. In fact, the latter was forced to resign as director in part because he defended the national monument. Second, the campaign was remarkably unacrimonious; even congressional opponents complimented Brower on his politeness.[5]

Third, in concluding the campaign, the club compromised. In 1956 Brower and Zahniser agreed to allow Reclamation to proceed with the Colorado River Project provided no reservoir constructed under the act be situated in whole or part in any national park or monument.

The proviso was to safeguard Rainbow Bridge National Monument as well as Dinosaur.[6] Before the club withdrew its opposition to the project, the Department of the Interior pledged "to take whatever steps were necessary to protect" Rainbow Bridge, including the construction of a protective dam one mile below the bridge. Neither Reclamation nor Congress honored the pledge. This was not the only compromise Brower would regret.[7]

The Bureau of Reclamation had also proposed to convert Glen Canyon on the Colorado into a reservoir. Preservationists debated the stance they should assume. Many considered the canyon of national park caliber, but it was not part of the national park system. Brower wanted it saved, but the club's directors decided they could not defend both Glen Canyon and Dinosaur. Director Alex Hildebrand, an engineer in charge of underground research for Standard Oil Company, concluded the club should not oppose "sound reclamation projects that did not invade the parks or wilderness areas. . . ." Thus Glen Canyon was sacrificed.[8] Almost ten years later, using photographs by Eliot Porter, Brower would publish *The Place Nobody Knew: Glen Canyon on the Colorado*.[9]

The tactics employed by Brower and his allies in the Dinosaur battle were harbingers of those the club would employ in defending the redwoods in the 1960s: the successful lobby, the newspaper advertisements, and book publication—in this case, working with Wallace Stegner on *This Is Dinosaur*. But in Brower's politeness and willingness to compromise as well as in the public unanimity of the nation's preservationists, Dinosaur differed from most of the controversies of the 1960s, including that prompted by the redwoods.

A barometer of developing environmental militancy during the 1950s was relations between the club and the Forest Service. During the interwar years they had been cordial. Club president Bestor Robinson served on the service's advisory board, and the foresters regularly conducted club directors on tours of the national forests to discuss forest practices. This friendliness was due to the service's wilderness policies, adopted in the 1920s and 1930s, and to lack of strong industrial interest in the national forests of the Sierra Nevada. Club members found the Sierra an unmolested land of personal adventure, a "gentle wilderness."[10] Club leaders mapped the range, garnered first ascents, built lodges, and named the mountains.

In the 1950s, however, the housing boom increased demand for timber from western national forests. The service strove to meet this demand to such an extent that some citizen activists came to doubt its commitment to wilderness and to push for congressional limitations on the agency's discretionary powers. There were several incidents that contributed to this growing distrust during the 1950s and early 1960s, from the logging of the Kern Plateau in the Sierra Nevada to the controversies over the proposed Oregon Cascades national park and the Three Sisters Wilderness Area in Washington's Cascade Mountains.[11]

No incident more clearly reveals the roots of future militancy, however, than does the logging of a small stand of Jeffrey pine along Deadman Creek near Mammoth Lakes in the Sierra Nevada. In December, 1954, the Forest Service had announced plans to cut this stand. Outraged, Brower argued it was "one of the few remaining virgin Jeffrey pine forests in the United States." The American Museum of Natural History had sent a team of experts to study it and create a $50,000 diorama for their New York museum. To make the move even more illogical to the club's executive director, the forest held only 3,000 acres of slow-growing, commercially inferior woods.[12]

The Forest Service maintained that it was an established timber management area and defended the operation as sanitary logging— the removal of trees hazardous to recreationists and prone to disease. Local residents called this a "falsification of the facts."[13] Brower, too, began to doubt the explanation that should hazardous trees fall on someone in a recreational area, the service would be liable. The attorney general's office had told him "a few minor changes in Forest Service regulations would end the liability." He suspected the service worked too closely with the local lumber company for it to exercise independent judgment. He became convinced foresters accepted wilderness and recreation only out of fear of Park Service competition for public land.[14]

Unable to dissuade the Forest Service, Brower publicly circulated a history of the controversy and reproductions of local residents' correspondence, including that accusing the service of falsifying facts.[15] Most club leaders were unhappy about Deadman Creek, and several had begun to question the practice of sanitary logging. But the directors did not share Brower's suspicions of the foresters' motives and were alarmed about the legal and political implications of his accusations. Alex Hildebrand thought the service's position "reasonable" and the men "able, sincere, dedicated." He admonished Brower not to hazard opinions on matters of policy where substantial elements of relevant professionals differed. Most of the directors preferred to cooperate with government and industry.[16]

Early in 1959 Brower issued a press release "blasting" as "phony" and "contrived" the California Highway Commission's contention that roads through the Sierra Nevada were needed for national defense.[17] In response to his outspokenness against the commission and the Forest Service, the club's directors resolved that henceforth "No statement should be used that expressly, impliedly, or by reasonable inference criticizes the motives, integrity, or competence of an official, bureau, or other responsible party."[18]

The directors' emphasis upon accommodation and objectivity is reminiscent of the league and earlier reformers in general. Brower was moving away from the league as well as from some within his own organization. The resulting tension would build through the 1960s. In the meantime, however, Brower would pull the more moderate elements in the club along with him, despite gestures like the 1959 resolution. Increasingly, he gathered such allies as the San Francisco physician Edgar Wayburn, club president and director through the 1950s and 1960s.[19]

The club would institutionalize Brower's militancy in the 1950s and 1960s in part because of its structure. From its inception the club had been an oligarchy. According to club leader Richard Leonard, through the 1940s, "Presidential leadership progressed in an orderly, almost predictable manner." Colby, LeConte, Huber, and Farquhar "simply decided" who would be club president "on their own"—a similar situation existed in the 1950s and 1960s. However, it was a structure sufficiently responsive to be described as a "consultive oligarchy"; that is, its board of directors was neither entirely self-perpetuating nor intolerant of decentralized decision-making.[20] Certainly this responsiveness was partially due to the strong role played in the organization by volunteers working through local chapters. In 1956 the club strengthened this role by establishing a central council to represent the chapters and advise the board. The directors were popularly elected by a paying and, after the early 1960s, unscreened membership.[21] From the late 1940s through the 1950s, members and leaders—proving stable in terms of individual persistence—moved slowly if unevenly toward a stronger defense of wilderness and alienation from technological growth. The men and women who first became members and directors in the 1960s would emphasize this shift. The employment of Brower as executive director in 1952 had been the first step in the development of an increasingly influential and strident staff. The 1959 resolution divides the old liberalism of most earlier preservationists from the militant liberalism that the club and Brower would epitomize in the 1960s.

By 1960, then, an apocalyptic vision had come to hover over the club. That spring Brower expressed this new perception in an article entitled, "A New Decade and a Last Chance: How Bold Shall We Be?" "What we save in the next few years," he prophesied, "is all that will ever be saved. . . ." He relished being charged with "extremism," defining it as distrust of authority, public attacks upon misguided expertise, and avoidance of compromise.[22] The battles of the 1950s had taught Brower and his allies three principles: do not trust agencies of the federal government, avoid compromise even when urged by allies, and audacity can sweep the field.

Events in the redwoods themselves had helped to engender this crisis mentality within the club. As late as 1947 vast tracts of old-growth redwoods still stood in Humboldt and Del Norte counties. However, as a result of the postwar housing boom, each year through the 1950s the redwoods fell at a rate three times that of any year prior to 1950, reaching in 1958 an annual cut unmatched before or since.

Figure 10. Arcata Redwood Company lands, south of Prairie Creek Redwoods State Park, 1965. This land was subsequently acquired for the Redwood National Park. Photo by Martin Litton. Courtesy of the Save-the-Redwoods League.

By the mid-1950s the effect of this accelerated logging on the land was evident. The tractor had made it feasible to log previously inaccessible slopes, and one of the first such areas to suffer was the Bull Creek watershed surrounding Humboldt Redwoods State Park. Two million dollars contributed by the Rockefeller family since the 1930s had saved the flat lining the lower creek, but the slopes above the Rockefeller Forest had remained the property of private landowners. Between 1947 and 1954 the stretches of pale, denuded lands grew on the aerial maps of the watershed, until only tiny Humboldt Redwoods State Park remained green. The lumbermen cleared the slopes of timber and gouged the hills with logging roads and tracks of the mechanical cat. Slash fires destroyed remnants of the land's cover. The steep walls of the upper basin, with their inner gorges angling as much as 75 percent, were delicately balanced before the cutting had begun. Now devoid of cover, the unstable soils washed away. Bull Creek grew muddy and wide. Along the lower slopes logging debris had collected, and downed trees stood piled for delivery to the mills.

The winter of 1954 and 1955 brought unusually heavy rains—the "one hundred year flood," experts said. Piles of logs were swept up into the muddy, raging waters of Bull Creek to form battering rams. The river tore at the soft alluvial banks of the flat. Within hours, dozens of trees two to three hundred feet tall had toppled. By the time the waters abated, 525 giant redwoods had been lost from the Rockefeller Forest. Fifty acres of the flat had washed away, and the creek had been maimed.[23]

The same year flood waters damaged Bull Creek Flat, the California

Figure 11. Bull Creek, Humboldt Redwoods State Park, 1923. The normally serene Bull Creek prior to extensive damage from floods. Courtesy of the Save-the-Redwoods League.

Figure 12. Bull Creek, Humboldt Redwoods State Park, 1959. Damage from the 1954-55 flood can be seen. Photo by Walter C. Lowdermilk. Courtesy of the Save-the-Redwoods League.

State Highway Commission began to rebuild the Redwood Highway through Humboldt Redwoods State Park as a freeway. The commission had decided to place the asphalt belt through, rather than around, the park because it was the shortest route and avoided costly condemnation of private lands. Preservationists had recoiled at the decision but found no channels for political protest. When it had established the commission in the 1920s, the California legislature had tried to ensure that the location of highways would be free from politics by retaining only the right to establish the termini of the roads. By law the commission's declaration was conclusive evidence that a route was compatible with the highest public good. In 1937 the legislature had given the commission complete power of eminent domain over state parks, and in 1959 the California Supreme Court would rule that freeway location was not a court matter. Nor did the governor retain any legal authority over the commissioners once he had appointed them.

Believing that protracted protest was futile and fearing the hostility of the pro-freeway northern counties, the league and the State Park Commission had compromised. The new highway cut the park in half, but narrowly missed the Rockefeller Forest and the Avenue of the Giants.[24] Undismayed, the league continued to purchase avenue groves.

The club condemned the compromise. To build the freeway, huge earth movers rolled onto the alluvial flats of the park. Giant trees were downed and their roots blasted. The engineers made cuts up to five hundred feet high into unstable slopes; top soil eroded down into the rivers, forming large alluvial fans. Club leaders warned that cuts through this dense forest would become wind tunnels, subjecting the shallow-rooted redwoods to windthrow. They said the freeway bypass would cut off ground water to downslope groves, changing the ecological balance that had produced them.[25]

It was clear that the old-growth redwoods were endangered. Logging had continued apace, so that by the end of the 1950s only about 10 percent of the original two million-acre redwood belt remained uncut. Even those redwoods in state parks were threatened by erosion and freeway construction. The disappearance of forested screens along the highways further shocked "conservationists into comprehending what the country would be like if more redwoods were destroyed." Everywhere the club's leaders heard the "snarling whine of the chainsaws."[26] To publicize the "apocalyptic devastation" of the redwoods, in 1960 the club's directors launched one of the first of the organization's "exhibit format" books, to be entitled *The Last Redwoods*. Conceived, designed, and edited by Brower, the volume reflected the organization's resolution, formed that same year, to seek federal assistance in saving the redwoods. Brower, Wayburn, and their allies were convinced that both the California redwoods state parks and the league's philosophy of accommodation and compromise were inadequate to meet the crisis.[27]

The events of the 1950s had dramatically changed the club but had only modified the league. Between 1949 and 1954 Anthony Smith, then with the National Parks Association, and Dewey Anderson, liberal Democrat and executive director of the Public Affairs Institute of Washington, D.C., had promoted federal action in the redwoods.[28] The league had given them no support. In 1953 Newton Drury had left Washington to serve as chief of the California Division of Beaches and Parks under Republican Governor Earl Warren. With the backing of Warren and with Drury as chief, the league had good reason to prefer state action. Drury told Smith that he would "much rather see the State do whatever is necessary to round out the Redwood parks rather than the Federal Government. This would be in harmony with the current philosophy with which I am in sympathy, as far as State responsibilities are concerned." Again he wrote in 1954, "One of the things that Dewey Anderson never seemed to get through his head was that the cream of the Redwood forest had already been preserved in the California State Parks."[29] Winter that same year, however, revealed the fragility of these parks.

The 1954–55 flood damage to Bull Creek and the Rockefeller Forest had made the fallacy of Frederick Law Olmsted's 1927 plan obvious: acquisition of the flats at the base of privately owned watersheds invited disaster. In 1961 the league employed Walter C. Lowdermilk, retired University of California professor and specialist in erosion, to study Bull Creek. He recommended that the state bulldoze a channel in the river of gravel advancing down the creek and reconstruct the banks with cement riprapping. He approved state construction of an earth-fill dam in the upper watershed. Above all, he emphasized that a forest cover had to be restored to the slopes. The league's directors voted to help the state acquire the entire basin. Although the landowners were willing to sell, the project would be costly and dogged by time. Each winter could again bring torrential rains and further damage. (It would take the league and the state twenty years to acquire the watershed, and floods would again damage Bull Creek in 1964.) The league also worried about the safety of Mill Creek Flat in the heart of Del Norte County's Jedediah Smith Redwoods State Park.[30] The Miller Lumber Company was clearcutting the drainages of the Smith River and its tributary Mill Creek.

Figure 13. Humboldt Redwoods State Park, south fork of Cuneo Creek, 1965. Erosion caused by 1964 flood. Photo by Howard King. Courtesy of the Save-the-Redwoods League.

In 1959 Aubrey Drury died, and his brother returned to the somber, brick Adam Grant building in San Francisco's financial district. Speaking to the league council that year, Newton explained that the group's success had been "due to its singleness of purpose, its clear definition of its program, and its steadfast adherence to that program."[31] Despite accelerated logging, the rise in stumpage rates, the lumbermen's growing reluctance to sell land, and threatened park erosion, the group continued to emphasize cooperation with industry as well as state and private reform. It continued to distribute to prospective members John Merriam's optimistic messages based on faith in progressive evolution and man's control of the physical environment.

The league's constancy stemmed from the continued reinforcement of shared values of the leadership and donors. It thrived on the conviction that came from being responsible for the state's ownership by 1963 of some 102,000 acres of redwood forest lands valued at over $11 million located in four well-administered parks of widely acclaimed quality.

As intended by its founders, the organization's closed internal governance also provided stability. The council and board of directors were self-perpetuating, so that in 1960 about one-fourth of the sixty councilors had held that position since the 1930s. Others were scions of deceased councilors or donors. Of the four officers in 1960, three dated their involvement prior to 1920 and the other to the 1930s. One was the early twentieth-century president of the University of California, Robert Sproul. Even as late as 1972, two-thirds of the council had either been members of that body in 1955 or were related to someone who had been. The strong, continuous presence of Newton Drury and his brother Aubrey similarly provided continuity. This stability made for moderation, as did the tendency for the council and board to be increasingly dominated by businessmen and patricians, while fewer academics were drawn into the organization's leadership in the 1950s and 1960s.

Still, the league's officers knew that the Sierra Club was promoting a redwood national park and were themselves concerned about the cost of acquiring both the Bull Creek and Mill Creek watersheds. The Rockefellers' Jackson Hole Preserve Incorporated was providing several hundred thousand for acquisition of the slopes above the Rockefeller Forest, but state funding was minimal. In fact, despite the support of the Warren Administration, state appropriations had lagged so far behind private donations in the mid-1950s that as chief of the Division of Beaches and Parks, Drury had arranged for the abandonment of the matching funds principle.[32]

Prompted by Drury, in 1960 the California Division of Beaches and Parks conferred with western regional director of the National Park

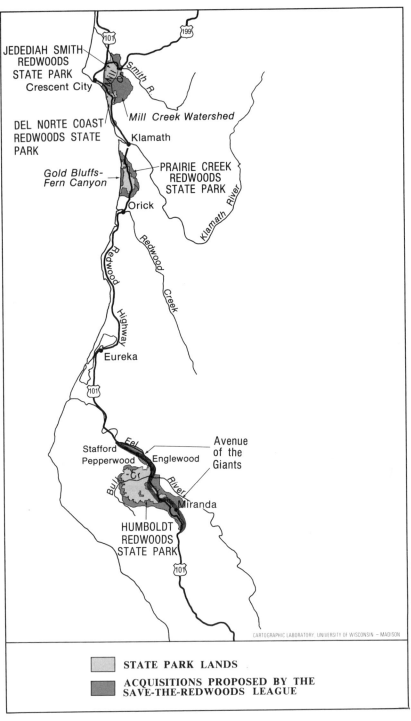

JEDEDIAH SMITH
REDWOODS
STATE PARK
Crescent City

Mill Creek Watershed

DEL NORTE COAST
REDWOODS STATE
PARK
Klamath

*Gold Bluffs-
Fern Canyon*

PRAIRIE CREEK
REDWOODS
STATE PARK

Orick

Eureka

Avenue
of the
Giants

Stafford
Pepperwood
Englewood

Miranda

HUMBOLDT
REDWOODS
STATE PARK

STATE PARK LANDS

ACQUISITIONS PROPOSED BY THE
SAVE-THE-REDWOODS LEAGUE

Map 3. California redwoods state parks and primary projects of
Save-the-Redwoods League, 1965.

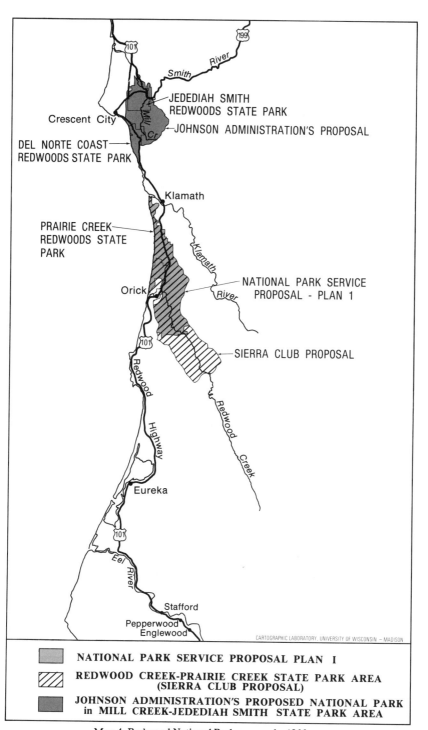

Map 4. Redwood National Park proposals, 1966.

Service, Lawrence Merriam, son of John. The division told Merriam that damage to the Rockefeller Grove proved the necessity of acquiring and reforesting the "now devastated watershed." This would cost some $1.5 million, "quite beyond any foreseeable State resources." "It was the consensus," Merriam told his superiors after the meeting, "that assistance in the matter was a proper Federal function."[33]

The league's new receptivity toward national intrusion accords with America's postwar acceptance of big government in general. Drury had himself acknowledged, over twenty years before, the existence "for good or for evil" of Washington's irresistible centripetal force.[34] The group, however, still advocated only minimal, well-planned federal involvement based on its traditional program. Drury wrote in 1960, "The same considerations we stated in the 1946 report are still pertinent to the question of a Redwood National Park: the four main projects of the League . . . represent the core of the areas of greatest caliber, worthy of being incorporated in a national park."[35]

That same year the league approached the National Geographic Society, whose president and editor Melville Bell Grosvenor was, as had been his father, a league councilor. Drury suggested that the society donate funds for a memorial grove along the Avenue of the Giants. Since the society was national, Grosvenor worried about contributing to a state park. He and Drury agreed that the society's grove might constitute the nucleus of a redwood national park or parkway. Drury believed that a combination of philanthropy and federal funding could be used to create a federal reserve perhaps administered jointly by Sacramento and Washington.[36]

The growing interest of citizen groups in a redwood national park was in part a response to changes in the nation's political climate. Historically, the National Park Service could do little to help the cause of the redwoods; to acquire private lands, the service depended entirely upon state and private funding. Only since the mid-1950s had the secretary of the Interior had the authority to use federal appropriations to acquire private lands and then only when this funding was matched by private individuals or groups, such as the National Geographic Society. The election of President John F. Kennedy in 1960, his Special Message to Congress on Natural Resources the following year, and his appointment of wilderness advocate Stewart L. Udall as secretary of the Interior all gave conservationists reason to hope that they were riding "a rising tide."[37] Their optimism proved warranted. In 1961 Congress established Cape Cod National Seashore, the nation's first parkland to be purchased entirely with federal funds. With the administration and Congress favorably disposed toward environmental concerns, citizen activists seized the opportunity to raise the issue of the redwoods.

At the Sierra Club's annual Wilderness Conference in 1961, the general secretary of the conference, Edgar Wayburn's wife Peggy, suggested to Secretary Udall that the Kennedy Administration support the establishment of a redwood national park.[38] Later that same year Brower wrote to Udall asking that the secretary make at least a "private expression" of interest in such a park so that the club might continue its efforts.[39]

The secretary was receptive. Indeed, he agreed to write the foreword to *The Last Redwoods*. But Udall was also aware of the magnitude of the proposal. In 1962 Congress reaffirmed the precedent of federal purchase by establishing Point Reyes National Seashore, at the dedication of which Brower was photographed with President Kennedy. Nevertheless, a redwood national park would cost far more than either Point Reyes or Cape Cod and would meet strong opposition from the lumber companies.[40]

In fact, national park appropriations were such that when in 1962 Grosvenor asked the Park Service to recommend a location for the redwood national park, the service lacked the funds to survey the redwoods.[41] So in March, 1963, the National Geographic Society agreed to provide the service with a $64,000 grant for that purpose.[42] In May the grant was made public.[43] That summer the chief of the National Park Service's Coastal Redwood Survey, Chet Brown, and *National Geographic Magazine* photographer Paul Zahl headed west to survey the redwoods.

From the beginning the league was convinced that if a national park were to be established, it should be located so as to complete one of Olmsted's four 1927 park projects. Bull Creek was too scarred to be of national park quality. Prairie Creek was a possibility, but the league favored Mill Creek, which was threatened and as yet undamaged. Drury told the Park Service that the 42,000-acre Mill Creek basin in Del Norte County was the best site for a national park.[44] Initially, both the society and the Park Service intended to follow the league's suggestion that the national park be centered on one of the state parks, preferably Jedediah Smith.[45]

At this point, the Sierra Club had no official position on location but considered the Klamath River and its tributary Blue Creek a possible site. The previous year Edgar and Peggy Wayburn had shown the area to the assistant secretary for national parks, John Carver. *The Last Redwoods*, which appeared in print in December, 1963, contained photographs of the river with the caption, "Redwoods—Going-Going on the Klamath." This watershed seemed an ideal national park site primarily because of its size and the recreational value of the broad river itself. However, much of the lower basin had been logged in the 1950s, and—true to the club's prophecy—the trees on the upper watershed and Blue Creek were cut shortly after Carver's visit.[46]

In the meantime, to help the Park Service select a site, Martin Litton, travel editor for *Sunset Magazine* and self-styled authority on the redwoods, offered to fly Zahl and Brown on an aerial reconnaissance over the redwood belt. Litton was a league councilor as well as a close acquaintance of Brower, Wallace Stegner, and Wayburn of the club. Litton had his own idea of where the park should be located. He thought that Mill Creek was of high quality and recommended federal aid to the state for the acquisition of the watershed but believed Redwood Creek's basin was "the ultimate Redwood wilderness."[47] In late summer he flew Zahl and Brown over the sweeping Redwood Creek watershed in Humboldt County. The basin was further off the highway than the state parks, and although it had been partially logged, it held at that time miles of virgin forests and several unlogged tributaries. Zahl was excited by the site. The Park Service, however, feared publicity could prematurely commit the service and induce defensive action by the lumber industry, so the National Geographic Society muffled public announcements.[48]

By fall the Park Service had narrowed its deliberations to Redwood Creek and Mill Creek, but several factors had begun to swing the balance against the latter.[49] For one thing, on a bend in Redwood Creek the Park Service and National Geographic team discovered redwoods taller than that previously considered the tallest living thing in the world—a redwood near Bull Creek dedicated to the league's founders.[50]

Further to the discredit of the state parks, the California State Highway Commission had announced in fall, 1963, that it intended to rebuild the northern portions of Highways 101 and 199 as freeways and align them through Prairie Creek and Jedediah Smith redwoods state parks.[51] The freeway would either follow the existing highway and bisect Prairie Creek's central groves and meadow, where the Roosevelt elk grazed, or go along the park's western boundary—Gold Bluffs Beach. The alignment proposed for Jedediah Smith would slice through Mill Creek basin. Any of these routes would eliminate the small parks—each no more than three or four miles wide—from national park consideration.

Through 1963 and 1964 the Department of the Interior repeatedly corresponded with the state and testified against the freeway proposals.[52] But the trucking lobby, lumber companies, and local

Figure 14. Prairie Creek Freeway Construction, 1964. Photo by Martin Litton.

residents favored the cross-park alignments as the shortest and most scenic routes. The club feared that the league and the State Park Commission would agree to a compromise, as they had with Humboldt Redwoods State Park. At a hearing of the California Highway Commission, Wayburn threatened to sue the commission, but the club was too unsure of its legal standing to sue to follow through. Finally, in late 1964 the Ford Foundation, which had donated the funds for the acquisition of Gold Bluffs Beach, encouraged President Lyndon B. Johnson to intercede. Pressure from the White House prompted the vacillating Governor Edmund G. Brown into opposing the alignments. The U.S. Department of Commerce also passed a requirement that all federal-aid highway projects, which included most of northern California's, give full consideration to the integrity of public parks. This threatened loss of federal funds saved Prairie Creek. However, the fate of Jedediah Smith would hang in the balance through 1966, undermining the league's campaign to make Mill Creek the site for the national park.[53]

In January, 1964, Paul Zahl, Chet Brown, Grosvenor, Secretary Udall, ex−National Park Service Director Conrad Wirth, and present Director George Hartzog met in Washington and decided on a tentative plan. They agreed federal aid should be arranged to help the state complete its four parks but that the national park should be on Redwood Creek. The Park Service, however, did not make its plan public. Its officials hoped to make headway in formulating and justifying their proposal before announcing a location so as to minimize local and industrial hostility.[54] The service also needed the support of the new administration before it could translate its plan into congressional action.

Fortunately for the redwoods, President Johnson had retained Kennedy's secretary of the Interior. In 1963 Secretary Udall's book *The Quiet Crisis* had appeared, in which he advocated use of the government's powers of taxation as a creative force for scenic preservation.[55] Responding to Udall's calls for bold park planning, President Johnson's 1964 Conservation Message proposed eight new national parks. In May of that year, Udall formally suggested the president initiate a specific new conservation proposal that would exemplify the convictions Johnson had expressed in his "great society" statement in Michigan the previous week. Udall said, "the most logical new proposal . . . would be the endorsement by the President of a Redwood National Park. 'Save the Redwoods' is still," he added, "the best understood and most honorable rallying cry of the conservation movement." At Udall's instigation, in June the president held a White House Conference, attended by congressional and conservation leaders, at which he expressed interest in a redwood national park and directed Interior to prepare a proposal for the administration to present Congress.[56]

One month after the White House Conference, *National Geographic Magazine* announced discovery of the "Mount Everest of All Living Things," a tree 367.8 feet tall on Redwood Creek. The society resolved to acquire a 140-acre Tall Trees Grove as the core of the future national park.[57] However, when Grosvenor sought to buy the Tall Trees from Arcata Redwood Lumber Company, Arcata's chairman of the board, C. Davis Weyerhaeuser, refused. Arcata owned about 6,400 acres of uncut timber and 3,000 acres of cutover land on the east side of Redwood Creek.[58] Weyerhaeuser explained that the company could not assess the monetary loss that would result from the sale of the 140-acre grove, "because it would be impossible to measure damage to the balance of the company's property by virtue of having a public park in the heart of our holdings." It would similarly be impossible, he added, to log the watershed without damaging the flat.[59] At this point the society began to find the park issue too political for its nonprofit blood and played only a minor role in the subsequent controversy.

But on September 4, 1964, the stark necessity of outside funding for land acquisitions that had impelled the Park Service to look to such organizations as the National Geographic Society diminished,

Figure 15. Redwood Creek area of the "World's Tallest Tree Grove," 1965. This photo was taken when this land was owned by the Arcata Redwood Company. The trees are now in the Redwood National Park. Photo by David Swanlund. Courtesy of the Save-the-Redwoods League.

although it did not disappear. On that day Congress passed the Land and Water Conservation Fund, making substantial funds available for national park purchases. Philanthropy, the time-honored method of redwood preservation, would play a decreasing role in the campaign for a national park.

In the meantime, the position of the Park Service had become increasingly untenable. Despite the agency's efforts at concealment, the lumber companies had somehow received information of its intentions and were issuing literature quoting details from the supposedly still-secret park proposal. The service concluded there was little reason to withhold from friends information already possessed by "the enemy." That September it released its report entitled *The Redwoods*, recommending a park on Redwood Creek. The proposal suggested three different plans for a park on Redwood Creek varying in size from 30,000 to 50,000 acres.[60]

The league reacted with displeasure. Drury and his directors conceded Redwood Creek was a larger area than Mill Creek, but they noted it had only narrow alluvial plains. The slopes sprouted even-aged stands a mere four hundred years in age and mixed with other species. In contrast, Mill Creek flat's "cathedral-like" groves were "noble gems." Mill Creek was, Drury argued, a higher quality flat, already publicly owned but endangered by upslope logging; Olmsted's 1927 park program should receive the highest priority. In contrast to the club, the league had not rejected the state parks because they were too small or close to highways. Through the 1950s and into the 1960s, in fact, the group continued to give acquisitions along the Avenue of the Giants top priority.[61]

Its closed governance and the principles of its leaders had locked the league into a world view in which man's technological modifications of the environment are of a whole cloth with the progressive action of evolution. The group had neither rejected its earlier faith in accommodation nor moved away from its belief that a park was a museum that must encompass the most striking evidences of evolutionary creation—the oldest and purest stands of redwood.[62] Despite the financial and ecological implications of the Bull Creek flood, the league steadfastly adhered to its political beliefs and its philosopher John Merriam, to whom the redwoods symbolized a triumph of progressive evolution.

The nation should not, Drury admonished the Park Service, strike out in a new direction in a watershed that would at best be only half in public ownership and therefore itself subject to erosion. In Mill Creek it would be possible to establish a national park encompassing an entire watershed theoretically safe from flood damage. Congress had never appropriated more than $35 million for a single park purchase, these moderates warned, making it unlikely that legislators would vote $160 million for Redwood Creek in the face of inevitable massive industrial opposition. They felt a 42,000-acre, $60 million park was "feasible."[63]

In contrast to the league, the Sierra Club immediately endorsed the service's designation of Redwood Creek, seeing it as the site of the single largest block of old-growth redwoods not yet preserved. Over the issue of park location there was an echo within the club of the internal schism that would continue through the 1960s. Several of the organization's directors and past presidents, two of whom also served on the league's board, wanted the club to defer to Drury's judgment that a moderate plan was the wisest solution. But Litton had convinced Brower, President Wayburn, and most of the directors that Redwood Creek was superior.[64]

Indeed, so sure were Wayburn, Brower, and their allies that the club could marshal the support necessary to establish a large park that they

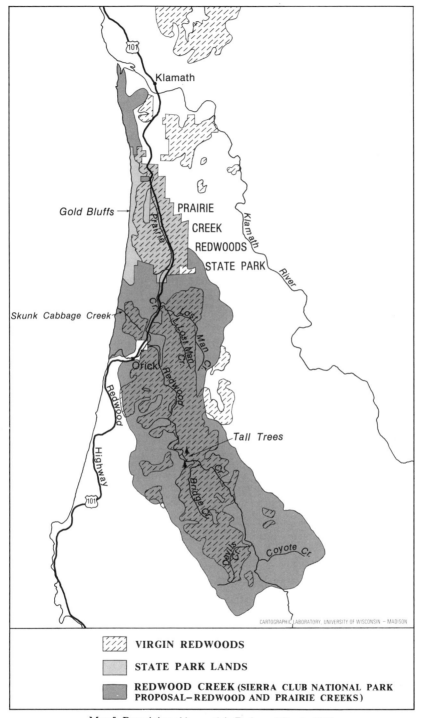

Klamath

Gold Bluffs →

PRAIRIE

CREEK

REDWOODS

STATE PARK

Klamath River

Skunk Cabbage Creek →

Lost Man Cr.

Orick

Redwood

Prairie

Tall Trees

Redwood

Highway

101

Bridge Cr.

Devils Cr.

Coyote Cr.

CARTOGRAPHIC LABORATORY, UNIVERSITY OF WISCONSIN – MADISON

VIRGIN REDWOODS

STATE PARK LANDS

REDWOOD CREEK (SIERRA CLUB NATIONAL PARK PROPOSAL–REDWOOD AND PRAIRIE CREEKS)

Map 5. Remaining old growth in Redwood Creek, 1966.

declared even the service's most ambitious proposal far too modest. They wanted at least 90,000 acres, or half of the Redwood Creek drainage. They believed such a park to be politically possible despite the estimated cost of $160 million.[65]

Between 1959 and 1964 the club's confidence had grown and with good reason. Its staff had gone from only a few in 1959 to thirty-three. The membership had increased at an average annual rate of 12−13 percent, and in 1964 jumped to over 22 percent. With 21,000 members, the club was a national organization, with chapters from the Atlantic to the Pacific Northwest.

Not only did the organization's leaders feel they could promote a large park, but they believed the very size of their proposal was a key to its realization. They saw the league's Mill Creek plan as evidence the group had "lost hope in the idea" of a national park. In speaking later of the decision in favor of a "big, bold plan for a Redwood National Park," Brower paraphrased the words of Chicago's city planner Daniel H. Burnham, "make no small plans because they don't have the power to inspire people."[66] He also deemed militancy crucial to success. In 1963 he told his board of directors that being "insistently critical" of government and industry won far more than "private diplomacy" and "being polite."[67] This strident attitude affected the organization's growing publication program. In 1963—the same year *The Last Redwoods* appeared in print—Brower wrote that "the club's publishing mission is to take sides—to be unashamed of good propaganda. . . ."[68]

And *The Last Redwoods* was good propaganda, with its photographs of beautiful old-growth redwoods juxtaposed against scenes of floodtorn rivers and eroding hillsides terraced to bed a freeway. Large, colored photographs portrayed fresh clearcuts with torn brown soil exposed, and speeding logging trucks bore away giant trees to smoky mills beside captions questioning the benefits of "the new technology."[69] Grey landscapes of burned snags and jagged stumps gave mute testimony to the club's crusade for a park. The book's very title was compelling.

Yet critics called *The Last Redwoods* a misnomer. League director and retired University of California professor of forestry Emanuel Fritz and Norman Livermore, Jr.—treasurer of the Pacific Lumber Company, former club officer, and soon to be Governor Ronald Reagan's resource administrator—attacked the title as unfair, inaccurate, and misleading. They argued that the timber companies were ensuring the species' industrial future. The club answered that tree farms and advertised reseeding projects were little more than public relations ploys and that the lumber companies had a long way to go before they would have an adequate supply of second growth once the virgin redwoods were liquidated.[70]

The environmentalists further pointed out that the title referred to old-growth giants, not saplings or commercial-size trees. Livermore and Fritz countered that there would always be giant redwoods in the state parks, to which the club retorted that these reserves were too small to tolerate heavy use and too close to the highway to offer a wilderness experience.[71] Stewart Brandborg, executive director of The Wilderness Society, wrote that state parks were "too small to support a National Park, with strictly limited groves of virgin redwoods—some of which have already been cut up by freeways and other man-caused impairments."[72] The club was even blunter: the state parks were "see-through roadside strips" and "almost as tall as they were wide."[73] Seeing the massive highway construction in postwar California, the organization had reversed its earlier policy in favor of Sierra Nevada roads and removed the phrase to "render accessible the mountain regions of the Pacific Coast" from its bylaws. By 1960, as a result in part of damage to the redwoods, its leaders viewed roads as the most destructive of all threats to parks.[74]

The club was adamant: the national park must be large and it must be on Redwood Creek. As it had earlier in the century, evolution still played a significant role in the rationale for redwood preservation and in the club's case for Redwood Creek. In *The Last Redwoods* Loren Eiseley's description of life's "immense journey" up from the ocean floor captioned photographs of small plants and animals silhouetted against giant redwoods.[75]

The message was beautiful but not reassuring. At the height of the redwood battle in the mid-1960s, Hugh H. Iltis, associate professor of botany at the University of Wisconsin, wrote in the *Sierra Club Bulletin*, "It is surely clear to all but the blindest of evolutionary optimists that the biological problems of both nature and human experience are now much more acute and are becoming increasingly urgent each day." Iltis warned against the idea that "technology has promised us a post-evolutionary heaven in which wild nature has no place."[76]

Most club leaders now believed with Iltis that any threat to the continuity of evolution endangered not only other species but man himself. In *The Last Redwoods* author François Leydet warned—as did the club in much of its literature on the redwoods—that man "if too impatient to care can end a chain of life, going back without interruption to an old eternity when life first strove to leave the mother sea." "We cannot," he said, destroy wilderness "without destroying something in us."[77]

Man was "inescapably a part" of his environment.[78] Theories of random evolution denied him authority over the earth. The club denounced the "hubris" of those who believed, as had John Merriam, that man was the apex of evolution and could manipulate his environment in

Figure 16. Jedediah Smith Redwoods State Park, Stout Tree, in the 1960s. Fence erected by state park officials to protect the Stout Tree against damage from visitor use. Photo by Howard King. Courtesy of the Save-the-Redwoods League.

full confidence of material and moral progress.[79] In a 1979 taped interview, Brower claimed that, looking at a redwood forest, Emanuel Fritz said, "nature never does anything right" and that Bestor Robinson believed "nature doesn't have any rights." Brower, of course, disagreed with both. Picking up the gist of Brower's line of reasoning, 1950s and 1960s club leader William Siri exclaimed, "We are all bloody accidents along the way. . . . We are the compilation of an enormous number of accidents." Brower objected, saying we were the products not of mistakes but of successes. Siri responded, "Accidents meaning casual, random effects that occur. I am talking," he added, "like a scientist."[80]

Martin Litton chided that man could take no credit for the redwoods, and the Wayburns argued that these trees were entitled to survive "even if there were no men at all."[81] These environmentalists did not believe that technology could ever obviate man's biological dependence upon evolution. "The best arguments against blind technological progress may be found," Iltis argued, in evolution.[82] In 1959 past president of the American Association for the Advancement of Science Paul Sears told the club that we cannot speak of "man's control of nature" or the "conquest of space."[83] Through the 1960s environmentalists repeatedly placed the efforts of the United States to conquer, physically and philosophically, the universe through space travel against the far more crucial need to protect man's evolutionary roots. The ancient redwood forest aptly symbolized these roots. A club advertisement warned, "History will think it most strange that America could afford the Moon and $4 billion airplanes, while a patch of primeval redwoods—not too big for a man to walk through in a day—was considered beyond its means."[84] William O. Douglas noted that it would be costly to save the redwoods but so was putting the first man on the moon. And it would be to the earth, not the moon, he said, that our descendants would look for their sustenance and survival.[85]

The club had abandoned the philosophy of LeConte for that of Eiseley, whose world view found no will, no knowledge beyond the natural order. To Eiseley, Brower, and many club leaders, the "apocalyptic devastation" of the redwoods proved that evolution might take man back into an "old eternity" of "lifeless darkness."[86] A nondirectional universe complemented a technology that appeared more destructive than beneficial. The postwar western landscapes seemed to verify Eiseley's assertion that human activity was merely the random movement of another parasite through one small sector of an indifferent universe. As a bold challenge to American industry and evolutionary proof against man's technology, club leaders demanded federal purchase of a 90,000-acre redwood wilderness on Redwood Creek. They refused to compromise, as had the league for decades, with the lumber companies and industrial needs.

In addition to accounting in large part for the club's increased militancy, the modern evolutionary synthesis and advances in experimental ecology had also changed the definition of parks and their functions. Theories of directional evolution had encouraged earlier preservationists to believe in man's capacity and right to select species that should be saved for his benefit as well as those whose continued existence man need not suffer. Theories of progressive evolution had also led these preservationists to see parks as museums, housing the very best examples of the most spectacular products of biological evolution and geologic change. As one club leader noted in the 1960s, the league still believed stands in Mill Creek to be "more typical of the 'climax of the species,'" the finest examples of a species that had emerged triumphant over centuries of progressive changes in the vegetation of the region.[87]

By way of contrast, postwar biologists and most preservationists emphasized the importance of all species and organisms. Each species was a link in the ecological balance, and without direction, evolution defined no plant or animal as superior, not even man. Hence, according to Iltis, the real thing to fear in our illusionary "post-evolutionary heaven" was that "life's diversity was threatened with imminent destruction." Wilderness parks, then, must preserve our "biotic wealth." The goal of environmentalists was to "sustain a livable earth for the diversity that can include us."[88]

Although the club followed National Geographic's lead in publicizing the Tall Trees, the attraction of Redwood Creek for Brower, Litton, Wayburn, and their allies lay in its great "genetic" or "ecological diversity." According to the club, unlike Mill Creek, Redwood Creek offered the entire ecological range of habitat for the redwood species, from groves at sea level to those at 3,000 feet, from wooded flats of "near rain-forest luxuriance" to drier "great slope" and ridge-top stands.[89] In Redwood Creek the redwoods also grew in all age classes. This great watershed also held a multiplicity of nonredwood ecologies, from the edge-of-the-sea to sunny inland hills covered with a broad spectrum of evergreens and deciduous trees.[90] In short, rather than simply the supposed climax of a single, distinctive species, Redwood Creek offered "superior faunal variety, geological variety and geographical variety." It was this variety that was, the club argued, "at the heart of the unparalleled uniqueness of the area."[91]

In addition to ecological diversity, the club believed a wilderness park had to be of significant size—a criterion the league had never employed. Club leaders thought that a broad terrain was necessary for a complete biome secure against recreational overuse. Redwood Creek's expansive vistas, together with its miles of coastline and rivers and the area's remoteness, promised a wilderness experience.[92] The 90,000-acre reserve would extend from the coast "far enough inland to reach beyond the fog into the sunshine."[93] Only a park of such size could offer a genuine escape from civilization, "a human experience" without "noise, visual distraction, pollution, and pernicious overcrowding."[94]

More important, size was essential to Redwood Creek's evolutionary continuity. Writing in 1962, Brower defined wilderness as the place wherein "the evolutionary force, in all its myriad forms, has gone on since the beginning of life, essentially uninterrupted by man and his technology." Brower warned that "this *un*interrupted requires a lot of space, and a wide buffer around it, for nobody is more pervasive than man and his technology."[95] By the 1960s environmental militants in the club had come to have a dynamic perception of a wilderness park. Rather than a preserve frozen in time, to them a wilderness park was a living organism within which disease, fire, and all natural processes must play a continuous and creative role.[96] Indeed, wilderness was less a state than a process.

The arguments in defense of Redwood Creek were in part propaganda rebutting the league's claim that Mill Creek held the best redwoods. There is, however, no doubt that club leaders genuinely sought a national park that would protect large ongoing forest, meadow, and maritime biomes rather than merely cathedrallike redwood groves. The militancy of their Redwood Creek proposal was, then, the result of a perception of evolution as a precarious and continuous process, rather than a cumulative one. Unfortunately, in the forthcoming battle for a national park, the club would fight so bitterly with the league in defense of its vision that there would be years when it was doubtful whether or not a redwood national park would be established at all.

8
The Redwood National Park: 1965–1968

THERE WERE three stages in what became one of the major conservation battles of the 1960s—the fight to establish the Redwood National Park. The first was from the National Park Service's 1964 report until January, 1966, when it became obvious the club had failed to prevent the Johnson Administration from abandoning the service's Redwood Creek proposal in favor of the league's more modest plan. In the second phase California's Republican Senator Thomas Kuchel sponsored the administration's redwood park bill in opposition to legislation introduced by club supporters in the liberal and pro-labor wing of the Democratic Party. The third stage opened in late 1967 as Senators Kuchel and Henry Jackson advanced a compromise and ended in October, 1968, when President Johnson signed a seriously weakened park act, the result of industrial opposition and the division among the citizen groups.

For the first year and a half after the Park Service's September, 1964, report recommending a large Redwood Creek park, the club's position had appeared stronger than that of the league. The White House received twenty petitions and some two thousand individual responses to the Park Service's report—all in favor of a park and two to one in favor of the largest proposal. Through summer and into early fall of 1965, Secretary Udall personally advocated a large reserve that would include at least a significant portion of Redwood Creek. National enthusiasm for conservation was quickening, and the redwoods were rapidly becoming symbolic of environmental deterioration in general. In a fall, 1965, CBS special entitled "Bulldozed America," Charles Kuralt changed Woodie Guthrie's song to read: "From the redwood forests, to the Gulf Stream waters, the bulldozers do their work, and the land is changed forever."

That same year Raymond Dasmann's *The Destruction of California* appeared in print with a photograph of the redwoods on the cover. Club leaders took heart as the Eighty-eighth Congress closed after authorizing ten new national parks.[1]

Still, they knew that precedents for federal land purchases were new, that the cost of earlier projects was insignificant compared to that of a redwood park, and that the league was still pressing for Mill Creek.[2] The state of California was also undermining the Department of the Interior's commitment to Redwood Creek. In April, 1965, Hugo Fisher, Governor Edmund Brown's administrator of Resources, told Udall, "We recommend against the Redwood National Park proposal on lower Redwood Creek." Echoing the league, Fisher argued that the southern basin could not provide complete watershed protection. In fact, the state opposed all plans for a redwood national park. According to Fisher, there was "inadequate continuous acreage of primeval redwood forest in any area of northern California, including the Redwood Creek, to constitute a National Redwood Park of proper scale and quality." Instead, Governor Brown proposed a national parkway to run from Muir Woods, up the Avenue of the Giants, and on to Grants Pass.[3]

When Udall ignored the proposal, Fisher called the National Park Service to offer "another idea for a possible national park." This was to include Humboldt Redwoods State Park and the King Range to the west, the latter a checkerboard of private and federal lands. The plan saved no new redwoods, which may be why it appealed to the Brown Administration. Fisher had personally denounced the scheme months before when the American Forestry Association had proposed it. It appears that Brown was responding to pressure from the industry and the North Coast.[4]

Having faced depression through the 1930s and 1940s, a flood in the winter of 1954—55, as well as another flood and a tidal wave in 1964, most Humboldt and Del Norte county residents now resented federal encroachments on their precarious economic recovery.[5] The timber industry relied upon this animosity and Brown to kill the park proposal. The various companies stirred up opposition among employees and local governing bodies, bluntly reminding Interior of the state's position.[6] Their strategy was sound; Congress traditionally grants its members broad autonomy in their own district.

The club decided to enlist local residents who favored the park. These individuals found that voicing their sentiments brought personal and economic harassment. Many "silent supporters" were afraid to arouse the ire of what one resident called the "sleeping giant" and of the unions whose members feared the loss of jobs.[7] In December, 1964, Brower transferred Michael McCloskey, a young lawyer who had served as the club's Pacific Northwest representative since 1961, to San Francisco to manage the redwood national park campaign, coordinating staff, officers, and volunteers. From December through February, 1965, working from a list of local park supporters supplied by the Park Service, McCloskey organized residents of California's North Coast counties who could be convinced to take a public stand. Constituting in large part students and professors from Humboldt State College, the Citizens Committee for a Redwood National Park remained an unofficial adjunct of the club. The committee helped the club recruit a network of supporters but did little to offset local animosity.[8]

McCloskey, however, played a significant role in the rest of the battle. In February, 1965, the club assigned him full-time to work as staff assistant to redwood task force leader Edgar Wayburn. In March McCloskey went to Washington to contact legislators. In October Montana's Senator Lee Metcalf together with California's representatives Jeffrey Cohelan and Phillip Burton—all Democrats—sponsored bills for a 90,000-acre national park to encompass over half of the Redwood Creek watershed and state park lands lining the tributary Prairie Creek. Introduced with club-arranged television coverage one day before adjournment of the first session of the Eighty-ninth Congress, the measures had no opportunity for passage. Yet McCloskey hoped that rushing the plan before Congress would allow for committee work prior to the next session. Wayburn understood that chairman of the House Committee on Interior and Insular Affairs Wayne Aspinall often used the chronological order of a bill's introduction to avoid taking it under consideration. The move was also calculated to call Redwood Creek to the public's attention before the president released his proposal.[9]

The club feared Johnson might abandon the large Redwood Creek proposal Interior had advanced, and it maintained a steady pressure on the White House.[10] This fear was well founded if premature. In June the Park Service formulated a second plan, this time for a two-unit park. The proposed southern unit was similar to that of the 1964 report: 56,000 acres, consisting of Prairie Creek Redwoods State Park and parts of Redwood Creek as well as the Little Lost Man and May Creek drainages. A 37,000-acre northern unit was to consist of Del Norte Coast and Jedediah Smith state parks and the remainder of the Mill Creek watershed. It was an ambitious proposal—some 93,000 acres, of which 68,000 were privately owned—to cost $120 million. In mid-July Bureau of the Budget Director Charles L. Schultze approved legislative submission of the plan to Congress. Schultze was receptive to Udall's suggestion that the park be paid for in ten yearly increments from the Land and Water Conservation Fund and that private support be solicited from foundations.[11] The report was not made public until November, 1965.[12] But from June to September, it was the basis of the Park Service's on-site inspections, Udall's negotiations with Governor Brown, and the department's legislative planning.[13] The new plan did indicate, however, that the club's premonitions were not entirely groundless. Should compromise prove necessary, Interior recommended that it be made in the southern unit, with the Mill Creek section left intact.

By November, 1965, it was obvious that Udall might well consider such a compromise advisable. On November 22 and 23, he held a series of conferences on the redwoods. He met with Arcata Redwood Company's chairman of the board C. Davis Weyerhaeuser and president Howard Libbey, and G. G. Evans and R. B. Pamplin of Georgia-Pacific. These firms had large Redwood Creek holdings, and their representatives argued strenuously against a national park in Humboldt County.[14]

Udall also faced the continued obstinacy of the state of California. Through the summer and fall, he had tried to buy Governor Brown's support for a redwood national park by offering to transfer public domain lands to the state. He told the governor that he, the league, and various foundations had met to discuss matching philanthropy with money from the Land and Water Conservation Fund for additions to the Avenue of the Giants. In July Brown had informed Udall that he regarded Mill Creek as a less objectionable site than Redwood Creek. On November 23 Udall repeated his offers to representatives from Brown's administration and presented them with a tentative plan for a park on Mill Creek.[15]

In the course of his conferences on the redwoods, Udall also saw Brower, who urged the secretary to press for what he called "the big one." The preservationist came away discouraged, however, and the club intensified its counterpressure.[16] Wayburn wrote the White House, comparing Mill Creek unfavorably with Redwood Creek, with its "broad spectrum of biota, climate and territory." Martin Litton—no longer active in the league—told Udall that Mill Creek was Newton Drury's "nearsighted obsession" and was not secluded enough from "shabby civilization."[17]

In December Udall wrote to Brower, counseling that "progress is usually the result of compromise. I think this may be the case with a Redwood National Park." He asked the club to maintain "a position flexible enough so that it gracefully can support the National Park proposal which the Administration adopts, even if it should be somewhat different from the first preference. . . ."[18]

Brower shot back that the club would be flexible about how much land was initially acquired but not "about where the buying is done." He reminded Udall of when he and writer Wallace Stegner had first brought the park proposal to the secretary's attention in the latter's office: "You turned to Wally and said, 'This would make Canyonlands look like a picnic.'" Brower called Mill Creek a "confession of failure." He warned that if the administration's proposal did not include Redwood Creek, "we have no alternative but to ask our members and the members of other conservation organizations not to support the Administration's bills. . . ."[19]

With the shrillness of the betrayed, the club attacked the White House and deepened the division between the once-friendly San Francisco groups into a nationally publicized schism. With the assistance of a San Francisco advertising firm, Brower, Wayburn, and McCloskey designed a full-page advertisement—borrowing the idea from the Dinosaur battle—to run in newspapers across the country. This was the first in a series of such advertisements that the club would use with great effectiveness through the 1960s. Framed as an "Open Letter to President Johnson on the Last Chance *Really* to Save the Redwoods," the advertisement accused the chief executive and those favoring Mill Creek of having been "intimidated by a powerful industry and its expensive public relations program."[20] The attack embarrassed Udall, since it appeared on the day he had called a meeting of representatives from the league and the nation's major foundations. In vain he had hoped to get financial support for redwood park acquisitions from such institutional philanthropies as Laurance Rockefeller's Conservation Foundation and the Ford Foundation.[21]

Despite the club's adamant posture, on January 5, 1966, Udall recommended to the White House a single-unit park on Mill Creek. It was to cost $45 to $50 million. He explained that the plan was the product of negotiations with the state of California, the counties involved, and various conservation organizations.[22] On January 25 President Johnson's budgetary message to Congress included a nonspecific proposal for a redwood national park. In February Udall transmitted to Congress the administration's proposal for a 39,264-acre park to encompass Jedediah Smith and Del Norte Coast redwoods state parks and the Mill Creek watershed. The plan was 4,000 acres smaller than Udall's recommendation but otherwise the same.[23] The league pledged strong support for the proposal.[24]

Brower and Wayburn publicly railed against Johnson's "self-defeating" plan to save 6,000 acres of old growth instead of the club's proposal, which would rescue 33,000 acres of virgin timber.[25] They denounced the sacrifice of Redwood Creek as benefiting "only the three lumber companies who own these remaining redwoods" and asked rhetorically how the interests of these "powerful and wealthy" companies could be weighted against the interests of the American people.[26]

In contrast to the assumption that productive cooperation with the timbermen was impossible, Drury had consistently maintained that the park "should and can be preserved only with proper concern for all interests involved: State, conservation organizations, the lumber industry, and local taxing authorities." He preferred quiet diplomacy to the club's confrontation politics and censured the rival group for having issued its publicity "before the program was better defined" and measures taken to alleviate the impact on the local economy.[27] He believed that the lumbermen would not wage a full-scale battle against a reasonable park plan if they were treated fairly.

The club's publicity had merely intensified, however, the industry's hostility. By 1964 the five major redwood companies had established a public relations firm to fight the proposed park. In the wake of the Park Service's 1964 report, the companies had made it clear they would fight condemnation. Oregon's Senator Wayne Morse threatened legislation to curb the Park Service's right of eminent domain.[28]

Meanwhile Drury argued that Mill Creek was at least somewhat "more acceptable to the lumber interests than the Redwood Creek proposal."[29] The northern plan demanded half as much old growth as the club's proposal and involved only the Miller Redwood Company. Miller could be compensated with timber from Forest Service land. The club was demanding 90,000 acres; industry offered 8,000 acres. The administration welcomed the league's claim that its plan was "feasible."[30]

Not surprisingly, McCloskey publicly accused the league of having, with the aid of the Bureau of the Budget and industry, "succeeded in reversing the Park Service."[31] Udall had hinted to Brower that cost had been a factor in the administration's decision. It was in fact commonly rumored that the bureau had set a $50 million limit.[32] Yet on the basis of Udall's advocacy of installment and private funding—methods for which there were precedents—the Bureau of the Budget had supported Interior's $120 million, two-unit proposal through summer and fall of 1965.[33] A $50 million ceiling did not necessarily dictate a Mill Creek site. Indeed, the club was willing to support a smaller park, as long as it was on Redwood Creek. By early 1966 war in Vietnam was threatening funding for domestic programs.[34] However, the Bureau of the Budget's supposed role in dictating a small Mill Creek park was in part a subterfuge for a Democratic administration that found it politically inexpedient to admit that it was bowing to industrial opposition.

The league no doubt had a part in the administration's reversal, as did the projected cost of the Park Service's Redwood Creek proposal, but it was one that opponents similarly oversimplified. Udall and Park Service Director George Hartzog announced publicly that the league had been pivotal in the administration's decision to back Mill Creek.[35] As past directors of the Park Service, both Drury and league councilor Horace Albright were members of its Advisory Board on National Parks, Historic Sites, Buildings, and Monuments. It has been suggested that the service would not seriously consider a project without the support of this advisory board.[36] Yet the advisory board had not been consulted before the service's 1964 report. Moreover, in October, 1965, the advisory group had recommended a two-unit park.[37] Drury and Albright had persuaded Interior to formulate a revised, two-unit proposal, but they had not convinced the department to abandon Redwood Creek. President Johnson and Governor Brown had done that. The league's influence upon Johnson was real but more indirect.

As special consultant to the president on the park, Laurance Rockefeller promoted the league's plan. As Edward Crafts, former assistant chief of the Forest Service and director of the new Bureau of Outdoor Recreation, later explained, Laurance "was a participant and privy to *all* of the things that were going on and he would deal directly with the President and Mrs. Johnson on this and was very influential," especially on the issue of park location, a matter about which "I don't think the President could have cared less."[38] Rockefeller's position within the administration had developed out of his father's support of the national parks. It rested, too, upon his own activities in conservation since 1958, making him in 1964 a logical choice for President Johnson's Task Force on Natural Beauty and the White House Conference on Natural Beauty. The relationship had grown as Rockefeller assisted Lady Bird Johnson in her dedication to beautification.[39] The alliance was cemented by his willingness to foster the LBJ State Park.[40]

If Johnson's reliance upon Rockefeller came logically from earlier events, the latter's commitment to Mill Creek was less than automatic. His first ventures into the redwood national park issue were attempts to reconcile the demands of preservationists and park opponents and did not involve the league. In 1964 he paid two professional foresters to study the impact various park proposals would have upon the economy and timber companies of northern California. Believing that a large national park would cause financial chaos, these foresters recommended the Rockefeller Forest and Humboldt Redwoods State Park be given national park status. Endorsed by the American Forestry Association, this proposal never received serious attention because of the freeway and flood damage to the park.[41]

In fall of 1964 Maurice Fred Smith, corporate businessman and conservation consultant to the Rockefellers, went to California at the request and expense of Bernie Orell of the Weyerhaeuser Company. Smith's goal was to negotiate with the lumbermen a plan more acceptable to them than that suggested by the Park Service's 1964 report. Smith met with seven of the companies, some of which reportedly told him they would provide land along the Redwood Highway, acreage adjacent to the state parks, and the Tall Trees grove. Udall immediately wrote to Rockefeller denouncing the "Smith compromise" as an attempt to undermine presidential intentions. Rockefeller replied that he had not yet seen the maps outlining Smith's proposal but said he agreed with Smith's desire to avoid "bitter conflict." Smith himself told Udall that no "Smith compromise" existed, but he added that both his sponsor and the president preferred a good park "without bloodshed" to the prospect of fruitless turmoil. Not even the league endorsed Smith's plan, and his efforts proved inconclusive. But the episode indicates that the White House had begun undermining Udall's position right after the Park Service had released its first study. Despite Rockefeller's efforts, as late as June, 1965, he had maintained a noncommittal stance publicly and called himself "pretty much of a bystander" on the park issue.[42]

But in July that same summer—five months before Udall delivered his report recommending Mill Creek—Rockefeller recommended to President Johnson that the park be on Mill Creek.[43] Guided in significant part by this advice, Johnson had defied the direction of his own party in Congress, backed the northern site, and played probably the pivotal role in forcing Interior to abandon its earlier plans.

In their book *The Rockefellers*, Peter Collier and David Horowitz correctly maintained that Rockefeller "orchestrated the forces for the Mill Creek site within the Johnson Administration," but they added that in order "to forestall criticism that this juggernaut was anticonservationist and to offset the Sierra Club opposition, Laurance enlisted the prestigious Save-the-Redwoods League."[44] The implication that the league's position was secured by the philanthropist is misleading. The stance of Drury and his councilors in 1965 was consistent with both their long-range program and their statements on the proposed national park dated as early as 1960.[45] Rockefeller had followed the San Francisco group, not vice versa.

Fred Smith explained that it was entirely logical for the philanthropist to be guided by the league. As had his father, Rockefeller maintained contacts with key men whose word could be trusted.[46] Drury had been well known to the family since John D. Rockefeller, Jr., had contributed to Humboldt Redwoods State Park in 1931. Albright had been the latter's conservation advisor in the 1930s and had subsequently become a trustee of the Rockefellers' Jackson Hole Preservation Fund and guided Laurance's appointment to President Eisenhower's Outdoor Recreation Resource Review Commission in 1958. It was logical for Laurance to turn to Albright and Drury for advice, and both men favored Mill Creek. However, were this the sole explanation for Rockefeller's action, he no doubt would have consulted them sooner.

It was not until summer of 1965 that Rockefeller and Smith journeyed west to tour the redwoods under Drury's guidance. Smith later recalled that Drury had shown them that many trees on Redwood Creek were "scraggly" and dying from the top down. The contrasting views offered of Mill Creek convinced the easterners. According to Smith, they were also persuaded by the belief that "everyone who was anyone was in favor of Mill Creek."[47]

Following that trip, Rockefeller had explained to the president that since 1960 he had sought means for minimizing industrial opposition. He now assured the chief executive that this reasonable proposal would meet "with a minimum of opposition and perhaps even with considerable support." Neither the foresters' study nor Smith's attempted compromise had brought a solution. The philanthropist had concluded that the league's position was the only one that would both lessen opposition and offer a respectable park. Echoing his father's trusted advisors, Rockefeller argued that Mill Creek was vulnerable and of higher quality than the "not very healthy and not-very-old" trees of Redwood Creek.[48]

Collier and Horowitz maintained that Rockefeller had capitulated to the lumbermen who decided that because Mill Creek was smaller and already had two state parks, "putting the national park there . . . would stop the spread of park blight."[49] But not all of the industry favored the northern plan. The elderly president and primary owner of the Miller Redwood Company, Harold Miller, fought bitterly against the northern plan, which would have required federal acquisition of the bulk of his holdings.

Those who said Mill Creek was the most acceptable site to loggers actually meant it was acceptable to the nationally powerful firms with holdings on Redwood Creek—Georgia-Pacific Corporation, Simpson Timber Company, and Arcata Redwood Company. The first two were large corporations, and the third was affiliated with the Weyerhaeuser interests. The chairman of the Arcata board of directors was C. Davis Weyerhaeuser, son of Frederick E. Other board members included John J. Pascoe, who was married to George Weyerhaeuser's sister, and Albert J. Morman, attorney to many family members. It was the administration's understanding that the small Miller Redwood Company, headed by a known maverick in the industry, had far less influence than the combined might of the three giants.[50] Miller's allies were the residents of Del Norte County, the Sierra Club, and his Washington lobbyist William Ragan, whose letters filled the files of the White House and the Department of the Interior.[51] In contrast,

Georgia-Pacific, Simpson, and Arcata relied upon chains of personal influence.

Laurance Rockefeller and the league believed Mill Creek would make a good park. They were also responsive to the needs of the lumber industry and to the realities of financial power. The league had maintained its program through periods of weak liberalism in part because it cooperated with the timber interests. One's demands must, Drury observed, be feasible.

In telling Udall—just one day after Rockefeller recommended Mill Creek to Johnson in July—that he regarded Mill Creek as the lesser of two evils, Governor Brown also appears to have responded to opposition from the Humboldt County firms. Brown's position reflected more than political pressure from northern California. The residents of Del Norte County were far more hostile to a park than were those of Humboldt County, and with good reason. The Miller Redwood Company was the county's only large employer, and the administration's bill would put it out of business.[52] The club was correct in believing that the opposition of the powerful Humboldt County timber companies had strongly influenced President Johnson's park proposal. The league's concurrence and its respectability had legitimized the plan.

Some of the club's leaders held Udall responsible for the administration's supposed betrayal, their anger in proportion to the expectations raised by the secretary's own "inspirational leadership and grand visions." As a result primarily of the redwoods, Wayburn would call him "the bitterest disappointment of my conservation career."[53] In fairness, Udall had held out for Redwood Creek from mid-July into fall, 1965. His capitulation involved not only budgetary problems and industrial opposition but perhaps his own insecure tenure as a Kennedy appointee within the Johnson Administration. Moreover, Udall's influence with the president was clearly eclipsed by that of Rockefeller, a man of great stature within conservation circles since the 1950s. It is not surprising that Udall finally concluded, "Mill Creek is the art of the possible."[54]

Shortly after Johnson's position had been announced, the role of the executive's official liaison with Congress passed from Udall to a less adamant preservationist and more seasoned negotiator with the industry, Edward Crafts.[55] Thus a first phase in the park controversy had closed. The club had failed to stem the administration's drift away from a large Redwood Creek park.

In March, 1966, Republicans Senator Thomas Kuchel and Representative Don Clausen introduced bills incorporating the administration's proposal for a 39,264-acre national park. Johnson's selection of sponsors was astute and well tailored to a compromise bid. Kuchel was a ranking minority member in the Senate, California's senior senator, and a member of the Committee on Interior and Insular Affairs. Clausen was a former Crescent City businessman and Humboldt County's congressional representative. The proposed park was to encompass Jedediah Smith and Del Norte Coast redwoods state parks, the Mill Creek watershed, and a 1,600-acre Tall Trees Unit on Redwood Creek. The administration described the plan as a "middle ground between the position of the lumber industry on the one hand and the Sierra Club on the other"; it involved "minimum disruption of the lumber industry and of the local politico-economic situation, consistent with a significant park."[56]

On the same day Kuchel introduced the administration's bill, Democratic Senator Lee Metcalf from Montana and Democratic Representative Jeffrey Cohelan of California sponsored amendments substituting the club's plan for a 90,000-acre park on Redwood Creek. Fifty-three congressmen from the liberal and pro-labor wing of the Democratic Party, including Robert and Edward Kennedy, introduced companion bills. The press paraded the battle as another example of the tension between the Kennedys and Johnson. Actually the Kennedys' role was incidental; McCloskey together with Congressmen Metcalf and Cohelan had orchestrated the Democratic opposition.[57]

Even without opposition in his own party, Johnson's bill faced serious hurdles. Despite Udall's continued efforts to solicit his support with one million dollars from the Land and Water Conservation Fund for the Avenue of the Giants, Governor Brown failed to follow through on his seeming willingness to accept a Mill Creek park. With Brown's quiet approval, Conservation Associates, a small nonprofit San Francisco conservation organization, continued to press the Humboldt-King Range plan. Meanwhile California's state legislators questioned the constitutionality of transferring the state parks to the federal government.[58] The club's plan would present a respectable park without Prairie Creek Redwoods State Park, but the administration's proposal was inadequate without the state park lands. Moreover, at hearings on the Kuchel bill in Crescent City that June, the Senate Interior Committee was made acutely aware of the hostility of Del Norte County residents and the Miller Redwood Company. Such feelings were becoming so intense that shortly after introducing the administration's bill in the House, Clausen had renounced his support of the measure.[59]

In late summer, 1966, another telling blow befell the administration's proposal. Miller Redwood logged right up to Jedediah Smith State Park's eastern boundary, breaking the continuous line of forest between the park and the projected national park in the eastern sector of the watershed. Udall immediately asked Harold Miller to stop the cutting until Congress could act and offered to arrange funding from private foundations and tax deductions to offset the economic loss. Miller refused, claiming it "would force the company to close down."[60] Udall retorted that the operation could be shifted without any employees losing their jobs and charged Miller with "spite cutting."[61] The club circulated aerial photographs of the now sharply defined park boundary.[62]

Figure 17. Southern boundary of Jedediah Smith Redwoods State Park, August, 1966. Aerial view of logging done by the Miller Redwood Company along the southern boundary of Jedediah Smith Redwoods State Park, separating the park from the area Congress was then considering for acquisition as the Redwood National Park. Photo by Martin Litton.

For some time Brower and Litton had been pressing the club to sue Arcata and Georgia-Pacific under the California Forest Practices Act to stop logging on Redwood Creek, but the club directors had considered the suit unlikely to succeed.[63] Now they asked Senator Metcalf to sponsor legislation to halt the cutting in both Mill Creek and Redwood

Creek.[64] The White House and Udall made the same request of Senators Kuchel and Henry Jackson. In the end it was Kuchel who on September 1 introduced a Senate resolution to revoke for one year Miller's cutting rights in the area proposed for park acquisition.[65] The Sierra Club was pleased. The league wanted the operation stopped but doubted the morality of taking property without just compensation.[66]

The other three major redwood lumber companies—Simpson, Arcata, and Georgia-Pacific—were similarly convinced the legislation was unconstitutional, but they did not want more public attention focused on Miller's blatantly defiant clearcutting. Simpson contacted Senator Jackson offering to negotiate.[67] As a result of these negotiations, in early September the three Redwood Creek companies agreed to a voluntary, one-year moratorium on cutting in all the areas being seriously considered by Congress for park status. In response to efforts of the industry-sponsored National Forest Products Association, Miller agreed to stop logging near Jedediah Smith and move his operations into the drier foothills two months earlier than usual.[68] According to Interior's sources, he continued to cut within the proposed park area but ceased logging next to Jedediah Smith Park.[69]

If anything, Miller's opposition to the national park was growing. Moreover, he was increasingly willing to forsake the other companies in his lobbying. His Washington representative, William Ragan, continued to exploit the schism between the league and the club, sending congressmen lists of the conservation organizations "against a Mill Creek park" and copies of the club literature calling the area unfit for national park status.[70] Ragan met with Metcalf to discuss common strategy, "since our interests—*albeit* for different reasons—are in the same direction as yours. . . ." Wayburn and Miller's general manager were "on friendly terms" and on occasion discussed their common opposition to the Johnson Administration.[71] Ed Crafts reported that the Miller-Rellim Company, Miller's production subsidiary, was "pretty much alone as far as the timber industry is concerned and that the industry is annoyed and . . . resentful of Rellim's apparent effort to join the Sierra Club in recommending a park be in Humboldt County and Redwood Creek. Mrs. Wayburn," Crafts continued, "reportedly has been making examinations of the Rellim property with this in mind and with company assistance."[72]

Despite the industry's efforts to exploit their division, neither the league nor the club attempted at this point to reconcile their differences. Through the spring and summer of 1966, the league reiterated its support for Mill Creek and ignored Redwood Creek. It urged that "all other conservation organizations join it in presenting a united front."[73] In contrast to this low-keyed intransigency, the club loudly denounced any compromises.

The club's refusal to support the Johnson legislation stemmed in part from the conviction—bolstered by the Park Service's 1964 report—that Redwood Creek was a better site. Sanctioning concessions to the loggers was unthinkable.[74] Club leaders believed succinct, uncompromising defense of a large park containing the Tall Trees had public appeal. "Extremism" was justified because this was a case of the people versus private interests. The organization's publicity demanded Americans stand up for their rights and provided coupons to convey this democratic will to Congress. A rejection of Redwood Creek would place the interests of the "powerful and wealthy" above those of the people.[75]

This conviction that it voiced the public will sprang from the power the club was demonstrating almost simultaneously in several major national campaigns, including those in behalf of the Grand Canyon and the North Cascades. The group's growth rate leaped to almost 30 percent in 1966. In six years the club had doubled in size and now had eighteen chapters across the nation.[76] Executive Director Brower was feted on the May, 1966, cover of *Life* as "the country's No. 1 working conservationist. . . . Knight Errant to Nature's Rescue."

At public hearings on the redwoods, 94 percent of the pro-park testimony favored Redwood Creek. The Wilderness Society of Washington, D.C., advocated both plans, while the American Forestry Association stuck by its old ally, the Save-the-Redwoods League. The majority of the nation's conservation groups, however, supported the Sierra Club. Even the league's long-time donor the Garden Club of America turned a deaf ear to Drury.[77] In addition to congressional support from the pro-labor faction of the Democratic Party, Walter Reuther's United Auto Workers also backed the club's proposal.[78] California's metropolitan newspapers as well as such nationally influential papers as the *Washington Post*, the *Christian Science Monitor*, and the *Los Angeles Times* similarly endorsed a large Redwood Creek park. Echoing Brower's group, the *New York Times* denounced the administration's "self defeating efforts to appease the lumber companies."[79] President Wayburn added the club's opposition to the clamor against the administration's bill at the Senate Interior Committee's hearing in Crescent City that summer.[80]

It was, however, Colorado's Democratic congressman Wayne Aspinall who delivered the coup de grâce to the administration's efforts to get an early compromise. A self-proclaimed defender of resource users, he had announced on March 1 that his Committee on Interior and Insular Affairs would not take action on the park issue during that session. Representative B. F. Sisk of California simultaneously reported that he saw no chance for the House bill to reach his Rules Committee. Although Aspinall later indicated that his committee would be willing to consider the bill in 1967, he adamantly maintained his opposition to moving the legislation forward in the present Congress.[81] Both the Kuchel and the Metcalf measures died in committee.

As the Eighty-ninth Congress drew to a close without further action on the park, the administration saw the club as its major obstacle.[82] In mid-September Kuchel had written to San Francisco lawyer Richard Leonard, a director of both the league and the club, urging him to use his "best efforts to bring about agreement between the warring conservation factions. Everyone with whom I speak assures me," he told Leonard, "that the Sierra Club will remain implacable and watch the lumber companies chop down the last remaining privately owned redwoods before 'compromising its principles.'" Leonard arranged a two-hour meeting of club and league leaders at the Bay Area's elite Bohemian Club in late September. He argued that Brower and Wayburn should defer to Drury. But Wayburn had opposed Drury's moderation and his park philosophy since the late 1950s when the latter was chief of the California Division of Beaches and Parks, and he refused to concede now. The group could agree only to meet again when the new bills were introduced.[83]

In October Jerry Verkler, staff director for the Senate's Interior Committee, met with representatives of Interior's Office of the Secretary. Verkler explained that the "Committee would consider any reasonable proposal for a Park upon which there could be some substantial agreement." He hoped the "conservation interests" could agree on a proposal because he and the senators found "the continuing disagreement over Park proposals among the organized conservation groups a major handicap. . . ."[84] Still, the two citizen groups held to their positions through October and November.

Worried about the damage Miller's cutting had done, the league in November gained permission from the company to have Lawrence Merriam visit the property. The son of the league's early president, Merriam had recently retired from the Park Service and was now acting as the league's advisor. He traveled north with league consultant Walter Lowdermilk, a retired University of California specialist in erosion control who was to report on whether or not recent logging had subjected Mill Creek to the erosion that had maimed Bull Creek. Lowdermilk noted that both creeks flowed through deep, walled valleys. The amount of rain and the advanced stages of plant succession also made the watersheds alike, yet he found no evidence of recent erosion in the northern basin. Moreover, he judged Miller's logging practices to be somewhat better than average. Thus Lowdermilk's study proved inconclusive.[85]

Merriam's report was less reassuring. By the 1960s only one part of the lower Mill Creek drainage outside of Jedediah Smith Park still held old growth, and that lay east of the park. (The Hobbs-Wall Company had logged to the west in 1911, and Miller had cut the southern sector in the 1950s.) Consequently, Merriam focused his attention to the east. There he found that between his previous visit in July and the November logging moratorium, the timbermen had chopped a strip 500 feet wide along the park boundary. They had also cut a wide road strip encircling this "last block of the very finest Old Growth Redwood." They had then logged an area of about 800 acres out of the middle of the stand. Merriam concluded, "The opening-up of the road strips and the actual logging . . . have seriously eroded the values in what should be the finest park area in the upper Mill Creek." Miller was trying to cut as quickly as possible the only area in Mill Creek outside of Jedediah Smith worthy of national park status; furthermore, road construction indicated that he intended to resume the operation.[86]

On December 1 the league's officers gathered, including the long-time club leaders Richard Leonard and Francis Farquhar and the elderly progressives Robert Sproul and Drury. They issued a public statement: "Our dream has been to preserve . . . in its primeval state the Mill Creek watershed. We have waited too long. It is now too late. . . . More in sorrow than in anger (although that might be justified) we have to note that since the national park program on the Mill Creek watershed has crystallized, serious inroads have been made by logging. . . ." A month later they issued a press release stating that both Mill Creek and Redwood Creek would make adequate national park sites. The league had compromised but not surrendered. The damage to Mill Creek was termed "deplorable" but not "fatal"; the area was still worthy of a national park.[87] The league refused to abandon Mill Creek to side with the club.

The club was even less accommodating. In December Ed Crafts and George Hartzog met with Wayburn and attempted to intimidate him into supporting the administration's bill. They failed. Wayburn accused Crafts of using the redwoods as a "political football" and told him, "I hope sincerely, Ed, that you will decide in favor of the American people."[88] However, on January 4, three days after the league's press release, the club's board of directors met. Leonard moved the club support a national park of maximum size with acquisitions of the last best virgin forests in both Redwood Creek and Mill Creek, with provisions for private funding to add those areas the federal government could not afford to purchase. The motion was passed.[89] Neither the club nor the league had given in, but they had lessened their mutual hostility.

In December Crafts had approached the Bureau of the Budget with a proposal he and the Park Service had devised for a two-unit park. He reported that the bureau seemed willing to accept a two-unit park in principle but not the need for additional funding, fearing such would harm other park projects.[90] Late in January Interior submitted to the White House draft legislation recommending a two-unit park, with a Redwood Creek unit of 36,800 acres to be acquired in part with private money.[91] A week later the club's ally Representative Cohelan called the league to ask if it would support a two-unit compromise. President Ralph Chaney said he thought two units infeasible but said the league would, as always, abide by whatever proposal the administration advanced.[92]

President Johnson now had three options. He could advance a two-unit proposal, presumably with the support of both the league and the club.[93] Secondly, he could propose a Redwood Creek plan, which the club would endorse and the league would not oppose. Thirdly, he could again opt for Mill Creek and club opposition. The two-unit park offered the best solution in terms of the citizen activists, but it would be expensive. The Bureau of the Budget was receptive to installment buying and private funding, but President Johnson was less enthusiastic; the lumber companies opposed the inconvenience of prolonged acquisition.[94]

To add to the dilemma, Johnson's plan now also faced the hurdle of California's recently elected Governor Ronald Reagan, representing the new conservatism sweeping the Republican Party. Upon assuming office in January, 1967, Reagan said he feared the park would adversely affect the industry and northern California's economy and questioned the transfer of state parks to the federal government. He announced his own Redwood Parkway and Recreation Plan, to consist of the state parks plus the opening of 35,000 acres of private forest lands for recreation. The plan necessitated no public acquisition of private land.[95] Reagan had previously assured the Johnson Administration the rumor that he had said "if you have seen one redwood, you have seen them all" was false.[96] Nonetheless, Udall and the White House felt keenly the potential for opposition from the governor.[97]

Despite the odds against success, Johnson was determined to advance the park. On March 11 Udall transmitted to the Ninetieth Congress the administration's proposal. Kuchel again sponsored it in the Senate, and Wayne Aspinall subsequently introduced it in the House. The plan demonstrated Johnson's tough pragmatism. Still cognizant of the opposition and influence of Georgia-Pacific and Arcata, Johnson once more proposed that the park be located on Mill Creek, owned by the seemingly less formidable foe, Miller.[98] Aspinall's support appeared to indicate that Johnson's attempt to maneuver through rather than face down the industry had a chance of success.

To placate the club, Johnson's new proposal called for a 17,000-acre unit on Redwood Creek—a reduction from Interior's draft bill. In deference to the Bureau of the Budget, this unit was to be acquired entirely through philanthropy. To appease Governor Reagan, the legislation also proposed to transfer to California—in exchange for the state parks—31,000 acres of federal land in the King Range of Humboldt County and Muir Woods National Monument.

Eager to follow through on his bid for support, Johnson asked Rockefeller to go to California and discuss Mill Creek "personally with Governor Reagan in an effort to persuade him to go along with this very urgent and meritorious proposal."[99] The eastern philanthropist plunged into broker politics. He arranged to buy endorsement for the administration's bill from Reagan and the lumber industry with a series of concessions from various federal agencies. Miller Redwood was to receive Department of the Interior lands in Oregon and the Forest Service's Northern Redwood Purchase Unit, an idea advanced by Udall as early as 1964 as a means of defraying the cost of the park.[100] Acquired by the service in the 1930s and 1940s, the Purchase Unit was located on the lower Klamath River and held 14,500 acres. Of this, approximately 8,000 acres were virgin; the rest had been selectively logged but held a lot of residual old growth, which Simpson and several small mills were harvesting. In return for the redwoods state parks, California was to receive several of the Department of Defense's marine beaches on the Pacific, including Camp Pendleton and Fort Ord. Interior was to reduce the projected boundaries of the Point Reyes National Seashore and renounce opposition to the road through Sequoia National Park, a concession vital to Walt Disney's proposed ski development in Mineral King —a project Reagan supported. Udall's department was also to forswear any intention of adding park units on Redwood Creek. The U.S. Bureau of the Public Roads was to accelerate freeway construction through the redwoods.[101]

In June the Bureau of the Budget forwarded its approval of the Rockefeller-Reagan package to Jackson and Aspinall, chairmen of the Senate and House Interior committees.[102] On October 12, 1967, Kuchel introduced a bill embodying the bargain.[103] The package had as many enemies as it had clauses. Only Udall acquiesced, conceding the Sequoia road; the Department of Agriculture opposed the transfer of its territory, and supporters of Point Reyes National Seashore sponsored a counter measure calling for additions to their reserve together with a small redwood national park. Most important, the Department of Defense adamantly refused to give up its beaches, arguing the Vietnam War necessitated practice areas for amphibious assaults. Even Reagan failed to find the bargain entirely satisfactory, waffling on what Interior had interpreted as his agreement to the transfer of Jedediah Smith and

Del Norte Coast state parks. The bill received little legislative attention.[104]

A meeting of the director of the Bureau of the Budget, the chief of the Forest Service, and Ed Crafts concluded that only one provision in Rockefeller's deal might prove useful. The Forest Service refused to consider the transfer of its Purchase Unit but might give Miller preferential treatment in the letting of timber contracts. Crafts determined to find out if Miller would accept such an arrangement. The answer was no, but outright transfer did interest him.[105]

Meanwhile Kuchel's Mill Creek bill was not faring well either. Despite Rockefeller's negotiations, Reagan's support was not forthcoming. The April, 1967, hearings of the Senate Committee on Interior and Insular Affairs showed that the New Yorker's efforts had not lessened local and industrial hostility. Moreover, Miller continued to exploit the club's hostility to a Mill Creek park.[106]

The club redoubled its opposition. Early in the Ninetieth Congress, Senator Metcalf had reintroduced his 90,000-acre proposal. Fifty-eight congressmen—all of the liberal and pro-labor faction of the Democratic Party—again sponsored similar bills. Club advertisements in six major newspapers pointed an accusing finger at the administration: "Mr. President: There is one great forest of redwoods left on Earth; but the one you are Trying to Save Isn't It. . . . Meanwhile they are cutting down both of them."[107]

In March, 1967, a private firm of consulting foresters reported that Redwood Creek had more virgin redwoods of superior size than did Mill Creek. (Mill Creek held compact groves of large old trees, but the far larger Redwood Creek basin actually had more of them.) In testimony before Congress Wayburn cited the study and demanded that the Department of the Interior "admit its mistake, and return to the proposal the professional planners in the Park Service originally gave them."[108] By fall of 1967 it was obvious that the club's opposition and the administration's inability to marshal support in California were dooming the Kuchel bill. Metcalf's bill was faring little better, faced as it was with the hostility of the large logging firms, budget-minded congressmen, and the administration. Under pressure from the White House, Udall and Hartzog had continued to defend publicly the Mill Creek proposal as "the most realistic approach to the major questions of suitability, feasibility, and economic impact."[109] Neither Kuchel's nor Metcalf's measures could be brought to a vote. The situation had reached an impasse.

Hoping to break the deadlock before Congress adjourned, in October and November, 1967, senators Jackson, Kuchel, and Alan Bible—a

Democrat from Nevada—offered a substitute for the administration's bill. They advanced a bipartisan, legislative compromise—a two-unit park.

The Senate's Committee on Interior and Insular Affairs, comprised of Kuchel, Jackson, and Bible, approved the measure that same month. In doing so, the committee commented that "public enthusiasm for creation of a redwood national park had been marred by a regrettable rift between conservation-minded citizens. . . ."[110] In an effort to appeal to a broad range of conservationists, the committee proposed a 61,654-acre park of the best stands on Redwood Creek and Mill Creek, with an emphasis upon the southern unit. In the Redwood Creek watershed, the federal government was to acquire 35,684 acres, consisting of Prairie Creek Redwoods State Park and 20,000 acres of privately owned lands. The remaining 25,970 acres were to be in Mill Creek, with only about 10,000 acres of private lands to be acquired in addition to the approximately 15,000 acres of Jedediah Smith and Del Norte Coast redwoods state parks. The bill also provided for the addition of lands through private funding.

The senators noted that the plan was devised to appease the club and to distribute the economic burden of the park over four companies and two counties. The committee emphasized that 70 percent of Del Norte County was already publicly owned, compared to only 21 percent of Humboldt County. The more southerly county could therefore better withstand any initial loss of taxes and employment that the park would bring. They did not recommend in-lieu taxes, believing the park would eventually bring economic compensations. Some congressmen were also afraid that tax remittance would establish a precedent and encourage other counties with national parks to demand equal treatment.[111]

The biggest bidding card in Kuchel and Jackson's hand was a provision to transfer the Forest Service's Purchase Unit to the Miller Redwood Company as compensation for the loss of Mill Creek. The measure would save the government some $40 million on the price of the park. More important, Kuchel knew Governor Reagan considered the exchange crucial to state support. Despite his early pronouncements against the park, Reagan had not become a hard-line opponent; his flexibility allowed Kuchel and Jackson to move their bill forward.[112]

Harold Miller immediately wrote to President Johnson explaining that transfer of the Purchase Unit would "make it possible for us . . . to continue our $30 million privately financed forest complex in Del Norte County." "I can assure you," Miller added, "without an exchange, our program must come to a prompt halt."[113] The North Coast Timber Association publicly endorsed the trade. The Kuchel-Jackson compromise was well engineered. It proposed to reduce the cost of the park with the Purchase Unit and with philanthropy. It received the support of both the club and the league. The proposal was well received by the press and had lessened Miller's opposition.[114]

But the Forest Service "vigorously and strongly objected" to its land being given to the industry so that the Park Service could increase its holdings. The move would, said Secretary of Agriculture Orville Freeman, "open the floodgate" to a new type of invasion of the national forests.[115] Both the club and Rockefeller urged Johnson to support the proposal. Kuchel and Jackson told Udall that deletion of the provision would "scuttle the Redwood National Park legislation."[116] Despite his years of work to ease the traditional friction between the departments of Agriculture and Interior, Udall agreed that the exchange was necessary.[117] But when he publicly expressed praise for Kuchel and Jackson's "adroit effort" at compromise, Johnson forced him to retract this seeming support for the legislation.[118] The president said he would not agree to the use of the national forests as "trading stock."[119]

Even without Johnson's endorsement, in November, 1967, the Senate passed the committee's bill for a two-unit park of 61,654 acres; the bill specified that the park was not to exceed 64,000 acres. The vote of 77 to 6 testified to Kuchel and Jackson's skill. Despite the president's position, the Senate defeated an amendment to disallow the trade of the Purchase Unit. As Senator Birch Bayh explained to Wayburn, the Senate believed the exchange was fair to the companies, reduced the cost, and did not set a precedent.[120]

The club was pleased with the Senate bill; however—as its critics would claim was inevitable—it was not satisfied.[121] Wayburn, Brower, and McCloskey still hoped that several areas might be added to the Redwood Creek unit through amendment in the House. The previous October Senator Jackson had negotiated with the timber companies to have the logging moratorium extended to the end of that session of Congress.[122] But the moratorium covered only those areas under serious legislative attention. The Georgia-Pacific Corporation now interpreted that to mean the Kuchel-Jackson bill. In late November the company declined the request by Cohelan and thirty-four other congressmen who had sponsored the club's proposal to stay out of areas immediately adjacent to the boundaries in the Senate bill. As the loggers moved close to the proposed park, the club's press releases announced, "Georgia-Pacific Invades the Emerald Mile," describing the area as a "magnificent 300 feet wall of virgin redwoods" that ran along Redwood Creek for two miles upstream from the Tall Trees. The club charged Georgia-Pacific with an "arrogant and defiant" attempt to define the final park boundaries "with its chainsaws."[123]

The company replied with a full-page advertisement in the *Wall Street Journal* and the *New York Times* saying, "Yes America's Majestic Redwoods Have Been Saved"—in California's state parks. Georgia-Pacific argued that "all the cathedral-like groves had been saved" and quoted Drury. The club riposted with its own full-page newspaper advertisement accusing Georgia-Pacific of "Legislation by Chainsaw," the headline underscoring a photograph of a clearcut.[124]

On January 22 the company wrote to Wayburn denouncing the charge as "inflammatory . . . hysterical and irresponsible" and threatening to sue.[125] Two days later Georgia-Pacific ran an advertisement to that effect in the *Wall Street Journal*. The Sierra Club demanded a public apology.[126] Wayburn said the club's lawyers were of the opinion that accusing it of "vendetta tactics" and the use of an "outright lie of defamatory nature and malicious distortion" was "libelous *per se*."[127] One club director asked the Internal Revenue Service to audit the corporation's lobbying expenditures.[128] For a short time the verbal warfare died down, only to erupt again in a March televised confrontation between a Georgia-Pacific official and Wayburn staged by San Francisco's Channel 2. The official again claimed the redwoods had been saved and cited league literature. Wayburn called this "a massive smokescreen . . . raised by the sawdust burners of the Georgia-Pacific Corporation to try to lull the American people. . . ."[129] Georgia-Pacific doggedly refused to extend the moratorium on logging beyond the boundaries in the Kuchel-Jackson bill, but shortly after this confrontation with the club, the corporation stopped cutting in the Emerald Mile.

Throughout this controversy the White House had allowed Udall to express no more than a private "pious hope" that Georgia-Pacific spare the area.[130] But Johnson had not abandoned the park. As the club and Georgia-Pacific battled, Johnson delivered his State of the Union Address to Congress. In it he reiterated the theme behind the Great Society: "If ever there were a people who sought more than mere abundance, it is our people." However, his attempt at optimism could not hide the pall that continuing war in Vietnam, the tightening budget, rising crime, and repeated urban disorders had cast over his term in office. One of the few passages in his speech that drew applause from Congress was his plea "to save the redwoods." No doubt he welcomed such an affirmation, however partial, of his administration.[131]

As the second session of the Ninetieth Congress opened, club attention focused on Aspinall's Committee on Interior and Insular Affairs. On April 17 and 18, the committee held field hearings in Eureka, California.[132] Club representatives pleaded for a park. Residents displayed bumper stickers reading, "Don't Park Our Jobs." The congressmen were feted by the Humboldt Chamber of Commerce in the Ingomar

Club's Carson House, the luxuriant woods of which testified to the success of the logging baron who built it. The committee had no money to take its members into the redwoods, so the companies took them up Redwood Creek and its tributaries on trips Martin Litton claimed were "rigged" to show only the logged areas.[133]

Wayburn and Litton hurriedly rented a small helicopter and airlifted five representatives into the Emerald Mile. The Democratic Irishman from New York City William Ryan walked out of Redwood Creek calling Georgia-Pacific's logging a "desecration." Democrats John Tunney, Thomas Foley, and Morris Udall had similar reactions. At the committee's hearings in Washington that May, the club again pleaded for the Emerald Mile. Wayburn hoped the House would produce a bill even larger than that of the Senate.[134]

Events in April and May seemed to indicate such optimism was warranted. Surprisingly, Reagan announced publicly that his administration would back a two-unit, 57,000-acre park—somewhat smaller but otherwise similar to the Senate's bill. He said he was now willing to permit transfer of the state parks to the federal government.[135]

Shortly thereafter President Johnson also did an about-face. As late as April he had persisted in defending Mill Creek and refusing to sanction what Kuchel called the single most essential provision in the compromise bill—the transfer of the Forest Service's Purchase Unit to Miller Redwood. But in May Udall announced to the House Interior Committee that the administration had abandoned Mill Creek and would support the transfer.[136] Johnson's move was pragmatic. Having recently announced that he would not run again for president, he was doubtless even less interested than he had been earlier in the actual character of the park and increasingly anxious for successes in his domestic program. Udall explained to Aspinall why the administration was now willing to endorse a proposal that placed the major portion of the park in Redwood Creek:

The indication in recent weeks is that each of the four major redwood timber operating companies in the area included in Senate-passed S. 2515 is more willing than heretofore to negotiate with the government and to make available a portion of its holdings for inclusion in a Redwood National Park.[137]

The timber companies had, after all, indicated a willingness to sell.

Miller had of course said as much the previous October, and Governor Reagan had been lobbying ever since for the transfer of the Purchase Unit. Miller had testified before the House Committee in April that he would be willing to negotiate the trade of some of his lands, although not as much as the original administration bill would have required.[138] The Forest Service had failed to convince Congress that its logging practices were sufficiently better than those of Miller to warrant congressional opposition to the transfer. There was the matter of the small mills dependent upon lumber from the unit, and Simpson Timber also drew heavily upon this source. But the voices of the small companies were easily dismissed in national calculations, and by the spring of 1968 Simpson was coming to see the transfer as a necessary evil.[139]

In fact, it was apparent in April and May that all of the major companies involved were now prepared in various degrees to negotiate. Both Simpson and Georgia-Pacific were willing to negotiate on some lands along Redwood Creek. More important, Arcata had indicated that it was prepared to sell a substantial portion of its holdings on Skunk Cabbage Creek and a strip along Redwood Creek.[140] The timbermen's decision had dictated the change in the position of both the Johnson and the Reagan administrations.

It is probable that the corporations had decided to negotiate as early as the previous fall when Kuchel and Jackson introduced their legislative compromise. Kuchel faced a primary race in June, 1968, and was sensitive to public support for the park in California. As a moderate Republican, however, he presumably did not wish to offend either the state's timbermen or the new Reagan Administration. Thus Kuchel's stewardship of the park bill may have been premised in part on the receptivity of Reagan and the timber companies.[141] Senator Jackson's role in the compromise was larger than that of Kuchel, and Jackson's constituency was dominated by the lumber industry. An aide to Kuchel at the time has since confirmed the bargaining role the timbermen played in the Senate Interior Committee's negotiations.[142]

Why did the lumbermen have this change of heart? Certainly the persistence of the Johnson Administration and the Sierra Club had played a role. The decision may also have been in part the result of the fact that the Federal Trade Commission had ordered the Simpson Timber Company to divest itself of 500 million board feet of redwood. This timber could be sold to Georgia-Pacific or Arcata, cushioning the impact of timber lost to the park.

However, the receptivity of Arcata was largely a product of the company's own history and program. In 1905 the Weyerhaeusers' Hill-Davis Company had acquired property on the east side of Redwood Creek. In 1945 Hill-Davis bought Arcata, and in 1958 all of the assets of the former became the property of Arcata. In the mid-1950s the company began serious logging and paid its first dividends. Its holdings on Redwood Creek, however, were small. In the words of the chairman of both the Hill-Davis and Arcata boards of directors, C. Davis Weyerhaeuser,

"With only 22,000 acres of land it was obvious from the start that a truly sustained yield operation which projected beyond the first cutting cycle was impracticable. The mill was, therefore, designed," he said, "to insure our employees and the local community a 30 to 50 year life on the existing lumber economy. . . ." After that the lands, "reforested with thrifty second growth, would be integrated into a pulp wood operation."[143] This was a familiar pattern in the redwoods except for two factors. First, the other major companies in Humboldt and Del Norte counties, including Simpson, Georgia-Pacific, Pacific Lumber Company, and Miller, had significantly larger redwood holdings. Second, unlike Arcata, Miller and Pacific Lumber were constructing their own pulp and hardwood mills with which to continue operations after liquidating their virgin stock. Simpson and Georgia-Pacific had local pulp and paper subsidiaries. At the rate Arcata was logging, the company would probably have liquidated its standing timber before the thirty years Weyerhaeuser had projected.[144] It is likely that Arcata would then have sold its cutover lands to one of the companies intending to stay. A cash return from the sale of virgin timber equal to the expected profits would simply speed liquidation. This contrasted with Miller, who insisted on a timber rather than a cash payment in order to maintain a sustained-yield operation.

In 1967 Arcata Redwood reincorporated as the Arcata National Corporation. Prior to 1967 Howard Libbey had been Arcata's president. A career lumberman raised in California's North Coast, he had been a staunch park opponent. In 1960 he had clearcut down to the Redwood Highway, a move that both timbermen and preservationists have said sparked the redwood national park battle. In 1967 Libbey retired, perhaps somewhat early, and was replaced as president by an eastern financier, R. O. Dehlendorf, who would guide the company through the financial complexities of the next years.[145] As Arcata National, the corporation was in a position, should the government take its old growth, to diversify with the cash payments. The move, coming as it did just before the introduction of the Kuchel-Jackson bill, signalled a possible lessening of Arcata's opposition to the loss of property.

Clearly the club's leaders had reason in May, 1968, to be optimistic, even though Aspinall was chairman and Clausen a member of the House Interior Committee. Thus the club was not prepared for the blow that followed. If Wayburn was correct in repeated assertions that a large park represented the popular will, the House betrayed that will.

In June it became known that Aspinall's House Interior Committee was considering a park of only 25,000 acres, to consist of Prairie Creek and Del Norte Coast state parks, and a nine-mile-wide strip up Redwood Creek. Shaken by this, McCloskey set out to have the bill amended in committee. By the time the full committee met on June 28, he believed he had sufficient votes and proxies pledged to have the Skunk Cabbage, Lost Man, and Little Lost Man creek areas added to the bill. By a vote of ten to seven, however, the committee defeated a motion by William Ryan to save these areas. According to McCloskey, Congressman John Saylor did not vote some of his proxies, and Morris Udall voted some the other way because, although "ostensibly friendly to the park," these two congressmen "dared not override the chairman." But the chairman, McCloskey continued, "sensed the precariousness of his control." When Ryan moved to add the Emerald Mile and its slopes, "Aspinall indicated he would not object and the motion carried on a voice vote." Aspinall did not allow any more amendments. McCloskey claimed a "small moral victory" but conceded "the overall plan was horrendous."[146] The House Committee reported onto the floor a bill to establish a strangely shaped park of only 28,500 acres, consisting almost entirely of state parks. The cost was to be $56,750,000 instead of the Senate's proposed $100 million.[147]

Preservationists were stunned. Metropolitan newspapers on the eastern and western coasts echoed their outrage. The fact that most of the old growth was to be on Redwood Creek did not console the club. The park would be a "fiasco." Club press releases denounced Aspinall's action as "a usurpation of Congress's right to create the decent park the American people want."[148]

Wayburn asked how the House, "where one-man-one-vote representation must surely respect the will of the people," could commit such a betrayal. He answered himself as follows: "In our democratic system of government, parks like pork barrels, are used for bargaining. They are used for power plays. In our system a single man on a single committee may have enough power to single-handedly call the shots."[149]

At the prompting of Wayburn, Brower, and McCloskey, seventy-three congressmen who had originally supported the club's proposal now signed a petition denouncing the chairman's move.[150] Aspinall, however, had brought the bill up under a suspension of the rules, a procedure that prevents amendment from the floor and is generally reserved for uncontroversial bills. Because of this and since adjournment was imminent, the club advised its legislative supporters to vote for the bill; the next Congress might bring even less success. The outgoing President Johnson wanted a park, and there was no assurance that the next president would sign a park bill. The moratorium on logging in the proposed park areas was due to expire with adjournment. The House-amended bill of 28,500 acres passed 389 to 15, with Aspinall's assurance that the final boundaries would be increased in conference.[151]

If Arcata and Miller had lessened their opposition to the park, why did Aspinall deliver what the club called an "emasculated bill"? McCloskey felt Aspinall "prided himself on never losing a bill on the floor" and thought the smallest park represented the smallest risk. If he had no love for the park, at least Aspinall realized public pressure necessitated action and wished neither to be responsible for defeat of the park nor to have the issue return to haunt him in the next Congress.[152] His actions probably had another rationale as well. The fact is the timber companies were willing to part with some of their land under certain circumstances. But neither the industry nor Aspinall wanted to risk the expansion of the park either in House committee or on the floor of the House, where the club had strong supporters. It would prove easier for the industry to control the boundaries and terms in Aspinall's conference committee than it would have earlier in the legislative process.

Park advocates had little choice but to turn their attention to the appointment of proper conferees. They met with limited success. The conference managers from the House were Aspinall, Roy Taylor, Harold Johnson, Theodore Kupperman, and John Saylor. Of these Aspinall and Saylor alone had been active in the redwood issue, and only Saylor's bill had met with club approval. The Senate conferees were more promising. They included Jackson, Kuchel, Bible, Clinton Anderson, and Clifford Hansen. All but Hansen had sponsored the Kuchel-Jackson compromise, and even Hansen had voted for it. Due no doubt in large part to the influence of the senators, the conference committee recommended—and Congress passed—a park of 58,000 acres.

The conferees did not explain the rationale behind their two-unit park. However, the roles of Kuchel, Bible, and especially Jackson were central in framing both the Senate and the conference bills.[153] The final measure was sufficiently similar to the Kuchel-Jackson bill that one can assume the conferees sought, as the Senate Interior Committee had, to divide the impact between the various companies and the two counties as well as to appeal to both the league and the club.

Of the 58,000 acres, 27,468 represented Prairie Creek, Jedediah Smith, and Del Norte state parks. Of the 28,101 acres of private lands acquired, only 5,625 were in the northern unit. They included a section of the Mill Creek watershed immediately south of Jedediah Smith and three coastal strips, generally one-quarter mile wide, between Del Norte Coast and Prairie Creek parks and southward. The southern

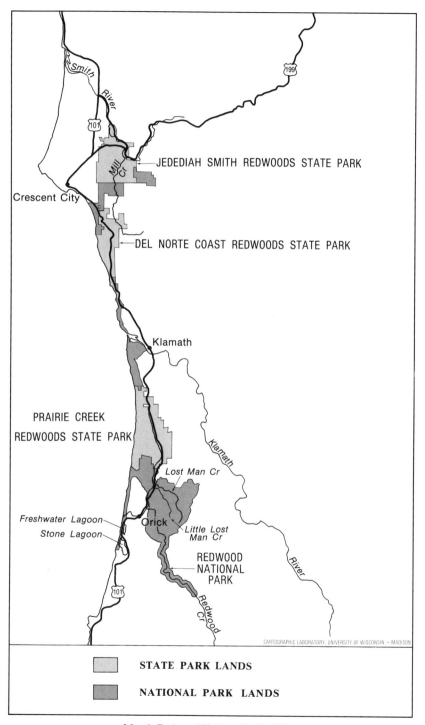

Map 6. Redwood National Park, 1968.

unit of the park included 22,476 acres of newly purchased private lands, of which 4,125 acres were located to the north, east, and west of lower Redwood Creek. A 4,200-acre park corridor one-half mile wide ran up Redwood Creek to the Tall Trees. Most of the additional 14,151 acres in the southern unit were on the Redwood Creek tributaries of Lost Man and Little Lost Man creeks, with some land south of Prairie Creek park and several coastal strips. (The location of 2,431 acres was not specified in the bill.)[154] Thus most of the private lands and almost all of the virgin timber purchased for the national park were in the Redwood Creek watershed. The new lands in the northern unit were essentially additions to link the state parks.

The park was to cost $92 million, about $40 million of which was to be paid for with the Purchase Unit. The park eventually cost about $198 million. As the single most expensive park purchase ever made by the United States government, the 1968 act was a triumph for the preservationists. But it saved only 10,876 acres of old-growth redwoods; the rest of the land had been logged. Moreover, the boundaries defied the contours of the land, passing at one point through the center of a lagoon. It was obvious almost immediately that erosion caused in part by logging above the Redwood Creek corridor—or what became known as "the worm"—would threaten the Tall Trees, located precariously on a horseshoe bend in the river. In both Redwood Creek and Mill Creek, the legislators had ignored the league's warning regarding the necessity for complete watersheds and the club's demands for park units of substantial size. Oblivious to mountain ridges and rivers, the park resembled the results of a taffy pull stretched the length of two counties. The illogical contours show that the conflict between the club and the league had taken a toll.

The influence of the timber companies was also evident in the park's boundaries. The final bill was considerably closer to the Senate version then to the House Interior Committee's bill, but it eliminated several thousand acres of private land and old growth included in the Kuchel-Jackson measure. In the end the companies had lost only 10,876 acres of virgin timber and received in exchange 14,500 acres, 8,000 acres of which was still uncut. The timber-rich Emerald Mile had been excluded from the act. Miller and Arcata had lost a much larger percentage of their lands than had the other companies. Miller was compensated with the Purchase Unit. Arcata lost 60 percent of its holdings, and as Arcata National, immediately began to diversify, using in part money from the sale of its land. Under its new president Arcata bought up printing companies across the nation to become one of the giants in the publishing business. Profits from logging were high, and the following year Arcata also bought the mills and largely Douglas-fir standing timber of the Simonson Lumber Company in Del Norte County.[155] That the conference committee considered the industry's priorities is evident in the park's size and shape. It is probably no coincidence that the final settlement contained the same acreage as the proposal Governor Reagan had said he would support that spring.

The terms of the act were generally if not entirely to the industry's liking. Thinking an eastern judge would be less sympathetic to the timbermen than would a western jury, the administration and the club had successfully argued for adjudication of the price in the United States Court of Claims in Washington, D.C. But under the act the government was precluded from initiating suit to precipitate a settlement; that right was reserved to the companies. Moreover, the bill contained an unprecedented declaration of legislative taking: upon its enactment, the lands became federal property. Although the club had welcomed the provision as a means of preventing escalation of the price and of protecting the land, it was Aspinall who championed it, claiming that the companies preferred to "know immediately and as precisely as possible where they stand."[156] For this same reason the timbermen had fought proposals for gradual acquisition and private funding. The lands became government property immediately, there was no provision for additions to the park, and it was up to the companies to decide when adjudication was warranted. In the meantime they received 6 percent interest—or $15,000 per day—on the unpaid balance.[157]

President Johnson signed the bill on October 2, 1968. McCloskey proclaimed that despite the park's obvious weaknesses, its establishment was "a great victory" over "the monumental opposition of the most powerful combine of financial interests that ever stood against a park." The league was circumspect; it had yet to save Mill Creek.[158] The final boundaries had not of course been a simple reflection of the respective powers of the two groups; the role of the timber companies clouded the story. Nevertheless, the battle showed something of the respective strength of each organization. A recent study of American philanthropy concluded that during the 1960s, nonprofit, charitable institutions dependent upon substantial donations had been eclipsed by organizations that subsist, as the club has, on small donations and strong membership involvement.[159] Yet as a traditional, paternalistic philanthropy, the league still exercised considerable political power. The personal influence of its donors and officers and their emphasis upon diplomacy and feasibility had swayed the bureaucracy. For a time the administration in turn had checked the club's legislative weight. The opponents were well matched, each with its own persuasive forum.

In the final legislative arena, however, the club demonstrated a superior might. The league's skills in fund raising and in seeking industrial cooperation were undercut by club publicity, as were Udall's efforts to coordinated federal funding and philanthropy. Moreover, the league understandably decided it could not afford to lobby for fear of losing its nonprofit tax-deductible status.[160] In contrast, Brower risked the club's tax-deductible status in defending the redwoods. The club's superior might was due to Brower's confrontation politics, Wayburn's persistence, and McCloskey's astute lobbying. McCloskey and Wayburn had a significant voice in both the final Senate bill and the conference bill. Neither Drury nor any of the league's allies had an input into this legislation.[161] Indeed, the national influence of such older conservationists as Drury, Albright, and Rockefeller was clearly ebbing in the 1960s.

Rockefeller's attempt to win Governor Reagan's support for a Mill Creek park represented nearly the last of his involvement with the redwoods. As McCloskey later observed, "there was a great mythology attached to Laurance Rockefeller's invincibility" in the 1950s and 1960s. "With his membership on major commissions and investing money in projects, he made himself indispensable to LBJ. But this power was waning. In the final stages of the Redwood National Park battle, Rockefeller had little influence." Symbolic of the relative shift in power, McCloskey recalled seeing Rockefeller waiting in 1968 for an appointment with Senator Jackson while McCloskey himself walked right into the office, having been given a desk there by the senator.[162]

Establishment of the Redwood National Park marked the club's emergence as a nationally influential lobby. The battle was a landmark in aggressive legislative advocacy; it was the club's most important introduction in the postwar period to the full legislative process of moving a bill along affirmatively—requiring success in each stage— in contrast to the easier defensive posture of most of the organization's early campaigns.[163] As McCloskey prophesied in 1968, the redwoods were "a harbinger of more sophisticated campaigns ahead."[164]

On August 27, 1969, Lady Bird Johnson dedicated the Redwood National Park. The ceremony was held in one of the few large groves of old growth actually saved by the park. Lady Bird played little role in the establishment of the park, but its formation was a credit to her husband's administration. From 1964 to 1968 Johnson personally made each decision regarding the administration's redwood policy, showing a surprising attention to detail and upon occasion undermining his secretary of the Interior. Although Johnson publicly committed himself to saving the redwoods in the first flush of the Great Society years, by

Figure 18. Lady Bird Johnson Grove dedication, August 27, 1969. Left to right: the Reverend Billy Graham, Governor Ronald Reagan, Congressman Don Clausen, Lady Bird Johnson, Secretary of the Interior Walter J. Hickel, President Richard M. Nixon, Pat Nixon, Former President Lyndon B. Johnson, Julie Eisenhower, David Eisenhower, Luci Nugent, Patrick Nugent, Lynda Robb, Charles Robb, Senator George Murphy. Courtesy of the Save-the-Redwoods League.

the time the park became a serious legislative issue in 1966, the war in Southeast Asia was threatening his domestic program. Yet neither Vietnam nor the urban crisis obliterated his attention to the park. They may even have increased his interest in conservation. In addition to whatever love for the land had motivated him to build upon Kennedy's interest in conservation, by 1968 Johnson may have seen the Redwood National Park as a tangible victory in the face of sinking public opinion polls—a monument to posterity.

Johnson's efforts to get park legislation through Congress were highly pragmatic. He was far less interested in the character of the park than in the fact of getting it established. Rather than ally himself with club-supporters in his own party and attempt to ram a bill through, perhaps consuming political currency he preferred to use elsewhere, he sought consensus. He would probably have succeeded in getting enacted fairly early a reasonable park, if not the best possible one, had the club and Harold Miller not intervened. In the end these two opponents foiled Johnson's strategy, and it was Kuchel and Jackson who ultimately devised a successful compromise to which the president wisely acceded.

Johnson's initial appraisal of the power of the timbermen had not been ill founded. The resolution of the park issue itself attests to the efficacy of compromise. Kuchel and Jackson designated a two-unit park proposal reasonably acceptable to both the companies and the preservationists. But even this solution did not escape Aspinall's hand. The tremendous public pressure the club had generated made it almost impossible for Congress not to pass a park bill, but the political power of Aspinall and the industry checked this ground swell. Had Miller and Arcata not lessened their opposition, there might have been no park because it had become politically difficult for Congress to select a site.

The environmentalists had forced a settlement, but the industry had done much to control the terms.

9
David Brower
and the Sierra Club:
1964–1970

IN 1968 the Sierra Club was at a height in its militancy, growth, and influence. At its urging, the second session of the Eighty-ninth Congress established the Redwood and Cascades national parks, expanded four wilderness areas, defeated three dams, and founded the scenic rivers, estuaries, and national trails systems. This power owed much to decades of accumulated support, political expertise, and anger. Club leaders from Brower and Wayburn to Leonard dated their activism to the immediate postwar years.[1] Between 1950 and 1963 the group's membership had grown steadily. But in the mid-1960s its combination of philosophical pessimism and pragmatic confidence caught the popular imagination fired by civil rights and opposition to the war in Vietnam. The militancy of the middle- and upper-middle-class professionals drawn to the environmental cause grew out of an alienation from industrial leaders and entrepreneurial values. Club members supported a staff even more strident than they. Unfortunately, the older liberalism of the group's established volunteer leaders was incompatible with this new "extremism." Thus at the zenith of its strength, the organization was rent by an internal struggle that would define the boundaries of environmentalism in the 1970s and of the next redwood battle.

In 1964 the club's annual growth rate jumped to over 22 percent and in 1966 to nearly 30 percent; these dramatic increases did not abate until 1972. In significant part this growth was a response to Brower's innovative advertising, begun with his first full-page adver-

Figure 19. Sierra Club Diamond Jubilee Banquet, December 9, 1967. Dr. Edgar Wayburn (standing) and David Brower. Courtesy of the Sierra Club.

tisements in 1964 and 1965 on the redwoods. Interestingly, those who joined in such large numbers in the mid- and late 1960s were similar to those who had belonged during the interwar years, when the membership had been characteristically young to middle age professionals or semiprofessionals.[2] William Devall's survey in the late 1960s shows that 80 percent of the members were still professionals— 49 percent upper-level professionals and 21 percent middle-level, such as school teachers, writers, and artists. Most were twenty-five to fifty years old. In a 1978 survey of club members, 68 percent of the respondents similarly listed themselves as professional, technical, and kindred workers.[3] The club's self-proclaimed "environmental revolution" attracted fellow travelers on campuses in the late 1960s, yet lawyers and professionals were still far more common than students within the organization. A staff member in the club's New York office wrote in 1967, "Last year, the New York lawyers began joining the club at such a rate that I was afraid we were going to become the New York Bar Association."[4] Before World War II most members had been college educated, and by the 1960s and 1970s over half had graduate degrees, a pattern repeated in a similar citizen group in the Northwest.[5]

If the constituency had remained constant, the rationale for membership had shifted. Those who had joined before 1940 had done so primarily to socialize and hike. But in the late 1960s, most members cited conservation as their main reason.[6] The years of greatest growth also suggest a larger political context of self-avowed protest. In 1964 and 1965 the paradox of civil rights was most clearly manifested; violence in Watts and Newark coincided with such successes as the Civil Rights and Voting Rights acts. One author stated, "It is difficult to imagine conservation and environmental groups as a social movement similar to . . . the Civil Rights movement and other such patterns of collective behavior." He argued organizations like the club were "not oppressed groups fit to be chased by . . . Alabama police dogs."[7] And yet there is a connection. In a Resources for the Future survey of Sierra Club membership in 1978, 18 percent of the members indicated that they had been active in civil rights efforts, and the overwhelming majority admitted strong sympathy with blacks.[8] According to one Berkeley activist, as civil rights and Vietnam had grown "uglier" and more "tangled"—he might have added less hospitable to the "blue-eyed devil"—young white Americans had moved into a cleaner crusade, against pollution.[9]

They saw it as a struggle in which no one could deny them a rightful place and an opportunity to expunge guilt. In the midst of the American middle class's "moment in the sun,"[10] its children preached self-denial and zero population growth—the resolve, in one young woman's words, not to reproduce "billions like us" in the face of the "spectacle of the starving child." The club's "ecotactics," or "activism against the enemies of the earth," was both self-effacing and self-directed: "We have met the enemy, and he is us."[11]

Behind the activism of the 1960s was the shadow of violence: the bomb, assassination, and war.[12] In the club's *This is the American Earth*, published in 1960, Nancy Newhall wrote that it was an age in which "the brutal fist threatens all life upon this planet."[13] Half a decade later militant environmentalism merged with the antiwar crusade. The poetry of Marianne Moore in the club's book on New York's Central Park wove together the need to live in peace with both the land and the Vietnamese people.[14] The *Sierra Club Bulletin* publicized the defoliation of the once green Vietnam. Brower saw the war as caused by "technological colonialism" and competition for resources. On May 14, 1969, fifty-eight of the nation's leading environmentalists, including many with the club, sent a telegram to President Nixon denouncing the war as an "ecological disaster" and asking for "a new, ecologically oriented foreign policy." The petition quoted Loren Eiseley: "The need is . . . for a gentler and more tolerant people than those who won for us against the ice, the tiger, and the bear."[15] In the 1978 Resources for the Future survey, 27 percent of the club's members testified to having participated in antiwar activities. A student wrote in 1970, "the primary question is not moral or immoral war. . . . The question is the re-creation of a total environment which encourages life and growth, rather than death and destruction."[16] As important as opposition to the Vietnam War was to the popularity of the club's ecotactics in the late 1960s, however, the group's militancy predated strong antiwar sentiments and rested on the support of those too old to be directly threatened by the draft.

The relationship between the various activisms of the 1960s was as much a continuity of participants as it was a commonality of philosophical pessimism. Historian Arthur Schlesinger, Jr., called the motif of the 1960s a "crisis of confidence." Microbiologist René Dubos described the "existential nausea," or "new pessimism." Student activists in the Sierra Club voiced a feeling of "helplessness."[17] Yet even the young among those attracted to the club were rarely children of the poor, black, or maimed. (In contrast to some of the other activism of the period, few were Jewish.) Theirs was an abstract despair, one induced less by personal conditions than by thought, one for which the naturalism of secular educational systems had prepared them. There were many manifestations of and reasons for the prevailing naturalism of the postwar world. But clearly among them were changes in the biological sciences that deeply affected those interested in protection of the natural world. It is not the denial of the supernatural in science, which had occurred decades before, that was significant—although a large percentage of college students in the 1960s were in fact atheists. Rather, it was the denial of design in nature and of purpose in evolution that was crucial to the postwar ecological perspective. As previously mentioned, when Eiseley, Garrett Hardin, or Dubos spoke of the chance-filled course of natural history, of evolution as "unconscious" and genetics as random, many educated Americans in the 1950s and 1960s felt they were correct and understood the implications.[18]

Naturalism is generally a logical reductionism; that is, if one has enough facts, the world is explainable. But in this period it became a despair, even of man's rational and empirical abilities. In 1959 Brower had referred to the idea of man being in a "terrifying sense" alone after destroying wilderness. Intimidated by the immensity of the universe and the complexity of the chain of life, scientists who sympathized with the club's cause emphasized man's crucial failures and the limits of his rational abilities. Wrote Eiseley, "The chill vapors of time and space are beginning to filter under the closed door of the human intellect."[19] The course of civil rights, Vietnam, and environmental pollution confirmed this suspicion.

Philosophical naturalism was also conducive to the challenge to authority and established values that characterized civil rights agitation, antiwar activities, and environmental activism.[20] If the world is explainable, moral authorities must exist; some people or institutions will explain things better than others. If the world is not explainable, as Eiseley claimed, then truth is subjective. Without natural order, there is no hierarchy; and without hierarchy, there is no authority. Changes in the education of the 1950s and 1960s had led students and young professionals to challenge progress, government, science, and rationalism. The result was a kind of epistemological democracy in many of the activist movements. Club leaders at the same time glorified the nonrational and employed the highly scientific.

Not all fears expressed in the environmental movement were so abstract. The club's rhetoric and policies after 1965 indicate that its followers found postwar demographic patterns disquieting. For two decades prior to World War II, America's population patterns had been stable. Immigration laws minimized changes in the nation's ethnic character, and the birthrate declined. After the war the birthrate jumped to a high in the late 1950s. Each of the various explosions—population, freeways, recreation, and suburbs—Lewis Mumford wrote of in 1960 had social as well as environmental implications.[21]

The early twentieth-century preservation movement had in part been sparked by notice of the closing of the frontier in 1890.[22] If historian Frederick Jackson Turner's essay on the significance of the frontier reflected a common turn-of-the-century anxiety that America's democracy and freedom had been the result of free land and wilderness, the frequent references by post–World War II environmentalists to him suggest that Turner projected a lasting impression of a connection between self-government, individualism, and unpeopled land. One conservationist suggested in 1961 that Justice William O. Douglas's love of wilderness was responsible for the justice's deep sympathy with the First Amendment. Shortly thereafter Douglas formulated a "Wilderness Bill of Rights."[23]

The tourist invasion of the western national forests and parks in the 1950s and 1960s resulted in a loss in the quality of the wilderness experience, or what Brower called "inner space."[24] Social claustrophobia—the specter of crushed individualism—resounded in the club as mass culture encroached upon western landscapes. The loss of beauty, psychological escape, and uniqueness was felt acutely by those whose travels to mountaintops expressed desire for exclusivity.

Most of the people joining the club after 1964 were, however, less interested in hiking than in opposing environmental deterioration in general, including that in the swelling metropolitan areas. The postwar baby boom was threatening the coastal valleys of California as well as the mountains. The metropolitan areas of the eastern and western seaboards—where interest in scenic preservation had always been and continued to be strongest—experienced postwar housing and freeway booms. California's population growth was especially dramatic. A club leader residing in the Santa Monica hills wrote of peering down upon Los Angeles's "sluburb." Members in Oakland, Berkeley, and San Francisco looked down at "ticky tacky" houses spreading across the Santa Clara Valley.[25] Each year there bloomed fewer valley wildflowers Muir had so loved.

Without denying crowding, pollution, and poor planning, it is possible to sense a social and psychological component in the club's reaction to population growth. The claustrophobia expressed by Eiseley's "cosmic prison" and the analogous "spaceship" earth was more than spatial. The fears Mumford expressed writing for the club of "featureless people," spreading across the "featureless landscape" and working toward the "same blank goals, cramping, dwarfing, dehumanizing," are of personal alienation and threatened individualism. Mumford told of suburban development exhibiting "vulgarity" and "dingy mediocrity." He called America's population growth a "flash flood of humanity," a cancerous spread reminiscent of "a microbiologist's view of fungus." Wrote one young club member, "We earth-bound humans are only digits now, crowded into anonymity, our lives and individuality diluted by the presence of rapidly doubling millions like us." Brower said that only wilderness prevents "Man's world from becoming a cage."[26]

In response to pressure from new members, the club in 1967 broadened its traditional role as defender of the wilderness to include the fight for urban amenities and zero population growth. To those educated on 1950s textbooks emphasizing world starvation widening from the human ant heaps of India, the rise in America's birthrate promised doom. Echoing biologist Paul Ehrlich, club leaders embraced population limitations as the only real solution to environmental preservation—although in fact most postwar deterioration in the United States might better be attributed to technological changes and increased per capita consumption than to growing numbers.[27]

Why did the postwar population boom generate social fears as well as environmental one? A large percentage of those joining the club in the 1960s were in their late twenties or early thirties,[28] born just before the baby boom. By 1970 the postwar generation itself was influencing the organization. For both that generation and those immediately ahead of it, the increase in numbers of the young was a brutal fact. From 1950 to 1970 there was a significant increase in the percentage of the population college educated and between twenty-five and thirty. This threatened job competition and lessened the uniqueness of professional status.

Educated Americans' ebbing faith in linear, progressive time related to a repudiation of material progress. Young, upper-middle-class professionals who joined the club in the 1960s sensed in technological progress a loss of control over the direction of their lives. So self-directing was Eiseley's cosmos that he did not even portray man as a conquerer in his destructiveness. Rather, man's outward thrust must be programmed by nature as a means of spreading disease, as with spores. Eiseley's spores were the "ticky tacky houses" the club saw obliterating "fields, forest, orchards, and meadows."[29] They were the symbols also of mass culture destroying individualism. Not only were the professionals growing in number, threatening their own uniqueness and success, but the affluence of the lower-middle class was rising. The American dream of a classless society that historian David Potter analyzed in the 1950s had become for some a nightmare in the following decade. The club's ecotactics, then, were in significant part a reaction to the physical and social implications of mass production, expanded affluence, and population growth.

In many respects the environmentalism of the 1960s was similar to the park movement of the early twentieth century. Brower sensed an affinity between himself and John Muir and also between the closing of the frontier in 1890 and the dramatic environmental changes in the postwar West. In both periods these changes coincided with a popular awareness of larger technological and political evils. The old and the new conservation alike appealed to professionals, especially lawyers and university professors. Both were reactions to abrupt demographic changes—in the early twentieth century, the shift away from a predominately rural, ethnically homogeneous nation; and in the postwar years, the baby boom.

Richard Hofstadter noted that rhetoric of the progressive period resounded with the theme of crushed individualism. Others have found, however, that most of those who participated in progressive reforms tended to be members of "a new middle class" confidently pursuing the ideals of efficiency and scientific revolution. Hofstadter himself wrote that for the universities the period marked ascendent power and status.[30] The environmentalists of the 1960s similarly combined the rhetoric of fear and threatened individualism with an obvious pragmatic confidence stemming logically from the growing numbers of young professionals—traditionally the type of people drawn to preservation—and the increased size of their supporting institutions, especially universities and colleges.

In contrast to the New Deal, preservation efforts of the progressive years and the 1960s were generally the work of citizen groups. These lay activists pioneered the tactics of mass movements—from Muir's efforts to save Hetch Hetchy and Newton Drury's campaign to establish the California state park system to Brower's books and full-page, professionally designed advertisements.

There were, however, differences. Both reform movements combined a broad spectrum of political sentiments, yet the activists of the 1960s tended to be more militant than those of the progressive years. A number of historians in the 1960s concluded that in fact most progressive reformers were actually not strenuously opposed to the new industrial order. Muir and Brower were kindred spirits, but the latter acknowledged a difference between himself and most of the club's progressive leaders—including William Colby, one-time University of California president Robert Sproul, and the public accountant Francis Farquhar.[31] On the basis of Muir's Hetch Hetchy campaign, it could be argued that the Sierra Club from its early years was less moderate than the league. Yet the league's efforts to acquire economically valuable private property were a stronger reform than the club's defense of what historian Alfred Runte has called "economically worthless" lands already in government ownership.[32] Certainly most of the league's earlier leaders had supported Muir, and a number had participated in his battle for Hetch Hetchy. Thus while the newer liberalism had much in common with the old, there was discontinuity.

In contrast to earlier park advocates who rebelled against laissez-faire and Social Darwinism but still held an essentially deterministic perspective, the more militant environmentalists of the 1960s like Brower criticized all authority. His popularity during that decade indicates many Americans were similarly inclined. He and his allies used science yet challenged its moral authority; they expanded the federal executive branch but limited its discretionary authority. These denials flowed from a repudiation of teleological hierarchy based upon power and legitimacy. In comparison to earlier preservationists, the militants in the 1960s neither believed in man's dominion over nature nor in the power of divine guidance over man.

In the absence of teleological hierarchy, they frequently idealized the pagan animism and arcadian pastoralism of the American Indian and the European barbarian.[33] The natural world seemed a mysterious, holistic prison—if largely benevolent and beautiful—in which man possessed little freedom and of which he had but a dim perception. In the absence of faith in the rational and empirical, they turned for guidance to the earth and, like Eiseley, to the animal nature of man.

In contrast to the position of most progressives, Brower and his militant allies now rejected, and were rejected by, older leaders in the movement who were affiliated with industry, such as 1950s club president Alex Hildebrand, who had been in charge of the Standard Oil Company's offshore drilling. Although it was obviously possible—as nuclear engineer Laurence I. Moss, club leader in the 1960s, demonstrated—for scientists and other professionals in resource development fields to be militant environmental activists, the incidence of such within the club declined significantly after the 1960s. As important, the faith that such people could operate effectively declined within the club, affecting the organization's strategies.[34]

Older leaders such as Richard Leonard—whose law firm handled industrial accounts—argued that the club should use liberally inclined industrialists and businessmen as sources of expertise, influence, and philanthropy. Prior to the 1960s club leaders like Bestor Robinson had found, as the league continued to do, an effective conservation strategy in service on boards advisory to the departments of the Interior and of Agriculture and such agencies as the National Park Service and the Forest Service. But the militants would not consent to compromise or discourse. Such cooperation connoted a sanction difficult for proponents of zero population growth. They did not trust government or industry and believed that the flattery and pressure of communicating with business interests or protagonists in government could seduce one from the truth, a process Brower called the "advisory council syndrome." He denounced advisory boards as "a device, through flattery, to take key conservation people, feed them a little private information, tell them not to spread it around, and make them support the agency rather than the organization that they were drawn from."[35]

Drury and older club leaders Richard Leonard, Francis Farquhar, and Ansel Adams were dismayed at this renunciation of diplomacy and open discourse with protagonists, echoing the consternation of professors bewildered in the 1960s by student attacks on supposedly liberal universities and disruptive behavior at open forums. Environmental militants found compromise fruitless, incompatible with commitment, even dangerous. This face of the period again reveals a streak of romanticism, the assertion of intuitive truth over objectivity, rationalism, and established expertise. As a result, the organization attacked the league and the Johnson Administration for compromising.

A young lawyer from the National Environmental Law Society head-quartered at Stanford University testified as *amicus curiae* for the club before the U.S. Supreme Court in 1970, stating that in the absence of administrative remedies, the environmentally aggrieved had only two alternatives—"relief in the courts" or "civil disobedience." Declared Brower, "If you have to choose between being naive or paranoid—I don't think there are any other choices—I guess I would rather be paranoid."[36]

Under his leadership, then, the club became increasingly antagonistic toward technology and corporate influence. Although this was partly due to environmental deterioration and the philosophical pessimism prevalent among America's educated classes, sociologist George Homans's exchange theories suggest another cause. He maintains that a strong empirical relationship exists between liking and interaction; that is, "an independent increase in interaction between persons is apt to be associated with an increase in liking between them."[37] Conversely, hostility between groups indicates a lack of interplay. Analysis of the club and its constituency offers an explanation for such a lack.

At first glance, it appears that the membership of the club was no different in the 1960s and 1970s than in the 1940s or earlier. As in the progressive years, the members were highly educated, white, middle and especially upper-middle class. There were, however, discontinuities in the participation of businessmen and the status of the professionals who joined.

Between 1950 and the 1970s, the percentage of the general population in salaried positions increased dramatically, in part the result of the bureaucratization of the professions. The 1978 Resources for the Future study of the club showed that this pattern was exceeded in the club. Sixty-eight percent of its members were professionals or specialized technicians and 12 percent managers or administrators; 20 percent of the membership earned its living in government and 27 percent in nonprofit organizations, especially schools. Of the total U.S. labor force, approximately 12 percent was employed in government, excluding education. There is no figure available for the percentage of the population working in the nonprofit sector, although 6 percent was in education at all levels. Presumably the majority of the club members in the nonprofit sector was in education. Nearly half of the club, then, was in government or nonprofit sectors—much higher than for the total population. Moreover, few businessmen—corporate or independent—were now either leaders or members of the club, a striking change for an organization founded in San Francisco's financial district by a group that was primarily businessmen. Other studies in conservation confirm that salaried professionals and other white collar workers at present constitute the backbone of such citizen groups.[38]

In his 1951 *White Collar*, C. Wright Mills noted that the ideologies of initiative and individualism required for success in the entrepreneurial world were quite different from those of the efficient executive prospering within a bureaucratic setting. Jacques Barzun called professors, for example, consumers—as opposed to the producers of the business communities.[39]

A concomitant shift within the politics of the club reflected this divergence of entrepreneurial and bureaucratic values. Until 1959 almost without exception club leaders registered Republican, including Brower. In the next decade, however, the militant leaders were more frequently although not exclusively Democrats. In the 1970s the membership at large also showed a Democratic majority. More important, in both decades the organization's political base was the liberal wing of the Democratic Party. The club received in these two decades far less backing from Republicans in Congress than from the Democrats. Yet prior to 1950 Republicans had supported conservation legislation only slightly less than did Democrats.[40]

The divergence of entrepreneurial and bureaucratic values probably explains the decrease in participation of businessmen in the club. Homans maintains that people spend their leisure time with those who share their values.[41] In the 1910s and 1920s, many businessmen participated both in the club and the league, finding the professionals within the organizations shared their entrepreneurial orientation as well as ethnic background, religion, and recreational and alumni affiliations. Clearly, activism in citizen groups was an option businessmen selected in decreasing numbers after 1960. Not only did professionals in government and nonprofit institutions no longer share their ideologies, but Sierra Club politics increasingly presumed and encouraged strong liberal oriented federalism, a position far more congenial to bureaucrats in government and nonprofit institutions than to businessmen.

In addition to suggesting that people associate with those sharing their values, Homans argues that personal interaction—even in the absence of shared values—promotes liking. Brower and other club militants obviously sensed this human tendency and feared its implications. As a result, they shunned direct negotiations with the "enemy" and discouraged activist participation of those associated with business. Not everyone in the club agreed with this. Yet Brower's intense alienation from industry struck a responsive chord among many new members. The Redwood National Park battle indicated a growing dislike for industrial leaders. Homans's theory suggests that this animosity was in part the result of a lack of personal interaction. Certainly this interplay Homans described was less common within the club in the 1960s than previously. More important, the encasement of professionals and administrators in nonprofit institutions and government decreased their interaction with businessmen in the work-place. Such bureaucratization was a particularly dramatic change for lawyers, who played an important role in the club from the 1890s through the 1970s.

Not only were more professionals in bureaucracies, but the nature of the organizations of which they were a part had also changed. Most relevant are the nation's colleges and universities, since professors and students have long been drawn to the club. Early in the twentieth century, most such institutions were private, and even the public University of California depended upon philanthropy. Federal subsidies for higher education began in the 1940s, creating a strong partnership with Washington. Tax dollars and funds from large foundations such as the Ford Foundation strengthened the financial base of America's colleges and universities. As a result, between 1953 and 1966 the budgets and enrollments of these institutions grew significantly.

In 1951 Mills argued that professors—in fact, most white collar workers—were incapable of genuine political alienation from the establishment.[42] But increasing financial independence from traditional philanthropy, together with strengthened tenure laws, isolated secular universities and colleges from the business and patrician communities. The 1960s represented a high point in both professors' salaries and the fiscal strength of their institutional base. This was especially apparent in the University of California—long a bastion of support for western environmentalism. The result was a political insurgency evident in the mid-1960s in the free-speech movement as well as in the size and militancy of such activists groups as the Sierra Club.

Professors and other white collar workers now found they could accomplish social change without traditional paternalistic philanthropy. Before World War II saving redwoods required millions from an individual such as John D. Rockefeller, Jr., and thousands solicited from names on social registers. Even through the 1950s federal funding was rare and state monies minimal. Yet in the 1960s Laurance Rockefeller was an encumbrance whose involvement angered militants. Moreover, they had the congressional influence to counter his weight within the Johnson Administration. The dramatic growth from 1950 through the 1970s in the percentage of the nation's population in white-collar employment—those traditionally drawn to citizen groups—made possible larger and more militant organizations supported by dues and having the political clout of large numbers.

The militant club leaders' view of a world polarized into business and nonbusiness interests, then, reflected new financial avenues for reform. It also reflected the militants' own reality and that of an increasing number—if far from all—of their constituencies. In 1967 a club staff member wrote to the San Francisco office that the Sierra Club was "becoming a force," which "the so-called power elite actively solicit and cultivate"—this because a Rockefeller had attended the club's book exhibit.[43] In contrast to alienation from the "power elite" obvious in this letter, in the 1960s Drury communicated easily with the Rockefellers but not with the universities.

Prior to the 1950s the Save-the-Redwoods League's council and board of directors had been divided between businessmen, industrialists, patricians, and professionals. In the 1950s and 1960s, liberal-minded businessmen and philanthropists continued to fill the ranks of the organization's leadership. Professionals also continued to do so but in decreasing numbers. Moreover, those who did tended to be independent professionals associated with the business community, such as the lawyer Richard Leonard or the accountant Francis Farquhar. In contrast to the earlier history of the league, 1960s leadership included few individuals from the federal land agencies. Moreover, the group had attracted few new scientists or professors; those on the council had served since the 1920s or 1930s. This was a striking change for an effort whose first offices had been at the University of California and whose founders had been predominately scientists and professors.

Like most citizen groups of the early twentieth century, the league relied upon philanthropy, a fiscal base that may often necessitate a relatively low profile. Newton Drury always found a moderate stance successful for raising funds and exerting personal influence. The organization relied less upon the political power of numbers than upon moral persuasion. The impeccable character of Drury—his consistency, humility, and reasonableness—was the league's hallmark for decades. Since the organization relied upon the interaction of professionals and businessmen, it sought solutions fair to all elements of the community.

In contrast, the Sierra Club had never depended upon paternalistic philanthropy. Its dues had generally covered operating expenses, and prior to 1960 it had not agitated for large-scale land acquisitions. Muir's Hetch Hetchy campaign offered a precedent for vigorous defense of public lands. But as Joel Hildebrand, club director from the 1930s until his resignation in 1965, explained, the group's power had traditionally rested with its board of directors, comprised as it was of "men of influence" who would "alert all their friends in the

East to apply pressure" when necessary. This style began to change as Brower followed in Muir's footsteps to defend public lands in the 1950s. And after passage in 1964 of the Land and Water Conservation Fund—for which the club lobbied—the organization pursued increasingly the politics of numbers. As Hildebrand bemoaned, its power came to rest on the size of its membership; it represented "voters, voting strength, and no official . . . wants to alienate a good many thousand of voters. . . . Our strength earlier was moral strength . . . and cogent argument rather than threats and confrontation."[44]

When Brower asked rhetorically whether you "catch more flies with vinegar or honey . . . should we be bold or should we be diplomats?" he answered himself: "private diplomacy belonged in the Bohemian Club but it didn't belong in the Sierra Club. We were trying to get the public to move, and the Bohemian Club type of operation is trying to get the leaders to move. You do that quietly. . . ." Some of the club's early affairs had filtered through the Bohemian Club, but in 1962 Brower told his directors that "being polite" brought little public support; "attention-demanding presentation of a problem" was necessary "to stimulate members to action." More bluntly, he declared, "if you're trying to get the public to move . . . there has to be controversy. . . ." Hence he relied upon full-page advertisements and "exhibit format" books. The club fought for a large Redwood Creek park in part because limited objectives would not inspire people. As Brower later recalled, "The big, bold plan for a Redwood National Park   is the one that really captured our imaginations." He saw this approach as a fulfillment of democracy, a system he greatly respected.[45]

The correlation between the league's and the club's bases of support and their politics is not unique. In 1975 the Commission on Private Philanthropy and Public Needs concluded that philanthropic groups relying upon the dues and activism of their members tend to be more radical than traditional, paternalistic ones. The same study indicated that membership-supported groups are also becoming more prevalent and powerful as citizen activism increases and philanthropy decreases.[46]

Homans's exchange theories relating liking to interaction suggest that the staff in such growing, consumer-based groups might tend to become more militant than their constituencies. They are economically and socially even more divorced from the business communities than are their members, and they must maintain a strident stance to attract a large following. This in fact is what happened to the club in the 1960s. The same forces that disrupted relations between the league and club caused a serious schism within the latter.

In May, 1969, the club fired David Brower. The controversies leading to his dismissal provided a backdrop to the redwood battle of the 1960s and would bear on the future of the Redwood National Park. The Brower affair involved a spectrum of often blatant, sometimes subtle differences of opinion as well as a diversity of charges and countercharges. The issues, however, fell into two broad categories. There were problems related to the administration of the club and its chronic fiscal deficit. There were also questions involving goals and methods in conservation. The principals involved fell into three groups: the old guard, a middle element, and the radicals.

In the late 1960s, the radicals shrilly charged that should their opponents win, the club would "revert to its days as a society of 'companions of the trail.'"[47] The club's old guard, voluntary leaders had been critical of Brower since 1959, yet they did not want the organization to be a mere society of hikers. They had strongly supported Brower's Dinosaur campaign and, with two exceptions, lauded the club's assumption of national leadership in conservation. The old guard's position was more subtle than the pro-Brower forces implied. From 1962 on the club ran a financial deficit, upsetting ex-presidents like Francis Farquhar, head of the California Society of Certified Public Accountants in the 1930s and 1940s. Almost to a man the old guard blamed Brower for the debt incurred by a growing staff and publications program.[48]

Since 1959 the club's past presidents had also continued to criticize Brower for publicly impugning motives and actions of opponents, from Forest Service officials to President Johnson. They charged the executive director with irresponsible and excessively emotional propaganda as well as with wrongfully challenging scientific expertise.[49] Bestor Robinson agreed with critics who considered *The Last Redwoods* a misleading overstatement. He and others of the old guard accused Brower of destroying essential cooperation between citizen groups, government, and industry. Those past presidents and vice-presidents who were also league directors—Farquhar, Sproul, Leonard, Horace Albright, and Walter Starr, who owned a pulp and paper mill on Puget Sound—shared Drury's faith in "feasible" demands and the value of the museumlike stands on Mill Creek and had challenged the club's Redwood National Park campaign.[50]

Of the twelve past presidents who opposed Brower, nine were independent professionals, one had been an engineer with Standard Oil, and two were retired University of California professors of science. They were older than the more radical elements in the club and by their seniority carried much influence into the 1960s. Robinson and

Alex Hildebrand were on the board through 1966; Leonard was a director until 1973. Yet the members of the old guard neither made a concerted effort to remove Brower prior to 1967 nor did they control policy at any time during the 1960s.

During most of that decade, the balance of power rested with those in the middle, who supported Brower at least through 1966. Most prominent among them were the photographer Ansel Adams, George Marshall, Edgar Wayburn, University of California biophysicist William Siri, writer and editor Paul Brooks, and Berkeley Radiation Laboratory technical writer Charlotte Mauk. They worried about the financial deficit that continued to mount after 1962 but hoped administrative changes might balance the books without necessitating a cutback or losing Brower, whom Adams called in 1963 the "top man in conservation." They supported expansion into national conservation and urban environmental issues. With the exception of Adams, they backed the strategy that Brower, Wayburn, and Michael McCloskey devised for the redwood park campaign.[51]

The third group consisted of the more militant directors together with Brower himself. Their representation on the board grew steadily from 1964 through 1968, although only from May, 1967, through April, 1969, did they constitute a majority. The most consistently adamant of them were *Sunset*'s travel editor Martin Litton, who was such a decisive influence in the redwood battle, and Fred Eissler, a Santa Barbara high school teacher. Others included lawyer Phillip Berry, University of Washington biochemist Patrick Goldsworthy, University of California hydrologist Luna Leopold, nuclear engineer Laurence I. Moss, photographer Eliot Porter, and *New York Times* editor and writer John Oakes. Thus they included two writers, a nuclear engineer, one photographer, one lawyer—who later became a professional environmental lawyer—and three scientists and educators. This was not different in broad outline from the old guard, but it can be noted that this group was generally younger and none had the strong, professional interaction with business of Leonard, Bestor Robinson, or Alex Hildebrand. From 1959 through 1966 club policy was generally too moderate to suit the radicals and too extremist for the old guard. The club's redwood battle represented only a majority opinion on proper goals and methods.

In 1966 the delicate balance within the club was upset. On the same day the United States Senate was to vote on the Bureau of Reclamation's proposal to dam the Colorado River above and below the Grand Canyon, Brower ran a full-page advertisement in five metropolitan newspapers denouncing the projects. The Senate voted down the bill. Less than twenty-four hours after this victory over Southwest power interests, the Internal Revenue Service delivered to the club's San Francisco office a letter revoking its tax-deductible status. The service ruled that the defense of the canyon had constituted a "substantial" effort to influence legislation. In taking its action, the service considered Brower's Grand Canyon advertisement as well as those on the redwoods. The directors had approved both the Grand Canyon and the Redwood National Park campaigns, yet some members considered the loss Brower's fault. More important, lost revenue and the $50,000 spent in two years of unsuccessful appeals deepened the fiscal crisis laid at his feet and drove a wedge into the already unstable ranks of club leadership.[52]

The group's internal stability was further damaged when Pacific Gas and Electric Company announced plans to build a nuclear power plant on the unique and wild Nipomo Dunes of California's San Luis Obispo County. Anxious to save these sand dunes, Conservation Associates offered to help the corporate utility select an alternate site. A nonprofit, San Francisco–based organization formed in 1960, Conservation Associates consisted of National Park Service retiree George Collins; wife of the founder of the electronics firm Varian Associates, Dorothy Varian; and Richard Leonard's wife, Doris. The three persuaded the company to put the plant in the nearby coastal valley Diablo Canyon. They had involved Sierra Club leaders in the process and now sought club sanction of the site.[53]

In May, 1966, club directors Ansel Adams and William Siri, supported by Richard Leonard, introduced a resolution before the board stating that the club considered "Diablo Canyon . . . a satisfactory alternate site to the Nipomo Dunes for construction of Pacific Gas and Electric Company generating facility. . . ." Referring to Mineral King and Glen Canyon, they noted that the resolution would be "in accord with the club's long tradition, and its most effective practice, of urging the selection of alternate sites. . . ." But Eissler injected, "it is not our business to select alternate sites," and Diablo Canyon was not—as proponents of the deal maintained—"a treeless slot." A long-time foe of nuclear power, he feared the vote could be regarded as condoning nuclear plants in general. Brower was not at that time an opponent of nuclear generators, but he did not approve of accommodation and objected to the speed of the decision. Several of the more militant directors were absent from the meeting, and the resolution passed eight to one, with two abstentions.[54]

Shortly after Pacific Gas and Electric and the press were informed of the motion, Litton wrote the company president calling the decision "a split vote," "fraudulently obtained."[55] He told the club's directors they should have learned their lesson with Glen Canyon, Rainbow

Bridge, and Mineral King. But other directors condemned Eissler for challenging "competent authorities in the nuclear field." At the fall board meeting, Eissler asked for a review of the resolution, describing Diablo Canyon as the only coastal area south of Humboldt County unmarred by highways or structures. A vote was taken, and Eissler lost.[56]

At stake was less a specific area than the question, as one participant put it, "What is the philosophy of the Sierra Club to be?" Another director asked, "Do we necessarily fight every conservation issue as a pitched battle; can we sometimes gain ground by an occasional compromise?" He answered that environmentalists cannot afford to despise "land modifiers." Ansel Adams declared the club must plan for development, "cooperate with reality"; Diablo Canyon had "proved that constructive cooperation was possible and effective." He called the reaction of Brower and his allies "evangelical," as opposed to "well considered." In rebuttal Eliot Porter maintained, "the Sierra Club should never become a party to a convention which lessens wilderness." Eissler charged that the club had been "infiltrated by industry." To him the evidence of "subversion" was "increasingly clear." The "PGE-AEC complex" had handed the club a "prepacked decision."[57]

In response to a petition from the membership, the Diablo Canyon issue was placed on the organization's April ballot. The referendum upheld the board's position. Press attention to the "inconsistent club" had impressed the members. The effort to reverse the directors' position had made Adams and some of the club's chapter leaders ardent foes of Brower.[58]

In that same April, 1967, election, however, the members returned a majority for pro-Brower supporters on the board, giving the faction a generally favorable balance of eight to five. The latter included such representatives of middle ground as Wayburn, as well as Leonard, the only one of the old guard left on the board after 1966. Yet before the new directors could assume office, ten past presidents together with Horace Albright addressed a letter telling the board either to control or remove Brower.[59] Several in the middle group joined with the militants to defeat the attempted ouster. The press heralded the executive director's triumph, and letters poured into the San Francisco office from the 50,000 membership, protesting the effort to remove "the symbol of the Sierra Club."[60]

In the April, 1968, election, Brower's allies further strengthened their majority on the board. Thus from May, 1967, through April, 1969, the militants controlled policy and defeated another attempted ouster of Brower. With Eissler urging "action, not principles," the organization reached a height of militancy, influence, and annual growth. In September, 1968, the board reversed the 1966 decision condoning the Diablo plant. Volunteer leaders at the chapter level angrily interpreted the move as defiance of the membership.[61] More ominous still, the club's financial deficit grew.

Since 1963 Brower had envisioned an "exhibit format" book on the Galapagos Islands, with Eliot Porter photographing and Loren Eiseley interpreting Darwin's and Melville's visions of the islands' rocky landscape. The club's Publication Committee had serious reservations about the project's financial wisdom. Still, Brower borrowed the funds, and Porter went to the islands in 1966. With the committee still dragging its feet, Brower kept the project rolling, telling Wayburn in 1967, "Watch what happens as we move . . . from Everest to Baja to Galapagos in preparation for . . . the International Earth Park. . . ."[62]

Then in 1968 Brower informed the directors that the club would soon receive a $70,000 gift in pound sterling to cover the cost of two volumes on the Galapagos. He added that only a British corporation could accept the block sterling. Determined that boldness and growth answered fiscal as well as conservation needs, Brower opened a London office from which he supervised printing of the Galapagos books. In December, 1968, both the books and the London office were accomplished facts that had cost more than the $70,000 gift. There was a showdown in the club's conference room in San Francisco, with Leonard, Adams, and now Wayburn maintaining that the books had not been authorized. They reminded Brower of their repeated attempts to limit his expenditures.[63]

Undaunted, on January 14 Brower arranged to have the *New York Times* run a full-page advertisement entitled, "Earth National Park." Above a satellite photograph of the globe, the copy announced that the club was initiating an exhibit format book series on the ecosystems of the world.[64] The following day club President Edgar Wayburn suspended Brower's financial authority. By a vote of seven to six the directors upheld the action. Brower's "insubordination" enraged even some who had previously sided with him, including Wayburn and a few of the militants, causing the seven to six vote by the generally pro-Brower board. Wallace Stegner publicly accused his old friend and ally of having been "bitten by the worm of power."[65]

Brower took a leave of absence and decided to run for the board in the April election. He and his allies dubbed their slate the Committee for an Active Bold Constructive Sierra Club, or the ABC forces.

Historically, nominees did not campaign for club office, and in 1967 the board had formally affirmed the tradition, but the ban went unheeded and was lifted in 1969.[66]

Electioneering began in March and continued through April, 1969. The ABC forces asked members if they wanted a bold, national club or a "society of 'companions of the trail.'" As a result of Diablo Canyon, Eissler and the others were convinced the basic issues at stake were ones of both methods and objectives: degree of cooperation with industry, stance toward development, posture in relation to government agencies, a nation-wide program, and other goals such as the opposition to nuclear power urged by Litton and Eissler.[67]

The ABC forces emphasized these issues as well as Brower's role in the organization's growth and power. One supporter wrote, "the club runs on passion and will." In obvious reference to Diablo, another said, "the land is not ours to compromise." Brower admonished, "Deferred pending study" is a trap that must be avoided along with the idea of condoning development "merely to accommodate population growth." Litton added, "We are not weaker for the battles we have lost, but rather for the battles we have not fought."[68]

Against the ABC slate and most of the club's young staff were arrayed all the club's past presidents and almost all the chapter leaders—that is, the bulk of volunteer leadership. Dubbing themselves the Concerned Members for Conservation, or CMC, these leaders argued that the club was "technically bankrupt." They accused Brower of "profligate spending" and "grossly irresponsible acts." Their anger focused on the Galapagos Islands books, the "Earth National Park" advertisement, and the proposed international series—none of which they said the board had authorized.[69]

Brower argued that the directors had known all along he was preparing the Galapagos volumes. He had for years been a step ahead of the directors—why now did they see his "energy" as hazardous? He and Eissler answered this question: Pacific Gas and Electric had infiltrated the club and was part of this concerted effort to remove them. Brower questioned the accounting procedures employed by his opponents, and he also claimed that "any environmental organization" that is not in financial trouble, "to paraphrase Dale Jones, isn't doing its job."[70] The CMC retorted that the issue was simply administrative responsibility.

For the old guard, however, the ideological and fiscal cannot easily be separated. Nor was the budget solely a fiscal matter in the eyes of the ABC forces. Brower had consistently refused to accept budgetary limitations that would restrict the club's "capacity to exert national leadership." His allies maintained that his politics had expanded the club. He said the membership had invested its funds in the Grand Canyon and the redwoods. When charged with overriding the budget by unilaterally opening an office in London in 1968, he answered, "operating deficits could be overcome by growth." He saw the budget as a means of controlling his militancy and argued that the deficit had been caused by the opposition's cries of doom. A less dynamic program would save money but would inspire "no one and lose wilderness."[71]

For several on the CMC slate the issues were largely fiscal and administrative, and had Brower not alienated such of these as Wayburn or Will Siri, he would have defeated the old guard. Wallace Stegner had supplied the opposition's most effective ammunition—the charge of egotism.[72]

Hostility to Brower further fed upon a growing tension between volunteers and staff. Most of the latter allied with the executive director, while the volunteer leaders of local chapters campaigned vigorously against him. The growth of the large staff had overshadowed the volunteers' power, so that many felt the club was becoming a "congregation with a priesthood."[73] The emphasis of the staff on lobbying, advertising, and book publication had left less time for the San Francisco office to coordinate volunteer conservation work. Brower was accused of not acting like "hired staff," and in return he chided the club for treating employees "as bodies."[74]

Following weeks of charges and counter charges, the membership voted in April. The CMC slate won a resounding victory: Wayburn, Adams, August Frugé, Raymond Sherwin, and Maynard Munger were elected to the board. All five of Brower's slate were defeated. The incumbents included Leonard as well as several of Brower's supporters, but the latter were outnumbered ten to five.

At the club's annual meeting in May, the executive director was forced to resign. John McPhee describes that event in his book *Encounters with the Archdruid*, the latter a reference to Brower himself. After calling the meeting to order, President Wayburn recognized Will Siri, who called Brower "the greatest spiritual conservation leader of this century" but added, "two great giants are in conflict— the body of the Sierra Club and the embodiment of David Brower. I move that his resignation be accepted." The motion was seconded by Leonard, long-time opponent of Brower but also one of his oldest friends and a man who had begun climbing with Brower in the 1930s when he was twenty-five and Brower was twenty-one. "My life," Leonard told McPhee the day before the club's May meeting, "depended on his judgment and ability for weeks at a time." Other old friends also voted to accept Brower's resignation. After a quiet farewell speech, he left the meeting. Later that same year he announced he would form Friends of the Earth. Most of the club's staff was either fired or voluntarily followed him into his new organization.[75]

It was a seemingly resounding defeat for environmental militancy. However, since the CMC campaigned primarily on the issues of administrative responsibility and impending bankruptcy, the membership vote reflected above all resentment and fear of Brower's supposed fiscal irresponsibility. This is indicated by the fact that the presidents elected from 1969 through 1975 were generally as suspicious of industry and accommodation as was Brower. For the next few years, Phillip Berry and Wayburn offered a strong continuity of the club's strident politics, despite the continued presence of Leonard and Adams on the board.

Laurence Moss, club director since 1968 and president in 1973-4, initiated and in 1973 the board passed a ruling that no one could serve as director for more than two consecutive three-year terms. In practice this ruling ended the approximately twenty-year tenure of Bay Area leaders such as Siri and Leonard. Adams had resigned in 1971. As a result, the older, more conservative elements left about the same time as did the militants Litton and Eissler. The new ruling broke the oligarchical tendency of the club's governance.[76]

Wayburn was the only leader of tenure to return to the board despite the six-year ruling. As in the 1960s, he served as director and often held the fulcrum of power on the board. He also launched a campaign for the expansion of the Redwood National Park. Leonard left to assume the vice-presidency and later presidency of the Save-the-Redwoods League. He continued to find the club's "extremism" disquieting.[77]

The direction the club had been moving through the 1960s was thus fixed. The bylaws were amended in 1969 to allow it legally to defend the environment as a whole. The national character of the group was confirmed. From 1960 through spring 1965, generally no more than one of the club's directors had been a non-Californian. In the 1965 and 1966 elections, the ratio of Californians to non-Californians became ten to five, a balance that was approximated through the rest of the decade. By 1974 the ratio of five to ten favored non-Californians, and the 150,000 members were in fifty chapters throughout the nation. The club embarked upon international conservation and took the stand in 1974 that nuclear power development should be suspended until the safety problems were solved.[78] Nor did the organization again help select alternate sites for development as it had with Diablo Canyon.

In 1969 and 1970 the club was buoyed by radicalism on college campuses and issued its most abrasive publication to date, *Ecotactics: The Sierra Club Handbook for Environmental Activists*. Defining the title as "the science of arranging and maneuvering all available forces in action against the enemies of the earth," the book was an anthology of generally young contributors who wrote of teach-ins, boycotts, advertising, and legal action.[79]

But the Indian summer proved short. In the early 1970s the club began curtailing its publications and issuing fewer books, in large part because after Brower left the fiscal deficit doubled. Income plummeted as the annual increase in membership dropped from the high of 30 percent to a low of 2 percent in 1971 and 1972. Although the years of dramatic expansion had correlated with Brower's innovative advertising, in 1971–72 membership growth also dropped for several of the nation's conservation organizations, including the militant Friends of the Earth and the National Parks and Conservation Association. In contrast, the league and The Wilderness Society experienced 10–15 percent increases that year. It is possible that this shift represented a cooling of the general population's militancy. It is also possible that the proliferation of more strident environmental groups decreased the membership draw of old and new alike.

Yet neither the club's militancy nor the size of its staff decreased. Brower's people were replaced. Michael McCloskey, the lawyer who had engineered the club's redwood lobbying in the 1960s, became executive director. Volunteer activism continued to be a potent force, although a smaller percentage of the members participated. Under McCloskey's low-keyed leadership, the organization moved increasingly in the 1970s into litigation and lobbying. The club still criticized industrialists and public officials but generally in the courtroom.

New boundaries had been set. The club was still militant if less evangelical. Its activism was absolute if more impersonal. The organization was no longer a California wilderness society controlled by a Bay Area oligarchy but rather a national environmental defense group. Optimistic fervor had been replaced by legal and legislative advocacy, stances more appropriate to the popular cynicism toward liberal causes of the years that followed.

Brower's new organization plunged into a strong antinuclear campaign and international conservation. Friends of the Earth, or FOE, did not ignore the courts, but favored education and propaganda, despite fiscal problems of its own. If the club and FOE pursued somewhat different avenues in the 1970s, their efforts were highly compatible. They were to cooperate in the fight to expand the Redwood National Park.

10
The Battle Rejoined:
1969–1977

FEW POLITICAL compromises have wrought a more untenable situation than the Redwood National Park Act, which devoted one narrow river valley to both clearcutting and wilderness recreation. The moment the park bill was signed in 1968, Arcata Redwood, Simpson Timber, and Georgia-Pacific began cutting their remaining old growth in the Redwood Creek watershed. Logging trucks rumbled along the ridges above the river. Within a short time, its once-canopied tributaries became sunswept gravelly creeks at the foot of bare slopes. Chainsaws outlined the park boundaries on the landscape. Tractor-made skid roads became gullies channeling topsoil into the rivers. A plug of rocks and dirt, in some places as high as fourteen feet, moved down Redwood Creek and threatened the Tall Trees. Some who came to the Redwood National Park sought peace and beauty. They left angry. Others came to Redwood Creek to make their living and became in the end no less angry.

Early in 1969 the California State Board of Forestry had granted the Arcata Redwood Company permission to harvest along Skunk Cabbage Creek, a lower tributary of Redwood Creek. The watershed held one of the few blocks of virgin timber remaining outside the park and formed an enclave between it, Prairie Creek State Park, and the Redwood Highway. That spring Arcata began cutting and by late summer had cleared about one hundred acres. In August the company also began building a logging road down the east slope of Redwood Creek, toward the national park boundary. Georgia-Pacific began logging down the western slope, along the Elam-McArthur Ridge.[1]

The Sierra Club had wanted these areas saved since the early

1960s.[2] Now the group and its allies—including The Wilderness Society of Washington, D.C., and Brower's new Friends of the Earth—believed these operations were causing downslope and downstream erosion that threatened the park.[3] Club President Edgar Wayburn repeatedly telegraphed secretaries of the Interior Udall and Walter J. Hickel that Congress had intended these areas be preserved and demanded they rescue them. He reminded them that the 1968 act empowered the secretary to adjust the park boundaries "with particular attention to minimizing siltation of streams, damage to the timber, and assuring the preservation of the scenery within the boundaries of the national park. . . ."[4]

Wayne Aspinall, chairman of the 1968 conference committee, replied that Congress had meant this section to allow for only minor border adjustments. He cited the legislative history as proof that Congress had not intended the park to be enlarged by Interior.[5] Aspinall's interpretation was in part accurate. Many who voted for the bill had wanted a larger park but accepted the loss of such areas as Skunk Cabbage Creek. The act clearly stipulated that under no circumstances was the total acreage acquired to exceed 58,000 acres. On the other hand, Congress had wanted the park protected and had granted Interior some discretionary authority, including the right to acquire if necessary a scenic screen hiding logging operations from travelers on the highway between Prairie Creek Redwoods State Park and the national park. Wayburn telegraphed Interior in April, 1969, asking if Skunk Cabbage Creek could not be rescued under this clause. Under Secretary Russell Train replied in the negative, explaining that department officials had visited the area since harvesting began, and Arcata was leaving a screen of trees between the road and its clearcuts.[6]

Train and Hickel seemed resigned to harvesting along Redwood Creek and its tributaries. Nonetheless, prompted by fears of erosion, the National Park Service's Western Regional Office had retained Edward Stone of the University of California's School of Forestry to study the problem.[7] In April, 1969, he reported that there were "a number of potentially destructive inputs from land adjacent to the Park and from watersheds tributary to the Park." The degree of damage would, he predicted, depend upon the nature of future logging practices. He suggested the three lumber companies voluntarily establish an 800-foot, no-cut buffer zone around the park. The Sierra Club's forester, Gordon Robinson, rebutted Stone's recommendations as inadequate.[8]

The Park Service's Western Regional Office studied the reports. It concluded that the Robinson study was designed to increase the "emerging tension" regarding the environment "for specific gain (an expanded park)" and was therefore "suspect." Neither did the office approve the Stone report, stating that its purpose seemed less a blueprint for a solution than "to disturb the conscience." On the other hand, the office said that although current industry standards "are less threatening than popularly portrayed . . . public concern dictates a new approach." "After all," the regional personnel told Washington, "it was just such practices which led to the companies' loss of lands and the establishment of the Redwood National Park." The office recommended "industry and Government working together coopera- tively." Instead of resource management by pressure groups, there could be management by a team of public officials and representatives of the relevant timber firms—"three of the nation's largest and most progressive companies." With the expertise available to them, these groups could develop a prototype in watershed management that would be "a standard for the nation."[9] In retrospect, this seems a great chorus singing a song of sweet reason.

Representatives from the Office of the Secretary of the Interior approached the companies with the Stone report and asked if they would adjust their operating plans so as to delay logging near the park. Arcata agreed, pledging not to log within the buffer until the secretary decided upon a permanent easement. Simpson proved similarly cooperative. Georgia-Pacific Corporation, however, the largest private landholder in the lower basin, informed Interior that it would soon log along Bridge Creek and the Emerald Mile and would cut immediately adjacent to the park. The Western Regional Office had known the company would not agree to Stone's recommended buffers.[10]

The department's Washington offices were given to understand that Georgia-Pacific intended to clearcut, "since the area is conducive to slides and erosion." "According to their experts," company repre- sentatives explained, "the large old growth heavy timber should be removed to reduce the threat of slides and erosion." The Bureau of Outdoor Recreation and the National Park Service asked company officials to delay the operation pending formulation of a master plan. They refused but did promise to log only alternate sites of twenty to thirty acres within the buffer and to build their first logging road a full 200 feet from the park boundary. A bright green belt of second growth would, they concluded, soon protect the park.[11] Interior accepted the corporation's arguments and assured concerned citizens that the operations were sound and located in areas of "non-critical buffer."[12] In 1971 and 1972 the company logged two areas of about fifteen acres each within the buffer zone, or what *Newsweek* was by then calling "a kind of token DMZ."[13]

The Sierra Club publicized aerial views of the clearcuts as they outlined the park's boundaries between the Redwood Creek tributaries of McArthur and Elam creeks, and it criticized Georgia-Pacific for clearcutting along Bridge Creek and Lost Man Creek. Wayburn also charged that immediately after the 1968 act was signed, Arcata had slashed the center of Skunk Cabbage Creek "to permanently deface the area."[14] If the park were to be safe, the club claimed that the government must acquire all of the lower watershed.[15]

Interior replied, "The integrity of the park is in no danger at the present time as a result of logging activities on private lands outside the park."[16] To further reassure those worried for the fate of Redwood Creek, the department explained that it had ordered two new studies, one by the Earth Satellite Corporation of Berkeley, California, and the other by Richard Curry, associate director of the National Park Service.[17]

Completed in 1972 and early 1973, the reports showed Interior's confidence misfounded. They echoed Stone: a buffer or management corridor was essential. The Curry Task Force suggested that at the very minimum the secretary regulate logging within the 800-foot and obvious upslope slide zones. If possible, control should extend to Redwood Creek's hydrologic boundaries. This could be done, the task force added, by acquiring either fee title to the land—which would allow direct federal control—or less-than-fee interests, which would permit Interior to stipulate logging practices and was well within the secretary's powers under the 1968 act.[18]

The department took no action and refused to make the reports public. The Sierra Club filed suit in Federal District Court to force release under the Freedom of Information Act. Anticipating the embarrassment divulgence of the reports would cause, on March 5 the department forwarded the Curry report to the Office of Management and Budget. The department hoped that at the least this might provide an excuse for inaction. That in fact is what happened. The White House promptly disapproved Curry's recommendations, explaining that the acquisition of even less than fee title to the 800-foot buffer would cost in excess of $15 million.[19] The Nixon Administration opposed expansion of federal interests in the redwoods.

Two weeks later the department sent Richard Curry to meet with representatives of the three lumber companies. He presented the results of his study and explained that Interior did not support acquisition of additional lands as a means of protecting the park. Instead, it sought cooperation from the timbermen. Curry told Washington that they appeared receptive.[20] Interior mailed the companies proposed guidelines for harvesting in Redwood Creek. By late summer it was apparent that industry expected financial compensation for modifying cutting practices. Interior was convinced it lacked authorization for compensation, and the White House opposed any such plan. Correspondence on the guidelines terminated that August. "We too are being sued by conservation groups," the department told the timbermen. "We had hoped for negotiations and not litigation. We regret that your response precludes such."[21] As the threat implied, Interior subsequently turned the matter over to the Department of Justice, asking for litigation against the companies. Despite this gesture, the administration had not abandoned its efforts at accommodation, and Justice showed little vigor in pursuing the issue. That December the director of the National Park Service, Ronald Walker, wrote to Senator Henry Jackson and Representative J. B. Hanson that his agency was still hoping industry would recognize Interior's proposals as "good business" and implement them voluntarily.[22]

Meanwhile in response to the club's suit, Interior released the Curry and Earth Satellite reports—although not without removing Curry's recommendations for action, which the White House had vetoed.[23] Even without the task force's final words, the club was convinced the studies proved its charges. Curry had identified harvesting activities on adjacent and upstream properties as "the greatest threat to the Park." Both in Redwood Creek and its tributaries, high sediment loads—produced in part by logging—were undercutting the river banks, toppling streamside redwoods, triggering landslides, and cutting gullies. It was "imperative," Curry asserted, "that present land use practices be revised."[24] The Earth Satellite Corporation named certain practices that were particularly destructive: the use of tractors to remove downed timber, construction of roads on steep slopes, and execution of clearcuts during the wet as well as dry seasons.[25] The club filed an Amended Complaint alleging that the Park Service was failing in its duty to protect the park.[26]

The decision to sue was characteristic of the club at this point in its history. In the early 1960s the group had relied heavily upon education and publicity. By the 1970s these methods had given way somewhat to a lower-profile, although no less belligerent, emphasis upon lobbying and legal action. Since legal action did not preclude strong publicity, the shift appears to indicate a decreasing attention to the need for public education.[27]

The turning points in the club's use of environmental litigation had been the *Scenic Hudson* and *Storm King* cases. In these the courts had waived the traditional proof-of-injury requirements in granting the club and other environmental groups standing to sue. Had the necessity for a claimant to show proof of personal injury measurable in dollars gone unchallenged, environmental litigation by citizen activists would have continued, as in the past, to be severely limited.[28] In the *Storm King* and *Scenic Hudson* cases—concluded in 1969 and 1970—the club and its co-plaintiffs were granted standing to sue the Federal Power Commission and the United States Department of Transportation, on the basis of direct if noneconomic interest in the fate of the Hudson River Valley.[29] In 1971 the club had institutionalized this new weapon by establishing the Sierra Club Legal Defense Fund, which two years later sued Interior in defense of the Redwood National Park.

In its bid to extend legal frontiers, however, the club had sustained a temporary setback in 1972. It had sued the Department of Agriculture, alleging the department violated legislative statute in granting Walt Disney, Inc., a permit to build a ski resort in Mineral King Valley in the Sierra Nevada. The club had claimed the right to sue on the grounds that it represented the public interest in "aesthetic, conservational, and recreational values." It also argued it had a legal right to defend the mountains. The United States Supreme Court ruled the club had not proved standing and threw the case out of court. The decision raised questions as to the future of environmental litigation. "It is uncertain," wrote an observer in 1972, "whether the Supreme Court's Mineral King ruling is a minor procedural adjustment or the beginning of more substantial curbs on citizen suits."[30]

In his dissenting opinion, Justice Harry A. Blackmun interpreted the ruling to mean that the club had merely to prove that its members actually used the area and would suffer injury by its development. Thus no special statutes, as the Federal Power Act in the *Storm King* case, or alliance with local citizens, as in *Scenic Hudson*, were necessary. Blackmun's 1972 dissent soon became precedent. That same year the Legal Defense Fund filed an amended complaint alleging that the club and its members had for years used Mineral King for recreational and aesthetic purposes, that members and allies owned or leased cabins there, and that the club had for decades spent time and money in protecting the area. The United States District Court in San Francisco ruled that the club had standing to sue.[31]

Citing this precedent, the following year the club claimed the right to sue in defense of the Redwood National Park, not in behalf of public interest or the trees but in the name of members who had hiked the Redwood Creek basin both before and after establishment of the park. The organization further claimed the right to contest on the basis that it had worked for the park's establishment and taken an active interest in its subsequent fate. The Federal District Court for the

Northern District of California accepted this liberal interpretation of traditional proof of injury. The precedent established by the Mineral King decision had held and been expanded.[32]

Having obtained entry into the courts to defend the redwoods in 1973, the Legal Defense Fund used the statutes governing Interior as the bases for accountability. Once again, the suit was typical of the club's tactics. That same year the Natural Resources Defense Council of Palo Alto, California, sued Arcata Redwood Company alleging that logging in Redwood Creek constituted a public nuisance and violated the new California Environmental Quality Act.[33] The club's policy, however, was to sue the relevant government agency rather than the corporate developer. In terms of standing and enforcement powers, it was easier for the government to defend its property than for the club to do so directly. It was easier to hold the government accountable than the timber companies. The federal regulatory and landed agencies were therefore both the club's worst enemies and its best allies.

The Legal Defense Fund charged that the National Park System Act of 1916 and the Redwood National Park Act of 1968 had imposed upon Interior the duty to protect the Redwood National Park and that the secretary had failed to discharge this obligation. In many of its suits, the club had successfully claimed that by taking a certain action, an administrative agency would violate one of the statutes governing its affairs. In this instance the group sought to limit administrative discretion by defining an action the department should have taken but did not. The club sought to prove that Interior served as a trustee of the national park and therefore had a duty to the plaintiff, club members, and other beneficiaries and users to preserve the park from damage due to improper upstream and upslope logging. The club had little trouble preparing a case for such damage. The group introduced Interior's own evidences: the now-public Curry report and the Preliminary Draft of a Master Plan made by Interior in 1971.

Interior's position was awkward, but its lawyers were optimistic. They believed the club's "public trust" claim would be found invalid. Past court decisions had in fact supported a broad interpretation of statutes giving discretion to administrative officials in condemnation of lands for public purposes and implementation of contracts or cooperative agreements. The courts had limited themselves to determining whether or not the secretary's actions were arbitrary or capricious. In *Citizens to Preserve Overton Park* v. *Volpe*, one of the Supreme Court's most important environmental decisions of the 1970s, the justices had acknowledged land management to be an administrative and not a judicial responsibility. Thus in the new case, all Interior would have to prove, according to its lawyers, was that there had been rational bases for the decision not to take stronger action in defense of the park.[34]

They told the court that neither the Curry nor the Earth Satellite reports had established a cause-and-effect relationship between logging and park damage. There was evidence of erosion in the Redwood Creek basin, the defendants conceded, but it was neither as significant as the plaintiff argued nor necessarily the result of logging; the area was geologically unstable. They claimed further scientific study must precede administrative action. In 1973 Interior had asked Dr. Richard Janda of the U.S. Geological Survey to do a three-year study of Redwood Creek. The department's solicitors assured the court Interior intended to base its master plan upon his results. They pointed out that the companies had voluntarily abstained from cutting within critical portions of the 800-foot buffer until 1973 and in resuming harvesting had done so in such a manner as to mitigate damage to the park.

Despite the lawyers' optimism, Judge Sweigert ruled against the defendants. He threw out each of their major defenses. He noted that the cooperative agreements to which Interior referred had not fully implemented even Curry's minimal recommendations and did not adequately protect the park. He ruled that time was of the essence; the secretary had moved too slowly, and additional studies were unnecessary. The companies may not have logged within critical portions of the 800-foot buffer until 1973, Sweigert conceded, but cutting had occurred during those years both within a 10,000-acre buffer the Park Service itself had proposed in 1971 and along tributary streams where Curry had advised a moratorium. The judge concluded, "the defendants unreasonably, arbitrarily, and in abuse of discretion have failed, refused and neglected to take steps to exercise and perform duties imposed upon them. . . ." He ordered them to perform their duties immediately and report their actions to the court no later than December 15, 1975.[35]

The adverse ruling sparked action. Interior redoubled its efforts to convince Congress and the court that it was without funds either to enlarge the park or to make cooperative agreements.[36] The entire $92 million Congress had appropriated in 1968 from the Land and Water Conservation Fund for the purchase of the park was gone. As of August, 1975, two of the major cases—that of the Georgia-Pacific Corporation and the Miller Redwood Company—were still pending in the U.S. Court of Claims, and yet over $117 million had already been spent. According to the department, these payments had exhausted its authorization for discretionary acquisition, as envisioned by the club under the 1968 act. The department maintained it could not ask Congress for more money. Such power rested with the president and was exercised through the Office of Management and Budget, which had vetoed the Curry Task Force's minimal recommendations. Interior was convinced that discretionary power to protect the park lay not, as the Sierra Club claimed, with the administrative branch but instead with the executive.[37]

Arguing it was without financial resources and yet impelled to act by Judge Sweigert, the department looked to nonmonetary solutions. In late summer and fall of 1975, the secretary made repeated and futile attempts to have the timber companies agree to an eighteen-month moratorium on logging in critical portions of the watershed. In December Richard Janda completed his three-year study, and a scientific team working under Luna Leopold of the University of California, Berkeley, concluded its investigations of Redwood Creek. Both reports warned that the park was in danger.[38] On March 1, 1976, the Office of the Secretary of the Interior mailed Arcata, Simpson, and Georgia-Pacific's successor, the Louisiana-Pacific Corporation, revised timber harvesting guidelines based upon the recommendations of Janda and Leopold. On March 2 the companies retaliated with their own, less stringent guidelines.[39]

That spring Interior asked the Department of Justice to sue the companies. By late summer Justice had taken no action. Interior's own lawyers said regulation of adjacent, nonfederal lands without compensation might be held constitutional under existing case law, but they were not certain. They advised against the suit as inviting, at the very least, an undesirable confrontation between the federal government and the California State Board of Forestry, which had ruled adjacent logging did not constitute a threat to the national park. They suggested instead that the department seek explicit legislative authorization for such regulation.[40]

Although there have been many instances in which activities on adjacent properties have threatened national parks, only once, in 1913, had Congress given the National Park Service explicit authorization, and that only temporary, to regulate adjoining lands: outside of Mesa Verde National Park. The service itself had always been unwilling to assert or even attempt to acquire such power. Nonetheless, assured by its lawyers that with an explicit congressional directive such regulation would be constitutional and pressed by the courts to defend the redwoods, Interior overcame this reticence. In February it had applied to the White House for legislation to regulate private forestry in Redwood Creek.[41]

The Office of Management and Budget vetoed the proposal, explaining that "By attempting to extend the degree to which the Federal Government can regulate the use of private property without creating a compensable taking, the bill would provide for a precedential and major expansion of the property clause of the U.S. Constitution which should not be undertaken."[42] The courts probably would have found such regulation constitutional, but insofar as it has been used in the United States, regulation of private forestry has been the prerogative of state authorities. The Ford Administration was not inclined to establish precedent in this matter.

Responding to the White House's philosophy, the Department of the Interior had tried to mobilize the traditional regulatory power of the state. Prior to 1973 there had been no question of getting help from the state of California. In its 1972 "Review of Redwood Harvesting," the California Division of Forestry had promoted clearcutting of redwood as producing, with even-aged second growth, a "healthier, more vigorous forest" than old growth.[43] The Board of Forestry had readily granted Arcata, Georgia-Pacific, and Simpson logging permits for clearcuts well over one hundred acres in size, even along steep slopes above Redwood Creek. Dominated by industrial representatives, the board left erosion control and reforestation to the discretion of the companies and to nature.

Meanwhile San Mateo County had been attempting to enforce more stringent redwood logging controls. Calling the effort a usurpation of state authority, county timbermen had sued. In 1971 the California Supreme Court had ruled that the state's Forest Practices Act was an unconstitutional delegation of authority from the legislature to an industry to regulate itself. The ensuing reform legislation, the Z'Berg-Nejedly Forest Practices Act, had been the product of compromise and had received support not only from the Sierra Club and the California attorney general but also from Governor Reagan and the forest industry. Passed by a large majority in the state legislature, the act had gone into effect in January, 1973.[44]

Encouraged by the new law and pressured by the club's pending redwood suit, Richard Curry of the National Park Service had met with Governor Reagan's Resource secretary, Norman B. Livermore, Jr., and representatives from the various Resource offices in March, 1973. Curry had presented the results of his study and asked the state for stricter enforcement of its Forest Practices Law and water quality standards in the Redwood Creek watershed. He relayed back to the secretary that the response was "noncommittal and less than enthusiastic."[45] Even after the State Forestry Board adopted new forest practice rules for the North Coast District in November, 1974, it continued to issue permits for operations in the Redwood Creek basin with no special consideration given to the presence of the national park.[46]

On January 19, 1975, the California State Supreme Court had ruled that the new Forest Practices Act was subject to the recently enacted California Environmental Quality Act. The State Forestry Board was again forced to amend its regulations for the North Coast. These new harvest regulations limited redwood clearcuts to eighty acres and forty acres on highly erosive soils.[47] About the same time the Reagan Administration, which seems to have identified strongly with industrial concerns, gave way to that of Governor Edmund G. Brown, Jr., who promptly appointed Sierra Club officer Claire Dedrick as his Resource secretary. Under her direction, the California Resources Agency completed a study on the rehabilitation of the Redwood Creek watershed, estimating the task would take twenty years and cost one million dollars a year.[48] The state did not intend to spend that sum itself, but at least the study indicated Resources was aware of the basin's problems. Legally prohibited from taking independent action to control cutting in Redwood Creek, that September Dedrick asked the State Board of Forestry to declare a moratorium on logging in critical parts of Redwood Creek.[49]

Buoyed by these new developments, that November Department of the Interior officials again approached the state for more vigorous regulation of forestry on lands adjacent to the park. They complained that although the state used a team of representatives from the Division of Forestry, the Department of Fish and Game, and the Regional Water Quality Control Board in its review of timber harvesting plans, negative votes by the latter two representatives went unheeded. Interior demanded that these two agencies and the National Park Service have a voice in the approval of harvesting plans for Redwood Creek. The department's officials further suggested the state enforce an 800-foot corridor around the park from which tractors would be barred and within which clearcuts could not exceed fifteen acres— with adjacent cuts delayed seven to ten years. They asked that on tributary watersheds the state enforce uncut streamside buffers 75 to 125 feet wide followed upslope by secondary buffers of 75 feet in which harvesting practices would be strictly controlled.[50]

That same month the State Board of Forestry held hearings on logging in Redwood Creek basin. The most striking testimony came from the attorney general of California, Evelle Younger, who described massive damage to the park's trees, fish, and soils. He named as causes the large size of clearcuts, disruption of soils by tractors, and unstable streamside environments.[51]

After hearing this and other testimony, the board deliberated for over a month. In January, 1976, it announced its decision. It ruled against a moratorium on logging near the park, voted not to adopt a rehabilitation plan, and declined to enforce special rules governing timber operations in the Redwood Creek watershed. The revised State Forest Practices Act limited clearcuts to thirty acres and required cable instead of tractor yarding in terrain such as that above Redwood Creek. The board regarded these as sufficient and refused the federal request for stronger measures.[52]

In early summer, 1976, after studying the litany of Interior's failures —with the state, industry, and Federal Office of Management and Budget—Judge Sweigert ruled that the department was "purged of its previously found failure to take steps to exercise and perform duties imposed" by law. The plaintiff had acted "in good faith and to the best of its ability" in attempting to protect the park.[53]

The decision upheld the so-called "trust theory" and expanded the rationale for judicial review beyond that established by the *Overton Park* decision. The case had spurred Interior into vigorous action, yet the Sierra Club's victory had proved empty. In this instance the courts could not replace either the legislative or the executive functions. The club filed a motion for rejoinder, with the president's Office of Management and Budget as a party to the suit. The court denied the motion. Said Judge Sweigert, "It follows that primary responsibility for the protection of the Park rests . . . squarely upon Congress. . . ." Only Congress could provide either the necessary funding or a new regulatory power. Throughout the legislative battle that followed, the judge's words would be quoted as justification for new legislation.[54] In this way, the judiciary helped stimulate legislative action.

As early as 1969 congressmen Reid of New York and Cohelan of California had introduced bills to add Skunk Cabbage Creek, Bald Ridge, and the Emerald Mile along Redwood Creek to the Redwood National Park. Each year through 1976 similar measures were presented to and subsequently dismissed by Congress.[55] By then Phillip Burton, Democrat from California and a close associate of Wayburn, had emerged as the House champion of the redwoods with his plan to enlarge the park by 74,000 acres. Each year the bills had been referred to the House Subcommittee on National Parks and Insular Affairs, the chairman of which—Roy Taylor, a Democrat from North Carolina —had refused to report them out of committee. Nor had the chairmen of the House Committee on Interior and Insular Affairs—Aspinall and, after 1972, Democrat James A. Haley from Florida—been favorably disposed toward the bills. Interior's legislative proposal for federal regulatory powers had not gotten past the administration; Burton's bills could not surmount the congressional committee structure.[56]

Attempting to break the impasse, in September, 1976, California's colorful Congressman Leo J. Ryan ordered a hearing by his Conservation, Energy, and Natural Resources Subcommittee of the House Committee on Government Operations. As an oversight subcommittee, it lacked the power to originate legislation; Ryan made it clear that the hearing was designed to publicize the redwood problem.[57] The preservationists found it a congenial forum.

The hearings disclosed that a bedload of gravel and sediment five to fourteen feet high was washing down Redwood Creek. This slow-moving plug was defacing the channel and threatening streamside groves in the national park. In the ballroom of San Francisco's Hyatt House that fall, the committee learned that winter rains could bring down the Tall Trees. Since about 90 percent of the Redwood Creek watershed had already been clearcut, the fate of the park became part of a larger national debate over that particular forest practice. In 1973 the President's Panel on Timber and the Environment warned of the possible ill effects of clearcutting. Staunchly defended by the U.S. Forest Service, this practice was repeatedly attacked by congressmen and citizen activists for its deleterious effect on the Monongahela, Bitterroot, and Tongass national forests. In 1976, the same year that Ryan's committee investigated clearcutting in Redwood Creek, Congress debated the compatibility of such harvesting with the Forest Service's 1897 directive to protect the nation's timber supply and watersheds and adopted guidelines for clearcutting on the national forests. Public attention was clearly focused on the issue.[58]

Ryan deliberately merged the larger question with that of the redwoods. In his opening remarks, he explained that the subcommittee was investigating "one of the most important and controversial environmental issues in the United States: The question of what constitutes proper forest management." He referred to the issues of "clearcutting on public lands in general" and "the unique clearcutting situation existing on private lands adjacent to the Redwood National Park" in particular.[59] Thus Redwood Creek became a test of the benefits and costs of harvesting as practiced on about 40 percent of the nation's western forest lands.

The hearing pitted preservationists against industrialists. There was sediment in the creek and erosion on the hillsides, but the protagonists could not agree on how much and what caused it. Wayburn called it "a man-made disaster" attributable to clearcutting, which always increases erosion on slopes.[60] Speaking for Arcata Redwood, Eugene Hofsted rejoined: clearcutting was the best harvesting method for regeneration; erosion was minimal and due to the area's natural instability, overgrazing in the upper drainage, fires, and faulty road construction. When pressed by Ryan, "Then you are maintaining that there is no significant erosion after clearcutting . . . ?" Hofsted shot back, "Erosion to where?" The soil "stays on the hillsides. It supports the trees that grow."[61] The industry was on the defensive with the testimony of both state and federal officials generally hostile. Public attention, together with raised emotions and self-interest, made subtle presentations difficult for both sides. Amid technicalities, truth on the issue was elusive although discernible.

Even before the intrusion of white men in the nineteenth century, the Redwood Creek area was physically active. On both sides of the long watershed, then as now, slopes rose precipitously. For centuries storms moved dirt and rock down into the rivers, and the redwoods flourished in the streamside deposits. However, a century of human activity had significantly magnified this erosion—how much no one can say exactly, but sufficient to disrupt streambeds and threaten the footing of downstream trees.

It is hard to apportion blame to various human activities there, but the logging practiced between 1950 and 1975 seems clearly the single most destructive cause of erosion. Over 90 percent of the approximately 150,000 acres in Redwood Creek basin was cut during these years. The industry moved rapidly down the long, narrow drainage. By the early 1960s an average of 3,000 acres of timber was falling each year. During this period the companies operated under what even Arcata's timber manager called "relatively weak and sparsely enforced forest practice rules." The companies made clearcuts of well over a hundred acres and often left no intervening forested barriers. They used trucks instead of the railroad and tractors instead of cables to remove the timber. This made possible the rapid pace of logging, but it also increased disruption to the land. As Alfred Merrill of Louisiana-Pacific hedged, "Whatever the amount of sediment in Redwood Creek caused by man's past activities in the watershed, it has been attributed primarily to large-scale, tractor clearcuts."[62]

Based on his study of Redwood Creek commissioned by the Department of the Interior in 1973, Richard Janda testified at the subcommittee hearings of the damage wrought by these large-scale tractor clearcuts. He described how tractors disrupted old hillside drainage patterns and forced the erosion of new gully networks. On steep, unstable slopes, soil was loosened to later wash away in the periodic floods to which northern California was subject. Concluded Janda, "Much of the sediment moving along the bed of Redwood Creek now is the result of the way that floods interacted with the inherently unstable hillslopes and the prior cutting history of the basin." Collaborative testimonies came from state Resource Secretary Claire Dedrick, Department of Justice attorney Peter Taft, California's deputy attorney general Alexander Henson, and Richard Curry.[63] It seems that clearcutting may often be good forest management for some species, but evidence from Redwood Creek indicates that large-scale clearcutting with tractor yarding produces erosion on steep, unstable hillsides.

The future of the basin raised even more difficult questions than did its past. Wayburn testified that for eight years Interior had pursued in vain state regulation, voluntary cooperation, and federal leasing. He said the only solution left was ridge-to-ridge acquisition—a 132,000-acre park—and rehabilitation of the land. Friends of the Earth offered collaborative testimony and encouraged immediate purchase of the approximately 10,000 acres of unprotected old growth still in the watershed. The Save-the-Redwoods League also spoke of the necessity for ridge-to-ridge acquisition, having resolved as early as 1971 to help the club protect the national park. The companies retorted that by limiting the size of clearcuts and substituting cable for tractor yarding near the park, they could harvest these last trees without increasing downslope or downstream erosion. They said the damage had already been done; to stop clearcutting of the small amount of timber left would not help the park.[64] To some extent, they were correct.

Janda agreed that most of the damage did indeed reflect earlier patterns and that improved methods were being practiced. He also noted, however, that much of the remaining privately owned old growth was located in areas that were even "more inherently susceptible to erosion" than most lands cut earlier and that current harvesting was being done, not in the headwaters, as in the past, but adjacent to the park. "Given the present overloaded condition of the creek," he warned, "even a small amount of additional sediment can do a disproportionately large amount of damage to riparian and aquatic resources." When asked by Ryan at the hearing's close if the Tall Trees could be lost in a flood, Janda replied, "there were certain numbers of trees that would be buried and certain numbers of trees that would be toppled. . . ."[65]

Despite the efforts of Congressman Ryan, no amount of scientific testimony would bring consensus on clearcutting, whether in Redwood Creek or the national forests. Good industrial forestry means efficient, economical removal of one crop and its replacement with another. According the the U.S. Forest Service and industrial spokesmen, properly executed clearcutting is in many instances admirably suited to do both. The service and the companies continually emphasized the regenerative powers of a clearcut. In defending practices on the Bitterroot, the service explained that the slopes in dispute had been replanted and were growing trees. In his outburst, "Erosion to where? . . . It supports the trees that grow," Hofsted expressed industrial logic: regeneration proves a healthy forest. Not all redwood companies clearcut, but those that did boasted that within one to five years even the rawest cut would be covered with the light green of new sprouts. Some species such as redwood and Douglas-fir thrive in the absence of competition for light and minerals clearcuts afford and the saplings are spared disease and infestation from older trees. Within twenty years a vigorous, even-aged stand provides good ground cover and promises a new crop. The companies wanted interim disruption to the land and streams balanced against the returns of even-aged management and the costs of other methods. Should it prove necessary for them to curtail or modify seriously clearcutting to protect downstream values, they maintained compensation was mandatory.[66]

In contrast to this view of a forest as a narrowly defined silvicultural unit, critics of clearcutting generally consider the entire forest ecology. Restocking does not by itself prove a healthy land; it does not necessarily stop erosion. Soils lost between the baring of the land and the maturation of new cover can harm downslope and downstream resources. In his concluding remarks, Janda showed photographs of a land cut in 1970 and 1971 and considered fully restocked under the California Forest Practices Act. He pointed to "actively eroding gullies and . . . roadfills which are actively contributing to stream channels." The land had, he noted, "clearly not healed from the point of view of stream sedimentation, although it is restocked from the point of view of forestry."[67] In its 1973 report the President's Panel on Timber and the Environment had warned, "it may be a wise precaution to avoid clearcutting the entire area of an intermediate size watershed within a brief time period—for example, five years—if high peak flows are both probable and detrimental to downstream values."[68] Such was the case in the redwoods.

The preservationists in the redwood battle wanted federal regulation of private forestry to make such values part of private land-use considerations. The National Parks and Conservation Association of Washington, D.C., in particular sought precedent in Redwood Creek for protection of all national parks, many of which, such as the Everglades, were similarly threatened by land practices beyond their boundaries.[69]

If clearcutting and erosion control are sometimes incompatible, much more so are clearcutting and outdoor recreation. No amount of refinements in harvesting would ultimately have satisfied those in the Sierra Club, Friends of the Earth, and the league who did not want old-growth redwoods to fall nor logging near the national park. Clearcutting was on trial in Redwood Creek, but behind that lay two more fundamental issues: federal regulation of private forestry and federal acquisition of valuable industrial land. The two issues stood out more starkly when state and federal officers finally persuaded the companies to sign cooperative agreements later that fall.

At the September hearings of Ryan's committee, a representative of the California attorney general's office had testified that his office had filed suit in Humboldt County Superior Court against Arcata, Simpson, and Louisiana-Pacific. The suit charged that clearcutting in Redwood Creek was threatening the national park and the entire region's soil productivity. The U.S. Department of Justice also testified that it hoped to persuade the industry to accept the guidelines Interior had formulated the previous March.[70]

Despite the apparent determination of these public officials and publicity adverse to industry from the hearings, closed-door negotiations dragged on through September and October. The companies were reasonably confident they would win. Precedents for state and federal suits were weak, and the companies planned to challenge the constitutionality of regulation without compensation. The industry knew it had an ally in the Ford Administration.[71]

That November the redwoods were once again a national issue. The day before the presidential election, Jimmy Carter announced that his administration would end the "insensitivity" Ford people had shown toward the redwoods. "I will call on the timber companies," he promised, "to initiate a one-year moratorium on further cutting in the sensitive area outside the Park. I will recommend immediate action next year to protect the Park and the Redwoods from further jeopardy."[72]

Less than a week after Carter's election, the three companies signed "Redwood Agreements" with the Department of Justice. The documents were compromises, weaker than Interior's earlier guidelines proposal. In fact, the agreements were procedural only. In return for relief from threat of federal suit, the companies agreed to furnish the Park Service with proposed timber-harvesting plans for Redwood Creek before submission to the state forester. A Park Service multidisciplinary team would review the site and the plan and make recommendations to the state. If the state forester should issue a permit that did not meet with the service's approval, there was a ten-day moratorium during which both sides would seek to settle their differences. Should there be an impasse, both retained the right to withdraw from the agreement and take legal action. The following January the state signed similar agreements with the four companies operating in Redwood Creek basin.[73]

When Ryan's subcommittee held a follow-up hearing on February 9, 1977, Starr Reed of Simpson Timber called attention to these federal and state agreements and asserted, "In short, the concerns of the Park Service, the Attorney General and the general public about park protection must be satisfied prior to implementing any harvest plan."[74]

The Park Service testified that the agreements were working out well and that it had rejected only three of the last twenty-eight harvest plans. Janda commended the companies for keeping their tractors and bulldozers out of the "equipment exclusion zone." He again expressed concern about some steep areas that might eventually be logged but said plans currently approved posed no significant danger to the park. The state's Resource secretary, Claire Dedrick, had spoken strongly in favor of park expansion and logging regulation at the September hearings, but now she stated the companies were meeting the criticisms of her agencies, the state attorney general, and the Park Service.[75]

In spite of such testimony, as the industry ruefully anticipated, the Sierra Club and its allies were not satisfied. Michael Sherwood, attorney for the Legal Defense Fund, told Ryan's committee that the agreements were merely "a hollow victory." He scoffed that after seven months of negotiations, the Park Service had won the right to make on-site inspections and issue recommendations. The service's criteria were weak, and it possessed no enforcement rights.[76]

The club and its allies wanted ridge-to-ridge acquisition of Redwood Creek basin, and their chances of success were improving. The political forces that had compelled the companies to cooperate had also improved the club's position. In addition to replacement in 1975 and 1976 of the conservative Reagan and Ford administrations with those of Brown and Carter, liberal Democrat Morris Udall succeeded Haley as chairman of the House Committee on Interior and Insular Affairs in 1977. Further, early that same year San Francisco's Phillip Burton had become chairman of the House National Park and Insular Affairs Subcommittee.

11
A Second Redwood
National Park Act:
1977–1978

DURING THE last year of the battle over park expansion, the loggers of northern California staged mass demonstrations and evoked the power of the national AFL-CIO. The timber companies denied clearcutting damaged the park, called its expansion a "land grab," and prophesied economic doom for the North Coast. The vice-president of the Arcata Redwood Company accused the Sierra Club of the "big lie technique." The club cited the industry's irresponsibility to the land and the workers; the organization's representative returned the "big lie" charge. The Save-the-Redwoods League neither condemned the companies nor lobbied for park expansion. Nonetheless, having found the state and industry uncooperative, the organization did join the club, Friends of the Earth, and other citizen groups in urging federal intervention. Drury's group also pledged $1 million to the Department of the Interior for the condemnation of private land in northern California.

Ideologically receptive to demands of organized labor and supported in the redwood battle by liberal and pro-labor Democrats in Congress, the club advocated unprecedented compensation to union loggers for losses due to park expansion. Faced with strong state and federal endorsement of the park, the timber companies and the unions conceded defeat. On February 9, 1978, Phillip Burton's Redwood National Park Enlargement bill came up for a vote before the House. In an unlikely juxtaposition of interests, the lobbyists of industry, labor, and the club stood in the wings urging an affirmative vote. California's Democratic Representative Burton and Senator Alan Cranston had brought the three major pressure groups into consensus. Each group, however, had exacted a price.

204

In January, 1977, eager to benefit from the president's campaign pledge and the environmentalist reputation of his new secretary of the Interior, Cecil Andrus, the club called upon the White House. The new administration was receptive if preoccupied.[1] It soon became apparent that Carter's people had fiscal reservations. In February Burton, Udall, and twenty-three similarly Democratic co-sponsors again introduced Burton's park expansion bill. Developed with the cooperation of Edgar Wayburn and other club leaders, it would enlarge the park from 58,000 to 132,000 acres. At the hearing of Ryan's subcommittee that same month, the conservative National Park Service testified that acquisition of 74,000 acres would cost $400 to $500 million, far more than had ever been spent for a federal land purchase. The club's lobbyist in Washington, D.C., Linda Billings, countered by quoting $150 million but to little avail.[2] Under pressure from Bert Lance and the Office of Management and Budget, the White House began to give serious consideration to a 21,500-acre proposal advanced by the National Park Service.[3] Secretary Andrus put forward a dead-center compromise—48,000 acres. With the support of the federal Council of Environmental Quality, he prevailed and in late April made public administration support for his plan. His recommendation simply eliminated 26,000 acres of cutover land in the upper watershed that Burton's bill had proposed be included in the park. Andrus explained state and federal regulation in this area would protect downstream resources.[4]

Burton's and Andrus's proposals were otherwise in substantial agreement. Both called for acquisition of the watersheds of Lost Man, Boyes, and May creeks—all now almost devoid of timber—and that of Skunk Cabbage Creek with its patches of old growth. Both would add to the park all lands upslope from Redwood Creek to the hydrologic divide and extend the ridge configuration upstream to include the Cooper Creek drainage and that of Devil's Creek with its heavy virgin stand. Even under Andrus's plan, the lower Redwood Creek basin and all streams directly tributary to the original park corridor would be in federal ownership. All remaining old growth in the watershed would be saved. Andrus noted that the acquisition would create "a sweep of park from the ocean to the first major inland ridge."[5] Burton's ambitious proposal and the administration's compromise were referred to the House Subcommittee on National Parks and Insular Affairs, which scheduled hearings for March and April.

The drought of the previous winter had permitted heavy logging in Redwood Creek. The club now anticipated a similarly heavy spring harvest of at least three hundred acres.[6] The California State Board of Forestry had approved clearcuts in the only block of old growth left on the east slope above the Tall Trees, on Skunk Cabbage Creek near the highway, and streamside in two of the last virgin tributaries. In January the club had begun lobbying for a moratorium on logging. It had soon enlisted the support of the four chairmen of the committees that would be considering the park legislation in the next session.[7] At the club's suggestion, in March Burton of the Interior Subcommittee, Morris Udall of the House Committee on Interior and Insular Affairs, Senator Henry Jackson of the Committee on Energy and Natural Resources, and Senator James Abourezk of the Subcommittee on Parks and Recreation petitioned President Carter to issue a plea for industrial cooperation. The president declined.[8] Nevertheless, following a similar request from the nation's citizen groups, Secretary Andrus joined Burton in a public appeal to the companies for a six-month logging moratorium in sensitive areas adjacent to the park. They explained that the administration was giving the matter highest priority.[9]

Club leaders held out little hope for voluntary compliance and pressed Interior to sue should the logging continue. The federal attorneys claimed they lacked grounds for a suit—which the club refuted—and noted that political considerations barred legal action.[10] Using the November agreements, Interior had blocked two harvest plans deemed crippling to the park, but the department said that voluntary compliance was the only way all harvesting near the park could be stopped.[11] The club was correct in distrusting such voluntarism. The companies replied to Andrus and Burton's plea by launching full spring operations in Redwood Creek as planned.[12]

Energized by Carter's election, the companies had moved to solidify their position. Through a Washington, D.C., law firm, they had retained ex-Congressman Jim O'Hara as a lobbyist. Public relations people told the nation that Redwood Creek's old growth and the second growth it would one day produce were vital to the companies' sustained-yield programs. They advertised that the best of the redwoods were already protected in California state parks. That January corporate officials had met in Eureka with 120 citizens of the North Coast—representatives of labor, chambers of commerce, the local press, and business. William Walsh, the persuasive senior vice-president of Arcata, outlined dire economic consequences of park expansion for the region and made his charge of Sierra Club politics as effective use of the "big lie."[13] Humboldt County residents and organized labor were ready allies for timber interests.

Through winter and into spring, rumors fed fears in this industry-dominated county. The anxiety exploded on April 13 when Burton's subcommittee held hearings in Eureka. Encouraged by local news media and city officials, several thousand townspeople took to the streets in protest. They rallied downtown, and from there a tractor trailer carrying local leaders led a procession to the municipal auditorium where the field hearings were to be held. There Mayor Sam Sacco's gravelly voice, amplified by a bullhorn, mouthed the crowd's anger at those who would take away their livelihood. Loggers pounded their axes on the wooden floor of the hall's stage and swung the wedged blades over their heads.[14]

At 10:00 that morning congressmen K. G. Sebelius, Phillip Burton, and district representative Don Clausen arrived under police escort. For the next seven hours they listened politely to loggers and union officials express the fear that park expansion would cost many jobs. Older loggers spoke of dim prospects for reemployment and anticipated loss of pension and social security benefits. Residents testified that a county in which public lands were already extensive could ill afford the reduction in the tax base that federal purchase of more land would entail. The park would be paid for with the diminished lives of local children, whose schools and colleges would lose tax funding and whose parents would be forced onto welfare. A few residents spoke in favor of park expansion: students from Humboldt State University, an Indian spiritualist, and an elderly woman whose frail voice met with respectful silence.[15]

Less polite was the reception accorded John Amodio, who charged the industry with forcing employees to oppose park expansion and who only a month before had returned industry's animus by accusing it of using the "big lie" in denying erosion in Redwood Creek. Amodio had become interested in the park as a student at Humboldt State University. As Sierra Club representative and founder of the local Emerald Creek Committee—or what he called preservationists "behind the redwood curtain"—he now described the gullies, gravel plugs, and barrenness that clearcutting produced.[16] Amid audience protest, he minimized the impact park expansion would have on the local economy.[17] Other residents denounced Amodio and his allies as "extremists" and "radicals." Cheers and standing ovations greeted the union leader who loudly declared the "stylish people" from out of town already had enough parks in which to play.[18] With that, a caravan of logging trucks, air horns blaring, roared out of town heading south so that their drivers might protest once more before Burton's subcommittee, this time in San Francisco. The loggers' arguments remained the same, their anger unabated.[19]

Debate no longer revolved around clearcutting and erosion. A report by Ryan's subcommittee and Judge Sweigert's ruling had established the rationale for enlarging the park.[20] At issue now were Humboldt County's economy and local control. National organizations of highly educated, mostly urban citizen activists confronted local people with rural values and industrial concerns. This dichotomy had plagued con-

servationists since the 1920s when Wyoming residents fought establishment of the Grand Teton National Park. After World War II such confrontations became more frequent with local residents often allied with
national industries and organized labor. Alaska and Florida have in the
1970s seen the same debate, involving whether national interests should
take precedence over local ones, and whether a congressman should
forsake the traditional reluctance to vote against another congressman
in matters concerning the latter's own district. Representative Don
Clausen from Humboldt County, a staunch opponent of park expansion,
answered no to both issues.

As the San Francisco hearings of April, 1977, made apparent, the
loggers' protest was not taken lightly. They had political power, and
their fears were rooted in fact. The Department of the Interior
estimated that expanding the park by 48,000 acres—because of the
10,000 acres of virgin timber involved—would cost about 1,000 jobs; the
industry estimated 2,000.[21] This was an ominous prospect for a
sparsely populated county where unemployment already wavered
between 14 and 18 percent.[22]

Local opposition might have been the preservationists' Achilles' heel
had they not turned the very nature and severity of the region's
economic depression to their advantage. In testimony before Ryan's
subcommittee the previous September, they charged that timber-
related jobs had declined almost 40 percent since 1960, not because of
parks but because the industry had replaced men with machines and
exported raw timber to Japan for processing.[23] In the future felling and
milling would become even more mechanized, and there would be
fewer big trees to log. In the 1960s the club had prophesied that
Humboldt County's old growth would be gone by 1980. Now it predicted
depletion within ten to fifteen years. The group's forester testified that
production would fall at least 45 percent and employment even more.[24]

The club and its more liberal allies such as the Emerald Creek Committee, FOE, and the Planning and Conservation League of San Francisco used these figures to portray the industry as a house of cards and
clearcutting as hit-and-run forestry.[25] Rather than offer solutions to the
problems of the redwood region, Amodio charged, the industry
employed "delaying tactics to allow them to liquidate the remaining
lucrative stands of old growth." The timber companies themselves,
"through conscious management decisions," were "responsible for the
faltering northcoast economy." Theirs was, he concluded, a "final
assault," an "execution," a "blitzkrieg" against the last redwoods.[26]

Industry spokesmen countered by saying that production was not
declining. They pointed to tree farms—which Amodio called "a joke"—
and green hillsides of second-growth conifers as proof of a continuing

timber supply. To ensure future production, they recommended the reduction of taxes on cutover lands, passage of zoning ordinances restricting the subdivision of industrial forest lands, and termination of park acquisitions. "Despite contentions that timber is a dying industry," Simpson's vice-president argued, "employment by the three companies had actually increased between 1968 . . . and 1976."[27]

If the club's and the Emerald Creek Committee's predictions were somewhat too pessimistic, the companies' optimism was also unwarranted. In 1963 a California Agricultural Experiment Station report stated, "Stands similar to the virgin redwood forest will never again be produced on a commercial basis. . . . Thus the . . . timber industries of the northern California coast face the irreplaceable loss of their primary resource base. . . ."[28] In 1968 the U.S. Department of Agriculture predicted that in fifteen years the old-growth redwood would be gone. In both 1975 and 1977 it prophesied a slow but steady decline in available timber and thus in production on the Pacific Coast.[29] In 1976 Secretary Dedrick noted that less than 12,000 acres of old growth remained in Redwood Creek. Since the three companies were harvesting 800 acres per year, in twelve to fourteen years it would be gone. Outside of Redwood Creek, Simpson had 12,000 acres of old growth in Humboldt County, Arcata 7,500 acres, and Louisiana-Pacific only 2,000 to 3,000 acres.[30]

Amid the conflicting, self-serving, and supposedly empirical evidences of the protagonists lay the harsh realities and uncertainties of any resource issue. Old-growth redwood will soon go out of production in this region, as did old-growth pine and hardwoods in the southern and eastern United States decades earlier. Dislocations will surely result. At least one company is divesting itself of mills and cutover land and moving on, partly because of timber lost to the park and partly because the returns from second growth are generally less than from original growth.[31] But others will stay, and second-growth conifers will support a significant if largely pulp and paper industrial base. Some firms, such as the Pacific Lumber Company, have successfully encouraged second growth, but much of the cutover land in Humboldt County has regrown a scrub forest of hardwoods, or weed trees. The expense and decades necessary to cultivate the small conifers that may or may not be present under the hardwood overstory make conversion of these lands into merchantable forests problematic although possible. Since mills must be converted to handle second growth and the new operations will be more highly mechanized than the old, employment will drop at a slightly higher rate than production. Production will decline when the old growth is gone, but estimates of regrowth are judgmental. So, too, are estimates of future tourism. It was nonetheless obvious in 1977 that park expansion would take an immediate toll in jobs and that the North Coast economy faced an impending crisis. Without mitigating measures, park expansion would speed the onset of this crisis but had not created it and should in the long run ease it.[32]

In the 1960s industry had been united with labor and county residents to such an extent that their separate interests were almost indiscernible. This was not so in the 1970s. In 1976 the city of Eureka published a report stating that between 1960 and 1973 there were 2,500 new jobs in tourism and a corresponding drop of 2,500 in timber-related jobs due to mechanization, the exporting of unmilled wood, and resource depletion. In 1975 the local press harped, "It is also undeniable that past logging practices were abominable and dumped an outrageous amount of soil and debris into the streams. It is hard to avoid the conclusion that most companies move only as fast as required by law to change such practices."[33] The anger of loggers and residents toward the industrial policy-makers was only a crack in an old alliance, yet together with outrage at park "extremists," it convinced labor to fight for its own interests.

On May 17 twenty-three logging trucks pulled out of Eureka heading east. The lead vehicle carried an eight-ton redwood carved as a peanut for delivery to President Carter in Washington. Organized labor, the lumber companies, and the merchants of the North Coast had arranged the convoy, confident it would generate publicity hostile to park legislation.[34] They miscalculated. Small town presses of northern California —the Eureka *Times-Standard*, Healdsburg *Tribune*, and Willow Creek *Klamity-Kourier*—had, as expected, consistently reflected local animosity toward the park.[35] But those of northern and central California's larger urban centers had backed the preservationists and continued to do so.[36] Similarly, the large metropolitan presses of the east and the west coasts had supported park expansion for years. The convoy evoked editorial sympathy but did not cool media enthusiasm for expansion.[37] This pattern could have been anticipated, since environmentalism has traditionally rippled out from the nation's urban centers—generally those on both coasts as well as in the Great Lakes region—often breaking on the opposition of local and more rural interests.

What was surprising was that the wave of publicity following the truckers across the country brought such strong endorsement of the club's position from the presses of mid-America and reflected a national cynicism toward claims of the frequently multinational timber companies. The day the loggers' convoy arrived in Washington, the club released press packets across the country.[38] Echoing the citizen activists' publicity, midwestern editors told their readers that even without additions to the park, the loggers' jobs would be gone within ten to fifteen years. They editorialized that the last redwoods should not fall simply to postpone the inevitable—or to supply the wood-starved Far East. The companies had, the club-prompted litany continued, caused their own woes by hit-and-run forestry and careless clearcutting adjacent to the park. Newspapers in Ohio, Nebraska, Kentucky, and Virginia accused the industry of "scare tactics," "injudicious logging," and a "Hell-with-tomorrow approach." The companies were "clear-cutting timber, felling every stick from sapling to giant, ruining vast stands." One press labelled the loggers' convoy loaded with giant downed redwoods "an ostentatious consumption of fuel," and others ran a cartoon by Judge showing Sally Edwards, age eight, of Horseź Breath, Montana, sending Congress "her thanks for the chance to see the spectacular California Redwoods up close."[39]

While the loggers bid for sympathy, Arcata Redwood defied public opinion. That spring all three companies had launched operations as usual. Arcata's plans, approved by the State Board of Forestry, in-volved Skunk Cabbage Creek, a lower tributary of Redwood Creek. The drainage formed an enclave between the coast, Prairie Creek State Park, and the national park. For several years preservationists had watched the baldness grow on the ridge above the creek, stark against the blue of ocean and sky. Now Arcata had begun cutting a parcel immediately visible from the Redwood Highway.

On May 23 the Save-the-Redwoods League pledged $1 million to the Department of the Interior to stop the operation. Using this money and its authority under the 1968 act to acquire a scenic screen along the highway, Interior seized thirty-five acres of Skunk Cabbage Creek. Arcata sued, but the U.S. District Court upheld the takeover.[40] The move saved trees up to 1,400 years old. In mid-summer the league pledged a second million to halt the other operation Arcata planned for the area, but because logging would be only fleetingly visible from the highway, the department felt its authority did not apply and rejected this second donation.[41] The offers, however, marked a turning point for the league, which had traditionally rejected federal action and con-demnation.

The change was no less dramatic for having followed years of abortive efforts at accommodation. Four years earlier league director Richard Leonard had contacted the vice-president of Arcata Redwood Company, who was also vice-president of the electronics firm Varian Associates. Leonard had incorporated Varian and served on its board for twenty-five years. As a business acquaintance, he arranged a meet-ing with the Arcata officer to ask if the league could buy Skunk Cabbage Creek. At the meeting he and Newton Drury explained that their organi-zation could pay the full market value of $15 to $20 million. It could contract to buy the area over the next decade, and Leonard assured the Arcata officer the stockholders would be in no way hurt. The company did not even reply; it had no intention of selling to the preservationists.[42]

The league was also desperately interested in saving the upper Mill Creek watershed. Like Arcata, however, the firm owning the basin, the Miller Redwood Company, refused to sell, and the state refused to condemn. Drury and his allies raised millions in funding but purchased little new in Mill Creek. By 1977 few areas of old growth remained outside of Jedediah Smith State Park. The league could hope only to acquire eventually the bared slopes for rehabilitation. Meanwhile it bought cutover lands above Bull Creek and the last, unprotected original growth along the Avenue of the Giants highway bypass.[43]

For thirty-five years the Pacific Lumber Company had refrained from cutting the Avenue's groves, holding them until the preservationists had funds for their purchase. The league pointed with pride to this gesture of accommodation, which actually owed much to the timber's prominence.[44] As Pacific's president proved in 1960 when he had begged Arcata not to clearcut down to the Redwood Highway, he respected public opinion.[45] Most timbermen shared this attitude. In 1970 Georgia-Pacific offered to exchange 734 acres "visually prominent to highway travelers" approaching the national park for 600 acres with a denser stand hidden in the heart of Redwood Creek.[46] Indeed, even Arcata argued that the price the league paid for the Avenue groves did not represent fair market value because the trees could not be logged.[47] Such industrial cooperation was limited to the more visible redwoods, if—as Arcata made doubtful in 1960 and again in 1976—it existed at all.

In the 1970s the league faced the limits not only of industrial cooperation but also of state reform. Just as the state of California proved averse to evoking its regulatory power to defend the national park, so too was it no longer an effective fiscal partner for the moderate reformers. The league's funding soared ahead of state expenditures, and in haste to buy the last of Bull Creek, the private organization received matching funds not from Sacramento but from the federal Land and Water Conservation Fund. Neither the conservative administration of Governor Reagan nor the more liberal one of Governor Edmund G. Brown, Jr., with its budgetary surplus, offered significant support. In 1974 and 1976 the group donated two parcels of land to the federal government, one in Del Norte County and one near Skunk Cabbage Creek.[48]

In fall, 1976, having resolved to back the campaign to protect the southern portion of the Redwood National Park, the league pledged one million dollars through the state's Resource Agency to acquire several parcels near the Tall Trees Grove. The company had refused to sell, and Resource Secretary Claire Dedrick was able to win no more than a temporary deferral of cutting on two parcels. The following spring the league publicly endorsed the Carter Administration's park enlargement bill.[49] Again in summer, 1977, the group applied to the state for a moratorium on logging near the park, with even less success —despite the fact that Dedrick had been working hard for federal acquisition of Redwood Creek, including lobbying in Interior's offices on Capitol hill.[50]

The league's aggressive endorsement of federal action coincided with Newton Drury's retirement in 1975 from the presidency and his assumption of the less active position of chairman of the board. Richard Leonard became the new president. The latter's thirty-five years as Sierra Club director and president reveal much about his philosophy. As club director, he had campaigned for the 1968 ouster of executive director David Brower because he thought the latter fiscally irresponsible and unnecessarily hostile toward government and industry.[51] At least in part Leonard was a moderate reformer.

His wife Doris's career with Conservation Associates reflected some assumptions shared by her husband. The association promoted preservation from Alaska to Puerto Rico but concentrated on expanding California state parks such as Big Basin Redwoods and establishing such new ones as the Forest of Nisene Marks—10,000 acres of redwoods in Santa Cruz County. When a scenic area came up for sale and the state could not purchase it, Conservation Associates often acquired it and either held it pending public funding or donated it to the state.[52]

In addition to preferring philanthropy and state action, Conservation Associates shunned publicity and solicited industrial cooperation. This conciliatory disposition had been evident when it helped Pacific Gas and Electric select Diablo Canyon as a nuclear power plant site, an act that had enraged those in the Sierra Club who opposed accommodation and atomic sitings anywhere along the coast.[53] In spite of opposition, construction was begun on the plant, and in 1973, hoping to facilitate environmentally sound development, Doris Leonard became a director of Pacific Gas and Electric. Thus it is not surprising the Leonards found the league congenial. In the mid-1960s, when forced to choose between that organization and the club, Leonard had sided with Drury.[54]

Still, he did not entirely share Drury's moderation. As an ally of Brower in the 1950s and early 1960s, Leonard had seen the effectiveness of inflexibility and "extremism" even if he had not always accepted them. In 1963 he had incorporated the Conservation Law Society, one of the nation's first firms devoted to environmental litigation. He sought accommodation but was willing to use legal action as well as prudent publicity and federal action.[55] If his reform strategies lacked some of the elegant simplicity of those of Drury or Brower, his assumption of the league's presidency foreshadowed modification of the group's policies. As early as 1971 the league had endorsed the club's campaign to control damaging logging in Redwood Creek. In 1975 and again in 1976, the league appealed publicly for federal initiative. To avoid the kin-strife of the 1960s, the group did not raise the issue of Mill Creek. Finding the state unable to protect Redwood Creek, Leonard's organization had donated a million dollars to Interior to condemn land on Skunk Cabbage Creek.

Arcata's roadside cutting in 1977 followed hard upon a request from Interior to inspect a series of parcels near the Redwood Highway that the State Board of Forestry had approved for harvesting. When the company refused both negotiations and on-site inspection, Interior had seized the land. Newspapers nationwide condemned Arcata's "arrogance" and commended the league and Interior.[56] Since the company had merchantable timber outside Skunk Cabbage Creek, the operation appeared needlessly defiant, especially to citizens of Humboldt County. Under the headline, "Just Who Are the Area's Friends?" the Eureka *Times-Standard* accused the corporation of courting the government seizure. Since "even an enemy could not deny that Andrus had acted legally in seizing the territory," the editorial concluded, "it is our unhappy belief that it may be part of a long-term plan to leave this area."[57] This was a charge the Sierra Club frequently made. Whatever its truth, Arcata had always insisted that it either log or be paid not to log, and in this case the latter does not appear to have been unwelcome. Unwillingness to sell all of Skunk Cabbage Creek to the league for fair market value did not imply a reluctance to lose highway parcels by legislative taking, a process which in 1968 had rendered Arcata and the other companies from whom land was taken rewards far higher than what the league considered fair market value. The Eureka paper had probed a critical assumption in all America's previous environmental settlements. Stocks, buildings, and lands were deemed property; jobs were not.

Prior to 1975 Congress had given virtually no consideration to compensation for jobs lost due to the establishment or enlargement of a national park. Even proposals—including those made during the 1960s in relation to the redwoods—to reimburse counties for the loss of property taxes due to parks received little legislative support. But the increasing orientation of environmentalism toward the Democratic Party prefigured a break in this pattern. It came in 1976 when Congress passed a bill giving in-lieu tax payments to counties in which national parks were located.[58] The next breakthrough would come in relation to the redwoods.

The Democratic administrations in Sacramento and Washington could not easily ignore the complaints of loggers and North Coast citizens. Secretary Claire Dedrick had coupled even her earliest endorsements of park legislation with pleas for federal aid to Humboldt County and the woodsmen.[59] On April 19, the day after the demonstrations in Eureka and San Francisco, the Department of the Interior announced that President Carter would push for legislation to mitigate the loss of jobs. Andrus told the press the administration was assembling a task force of economists, foresters, and other specialists to study Humboldt County.[60] In his Environmental Message to Congress on May 23— delivered while logging trucks rumbled through the capitial and the league announced its one-million-dollar rescue of Skunk Cabbage Creek —Carter requested every effort be made to cushion the effect of temporary unemployment caused by park expansion. He directed the departments of Interior, Commerce, and Labor to analyze the potential employment impact and, using existing state and federal programs, develop plans for job training, placement, unemployment insurance, and economic aid to the county. In July Andrus announced that the Department of Commerce's Economic Development Administration had granted $200,000 for economic planning in Humboldt County.[61] That same month he recommended to Morris Udall, chairman of the House Committee on Interior and Insular Affairs, that Burton amend his bill to provide compensation for job losses.[62]

Burton's response exceeded the administration's expectations. On July 29, Burton, Udall, and twenty-three similarly Democratic co-sponsors introduced—with the club's support—a new redwood national park enlargement bill, Title I of which incorporated the administration's plan for a 48,000-acre enlargement of the park instead of Burton's original 78,000-acre plan and included Carter's property tax and job compensation program. Title II called for affected woods and mill employees to receive even more extensive federal benefits and income protection.[63]

Two days later Senate Majority Whip Alan Cranston introduced the administration's bill for a 48,000-acre expansion. This was in part a victory for the club, which has been working for some time to get him to sponsor the Senate bill and to dissuade him from the Park Service's 21,500-acre proposal. The Cranston-administration measure contained only the administration's employment and county compensatory provisions, but Cranston personally endorsed Title II. On August 1 the bill was referred to the Committee on Energy and Natural Resources. With Cranston's support, Senator Abourezk intended to add Title II in committee.[64]

Title II was the brainchild of Burton, chairman of the House Education and Labor Subcommittee and champion of black lung and minimum wage legislation. It was framed in response to the loggers' protests, yet the preservationists and not the unions gave it immediate endorsement.[65] The club's backing of Title II was more than a political expedient. Having moved away from the moderate orientation of earlier preservationists, the group found Burton's proposal ideologically congenial. Occasionally the CIO had supported earlier park efforts, such as the Douglas bill of the 1940s or Dewey Anderson's redwood national park proposal of the 1950s. At that time both the club and the league had shied away from association with labor.[66] But in the 1960s the club —if not Drury's group—courted organized labor with some success.[67] In the 1970s it intensified the activity. In 1977 the club initiated a major effort to build coalitions with women's groups, inner city people, and labor unions. This effort included the endorsement of labor law reform.[68] Far from the hostility it accorded financial concessions to industry, the club consistently supported Title II.

Lobbyist Linda Billings explained the group's position to bill opponent Oregon Republican Senator Mark Hatfield:

We genuinely believe that there was an equity issue at stake. Our major premise was that since the timber companies are to be paid for their land, then the workers who are currently employed in jobs harvesting and milling timber from that land deserve some compensation and protection also in the event they suffer loss in employment and benefits.[69]

Similarly, in accusing the multinational timber corporations of cut-and-run operations in the West, migration to foreign soil, and abandonment of American jobs, the literature of these citizen activists resembled that of organized labor.[70] Concerning labor and environmentalists, Billings commented, "We face a common enemy—industry."[71] Labor's redwood lobbyist agreed with this summation, yet when the club approached representatives of organized labor hoping to gain their support for Title II, labor held back from alliance with the environmentalists.[72]

In orchestrating support for Title II, however, the club did find many allies among the nation's preservationist groups. A few, most notably the league, did not endorse Title II, but Brower's FOE had for several years actively sympathized with the cause of organized labor and immediately backed Title II. So also did the National Audubon Society, American Rivers Conservation Council, Defenders of Wildlife, Natural Resources Defense Council, Environmental Defense Fund, Environmental Action, The Wilderness Society, Conservation Foundation, and the Environmental Policy Center.[73]

Sierra Club leaders deemed Title II necessary to ease immediate problems of transition, but they saw the administration's employment replacement program as ultimately "the best solution to the problem of job loss due to expansion."[74] The Cranston bill and Burton's Title I guaranteed opportunities for displaced workers through public works projects, economic diversification programs, and Economic Development Administration plans. In assisting Humboldt County, the bills evoked all existing federal and state employment programs and directed the secretaries of Labor, Commerce, and Interior to devise new means for providing jobs to those affected by the park's expansion. In addition, the administration's plan guaranteed affected woods and mill workers preference in hiring for jobs in the rehabilitation, protection, and improvement of the Redwood Creek watershed—for which another $12 million, later $33 million, was provided.

The cooperative efforts of the White House, Interior, Cranston, and Burton produced these unemployment compensation provisions, but the philosophy behind the rehabilitation program also had origins in northern California itself and in the preservation movement. One of the first to suggest federal funding for employment of displaced loggers in reforestation, stream clearance, and reconstruction was Rudolf Becking, a Humboldt County forestry consultant, in a 1975 report commissioned by the National Park Service.[75] Two years later the Center for Education and Manpower Resources of Ukiah in Mendocino County issued a study—financed in part and distributed by the Sierra Club—based upon the premise that native materials and hand tools could be made to generate local jobs in watershed reconstruction. The author, Mēca Wawona, was a former resource management major at the University of California, Santa Cruz, who had left school in 1972 to homestead near the Ukiah Valley and had for several years advocated "a return to people power resource production." Her report detailed how, using "old skills" and new ones, hand tools and scientific techniques, ex-loggers could build check dams, waterbreaks, and water ladders in Redwood Creek—"And what delightful work!"[76] Like Milton Lott's fictional buffalo hunter in *The Last Hunt*, who supported his last days gathering the huge animals' bones on the empty prairie, displaced loggers were to find employment erecting small dams out of local materials and planting trees on the bare slopes of Redwood Creek.

Unlike the Becking study, Wawona's plan was completed on the eve of the introduction of Burton's and Cranston's bills and thus contributed little more than refinements to the actual legislation. The study underscores, however, how very congenial the administration's approach was to many citizen activists. Although the club and the Emerald Creek Committee were the only groups directly involved with the Ukiah study, most of the nation's preservation organizations endorsed its legislative embodiment, including the league. After all, the administration's pro-

gram incorporated a philosophy that many in the club and Friends of
the Earth especially had been interested in since the 1960s. Labor intensive reconstruction of the environment provided an answer to the
seeming incompatibility of environmental protection and economic
survival, to the charges of elitism, and to the antagonism of the labor
lobbies.[77]

If Burton and Cranston were bidding for labor's support, they began
with no such concessions to industry—much to the club's pleasure.[78]
Both Burton's amended legislation and the Cranston-administration
bill authorized the secretary of the Interior, upon finding state regulation inadequate to protect the national park, to regulate logging,
rehabilitation, and management practices on nonfederal lands in the
upper Redwood Creek drainage, a provision the department advocated
as essential for protection of the park.[79] The bills also authorized any
citizen group to sue the secretary of the Interior for alleged failure to
protect the park and gave the courts discretion to award such activists
litigation costs, including attorney and expert witness fees—a boon the
club sought in many suits. In addition to the prospect of federal regulation at the behest of citizen activists, Burton's bill presented the lumbermen with the possibility that upon its passage, all downed timber—that
is, logs cut but not yet removed—in the region of park expansion would
become the property of the United States, to be resold to the companies
only at the discretion of the secretary of the Interior. This could deny
timbermen access to logs that would keep the mills running in the
months of transition following park expansion.

In another swipe at the industry, Burton's and Cranston's bills proposed that adjudication of the purchase price of the park lands be in the
district court rather than, as with the 1968 settlements, in the U.S. Court
of Claims. In 1968 the club had preferred the latter, thinking eastern
judges would be more sympathetic than western juries. By 1977 the
club, the league, Burton, and the Carter Administration were convinced that the Washington, D.C., court had awarded the industry
compensation far in excess of equity. The club still worried about the
adverse affect of localism and hoped to avoid state courts, but it tended
to agree with the administration and Burton that a jury in the district
court of San Francisco might render a better decision than had the
Court of Claims.[80] In contrast to the first park bill, Interior was also to
be provided with $5 million from the Land and Water Conservation
Fund for initiation and defense of claims proceeding from the act and
for development of expert testimony and professional services otherwise
not available to the Department of Justice.

After introducing his new bill, Burton substituted its text—48,000
acres, Title II, revised adjudication procedures, and all—for that of his

original bill and introduced it into deliberations of the House Interior
and Insular Affairs Committee. Not surprisingly, the five-hour mark-up
session that followed disclosed opposition to the unprecedented provisions—federal regulation of private forestry and employment compensation. Several of the committee's Republican members objected to the
cost of Title II, its introduction subsequent to the committee's hearings,
and the absence of testimony from the White House. (For fiscal reasons,
the administration did not support Title II.) The Republicans on the
subcommittee were, however, relatively inactive during the mark-up
session, and rather than exploit the controversial items, committee
member and leader of the opposition Don Clausen helped Burton fend
off conservative hostility to Title II. Should the bill pass, Clausen
wanted maximum protection for his constituents.[81]

Representative Lloyd Meeds, a Democrat from the timber industry's
stronghold of Washington State—where the Simpson Timber Company
was headquartered—introduced an amendment to remove federal
regulation of private forestry from the bill.[82] Several congressmen noted
that the state of California had submitted a statement that state regulation already provided sufficient park protection. Proponents of the bill
had not encouraged state officials to testify at the committee hearings.
Although the Brown Administration supported park expansion, the
Resource agencies and state foresters would have claimed damage to
the park had already been done and California regulation would prevent further deterioration. Such testimony might have persuaded some
members that federal regulation and acquisition were unnecessary.
However, the committee's Democrats outnumbered the Republicans,
32 to 14, and the former defeated Meed's amendment. In early August,
as a result of the efforts of chairmen Udall and Burton, the committee
recommended by a strongly Democratic vote of 38 to 8 that the bill be
passed with its controversial provisions intact.[83]

The dissenting Republicans issued a statement denouncing the
measure as "the most expensive park bill ever sent to the House" and
had it referred to the Appropriations Committee, where they hoped the
price tag of some half a billion would at least bring a delay. But on
September 23 the committee issued a report without recommendations.
It noted the bill's high cost and discussed problems associated with
legislative taking but did not oppose the measure and emphasized the
necessity of prompt action in defense of the park.[84] Signs looked good
for early passage in the House.

The timber companies began to shift their tactics. Initially confident
of defeating the park effort, they had waged all-out battle. Now they
began to consider terms. Pleased with the Court of Claims's awards,
they lobbied against the attempt to get adjudication changed to the

district court.[85] They also told the press that the government should offer an equivalent amount of national forest land, as it had in 1968 with the Redwood Purchase Unit.[86] Even before the bill was out of the Interior Committee, they began pushing for an amendment to increase the allowable cut on the Six Rivers National Forest in Del Norte County.[87]

Similarly convinced it could not block the park bill, labor was also considering terms. The Carpenters' Union was not totally pleased with the House Committee's measure. Despite Burton's generally pro-labor position, he had not consulted with the union about the labor provisions of his bill. Organized labor was not at all impressed with Carter's provisions in Title I and felt that even Title II's provisions were inadequate. The union feared that the wording of Title II was too broad and would not hold up if challenged in the courts.

A telephone call from a staff member in liberal Democrat and House Speaker Tip O'Neill's office advised the Carpenters' Union that the measure might well reach the floor shortly. The union contacted George Meany. Believing the bill would pass should it reach the floor, Meany personally called O'Neill to ask for a postponement. This was an unusual step with minor legislation, but the Speaker was obliging.[88]

On October 7 O'Neill told the press that the Burton bill would not make it to the floor during that session. O'Neill had had little trouble getting Democrats Dick Bolling and B. F. Sisk of California, both of the Rules Committee and neither an admirer of Burton, to table the bill, blocking action until the following year.[89] Fearing postponement could cost the bill, the club pressured the Speaker, to no avail. Thus O'Neill had given the AFL-CIO six months to arrange a compromise with Burton.[90]

One week after O'Neill's announcement, the Senate Energy and Resources Committee held a three-hour mark-up session on the Cranston bill. It passed an amendment by Senator Abourezk to increase the appropriation for rehabilitation from $12 to $33 million. But his amendment to add Title II was tabled by a vote of 10 to 8, despite Cranston's support. Of the 11 Democrats generally favorable to labor, two voted against the amendment to add Title II to the bill. Jay Power, legislative advocate for the Carpenters' Union, had thought he had the votes of all of these Democrats and failed to contact the members. After this loss in committee, he did not press for amendment from the floor, fearing defeat by fiscal conservatives. Instead, he concentrated on the House bill.[91]

The timbermen had been more successful than labor in the Senate committee. Facing 11 Democrats and 7 Republicans, Cranston and Abourezk bid for support with amendments favorable to the industry and drawn up in consultation with Republican Clifford Hansen of Wyoming. One was a key amendment proposed by Washington's Senator Henry Jackson. As introduced into the committee, the Cranston bill authorized Interior to establish regulatory zones on nonfederal lands in the upper Redwood Creek drainage. The provision had been the administration's answer to the club and Burton's 74,000-acre proposal. Because of intense opposition to any precedents in federal regulation voiced by Republican committee members Hansen, James McClure, and Dewey Bartlett—and no doubt expressed to Jackson by timber interests in his home state—the committee deleted stand-by regulatory authority and substituted authorization for Interior to acquire if necessary lands within the upper-protection zone. The committee report explained that the "regulatory concept" was a new approach to national park protection, and the problems of Redwood National Park were "too urgent to place reliance on such a new concept."[92] Still, through the 1970s, the redwood companies had consistently maintained that they would either cut their trees or the government must pay them compensation. In fact, since the 1940s the entire industry had fought periodic threats of federal regulation of private forestry by the U.S. Forest Service. It did not intend to accept from Interior what it had successfully denied Agriculture, and the position of almost every congressman from the Pacific Northwest, Democrat or Republican, reflected this determination.[93]

Both the National Parks and Conservation Association and the Sierra Club had lobbied hard for federal regulation, hoping to use it as precedent in the defense of other national parks. They staunchly defended the provision's constitutionality, citing precedents under the property and commercial clauses of the Constitution. The National Parks and Conservation Association was sorely disappointed by Cranston's capitulation, but the club felt the amended bill still offered sound protection for the redwoods and the possibility of eventual acquisition of the entire 74,000 acres.[94]

In addition to dropping federal regulation, the Senate committee deleted downed timber from legislative taking and dropped the $5 million government defense fund, changes the club did not support. Out of deference to the Republican minority, the committee also removed, as the House committee had with Burton's bill, the provisions authorizing citizen group suits and financial compensation, a concession the club fought to reverse without success. In fact, the loss was of limited harm to the organization. In the absence of explicit legislation, the club had already won standing to sue in the courts. Moreover, the committee inserted into its report a statement saying the right of citizens to sue the government had been established.[95]

Despite these compromises, the timber companies were not entirely happy with the Cranston bill as it was reported out of committee. If they regarded the provision authorizing stand-by acquisition as preferable to stand-by regulation in the upper drainage, the companies—and committee Republicans James McClure and Dewey Bartlett—still considered the former excessive federal interference with private property. Moreover, since the expanded park would come between Highway 101 and their timberlands in the upper watershed, they had wanted all roads excluded from park acquisition. Cranston and Abourezk did not agree to this, although the amended bill offered the companies guaranteed access over all park roads. Last, and far from the least of the industry's objections, the committee did not change the bill's authorization of adjudication in the district court. Yet Cranston and his allies had been successful in meeting some of the industry's objections, and this was reflected in the committee's vote of 15 to 2 in favor of passage—with four conservative Republicans voting yes.[96]

The Senate bill was then given a fifteen-day sequestial referral to the Appropriations Committee, one week before the November 4 deadline for congressional action on all but conference reports. At the request of Cranston and in response to pressure from fourteen of the nation's leading citizen groups,[97] Majority Leader and chairman of the Interior Appropriations Subcommittee, Robert Byrd, prompted committee action on November 2. The committee's report carried no recommendation. It explained that the bill would seriously disrupt the normal spending priorities of the Land and Water Conservation Fund and commit the government to obligations over which it would have no control, but the report added that the need to protect the redwoods overrode these issues.[98] The measure was ready to go to the Senate for a vote. To the club's dismay, however, the strenuous opposition of California's Senator S. I. Hayakawa together with the limited time available precluded consideration of the bill for the rest of the year.

As forces worked behind the scenes preparing for the Senate and House votes, preservationist eyes were upon California, where sediment loads continued to threaten Redwood Creek through the winter and Sacramento offered the only hope for preventing the loss of several hundred more acres of virgin redwoods before Congress could next act.[99] Having changed its character with the infusion of Brown appointees and responding to the 1976 cooperative agreements, the State Board of Forestry had the previous spring rejected three of the more environmentally harmful harvesting plans scheduled for Redwood Creek. Arcata and Louisiana-Pacific had promptly brought suit to test the new State Forest Practices Act and the California Environmental Quality Act under which the board acted. In September, 1977, the

California Superior Court upheld the board's authority to reject logging plans on strictly environmental grounds and in fact ruled that the board must consider environmental protection.[100]

Armed with this decision and bolstered by the seeming proximity of congressional action, the California board had voted in October to postpone until November approval of all harvest plans downstream from the Tall Trees and within the proposed area of park expansion. So now, with Meany holding up the House vote and the calendar blocking Senate action, environmentalists again looked to Sacramento for help. There on November 8 and again in January, under pressure from both the state's Resource secretary and Interior, the board extended the logging moratorium.[101] The state's position had not fundamentally changed; the board's reservations were temporary only and made without prejudice. Nor would the state go beyond regulation. Despite overtures from Interior and indignant speeches in Congress, the California Resource agencies repeatedly made it clear that any assistance the state might offer in the rehabilitation of either Redwood Creek or the local economies would be advisory only. They maintained the problems of the redwood region—its resources and its people—were the financial and legal responsibility of the federal government.[102] And yet the state had saved the day with its moratorium. Even the weather cooperated; the winter passed an uneventful second year of drought. The Tall Trees stood. Although vandals slashed trees in Humboldt Redwoods State Park, chainsaws did not break the quiet of Redwood Creek.[103]

On January 31, 1978, the Senate took up the Cranston bill. Senator Hayakawa led the opposition, vocally supported by Republicans Curtis, Stevens, McClure, and Laxalt. Democrats Abourezk, Cranston, and Bentsen spoke in favor of the bill. However, Abourezk did not introduce Title II as an amendment. He and Jay Power of the Carpenters' Union calculated that the bill would go to a conference committee, providing an atmosphere more congenial than the Senate floor. Hayakawa offered the only amendment, to restore adjudication to the U.S. Court of Claims. Defeated by a strongly Democratic vote of 36 to 57, this was the only challenge to the bill. The measure passed 74 to 20. Of the yes votes, 57 were Democratic. Only one Democrat, Senator Allen from Alabama, voted against the bill.[104]

Meanwhile organized labor had been working with Burton. Not only had he initiated Title II without union input, but he had also tried to get other unions to pressure the Carpenters' Union into accepting it. But once Meany had intervened, Burton cooperated enthusiastically. He assigned Nat Weinberg, formerly with the United Auto Workers, to reframe Title II. Acting as consultant to the House subcommittee, Weinberg worked closely with Burton and Alfred Lasley, secretary of northern California's Local 2592 of the Carpenters' Union. During fall and winter the three reframed Title II's provisions to bring them into accord with the Union's collective bargaining agreements with the industry.[105] The new and essentially unprecedented Title II directed the government to pay full salary, layoff, vacation, and pension benefits to woods and mill employees with over five years' creditable service who were dismissed as a result of the bill. The Department of Labor was to determine who was eligible but was instructed to give the broadest possible interpretation of the park's impact. Payments were to be made until an employee either accepted severance payment or for a period equal to the employee's seniority, not to exceed six years.

For hundreds of loggers this would mean full pay and benefits for six years. The government was further to provide allowances for retraining, job search, and relocation. Once more, Burton framed the bill to make these benefits an entitlement, removing the unions from the necessity of going back to Congress for an appropriation each year. Labor's benefits would total over $40 million.

As the bill passed the Senate, O'Neill publicly divulged he "had never seen a redwood" and complained of being bombarded with criticism from the press and with mail, much of it club-inspired, urging him to move the House version.[106] Under attack for possible links with the Korean influence-buying scandal and not making public his income tax returns, he had little desire for more adverse publicity. Moreover, Burton threatened to delay action on the Carter bill to create the Chattahoochee Rivers National Recreation Area in Georgia.[107] In early February the Rules Committee released the measure onto the floor, and the Speaker endorsed it. Although this may have been in part a response to public pressure, it also signalled consensus among the various protagonists.

The unions believed they lacked the power to defeat park enlargement. Environmental legislation was one of the few situations in which many northern, liberal Democrats might abandon organized labor. This fact, the beneficence of Title II, and nagging doubts as to the future of jobs even without the park combined to induce the Carpenters' Union to support Burton's bill. Jay Power felt confident that a conference committee would support Title II and looked forward to House passage of the Burton bill.[108] The timber companies maintained public opposition, but they too were convinced the bill would pass and were eager to compromise.

When the bill came onto the House floor on February 9, it contained a number of provisions not to the liking of the industry.[109] Having threatened the companies, however, Burton now offered a series of amendments to court them. He removed federal regulation of private forestry from the measure. Instead, as in the Senate measure, Interior was given discretionary authority to acquire lands as needed in the upper drainage zone. Burton further proposed to guarantee the companies the right to remove all trees cut after December, 1974, and before February, 1978. Although this provision placed upon Interior the burden of policing removal to protect second growth, the department supported it as a means of lessening the price of acquisition and avoiding the disagreements downed timber had caused following the 1968 act.[110] Burton also offered an amendment guaranteeing the companies continued use of all park roads. This provision did much to placate the timbermen. It also lessened the cost of park expansion, as the lumbermen would have added expenses incurred for access to severance damages.[111] These changes were concessions the Senate had already offered the companies.

Burton, however, offered two more. The secretary of Agriculture was to transmit to Congress a study of timber harvest schedule alternatives for the Six Rivers National Forest. Simpson and Louisiana-Pacific as well as the Carpenters' Union had been agitating for this since the previous fall. They hoped to persuade the Forest Service to increase the allowable cut on this Del Norte County national forest. Burton's final amendment assigned adjudication to the Court of Claims, thereby removing what he termed "the last obstacle to the assurance of the passage of the bill."[112]

The club and its allies wanted settlement in the district court as well as strong restraints on industrial use of park roads and on removal of downed timber.[113] To the union's anger, the club lobbied against increasing the cut on Six Rivers because it would "foreclose options for designating these areas as wilderness."[114] Through the winter the organization had fought to convince Burton that the cause of park expansion was strong enough to render unnecessary the concessions to industry he was contemplating.[115] But by February the citizen groups were ready to accept Burton's amendments with an assurance written into the legislative history that changes in the Six Rivers harvest schedule be consistent with multiple-use and sustained-yield principles.[116]

On February 9 Burton's bill came up for a vote. By the House doors stood labor's Jay Power; Jim O'Hara, the industry's spokesman; and club advocate Linda Billings. As the legislators filed onto the floor, all three urged a yes vote. More than one representative returned to see if he had heard correctly.[117] It was a strange political marriage, one that testified to Burton's political skill. There was little discussion on the floor. Evidently fiscal conservatives failed to realize in time that Title II was an entitlement. O'Hara had no desire to call Republican attention to Title II, lest the unions oppose the companies' benefits.

If the interest groups were placated, the White House was not. All winter the administration had tried to establish—with a united front of Interior, Commerce, and Labor—that its proposals together with the economic stimulus of the park itself were sufficient to offset the effects of expansion on employment. As the House prepared to vote, the Office of Management and Budget notified Congress that it considered Title II too costly and unnecessary. Carter's opposition, however, was ineffective. The bill passed by a heavily Democratic vote of 328 to 60.[118]

The Senate insisted upon its provisions and requested a conference. Since the conferees were selected either directly or in effect by committee chairmen Burton and Abourezk, it is not surprising that the conference committee was dominated by pro-park, pro-labor Democrats. Minority members such as Hansen settled for minor concessions.[119]

The park was increased by 48,000 acres, and an upstream protection zone of 30,000 acres was established within which Interior could acquire lands if necessary. All of the concessions to industry remained, except that adjudication reverted to the district court as the Carter Administration wanted. The House conferees agreed to the Senate's larger $33 million for rehabilitation of Redwood Creek, and the Senate conferees conceded Title II. Congress passed the conference bill by wide margins.[120]

Despite opposition from the Office of Management and Budget, on March 27 at the urging of Secretary Andrus, President Carter signed the act enlarging the Redwood National Park.[121] About seventy thousand acres of Redwood Creek drainage now belonged to the federal government. At last 8,990 acres of virgin redwoods became part of the public heritage. The act did not estimate how much it would cost to buy the land. But it is clear Congress anticipated that the purchase price would be at least $359 million, the figure used in earlier versions of the bill.

In addition to being the most costly land acquisition measure ever passed by Congress, the 1978 measure was labor legislation and regional land planning reminiscent of the New Deal. Aid to the North Coast was no doubt essential to passage of the park act, but Title II was not. Both company and union advocates were convinced that with the pro-environmental sentiments of the House and Senate committees and the determination of Burton, they could not defeat park expansion. Title II was as much a result of Burton's championship of labor as it was of expediency.[122]

Enormously pleased with the final bill, the Carpenters' Union advocate called it a "set piece of the principle that whenever the government interferes it must compensate labor." It is a precedent organized labor may apply in future settlements, from federal land reservations to

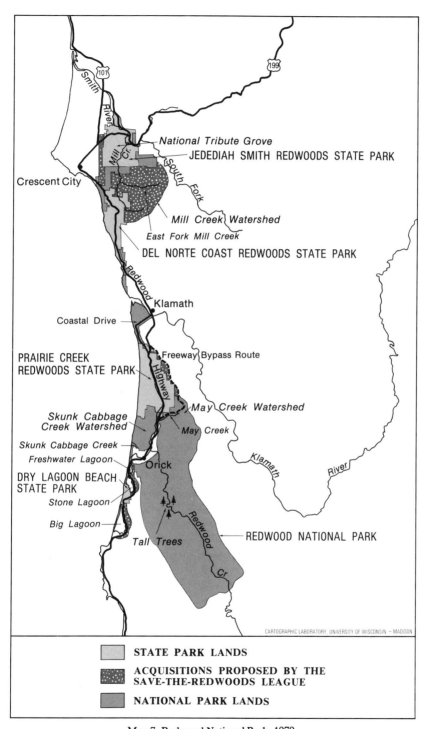

Map 7. Redwood National Park, 1979.

antipollution decisions and technological unemployment.[123] The club will probably support some of these applications, thus strengthening the environmental lobby.[124] The act was a logical outcome of the activists' strength within the liberal and pro-labor wing of the Democratic Party, their ideological drift leftward, and their wish to defuse labor's opposition. The act's passage is evidence that the Sierra Club had become one of the most powerful lobbies on the Hill.

12
No Place to Stand: Saving the Redwoods, 1917–1978

THE PROGRESSIVE years of the early part of this century are unique in the attention they garnered from historians in the 1950s and 1960s. As sons discovering the clay feet of their fathers, these generally liberal historians found the progressives weak in their commitment to social change. Richard Hofstadter compared reformers of the 1900s and 1910s unfavorably with the more realistic and constructive New Dealers. Samuel Hays described such progressive conservationists as Gifford Pinchot as being concerned about the limited issues of efficient resource use rather than the social implications of resource ownership or the corporate structure. Biographers of Theodore Roosevelt and Woodrow Wilson emphasized these presidents' failures to move against the industrial trusts of the period, describing them as conservative progressives. Gabriel Kolko and other historians of the New Left labelled progressivism the conservative triumph over nascent radicalism. More recently, Alfred Runte noted that early park advocates saved only lands that were economically "worthless."[1] Activists in the 1960s similarly set themselves against many established reformers, some of whom had been active since the early decades of the century.

Despite obvious continuities of goals, methods, and even individuals, discontinuity has in fact characterized the twentieth-century environmental conservation movement. Strong if generally moderate from the 1890s into the 1920s, citizen activism was relatively quiet during the 1930s and 1940s. Then in the mid-1950s the anger and influence of participants burst forth, to flourish in the 1960s. As the movement became less evangelical in the subsequent decade, militants channeled their hostility toward developers and industrialists into environmental litigation and legislative advocacy. The 1950s, then, divide recent environmental militancy from the older, optimistic reformism of the early park movement.

Although those who established and led the league in the 1910s and 1920s were capable of vigorous action to save what they regarded as the best of nature's wonders, theirs was a typically moderate early twentieth-century reform effort.[2] The politics of the league's leaders can be defined succinctly: balancing their desire to save redwoods was a strong respect for the rights of private property and the needs of industry, an aversion to disruptive social action, a distrust of concentrations of power, and a strict attention to the means as well as the goals of reform. They established four redwood state parks but in doing so tried to avoid the use of economic boycott, eminent domain, and publicity adverse to the timbermen. Out of necessity and conviction, they turned to state and private reform. Like most reformers from the progressive years who survived into the 1930s, they opposed the New Deal.

An ally of the league, the Sierra Club showed a similar moderation. The organization's 1892 bylaws announced among its purposes to "render accessible the mountain regions of the Pacific Coast," and from the 1890s through World War II, its members proposed roads into Yosemite and across all the highest passes of the Sierra Nevada. The club waged a national battle to prevent the conversion of Hetch Hetchy Valley in Yosemite National Park into a reservoir; however, it was only with difficulty that John Muir had enlisted a club majority behind him in this battle. According to Donald Fleming, the early club was a "highly imperfect instrument for propagating" the wilderness ideal, "for by no means all the club's members were singlemindedly committed to wilderness values."[3] Despite this major controversy, the organization for the most part restricted its efforts to protecting areas already in public ownership. Since there was minimal economic pressure on the Sierra Nevada before World War II, this defense only occasionally brought the club into conflict with resource users. During the interwar years especially, the group was only moderately active in conservation and opted for accommodation rather than confrontation with resource users. Yet by the 1960s the club was a leader in the national wave of protest. This metamorphosis was rooted in mid-century environmental, social, and scientific changes.

No decade in American history had sustained rates of urbanization, population growth, and resource consumption equal to those of the 1950s. Inroads into the wildernesses of the Far West were significant enough to constitute the closing of a latter-day frontier. The pioneers had passed lightly over the mountains and forests of the West, but postwar extractive industries spared little from the Cascade Mountains to the coastal redwoods. Political conservatism allowed massive deterioration of the nation's landscapes to go unchecked. Suddenly realizing the extent of the destruction, in the mid 1950s such wilderness advocates as David Brower turned militant. During the Kennedy and Johnson years, he and his allies found Washington's political atmosphere relatively congenial.

Between 1964 and 1970 club membership grew at the average rate of 25.6 percent a year, as concern for the land merged with the larger context of social protest and opposition to the war in Vietnam. Young, white activists deposed from the increasingly complex civil rights movement by black power launched their own "revolution" and sensed an affinity between international peace and peace with the land. Most of those who joined the club in the 1960s—as well as the 1970s—were highly educated, young and middle-aged urban professionals or semi-professionals, the same people who had been consistently drawn to the organization since its founding in the 1890s.[4]

Yet neither the club nor the league had been militant during the early decades of the century or the interwar years. Historian Robert Wiebe has written that progressives were imbued with "bureaucratic thought."[5] This was true of early park reformers. They were not, as Samuel Hays has suggested, reactionaries who opposed rational land planning or saw conservation as an antidote to urbanization and industrialization.[6] Despite their romanticism, those in the early league and club were in the mainstream of western science. They saw parks as a way of improving the future, not restoring the past. They were geologists, paleontologists, geneticists, landscape architects, as well as successful businessmen, lawyers, and other professionals. They were members of what Wiebe has called the "new middle class."[7] They fought for efficient, centralized, professional land planning and management.

Nevertheless, those in the league and the club, as most early reformers, still lived in an essentially entrepreneurial world. Non-academic professionals were independently employed within their local business communities. The institutions of higher learning and research supplying the scientists and professionals vital to the preservation effort were small, lacked strong tenure protection, and depended upon philanthropy. Moreover, reform depended upon charity; Stephen Mather's use of private wealth to establish the national park system shows that not even government offered economic independence before the 1930s. The lawyers, scientists, and academics who spearheaded public resource planning were neither economically independent nor socially isolated from their local business communities, which themselves contributed heavily to early reform. This interaction with the world of commerce helped limit their reformism, even into the 1930s.

In contrast, by the 1960s and 1970s businessmen played little role in the club, and the professionals and semiprofessionals who constituted its strength were largely salaried employees, most notably in the public and nonprofit corporate sectors. These institutions separated them socially and economically from both corporate and especially independent businessmen, which may help explain why these professionals and semiprofessionals were willing to demand strong federal curbs on industrial prerogatives and to agitate for strict limitations on the discretion of federal agencies working with developers. Quite different was the Save-the-Redwoods League, the closed and aging governance of which sealed it against change. While the league still sought accommodation with the timbermen, Sierra Club publicity set the people against private interests, a stance it translated into environmental litigation in the following decade. The club no longer identified with business and the Republican Party, as had most earlier park advocates, but now generally received political support from the liberal and pro-labor wing of the Democratic Party and, in the 1970s, proved ideologically receptive to pragmatic alliance with organized labor. The bureaucratization of professionals as well as the economic strength of government and institutions of higher learning in the 1960s enabled activists in the club to respond to environmental depreciation less as producers than as consumers.

Scientists have always been pivotal in the environmental preservation movement. But their changing perceptions of the natural world have reinforced the historical discontinuities of the movement. In the twentieth century the theory of evolution passed through three stages. Between 1890 and 1930 most scientists questioned whether or not natural selection was the controlling force in evolution and assumed that changes in natural history tended to be directional. During the 1930s and 1940s, mathematical genetics and studies of natural populations established a new model based upon a synthesis of opportunistic natural selection and random genetic change. For the past thirty years, this chance model of evolution has affected American thought and culture, much as directional theories shaped earlier perspectives.

The popularity of the latter before 1930 was due in part to the influence of Christianity and nineteenth-century notions of progress. Such is particularly evident in the writings of such turn-of-the-century dualists as geologist and club leader Joseph LeConte, who reconciled religion and evolution by making the latter a divine plan for the material order. By 1910 such overtly vitalistic or theological interpretations were in scientific disrepute, yet directional assumptions persisted. These were most obvious among proponents of mechanical theories of orthogenesis, orthoselection, and orderly mutation—all of which postulated the existence of some chemical force either in the organism itself or the environment that accounted for the progressive momentum of natural history. In addition to the inability of many early twentieth-century scientists to accept the idea that such complex beings as ourselves had emerged by chance, the state of the sciences themselves encouraged the prevalence of perfectionist theories.

Early paleontologists ordered their meager fossils with what appeared to them the most modern organisms at the top and the seemingly more primitive at the bottom, drawing a straight, often causal, link between them. The parallel development of characteristics in different environments, the supposed law of the "irreversibility" of evolution, contemporary underestimates of geologic time, the presence of characteristics without advantage before fully developed, and the existence of neutral or disadvantageous characteristics all seemed to indicate the weakness of Darwin's theory of natural selection and the existence of an orthogenetic force. Without an adequate theory of inheritance, selective adaptation seemed to make for equilibrium; species would appear to drift toward the statistical mean of adaptability rather than producing genetic variation and speciation.

Despite advances made between 1890 and 1910 in analyzing inheritance, geneticists were unable to offer a convincing model of evolution. They favored the theory of evolution by mutation over Darwin's emphasis upon small adaptive changes, generating a schism between geneticists and selectionists that delayed formulation of a widely accepted explanation of the evolutionary mechanism. In this theoretical chaos, directed theories and assumptions flourished and were scientifically respectable. Advocates of perfectionist interpretations were among the most popular scientists of the day. As late as 1934 a founder of the league and exponent of a variant of orthogenesis, Henry Fairfield Osborn, represented the majority of naturalists in his skepticism that selection was the controlling force in evolution. As president of the New York Museum of Natural History, he was also more influential than many geneticists whose work would outlast his. The same could be said of John Merriam—league president and head of the Carnegie Institution from 1919 to World War II.

Whatever their interpretation of the causes of evolution, a large percentage of geneticists, paleontologists, and biologists prior to the 1940s believed that evolution was perfectionist. A number of these scientists were active in the early national and state park movements.

From Merriam, Osborn, and Vernon Kellogg of the league to Muir, LeConte, and David Starr Jordan of the club, these scientists carried the belief that the universe was ordered into their preservationist efforts. They saw parks as a means of preserving the evidence of cosmic design and sought to save the most spectacular results of the culminant processes of evolution—such as the climax forests of the California coastal redwoods.

Most of them were reform Darwinists; they believed that humans could realize greater physical and social progress through social cooperation than through survival of the fittest. Such cooperation was to range from advances in eugenics to the establishment of scientifically managed public parks. Yet their faith in directional evolution indicates an essentially deterministic perspective. Scientific evidence of the inevitability of progress helped limit their advocacy of reform, prevented them from denying human control over the natural world, and affected their definition of parks. Orthogenesis, orthoselection, and other such explanations and assumptions presumed that nature produced ever more complicated, powerful, and adaptive creatures and that man's brain was the summit of this process. Technology, then, was not a violation of nature but a fulfillment of natural history.

In the 1930s and 1940s, scientific evidence against theories and assumptions of directional evolution grew, and by 1950 they had been discredited. As more fossils were classified, each case of supposedly straight-line phylogenetic development grew more complex. Evidence verified that genetic changes were random. As the known range of geologic time was pushed backward from 100 million years in 1920 to 7,500 million in the 1950s, explanations of meandering development became increasingly palatable. Paleontologists reached a point where they could explain evolution as a process, each step of which had been immediately advantageous to the species involved.

The demise of directional assumptions in the United States and England was, however, more than a matter of the specific disproof of proponents' arguments. Between 1930 and 1950 advances in the natural sciences, especially mathematical genetics, enabled scientists to overcome the communications gap and hostility that had divided geneticists and selectionists. With a better understanding of genetic materials and the significance of population size and structure, evolutionists developed a convincing synthesis that refined and merged Darwin's theory of natural selection and Mendelian inheritance.

The affinity between this mid-century evolutionary model and the modern ecological perspective is obvious. Indeed, according to one philosopher of science, "Ecology is the study of short-term evolution."[8] The evolutionary synthesis served to do three things: it removed from scientific respectability assumptions of cosmic order and progress, redefined man's place in natural history, and underscored a rethinking of goals within the wilderness and park movements.

Historian Donald Fleming noted that the "New Conservation" would have been incompleted without "an alternative schema of history portraying the doctrine of progress itself as . . . a fundamentally mistaken attitude toward life."[9] By merging theories of random genetic drift and opportunistic natural selection, the mid-century synthesis supplied such a chance model of change. In the 1950s leading geneticists attacked finalistic interpretations as empirically and methodologically untenable. Garrett Hardin, René Dubos, Marston Bates, Loren Eiseley, and others carried philosophical naturalism into the environmental movement of the 1950s and 1960s. Most of the postwar college-educated professionals and semiprofessionals who now joined the Sierra Club understood what Hardin and Dubos meant when they called evolution "unconscious." In 1959 Hardin asked rhetorically if the concept of progress was in any way relevant to natural science. No, he answered, the evolutionary process consists of shifts from one cybernetic system to another and cannot "be said to involve direction at all." Nor can the fitness of a species be judged superior in any absolute sense. Julian Huxley wrote that selection "does not ensure progress, or maximum advantage, or any other ideal state of affairs."[10]

Many early park advocates had believed that the evolutionary sciences would supply not only descriptions of the natural order but ultimate answers as to purpose. By the 1960s teleological assurances had been undercut, and many who joined the environmental movement found science unable to contribute to the definition of goals. Indeed, as Leo Marx stated, "By the late 1960s . . . a large audience was prepared to accept the neo-romantic critique of science at the core of the dissident counterculture"—the latter including the more militant exponents of "ecotactics."[11]

Denunciations of science were not, of course, unique to the 1960s. What was new was its condemnation combined with its use. Many modern environmentalists were themselves scientists. They used empirical data in their battles and defined goals in ecological terms. Their disillusionment with science was due to its historical association with teleological assumptions and technology. But the denunciation was also a result of the self-defined epistemological limits of the postwar natural sciences, with their proponents' emphasis upon objectivity and a disinclination to define goals or values.

Such images as "the cosmic prison" and "spaceship earth" reveal the affinity between the naturalism inherent in the modern view of evolution and the ecological perspective. Many environmentalists believed the world was not only man's physical prison but his spiritual one. The Sierra Club's increased militancy represented rejection of a universe of spiritual infinity and expanding material possibilities. The teleological world view of LeConte and Merriam had demanded transcendence of the natural order to grasp greater intelligence and purpose. Scientists had abandoned this vision; in the absence of escape, empirical evidence supported only the belief that randomness characterized the universe.

Biology revealed interdependence, specialization, and adaptation but allowed for no judgment as to direction or superiority of species. Man was a genetic accident. In the face of overpopulation, random mutation was translated into man seen as a spore, a weed, a cancer, a disease of nature. Condemning the construction of freeways in 1959, David Brower quoted the physicist J. A. Rush in saying that when he obliterates wilderness, man repudiates the evolutionary force itself and then "in a deeply terrifying sense" is on his own.[12]

The controlling concept in the modern view of both evolution and ecology is the interrelatedness of all species and the environment. This interrelatedness presumes an ontological equality—that is, men are not better than trees. In a survey by the Resources for the Future in 1978, 83 percent of the club members disagreed with the statement that "plants and animals exist primarily for man's use."[13] In the late 1960s and early 1970s, the club went to the United States Supreme Court to establish the principle that elements of the natural world had the right to stand before the courts without reference to interests of human claimants. The theoretical denial of man's place at the apex of evolution complemented the practical findings of such individuals as Aldo Leopold and Rachel Carson that manipulation of nature can have unanticipated consequences.[14]

The mid-century evolutionary synthesis also contributed to a shift in the definition of wilderness itself. Earlier wilderness advocates emphasized the preservation of spectacular examples of natural processes. Men such as Merriam were confident that they could decide what were the highest and most useful manifestations of natural history. Like those in the natural sciences who influenced their thinking, modern environmentalists have been less willing to make such judgments.

For them the essence of wilderness became process and diversity, the interaction of all natural elements. This shift of attention from the accident to the essence of nature had specific manifestations. Although recent attention to the Tall Trees shows "monumentalism" has not entirely lost its appeal,[15] environmentalists have generally moved away from a preoccupation with great sweeping evidences of evolutionary and geologic forces that so intrigued the first generations after Darwin.

In the 1960s and 1970s, the club pushed for the preservation of *all* forms
of wildlife as well as representative ecosystems. Wilderness advocates
were now as fascinated by the smaller evidences of diversity and the web
of life. Scientific attention to the redwoods gave way to study of the
Drosophila, or fruit fly. Demands that national parks be restricted to
such splendors as Yosemite and Yellowstone gave way to the campaign
for a prairie grass national park.

Early leaders of such citizen groups as the league, the club, and the
National Parks Association had defended national park standards. Their
purism was a component of a sense of evolution as a culminant rather
than an ongoing process. However, in the 1960s and 1970s, the club and
many other citizen groups were increasingly receptive to the idea that
parks and wilderness areas need not be entirely primitive. At the same
time they were even more adamant than the early purists in arguing that
once a park or wilderness area had been established, its manipulation—
be it for access, insect control, or fire protection—must be minimized if
not eliminated.

The divergence between the older and newer movements became
clear in the schisms of the 1960s. From 1959 through 1969 the club
experienced internal conflict, as generally older leaders objected
to the methods and ideology of militants. The league and the club
similarly became combatants, and this kin-strife nearly prevented
establishment of the Redwood National Park. While the club had
recently incorporated the energies of many young individuals,
especially academics and scientists, the league had not. As a result,
it clung to the methods and goals laid down by its early president
and proponent of directional evolution John Merriam.

The Sierra Club demanded a large wilderness park, a preserve
defined more by its size and the diversity of its landscapes and species
than by either its totally virgin state or the purity and age of its
stands. The organization denounced the league's conciliatory attitude
toward the lumbermen and its small, museumlike parks designed
to save the oldest and densest groves. In denouncing the more moderate
organization, the club was rejecting an image vaguely like an old
photograph of itself.

The club prevailed because of its greater political power and because
its combination of philosophical naturalism and pragmatic confidence
captured the mood of many Americans, especially urban professionals
and semiprofessionals. The growing militancy and popularity of
conservation during the past quarter century has been a result of
awareness of environmental deterioration and its implications as
etched in the chain-of-life studies by scientists from Leopold to
Barry Commoner. This increased strength also resulted from political

and social changes that led some white collar Americans into protest and consumer groups less sympathetic to demands of developmental industries than to the need for clean air, safe water, and open space. The ecological implications of the new evolutionary synthesis both mirrored and reinforced discontent generated by postwar population growth and environmental problems.

If the redwood battles from the 1910s through the 1970s have been preeminently political, they also show the extent to which politics is often rooted in philosophical issues. One suspects few will challenge the idea that an organization and its goals are shaped by the social and economic position of its constituency. But less popular today may be the assertion that one's assumptions about the natural world affect one's politics. Yet ideas do mobilize material forces; this is especially true of environmentalism. First, its participants have been highly educated and articulate. They have acknowledged the influence upon their actions of scientific thought. They have not been a significantly religious people—at least in the sense of measurable allegiance to formal institutions. For them ecology may have become a substitute for traditional religion; certainly it explains origins, function, and even purpose. Second, the character of the redwood battles lends credence to the movement's intellectual component. If sentiment for the preservation of the redwoods—as with Alaska and many other scenic and wild areas—is far stronger in New York or San Francisco than it is in northern California or Alaska, what is the motivating force if not that of an idea?

Lewis Mumford had pointed out that Darwin stood for a "fresh vision of the entire cosmic process."[16] This vision went unappreciated until the past quarter century. Historian Susan Flader suggested that evolution's ecological implications had been lost earlier "in the furor over the very fact of evolution."[17] Added to this was the tendency of early scientists to subscribe to theories and assumptions of directional evolution. Such explanations masked the ecological implications of evolution by superimposing hierarchy and purpose on the natural world. Darwin's vision went unappreciated because western scientists did not fully embrace a random model of evolution until after World War II.

Citizen Activism

If the history of redwood preservation suggests something of the scientific and social forces behind American reform, it also offers insights into the character of citizen activism. Since the turn of the century, citizen groups have emerged as a third force shaping the nation's land-use patterns and balancing government and industry. These organizations tend to fall into three categories—the moderate, evangelical, and consumer advocate. Nature Conservancy, the Audubon Society, the Sempervirens Club, and Conservation Associates, for example, have operated in a manner similar to that of the league. They might well be called the moderates, or perhaps "the conscience of the establishment." In addition to relying upon traditional paternalistic philanthropy, they often prefer state to federal initiative, are shy of popular crusades, and favor accommodation over confrontation.

Strident reformers have occasionally denounced such groups, yet as of 1979 the league was responsible for the preservation of some 150,000 acres of redwoods—in contrast to the 78,000 acres saved by the national park acts of 1968 and 1978. It prevailed through dogged consistency and the ability to function in such periods of ebbing liberalism as the 1950s and the Nixon and Ford administrations. On several occasions in the 1970s, its annual membership growth exceeded that of the club. But the league has also acted as a brake on reform during high tides of liberalism. It defeated New Deal efforts to establish a redwood national park, and through the 1960s it clung to Frederick Law Olmsted's 1927 master plan rather than support the club's more ambitious proposal.

A recent study of American charity concluded that paternalistic philanthropies are on the wane because large-scale, nonreligious giving has declined. The league's private financial support has in fact grown, but its other premises—gradualism, limited goals, accommodation, and state support—have been undercut. Since World War II accelerated resource use has rendered piecemeal reform less adequate to meet either crises or long-range acquisition goals. Tractor clearcutting has caused sufficient erosion to render untenable Olmsted's plan calling for the acquisition of representative flats without the surrounding watersheds. Resource scarcity has made industrial cooperation rare. Because of financial limitations and the hostility of local residents to public land acquisitions, the state has proven less responsive.

Environmental preservation has traditionally involved the imposition of national or regional will over local interests, increasingly so since World War II. Once initiative passes to the federal level, the influence of traditional philanthropies declines, primarily because of the 1954 law barring nonprofit organizations from lobbying. In the 1960s the league was able to sway the Johnson Administration through the personal influence of its officers and its donor, Laurance Rockefeller, but it could not match the club's lobbying in Congress.

Since 1964 the moderate reformer's position has been further undercut by the new conservatism of the Republican Party. The league's leadership has traditionally been Republican, and until 1950 that party gave conservation almost as much support as did the Democratic Party. In the 1960s liberal Republican Thomas Kuchel sponsored the administration's moderate park proposal, but in the 1970s all active support for redwood preservation was Democratic.

If the moderates have suffered from the nation's political and social polarization, the militants may have profited from it. The club incorporated postwar liberalism in part because—in contrast to the league—its members elected the organization's directors and therefore affected policy, making the club responsive to the nation's changing moods and Brower's self-proclaimed "extremism." Unlike the league, the club developed a large, young militant staff and a corps of professional consultants. The two organizations were also shaped by the personalities of their executive directors. In the 1970s Brower could still recall having been deeply moved by Newton Drury's appointment as National Park Service director in 1940. Yet the 1960s pitted the elderly and moderate Drury against the younger, ardent, and mercurial Brower.[18]

The Sierra Club of the 1960s and Brower's Friends of the Earth might be called evangelical citizen groups. They have been characterized by charismatic leadership as well as by effective use of propaganda and moral outrage. The Wilderness Society, the National Parks and Conservation Association, and the Emerald Creek Committee are similar organizations that have participated in the redwood park battles. Supported by membership dues rather than patronage, they can assume positions hostile to industry. Their strength lies in boldness and unwillingness to compromise. However, the weakness of this type of activism is its dependence upon a favorable political climate.

In the 1970s the club's goals remained little changed, but its methods now had much in common with those of Ralph Nader. In fact, the club might be called a consumer protection group. Although continuing to advertise and publish, it relied increasingly upon environmental litigation and lobbying. The loss of tax-deductible status freed it to lobby without legal limitations, and precedents establishing standing to sue opened the courts to citizen suits. The organization's local chapters and volunteer network accounted in large part for its ascendancy to power, and they continued to form the backbone of its political influence in the 1970s. It has also, however, used increasing numbers of professional lobbyists and lawyers as well as ad hoc task forces. In view of the legal and legislative precedents established in the 1960s plus the low level of public activism in the

1970s, it is not surprising that the nation's newer citizen groups have relied heavily upon the courts. Such organizations include the Natural Resources Defense Council, the Planning and Conservation League, and the club's affiliated Legal Defense Fund—all participants in redwood issues.

The club maintained its effectiveness in the 1970s by entrenching itself as a pressure group within the liberal and pro-labor wing of the Democratic Party. Despite the vote removing Brower, the organization did not revert to industrial accommodation. It embraced the notion that wilderness and environmental defense require the imposition of national over local will and advanced federal regulation of forestry and, in the early 1970s, national land planning.

Both in the 1960s and 1970s, militancy proved well suited to a bureaucratic state. The Park Service official Frank Kittredge once explained why to Richard Leonard:

A bureaucrat is held upright by pressure from all sides. The administrator always has to compromise between the ideal and what he has money for or political strength to get. If the timber interests are on one side and you call that black, and if the Sierra Club isn't way over on the white side but instead somewhere in the grey, then the compromise will be part way between the grey and the black instead of between white and black.[19]

In a similar vein, the Izaak Walton League wrote in the 1960s, "Thank God for David Brower; he is so extreme he makes the Izaak Walton League look reasonable."[20] The club's willingness to lobby for legislative restrictions on administration discretion and to sue to enforce these limitations brought success. By adopting techniques long employed by industry, the environmentalists balanced somewhat the pressure of resource users.

There are those who ask if the club would not accomplish more by being reasonable. Such was the assumption of many, especially older moderate reformers. But the American political system does not function simply according to right or wrong. Moderate progressives correctly sensed in the 1930s that federal bureaucratization threatened the influence of private reformers who relied upon what Joel Hildebrand called "moral strength rather than numbers." Judges, congressmen, and federal administrators may distrust "extremism," but they respond to its existence in the spirit of old-fashioned horsetrading.[21]

C. Wright Mills predicted in 1951 that America's professional classes were incapable of genuine opposition to established values and economic interests.[22] At that time the history of the environmental preservation movement supported his contention. Since Mills wrote *White Collar*, however, opposition to technology and industry from environmentally concerned American professionals has stiffened dramatically. Participants still rarely see their cause as a means of inducing broad social reform. In fact, they have been strikingly nonideological. Nevertheless, the conservation movement has grown in strength and militancy. The rise of citizen groups has also made land and resource-use decisions more democratic. Groups dependent upon membership dues and activism have grown faster than traditional philanthropies, further broadening public participation. But it must also be said that the fate of the redwoods indicates that even militancy and popular enthusiasm have been of limited effectiveness in preserving an economically valuable resource.

The Future of the Redwoods

The 1968 and 1978 Redwood National Park acts were the most costly land purchases in American history. They were significant victories for the nation's preservationists. Yet the 1968 act was a compromise for which the government paid an exorbitant price and because of which Congress was forced ten years later to spend millions more, most of that to buy lands cut over in the interim. Moreover, as soon as the second act passed, the timber companies let it be known that the $359 million anticipated by Congress would not cover the cost of lands taken from them, even though the vast majority of the acres would have had no industrial value for decades. It has proven costly to buy the last of a resource controlled by a handful of large corporations. Despite the 1978 act, the park visitor today is still aware of the onslaught of logging trucks and smoke spewn into the sky by the lumber mill in the middle of Redwood Creek basin.

Viewed from its riverbed, lower Redwood Creek presents a striking old-growth forest. But much like the Redwood Highway's scenic screen, the Tall Trees hide a largely denuded watershed. Only about one-fifth of the acreage transferred to the federal government by the two acts holds old-growth redwoods. This is found in the Tall Trees grove, in small patches scattered throughout the main watershed, and on the steep slopes along the tributaries of Devil's Creek, Panther Creek, and Bridge Creek. Over 90 percent of Redwood Creek was logged over or clearcut in the last twenty-five years, and much that is closest to the park in the past decade. Viewed from the valley's ridges, the full impact of these operations is harsh. Environmentalists envision one day a dramatic park extending from Gold Bluffs Beach and the virgin stands of Prairie Creek through the second growth of Redwood Creek and into the upper watershed with its Douglas-fir forest and open meadows. Hikers will walk from fog-shrouded bluffs through deep forest and mixed conifers up into the sunshine. Today,

Figure 20. Prairie Creek Redwoods State Park from Gold Bluffs Beach looking south, July, 1966. Photo by David Swanlund.

however, the park is scarred and vulnerable to erosion, necessitating millions of dollars in rehabilitation work.

The state redwood parks are of higher quality than the national park but small and close to the highways. They are threatened by recreational overuse and eroding watersheds. The Save-the-Redwoods League and the state have purchased the upper Bull Creek drainage and are reforesting its steep slopes. Concrete riprapping along Bull Creek's banks remind those who visit the Rockefeller Forest of the ever-present threat from floods. Del Norte and Prairie Creek state parks are located on more stable watersheds, but upstream operations make the future of Jedediah Smith's Mill Creek Flat more problematic.

About 4 percent of the original almost two million acres of redwoods has been saved. There are about 20,000 acres of virgin forest in the Redwood National Park plus 56,000 acres in state and county parks. This old growth is scattered along California's northern

Figure 21. Del Norte Coast Redwoods State Park and the Redwood National Park looking south, 1966. False Klamath River and False Klamath Cove in foreground. Photo by David Swanlund.

coast from Monterey Bay to Oregon. If gathered together, it would make a square about ten miles to each side. When the logged-over portions of the state and national parks are added to the virgin acreage, the total redwood producing lands that have been preserved represent about 10 percent of the original belt. Second growth will be added to the parks, but little old growth remains to contest.

Between 1917 and 1979 the redwood region moved from a resource-rich frontier to a land facing depression and high unemployment due to resource depletion. This transition paralleled the life of one man. In 1919 the league's founders hired the young progressive Newton Drury to manage the organization. A man of modesty and dedication, he devoted the next sixty years to wilderness and scenic preservation. On the eve of his death in 1979, he was chairman of the league's board and still active in its affairs. That one individual's life can span the disposition of a forest as vast as that of Humboldt and Del Norte counties underscores the urgency of environmental decisions. For the moderate reformers—as for the old redwoods—there is no place to stand.

Reference Matter

NOTES

A KEY to the abbreviations used in the notes appears on pages 321-23.

Chapter 1: Progressives and Scenic Preservation

1 Quotes from John Merriam, "Forest Windows," *Scribners Magazine* 83, no. 6 (June 1928): 733. See also M. Grant to Everett Griggs, 16 September 1919, Save-the-Redwoods League, Files, History Folders (SRL/F/History) [hereafter all repository and collection designations are abbreviated]; Merriam to Childs Frick, 4 August 1917, LC/JM/195.

2 Merriam, "Forest Windows," pp. 733—34.

3 Osborn and M. Grant to Governor William Stephens, 8 August 1917, M. Grant to J. D. Grant, 26 August 1918, SRL/F/History; Merriam to M. Grant, 8 August 1930, 12 August 1932, LC/JM/82; Newton Drury, "Parks and Redwoods: 1919—1971," interview conducted by Amelia Fry and Susan R. Schrepfer (Berkeley: University of California Bancroft Library Regional Oral History Office [hereafter abbreviated ROHO], 1972), p. 106.

4 Quote from Joseph D. Grant, "Twenty Rings in the Redwoods: An Informal History of the Save-the-Redwoods League" (1940), p. 1, manuscript held by the Save-the-Redwoods League [hereafter abbreviated SRL]. Madison Grant, *The Origin and Relationship of the Large Mammals of North America* (New York: New York Zoological Society, 1904); Madison Grant, *The Passing of the Great Race* (New York: Charles Scribner's Sons, 1916, 1917); Frederick Woods, review in *Science* 67, no. 1243 (25 October 1918): 419—20; Merriam to Osborn, 7 February 1906, B/JM/1:1; Merriam to Frick, 22 August 1917, Merriam to M. Grant, 15 September 1917, LC/JM/195.

5 Henry Fairfield Osborn, *The Age of Mammals in Europe, Asia, North America* (New York: Macmillan Company, 1910); *Men of the Old Stone Age: The Earth Speaks to Bryan*; and *Impressions of Great Naturalists* (New York: Charles Scribner's Sons, 1925, 1928).

6 William Gregory, "Dr. Merriam's Contributions to the Development of Vertebrate Paleontology on the Pacific Coast," *The Scientific Monthly* 42,

no. 4 (April 1936): 377—80; Ralph Chaney, "John Campbell Merriam," *American Philosophical Society Yearbook* (1945), pp. 381—87; Chester Stock, "J. C. Merriam as Scientist and Philosopher," *Cooperation in Research* (Washington, D.C.: Carnegie Institution, 1938), pp. 765—78; Merriam, "Asphalt Beds of Rancho La Brea," *Published Papers and Addresses of John Campbell Merriam*, Carnegie Institution of Washington pub. no. 500, (Baltimore: Waverly Press, 1938), 2:848—49.

7 John Merriam, "Statement Concerning Research Work of J. C. Merriam transmitted in reply to University of California Research Board Circular of January 5, 1917," pp. 1—2, LC/JM/197; Ralph Chaney to R. M. Field, 5 January 1931, LC/JM/40.

8 Merriam, "Ultimate Values of Science" and "Science and Human Values," *Published Papers*, 4:2104—24.

9 George Sudworth, *Forest Trees of the Pacific Slope* (Washington, D.C.: GPO, 1908), p. 146; Ralph Chaney, *Redwoods of the Past*, rev. ed. (San Francisco: SRL, 1965), p. 1.

10 Quote from John Merriam, *A Living Link in History*, rev. ed. (San Francisco: SRL, 1968), pp. 5—6. See also M. Grant to Merriam, 30 May 1928, LC/JM/82.

11 Quotes from Henry Fairfield Osborn, "Sequoia—the Auld Lang Syne of Trees," *Natural History* 19 (November—December 1919): 601. See also Madison Grant, "Saving the Redwoods," *National Geographic Magazine* 37, no. 6 (June 1920): 525.

12 W. G. Bonner, "The Trail in the Redwoods," *Overland Monthly*, 2d ser., 37, no. 6 (June 1901): 1062.

13 Grant, "Saving the Redwoods," p. 527.

14 C. Raymond Clar, *California Government and Forestry*, vol. 1 (Sacramento: Department of Natural Resources, 1959), p. 68—78; "The Fate of the Redwoods," *Pacific Coast Wood and Iron* [*Pioneer Western Lumbermen*] 11 (June 1889): 150.

15 Quotes from Bertha F. Herrick, "The California Redwoods," *Sunshine* 11, no. 2 (July 1889): 99. For similar sentiments, see H. W. Plummer, "The Redwood Lands of California," *Timberman* [*American Lumberman*] 21 May 1887, p. 4; Ernest Ingersoll, "In a Redwood Logging Camp," *Harper's New Monthly Magazine* 66, no. 391 (January 1883): 203.

16 Robert Sterling Yard, "Historical Notes on the Primitive in National Parks" (1932), pp. 5—6, mimeographed, in Library of Congress.

17 Quote from Alfred Runte, "Origins and Paradox of the American Experience," *Journal of Forest History* 21, no. 2 (April 1977): 70. See also Alfred Runte, "'Worthless' Lands: Our National Parks," *American West* 10 (May 1973): 4—11; Alfred Runte, *National Parks: The American Experience* (Lincoln, Neb.: University of Nebraska Press, 1979), pp. 33—64.

18 Interview with Enoch P. French conducted by Susan R. Schrepfer, 15 September 1969, Arcata, Calif.; Plummer, "The Redwood Lands of California," p. 3.

19 Sherwood D. Burgess, "The Forgotten Redwoods of the East Bay," *California Historical Society Quarterly* 30, no. 1 (March 1951): 1—13.

20 Nathan Rosenberg, *Perspectives on Technology* (London: Cambridge University Press, 1976), p. 44.

21 Roderick Nash, *Wilderness and the American Mind* (New Haven: Yale University Press, 1971), pp. 8−43.

22 C. D. Robinson, "The Two Redwoods," *Californian* 5, no. 30 (June 1882): 481−91; "Humboldt County," *Pacific Coast Wood and Iron* 8 (August 1887): 20; Charles Shinn, "The Great Sequoia," *Garden and Forest* 2 (25 December 1899): 614−15; W. G. Bonner, "The Trail in the Redwoods," pp. 1061−67; Val Shaw, "The Rape of the Redwoods," *Overland Monthly*, 2d ser. 39 (March 1902): 738−42.

23 First quote from Ingersoll, "In a Redwood Logging Camp," p. 201; second quote from Ninetta Eames, "Staging in the Mendocino Redwoods, " *Overland Monthly*, 2d ser. 20 (1892): 273.

24 Hyman Palaid and Earl Roberts, "The History of the Lumber Industry in Humboldt County," *Pacific Historical Review* 19, no. 1 (February 1950): 16.

25 Quote from Douglas H. Strong, *The Conservationists* (Menlo Park, Calif.: Addison-Wesley Publishing Company, 1971), p. 33; George Perkins Marsh, *Man and Nature: Or Physical Geography as Modified by Human Action* (New York: Scribner's Sons, 1865), pp. 3−8, 35−44.

26 William Thomas, Jr., ed., *Man's Role in Changing the Face of the Earth* (Chicago: University of Chicago Press, 1962), pp. 200−204; Robert Albion, *Forests and Sea Power* (Hamden, Conn.: Archon, 1926), pp. 121−38; Paul Bamford, *Forests and French Sea Power, 1660−1789* (Toronto: University of Toronto Press, 1956), pp. 70−94.

27 Clarence Glacken, *Traces on the Rhodian Shore* (Berkeley: University of California Press, 1967), p. 704.

28 Bernhard E. Fernow, *Economics of Forestry* (New York: Thomas Y. Crowell and Co., 1902), pp. 90−91.

29 Douglas H. Strong, *Trees or Timber? The Story of Sequoia and Kings Canyon National Parks* (Three Rivers, Calif.: Three Rivers Press, 1968).

30 Holway Jones, *John Muir and the Sierra Club: The Battle for Yosemite* (San Francisco: Sierra Club, 1965).

31 Gifford Pinchot, *The Fight for Conservation* (1910; reprint ed., Seattle: University of Washington Press, 1967), p. 42; *Oxford English Dictionary*, s.v. "conservation"; Samuel P. Hays, *Conservation and the Gospel of Efficiency* (Cambridge: Harvard University Press, 1959), pp. 40−42, 142−46.

32 Josephine McCracken, "About the Big Basin," *Overland Monthly*, 2d ser. 37 (August 1900): 135−37; William Dudley, "The Big Basin Redwood Park," *Forester [American Forests]* 7 (July 1901): 157−64; Arthur Taylor, *California Redwood Park* (Sacramento, Calif.: William Richardson, 1912), pp. 25−26; *Save the California Redwoods* (San Francisco: n.p., 1901), pp. 11−16; Charles Reed, "Petition to the Legislature of the State of California," 8 January 1901, in Bancroft Library, Univ. of California, Berkeley [hereafter Bancroft Library].

33 Act of 16 March 1901, ch. 162, p. 517.

34 Carrie W. Walter, "The Preservation of Big Basin," *Overland Monthly*, 2d ser. 40 (October 1902): 355.

35 "School Children Petition Preservation of California's Redwoods," *Journal of Education* 67 (5 March 1908): 278; *Congressional Record*, 62d Cong., 2d sess., 1912, 48, pt. 3:4068; *Humboldt Times*, 7 February 1912; *Humboldt Standard*, 11 March 1912; *Eureka Herald*, 9 and 14 January 1912.

36 *Humboldt Standard*, 4 September 1913, 20 October 1913, 10 November 1913; *Humboldt Times*, 6 September 1913, 11 January 1914; George Burchard, "Save the Redwoods," *Outlook* [*New Outlook*] 124 (10 March 1920): 428−29.

37 "Statement Made by William Colby of San Francisco, President of the Sierra Club, on March 15, 1918 to Mr. Stephen T. Mather," SRL/F/Mather; Theodore Roosevelt, "Remarks at Leland Stanford Jr. University, Palo Alto, California, May 12, 1903," *California Address* (San Francisco: California Promotion Committee, 1903), pp. 68−71; Donald Swain, *Wilderness Defender: Horace M. Albright and Conservation* (Chicago: University of Chicago Press, 1970), pp. 247, 289−91, 320.

38 *Congressional Record*, 63d Cong., 1st sess., 1913, 50 pt. 1:92; *Humboldt Times*, 4 April 1913.

39 Osborn to Alden Sampson, 16 October 1913, Osborn to Joseph Choate, 7 November 1913, Osborn to Johnson, 1 December 1913, Osborn, George Kunz, and Johnson to William Kenyon, 4 December 1913, Bancroft Library, Robert Underwood Johnson Papers; Merriam to Muir, 2 October 1906, 17 May 1907, B/JM/1:2; Merriam to Edward Taylor, 17 March 1909, B/JM/1:5; Merriam to A. F. Lang, 27 December 1909, 27 February 1910, B/JM/2:3; Merriam to C. Weaver, 20 February 1918, Merriam to P. Gregory, 29 June 1917, Merriam to M. Grant, 15 and 24 September 1917, LC/JM/195−97.

40 See Merriam-Grant correspondence, 27 August 1918 to 15 January 1919, in LC/JM/195 and SRL/A/Grant; M. Grant to J. D. Grant, 26 August 1918, SRL/A/Grant; Mather to Merriam, 11 March 1918, SRL/F/Mather; Merriam to Sproul, 25 November 1918; "Conference M. Grant and J. Merriam with Secretary Lane, October 31 [1918]," SRL/F/History; letters of acceptance, B/SRL/4:1.

41 U.S., Department of Agriculture, *Lumber Production in the United States, 1799−1846* (Washington, D.C.: GPO, 1948), p. 208.

42 Ayer to Mather, 20 June 1919, A/I/12-0.

43 Minutes, SRL Council, 2 August 1919. All minutes of the council, executive board, and directors are located in the Minute Books, SRL office, San Francisco.

44 George E. Mowry, *The California Progressives* (Chicago: Quadrangle Books, 1951), pp. 87−89.

45 Peter Filene, "An Obituary for 'The Progressive Movement,'" *American Quarterly* 22, no. 1 (Spring 1970): 20−34.

46 Samuel P. Hays, "The Social Analysis of American Political History," *Political Science Quarterly* 80 (September 1965): 373−74; Samuel P. Hays,

Conservation and the Gospel of Efficiency (New York: Atheneum, 1974), pp. 1–4, 145–46.

47 Hays, *Conservation and the Gospel of Efficiency*, pp. 1–4, 145–46.

48 Robert H. Wiebe, *The Search for Order, 1877–1920* (New York: Hill and Wang, 1967), p. 112.

49 Ibid.

Chapter 2: Citizen Reform

1 *Congressional Record*, 66th Cong., 1st sess., 8 July 1919, 58, pt. 3:2304; 2nd sess., 13 May 1920, 59, pt. 6:6479.

2 Donald Bruce, M. B. Pratt, and R. F. Hammatt, *Report on Investigation for Proposed Redwood National Park* (October 1920), SRL/A/RNP; Drury to M. Grant, 29 July 1920, SRL/A/Grant.

3 Mather to Lane, 19 July 1919, Lane to Mather, 21 July 1919, A/I/12-0; T. Nicolas Sinnott to Interior, 1 August 1919, Alexander Vogelsand to Sinnott, 8 December 1919, A/I/12-0; H. Rept. 871: U.S., Congress, House, Committee on Public Lands, *National Redwood Park: Report to Accompany H. Res. 159*, 66th Cong., 2nd sess., 26 April 1920.

4 U.S., National Park Service, *Report of the Director to the Secretary of the Interior for the Fiscal Year Ending June 30, 1920* (Washington, D.C.: GPO, 1920), pp. 37–39; Washington League for Preservation of Natural Parks to Mather, 19 November 1919, SRL/F/History; M. Grant to Merriam, 25 August 1919, Herbert Evison to M. Grant, 9 December 1919, M. Grant to Governor Olcott, 27 September 1920, SRL/A/Grant.

5 Jackson Putnam, "The Persistence of Progressivism in the 1920's: The Case of California," *Pacific Historical Review* 4, no. 66 (November 1966): 395–411.

6 Merle Curti, "The History of American Philanthropy as a Field of Research," *American Historical Review* 62, no. 2 (January 1957): 361; Merle Curti, "American Philanthropy and the National Character," *American Quarterly* 10 (Winter 1958): 436; Robert H. Bremner, *American Philanthropy* (Chicago: University of Chicago Press, 1970), pp. 123–30.

7 Quote from Bremner, *American Philanthropy*, p. 140. See also Russell Sage Foundation, *Report of the Princeton Conference on the History of Philanthropy in the United States* (New York: 1956).

8 Robert Shankland, *Steve Mather of the National Parks* (New York: Alfred A. Knopf, 1970), p. 294.

9 Mather to Merriam, 11 March 1918, 9 December 1919, SRL/F/Mather; U.S., National Park Service, *Report of the Director to the Secretary of the Interior for the Fiscal Year Ending June 30, 1919* (Washington, D.C.: GPO, 1919), p. 34.

10 Minutes of the Council, SRL, 2 August 1919; Executive Council, SRL, 20 August 1919.

11 Grant and Osborn to Governor Stephens, 8 August 1917, M. Grant to Everett Griggs, 16 September 1919, SRL/F/History; M. Grant to Merriam,

25 September 1917, 6 October 1917, Merriam to M. Grant, 25 October 1917, LC/JM/195; Mather to Lane, 9 August 1919, A/I/12-0.

12 N. D. Darlington to Mather, 19 November 1919, Darlington to Drury, 7 August 1920, B/SRL/5:12.

13 *Humboldt Times*, 8—9 August 1919; Putnam to M. Grant, 15 December 1919, SRL/A/Grant; *Humboldt Standard*, 15 January 1932; M. Grant to Emmert, 9 October 1919, SRL/A/Grant; Mather to Lane, 9 August 1919, A/I/12-0; M. Grant to Griggs, 16 September 1919, SRL/F/History; M. Grant to J. D. Grant, 6 January 1920, LC/JM/82.

14 Quote from Madison Grant, "Saving the Redwoods," *National Geographic Magazine* 37, no. 6 (June 1920): 520. See also Samuel Blythe, "The Last Stand of the Giants," *Saturday Evening Post*, 6 December 1919, pp. 8, 9, 149, 154; "Our Big Trees Saved," *National Geographic Magazine* 31, no. 1 (January 1917): 1—11; "A National Redwood Park," *Timberman*, June 1918, p. 1; Mather to Merriam, 17 February 1919, Cornwall to Mather, 11 January 1919, SRL/F/Mather.

15 For councilors' successful efforts to solicit a donation from William Harkness, see M. Grant to Merriam, 8 December 1920, LC/JM/195; Crocker to Merriam, 30 October 1930, "Memorandum," 18 October 1930, Crocker to Harkness, 5 November 1930, Aldrich to Crocker, 20 November 1930, LC/JM/50—59.

16 Merriam to M. Grant, 22 January 1919, 3 February 1919, M. Grant to Merriam, 30 January 1919, SRL/A/Grant.

17 Shankland, *Steve Mather*, p. 68; Donald Swain, *Wilderness Defender: Horace Albright and Conservation* (Chicago: University of Chicago Press, 1970), p. 48; *San Francisco Examiner*, 31 July 1928; *Oakland Tribune*, 6 August 1928; Newton Drury, "Parks and Redwoods: 1919—1971," interview conducted by Amelia Fry and Susan R. Schrepfer (Berkeley: ROHO, 1972), p. 254.

18 Drury to Merriam, 23 August 1921, B/SRL/1:21.

19 Quote from Merriam to Sperry, 31 December 1920, LC/JM/167. See also Minutes of the Council, SRL, 4 October 1919; SRL, *Annual Report, 1920*.

20 Quote from Henry Fairfield Osborn, "Sequoia—the Auld Lang Syne of Trees," *Natural History* 19 (November—December 1919): 612. See also J. D. Grant to M. Grant, 2 December 1921, SRL/A/Grant; Minutes of the Board of Directors, SRL, 23 November 1926.

21 Mather to Merriam, 12 March 1919, SRL/F/Mather.

22 Quote from Merriam to Sproul, 25 November 1918, SRL/F/History. See also Merriam to Grant, 3 February 1919, SRL/A/Grant.

23 By-Laws, SRL (14 October 1920; amended 20 August 1934).

24 Quote from Arno Cammerer, "Selling the National Parks," *Western Advertising* (Fall 1920), pp. 2—6. For N. Drury's reaction to article, see Drury to Cammerer, 11 November 1920, SRL/A/RNP. For N. Drury's career, see Merriam to Sperry, 31 December 1920, LC/JM/167; Drury to Merriam, 16 April 1924, 11 February 1927, B/SRL/1:25; Drury, "Parks and Redwoods," pp. 43—97, 102, 120—22. See also Bremner, *American Philanthropy*, p. 140.

25 *Humboldt Times*, 16 September 1919; Connick to M. Grant, 24 December 1919, SRL/A/Grant.

26 Merriam to M. Grant, 16 October 1919, Putnam to M. Grant, 15 December 1919, SRL/A/Grant; M. Grant to Griggs, 16 September 1919, SRL/F/ History; Mather to Lane, 9 August 1919, A/I/12-0; Cutler to Merriam, 13 December 1919, B/SRL/10.

27 "Save the Redwoods' Reception and Banquet to California State Highway Commission, State Forestry Commission and Executive Committee, 'Save the Redwoods League,'" 6 September 1919, SRL/F/History; Merriam to Wilbur, 8 September 1919, B/SRL/4:1.

28 Quote from Connick to Merriam, 20 January 1921, LC/JM/48. See also F. A. Cutler to Merriam, 15 December 1919, B/SRL/10; Merriam to Drury, 5 January 1921, Sperry to Merriam, 19 January 1921, 2 and 4 February 1921, Drury to Merriam, 4 March 1921, B/SRL/1:21.

29 Merriam to Drury, 5 January 1921, Drury to Merriam, 14 January 1921, B/SRL/1:21; Cutler to M. Grant, 5 May 1921, LC/JM/82; Drury to Cutler, 16 June 1921, B/SRL/10:1. S.B. 64: California, Legislature, Senate, *Journal*, 44th sess., 10 January 1921, p. 61; A.B. 80: Assembly, *Journal*, 44th sess., 11 January 1921, p. 77.

30 Drury to Merriam, 10 April 1921, B/SRL/1:21; Minutes, Board of Directors, SRL, 16 March 1921.

31 F. Baegley to T. Ingram, 2 March 1921, C. S. Smith to SRL, 7 March 1921, Drury to Merriam, 8 March 1921, B/SRL/1:21. A.B. 80: California, Legislature, Assembly, *Journal*, 44th sess., 14 April 1921, p. 1526.

32 California, Legislature, Assembly, *Journal*, 44th sess., 14 April 1921, p. 1525.

33 "Save the Redwoods League, Publicity Campaign Redwoods Legislature Appropriation January–February, 1921," SRL/F/History; Drury to Ayer, 11 April 1921, B/SRL/1:3. A.B. 80: California, Legislature, Assembly, *Journal*, 44th sess., 20 April 1921, p. 1939; Senate, *Journal*, 44th sess., 28 April 1921, p. 2217.

34 For tax bill (S.B. 855), see California, Legislature, Senate, *Journal*, 44th sess., 28 February 1921, p. 378 and Assembly, *Journal*, 44th sess., 5 March 1921, p. 454. Drury to Merriam, 21 January 1921, 10 February 1921, Merriam to Drury, 20 April 1921, B/SRL/1:21; Drury to M. Grant, 4 February 1921, SRL/A/Grant.

35 Quote reported in Drury, "Parks and Redwoods," p. 136 and Shankland, *Steve Mather*, p. 199.

36 Drury to Merriam, 25 November 1927, B/SRL/2:3.

37 For discussion of conservatism of charities, see Robert Wiebe, *The Search for Order, 1877–1920* (New York: Hill and Wang, 1967–68), pp. 175–76.

38 For middle-class origins of business elite, see C. Wright Mills, "The American Business Elite: A Collective Portrait," *Journal of Economic History* 5 (December 1945): 20–24; William Miller, ed., *Men in Business: Essays in the History of Entrepreneurship* (Cambridge, Mass.: Harvard University Press, 1952), pp. 193–204, 288–89.

39 Quote from James Curwood, "My 2000-Year-Old Friend," *Hearst's Inter-*

national [*Cosmopolitan*], January 1926, p. 13. See also Drury to Sperry, 14 January 1926, SRL/A/Sperry; Drury to Merriam, 14 January 1926, B/SRL/2:2.

40 Drury to Merriam, 14 November 1925, Merriam to Drury, 19 November 1927, Drury to Merriam, 25 November 1927, 11 March 1929, B/SRL/2:1−3.

41 First quote from Madison Grant, "Saving the Redwoods," p. 529; second quote from M. Grant to Merriam, 13 June 1921, LC/JM/82.

42 Roderick Nash, ed., *The American Environment* (Menlo Park, Calif.: Addison-Wesley Publishing Company, 1968), p. 97.

43 Donald C. Swain, *Federal Conservation Policy: 1921−1933* (Berkeley: University of California, 1963), p. 160.

44 George Mowry, *The California Progressives* (Chicago: Quadrangle Books, 1963), p. 290.

45 Newton Drury, interview conducted by Ann Lage, June 1977, San Francisco.

46 Quotes from William L. O'Neill, *The Progressive Years: America Comes of Age* (New York: Dodd, Mead & Co., 1975), pp. 55−58. See also James Weinstein, *The Corporate Ideal in the Liberal State, 1900−1918* (Boston: Beacon Press, 1968), pp. 6, 143−55.

47 Gabriel Kolko, *The Triumph of Conservatism: A Reinterpretation of American History, 1900−1916* (Chicago: Quadrangle Books, 1963), pp. 1−10.

48 Daniel E. Griffiths, ed., *Behavioral Science and Educational Administration* (Chicago: National Society for the Study of Education, 1971), pp. 33−57.

49 Ralph Chaney, taped speech at dedication of Newton Drury Memorial Grove, 1969, Humboldt County, in Bancroft Library.

50 Norman M. Wilensky, *Conservatives in the Progressive Era: The Taft Republicans of 1912*, University of Florida Monographs, Social Sciences, no. 25 (Winter 1965), pp. 32−51.

51 A.B. 912: California, Legislature, Assembly, *Journal*, 45th sess., 1 February 1923, p. 335; S.B. 55: Senate, *Journal*, 45th sess., 17 January 1923, pp. 130−31; Assembly, *Journal*, 45th sess., 17 January 1923, p. 140; Drury to Merriam, 15 March 1923, LC/JM/64; Drury to Merriam, 4, 10, and 19 April 1923, B/SRL/1:23.

52 Merriam to Drury, 27 January 1923, B/SRL/1:23; Drury to Merriam, 9 February 1923, LC/JM/64; Mather to Hugh Pomeroy, 15 March 1923, Mather to Drury, 1 May 1923, SRL/F/Mather.

53 Quote from J. D. Grant to Merriam, 20 January 1923, B/SRL/1:23. See also Merriam to Drury, 27 January 1923, 18 April 1923, B/SRL/1:23; Drury to Mather, 4 April 1923, LC/JM/119; Merriam to Henry Graves, 11 May 1923, LC/JM/83.

54 First quote from Merriam to Drury, 18 April 1923, B/SRL/1:23; second quote from Drury to Merriam, 10 April 1923, B/SRL/1:23; third quote from Merriam to Graves, 11 May 1923, LC/JM/83. See also J. D. Grant to Merriam, 20 January 1923, B/SRL/1:23; Drury to Merriam, 9 February

1923, 15 March 1923, LC/JM/64; Merriam to Graves, 19 May 1923, LC/JM/83.

55 Drury to William Badé, 9 March 1923, Kent to Drury, 23 March 1923, B/SRL/1:7−9; Merriam to Drury, 15 March 1923, Drury to Merriam, 19 April 1923, B/SRL/1:23; Drury to Merriam, 29 September 1925, B/SRL/2:1.

56 A.B. 106: California, Legislature, Assembly, *Journal*, 45th sess., 8 May 1923, p. 2018, 17 May 1923, pp. 2391−92; Drury to Merriam, 19 April 1923, B/SRL/1:23; Drury to Merriam, 2 May 1923, LC/JM/63; J. D. Grant to E. E. Ayer, 3 May 1923, B/SRL/1:3; J. D. Grant to Kent, 10 May 1923, B/SRL/1:9; J. D. Grant to Merriam, 12 May 1923, LC/JM/82.

57 Drury to Merriam, 19 April 1923, B/SRL/1:23. S.B. 608: California, Legislature, Senate, *Journal*, 46th sess., 23 January 1925, p. 228.

58 Merriam to Cornwall, 1 September 1919, B/SRL/5:12.

59 Connick to M. Grant, 24 December 1919, SRL/A/Grant; F. A. Cutler to Merriam, 15 December 1919, B/SRL/10; Drury to Merriam, 5 August 1924, B/SRL/1:24.

60 S.B. 185: California, Legislature, Senate, *Journal*, 46th sess., 20 January 1925, p. 133.

61 Drury to Kent, 5 August 1922, J. D. Grant to Kent, 10 August 1922, B/SRL/1:9; Merriam to Graves, 19 May 1923, Drury to Merriam, 18 November 1924, LC/JM/83; Drury to Duncan McDuffie, 3 October 1925, B/SRL/1:12; Graves to Merriam, 13 April 1926, LC/JM/83; Drury, "Point Lobos Reserve," speech at Regional Conference on State Parks, 31 August 1936, B/SRL/2:12.

62 Drury to J. D. Grant, 22 December 1924, Drury to Sperry, 2 January 1925, Drury to McDuffie, 7 and 22 January 1925, Drury to A. H. Breed, 19 January 1925, SRL/A/SPL.

63 Drury to Colby, 2 January 1925, Drury to Breed, 26 February 1925, Drury to Sperry, 18 June 1925, SRL/A/SPL; Minutes, California State Board of Forestry, 16 February 1925; M. B. Pratt to Drury, 18 February 1925, SRL/A/SPL; Drury to Mather, 15 March 1925, Mather to SRL, 19 March 1925, Drury to J. D. Grant, 10 April 1925, SRL/A/SPL; Merriam, "Memorandum," 4 November 1925, CI/JM/Merriam and Associates. Merriam organized the Committee on the National Relations of the Redwoods composed of national organizations endorsing California's legislation; see Barrington Moore to John Payne, 4 May 1925, LC/JM/126; Theodore Roosevelt, Jr., to J. D. Grant, 9 January 1925, Harlean James to Colby, 11 May 1925, SRL/A/SPL.

64 Drury to Merriam, 21 April 1923, 27 September 1923, 19 November 1923, B/SRL/1:23; Drury to Merriam, 10 July 1928, LC/JM/60; Drury to Merriam, 29 May 1926, B/SRL/2:2.

65 Drury to Mather, 15 March 1925, Drury to Breed, 25 March 1925, SRL/A/SPL; Drury to J. D. Grant, 19 April 1925, SRL/A/I; Drury to Merriam, 2 and 22 April 1925, LC/JM/63. S.B. 185: see California, Legislature, Assembly, *Journal*, 46th sess., 9 April 1925, p. 1333.

66 Quotes from *San Francisco Chronicle*, 10 January 1925. See also *Fresno*

Republican and *Santa Cruz Sentinel*, 10 January 1925; McDuffie to Drury, 28 January 1925, SRL/A/I; Drury to McDuffie, 10 January 1925, Drury to J. D. Grant, 10 April 1925, Drury to Sperry, 8 June 1925, SRL/A/SPL.

67 Quote from Greeley to SRL, 21 March 1925. See also Pardee to J. D. Grant, 29 January 1925, Pardee to Breed, 4 February 1925, Drury to Merriam, 22 April 1925, Mulford to Drury, 28 April 1925, SRL/A/SPL.

68 Samuel P. Hayes, *Conservation and the Gospel of Efficiency: The Progressive Conservation Movement, 1890–1920* (New York: Atheneum Press, 1974), p. 194; Osborn and Kunz to Kenyon, 4 December 1913, Graves to Johnson, 13 November 1913, Robert Underwood Johnson Papers, Bancroft Library; M. Grant to Sperry, 12 June 1920, SRL/A/Grant; Elmo Richardson, "The Struggle for the Valley: California's Hetch Hetchy Controversy, 1905–1913," *California Historical Society Quarterly* 38, no. 3 (September 1959): 249–58.

69 Fifty percent of the Senate Conservation Committee were lumbermen; Drury to Merriam, 2 April 1925, SRL/A/I; Drury to Merriam, 22 April 1925, LC/JM/63. S.B. 185: California, Legislature, Senate, *Journal*, 46th sess., 10 April 1925, pp. 1386–87, 1394–95, and Assembly, *Journal*, 46th sess., 22 April 1925, p. 2377. S.B. 608: Senate, *Journal*, 46th sess., 10 April 1925, p. 1387, and Assembly, *Journal*, 46th sess., 22 April 1925, p. 2378.

70 Mowry, *The California Progressives*, pp. 286–87.

71 *Sacramento Union*, 5 June 1925; Drury to Merriam, 22 April 1925, 6 June 1925, LC/JM/63; "Statement received by SRL from Governor's Office on S.B. 185," n.d., Drury to Albright, 17 June 1925, SRL/A/SPL; Drury to J. D. Grant, 10 April 1925, SRL/A/I.

72 Quote from Drury to Olmsted, 30 August 1926, B/SRL/2:1. See also Drury to Olmsted, 20 October 1926, B/SRL/2:1; McDuffie to Olmsted, 21 October 1926, LC/JM/GC120.

73 Quote from Drury to McDuffie, 4 November 1926. See also Olmsted to McDuffie, 25 October 1926, B/SRL/2:1.

74 Quotes from Drury to McDuffie, 4 November 1926, B/SRL/2:1. See also Drury to Kent, 5 April 1922, J. D. Grant to Kent, 10 August 1922, B/SRL/1:9; "Memorandum of Remarks to J. C. Merriam," before SRL, Council, August 1922, Merriam to Drury, 14 October 1924, B/SRL/1:22–24; Merriam, "Memorandum," September 1925, LC/JM/157; W. A. Cannon, "Studies on Roots," Carnegie Institution of Washington, D.C., *Yearbook*, no. 25 (1926), pp. 317–25.

75 Hays, *Conservation and the Gospel of Efficiency*, p. 145.

76 Quote from Samuel P. Hays, "The Politics of Reform in Municipal Government in the Progressive Era," *Pacific Northwest Quarterly* 55 (October 1964): 241. See also pp. 157–169 and Samuel P. Hays, "The Social Analysis of American Political History, 1880–1920," *Political Science Quarterly* 80 (September 1965): 373–74.

77 S.B. 439, 440, and 441: California, Legislature, Senate, *Journal*, 47th sess., 19 January 1927, p. 240. A.B. 1176: Assembly, *Journal*, 47th sess., 4 March

1927, p. 516. S.B. 439: Senate, *Journal*, 47th sess., 10 March 1927, p. 598; Barrington Moore to John Payne, 4 May 1925, LC/JM/126. For progressive control, see Putnam, "The Persistence of Progressivism," pp. 408–9.

78 Minutes, Board of Directors, SRL, 23 November 1926.

79 Bremner, *American Philanthropy*, p. 108.

80 Drury to McDuffie, 4 November 1926, B/SRL/2:1.

81 Drury to McDuffie, 22 January 1925, SRL/A/SPL; Minutes, State Parks Council, 7 February 1927, SRL/A/SPL.

82 Drury to Merriam, 9 November 1926, B/SRL/1:15; *Santa Monica Outlook*, 5 August 1928; correspondence between Williamson and Drury, 1927–1928, SRL/A/SPL.

83 For campaign, see SRL/A/SPL, SRL/A/McDuffie; State Parks Council Papers, in Bancroft Library.

84 Paul Redington to Drury, 17 February 1927, Rolland Vandegrift to Drury, 13 April 1928, SRL/A/SPL; Drury to Merriam, 29 May 1927, B/SRL/2:2.

85 Drury to McDuffie, 9 June 1928; letters of appreciation by J. D. Grant, 10 November 1928, SRL/A/SPL.

86 A.B. 1176: California, Legislature, Senate, *Journal*, 47th sess., 30 March 1927, p. 1206 and Assembly, *Journal*, 47th sess., 4 April 1927, p. 1515. S.B. 439: Senate, *Journal*, 47th sess., 15 April 1927, p. 1683 and Assembly, *Journal*, 47th sess., 28 April 1927, p. 2515. S.B. 440: Senate, *Journal*, 47th sess., 15 April 1927, p. 1683 and Assembly, *Journal*, 47th sess., 28 April 1927, p. 2516. S.B. 441: see Assembly, *Journal*, 47th sess., 25 April 1927, p. 2249 and Senate, *Journal*, 47th sess., 27 April 1927, p. 2151.

87 See SRL/A/SPL and State Parks Council Papers, in Bancroft Library.

88 State of California, Office of the Secretary of State, *Statement of Vote at General Election Held on November 6, 1928, in the State of California*, compiled by Frank C. Jordan (Sacramento: California State Printing Office, 1928), p. 31.

89 Ibid., pp. 30, 31, 35, 39; General Election Returns, Los Angeles County, November 6, 1928; Recapitulation of Constitutional Amendments, Charter Amendments, Propositions and Bond Issues, City of San Francisco, November 6, 1928.

90 Quote from Merriam to Sperry, 22 September 1920, LC/JM/167. See also J. D. Grant to Sperry, 13 December 1920, SRL/A/Sperry; SRL, *Annual Report, 1920*; M. Grant, "Saving the Redwoods," pp. 527, 533.

91 Frederick Law Olmsted, *A State Park Survey of California* (Berkeley: SRL, 1927).

92 Bremner, *American Philanthropy*, p. 194. The league paid $532,677 for 3,347 acres; SRL, "Summary Redwood Lands Acquired as of May 15, 1930," San Francisco, 1930, in SRL office.

Chapter 3: Ideology of Reform

1 When first discovered in 1838, *Sequoia* cones from the Tertiary of Europe were referred to the genus *Steinhauera*; see Chaney to Merriam, 19 October 1932, LC/JM/40; Ralph Chaney, "Abstract of Paper to be Presented to

the Cleveland Meeting of the Paleontological Society of America," 25 November 1927, LC/JM/40.

2 Asa Gray, *Sequoia and Its History: An Address by Professor Asa Gray . . . delivered at the meeting held at Dubuque, Iowa, August, 1872* (Salem, Mass.: The Salem Press, 1872).

3 John Merriam, *The Garment of God: Influence of Nature in Human Experience* (New York: Charles Scribner's Sons, 1943).

4 Merriam to J. P. Buwalda, 21 December 1921, LC/JM/30; see also William Gregory, "Dr. Merriam's Contributions to the Development of Vertebrate Paleontology on the Pacific Coast," *Scientific Monthly* 42, no. 4 (April 1936): 377−80.

5 Chaney's research was funded by the Carnegie Institution of Washington, D.C., of which Merriam was president; Ralph Chaney, "Ralph Works Chaney, Ph.D., Paleobotanist, Conservationist," interview conducted by Edna Daniel (Berkeley: ROHO, 1960); Ralph Chaney, *Redwoods of the Past* (San Francisco: SRL, 1934).

6 Ralph Chaney, "Abstract of Paper to be Presented at the Cleveland Meeting of the Paleontological Society of America," 25 November 1927, Chaney to Merriam, 28 January 1928, LC/JM/40.

7 Quote from Chaney to Merriam, 24 and 25 November 1930, LC/JM/40. The following year the Carnegie Institution funded an expedition under Chaney's direction that confirmed fossil findings; see Ralph Chaney, "Report of Paleobotanist Investigation and Instruction for the Year April 1, 1931 to April, 1932," Carnegie Institution, Washington, D.C., LC/JM/40.

8 "Redwoods Once Covered Continent," *Oakland Tribune*, 20 February 1931; "Bridge of Redwoods Emigration Is Found," *San Francisco Examiner*, 15 March 1931.

9 Ralph Chaney, "A Comparison of the Bridge Creek Flora with the Living Redwood Forest," 17 December 1923, LC/JM/41; Chaney to Merriam, 8 January 1929; Ralph Chaney, "Report of the Occurrences of Fossil Plants Four Miles Southwest of Garberville, California," 12 October 1929, LC/JM/40; Ralph Chaney, "The Miocene Occurrence of Sequoia and Related Conifers in the John Day Basin," *Proceedings of the National Academy of Sciences* 35, no. 3 (March 1949): 125−29.

10 Ralph Chaney, "Plant Distribution as a Guide to Age Determination," 22 May 1936, LC/JM/39; Ralph Chaney, "Trees and History," in *Science in the University* (Berkeley: University of California Press, 1944), pp. 247−54.

11 Merriam to Albert W. Atwood, 3 January 1936, LC/JM/13; Julian Huxley to Merriam, 8 March 1937, Merriam to Huxley, 19 March 1937, LC/JM/98; "Death Trap of the Ages," *The Wasp*, 16 January 1926; Chester Stock, "John C. Merriam as Scientist and Philosopher," *Cooperation in Research*, Carnegie Institution of Washington pub. no. 501 (Washington, D.C.: Carnegie Institution, 1938), pp. 765−78.

12 John Merriam, "Conservation and Evolution in a Changing Social Program," *American Philosophical Society Proceedings* 73, no. 5 (1934): 2280.

13 Emanuel Fritz, *Story Told by a Fallen Redwood* (San Francisco: SRL, 1934), pp. 2−4. For the study of precipitation in the redwoods, see Chaney to Merriam, 8 January 1929, LC/JM/40; Ralph Chaney, *Redwoods of the Past*, pp. 2−4; Willis Jepson, *Trees, Shrubs and Flowers of the Redwood Region* (San Francisco: SRL, 1935).

14 Quote from Merriam, "Conservation and Evolution in a Changing Social Program," p. 2279. See also Merriam to Henry Wallace, 14 January 1936, LC/JM/117; Albert W. Atwood, "Nature as Created," *Saturday Evening Post* 197 (28 February 1925), p. 16.

15 Laurence F. Schmeckebier, "The National Parks from the Scientific and Educational Side," *Popular Science Monthly* 80 (June 1912): 531; A. Hunter Dupree, *Science and the Federal Government* (Cambridge: Harvard University Press, 1957), pp. 1, 232, 239; Samuel P. Hays, *Conservation and the Gospel of Efficiency: The Progressive Conservation Movement, 1890−1920* (Cambridge: Harvard University Press, 1959), pp. 1−3; Donald Swain, *Federal Conservation Policy, 1921−1933* (Berkeley: University of California Press, 1963), pp. 1, 132.

16 Harold Bryant and W. W. Atwood, *Research and Education in National Parks* (Washington, D.C.: GPO, 1932), pp. 39, 45. Both of these men were Merriam's colleagues in the development of the educational program of the parks.

17 Raymond B. Fosdick, *The Old Savage in the New Civilization* (Garden City, N.Y.: Doubleday, Doran and Company, 1928); Robert A. Millikan, *Science and the New Civilization* (New York: Charles Scribner's Sons, 1930); Francis Mason, *The Great Design: Order and Intelligence in Nature* (New York: Macmillan Company, 1934); Merriam to Alfred Noyes, 24 May 1932, LC/JM/135; Glenn Frank, *America's Hour of Decision: Crisis Points in National Policy* (New York and London: Whittlesey House, McGraw-Hill Book Company, Inc., 1934).

18 Merriam to Charles Merriam, 28 March 1935, LC/JM/122. J. Merriam was active in the American Association for Adult Education founded in 1926; "Dr. Merriam Declares Adult Education is Vital to the United States," *Berkeley Gazette*, 14 July 1932; Merriam to Editor of *Century Magazine*, 22 September 1910, B/JM/2:4; John Merriam, "Making a Living or Living," *Published Papers and Addresses of John Campbell Merriam*, Carnegie Institution of Washington pub. no. 500 (Baltimore: Waverly Press, 1938), 4:2033−38.

19 For a discussion of the high degree of faith in all forms of education during the 1920s, see John D. Hicks, *Republican Ascendancy, 1921−1933* (Harper and Row, Harper Torchbooks, 1960), pp. 186−88; see also Philip N. Hicks, "The Development of the Natural History Essay in American Literature" (Ph.D. diss., University of Pennsylvania, 1924), pp. 6, 160−61; Francis Halsey, "The Rise of the Nature Writers," *American Monthly Review of Reviews* 26 (November 1902): 567−71.

20 Merriam was highly pleased when the collection of his natural history essays, *The Living Past*, quoted above (New York: Charles Scribner's Sons,

1930), p. 50, was recommended to schools and other educational institutions by the U.S. Department of Education; see Merriam to Chaney, 19 May 1931, LC/JM/40. Examples of Merriam's lectures include "An Open Book," *New York Times*, 19 August 1927; "Early Man Lived in America," *New York Sun*, 22 November 1933; "Recent Discoveries," *New York Herald Tribune*, 26 November 1933.

21 Schmeckebier, "The National Parks from the Scientific and Educational Side," pp. 533, 540, 547; Charles M. Goethe, *Seeking to Serve* (Sacramento, Calif.: Keystone Press, 1949), p. 99.

22 Organizations included: the National Parks Association, the American Association for the Advancement of Science, the National Conference on Outdoor Recreation, the American Association of Museums, and the Laura Spelman Rockefeller Memorial Fund.

23 First quote from Stephen Mather, "The University of the Interior," *Outdoors Pictorial* (June 1925); second quote from Robert Shankland, "The Yellowstone National Park as an Open-Air School," *School and Society* 24, no. 605 (31 July 1926): 132−33. For the history of interpretive work, see Bryant and Atwood, *Research and Education in the National Parks*, pp. 49−52; Minutes of the Meeting of the Trustees of the National Parks Association, 31 May 1928; Freeman Tilden, *Interpreting Our Heritage: Principles and Practices of Visitor Services in Parks, Museums, and Historical Places* (Chapel Hill: University of North Carolina Press, 1957).

24 Merriam to Mather, 24 December 1924, 6 May 1927, 14 November 1927, Mather to Merriam, 5 May 1928, Merriam to Mather, 6 October 1928, LC/JM/119; Merriam to J. P. Buwalda, 20 October 1928, Buwalda to Merriam, 15 November 1928, LC/JM/30.

25 John Merriam, *The Highest Uses of the Redwoods: Messages to the Council of the Save-the-Redwoods League, 1922 11* (Berkeley: SRL, n.d.).

26 Fritz, *Story Told by a Fallen Redwood*; John Merriam, *A Living Link in History* (San Francisco: SRL, 1934); Jepson, *Trees, Shrubs and Flowers of the Redwood Region*; Chaney, *Redwoods of the Past*.

27 Sir Arthur Conan Doyle, *The Lost World* (New York: A. L. Burt Company, 1912). Doyle located his "Lost World" in South America, but the *Pacific Rural Press*, 14 July 1928, suggested he should have placed it in the redwoods. For Merriam's comments on the book, see Merriam, *The Garment of God*, pp. 94−95.

28 Eugene O'Neill's *The Hairy Ape* (1922) and *The Emperor Jones* (1920) celebrated the primitive impulses of man. See also Merriam to C. K. Field (*Sunset Magazine*), 21 February 1910, B/JM/2:3; Drury to J. D. Grant, 21 April 1926, SRL/A/I.

29 Chaney to Merriam, 14 January 1927, LC/JM/40.

30 See front-page articles by Milton Silverman in *San Francisco Chronicle*, 25, 26, 29 March and 5, 6 April 1948; "Sequoia Saga," *Fortnight* (May 7, 1948), p. 18.

31 L. T. Sanderson, "There Could Be Dinosaurs," *Saturday Evening Post* 220 (3 January 1948): 17.

32 Quote from Francis Galton, *Essays in Eugenics* (London: The Eugenics Education Society, 1909), p. i. See also Francis Galton, "Eugenics: Its Definition, Scope and Aims," *American Journal of Sociology* 10 (July 1904): 1—25; Thomas Gosset, *Race: The History of an Idea in America* (New York: Schocken Books, 1965), pp. 370—408; John Higham, *Strangers in the Land: Patterns of American Nativism, 1860—1925* (New York: Atheneum, 1963), pp. 150—51.

33 Madison Grant, *The Passing of the Great Race: Or the Racial Basis of European History* (New York: Charles Scribner's Sons, 1921); the 1916 and 1917 editions had a preface by Henry Fairfield Osborn; Goethe, *Seeking to Serve*; Vernon Kellogg, *Mind and Heredity* (Princeton: Princeton University Press, 1923).

34 *Congressional Record*, 64th Cong., 1st sess., 27 March 1916, 53, pt. 5:4777; Lorimer obituary, *New York Times*, 24 October 1937.

35 Drury, "Note to Duncan McDuffie," 27 July 1928, B/SRL/1:11.

36 Ann and Myron Sutton, "Harold C. Bryant, Pioneer," *Nature Magazine* 48, no. 1 (January 1955): 38—40.

37 Benjamin Ide Wheeler, *Dionysos and Immortality: the Greek Faith in Immortality As Affected by the Rise of Individualism* (Boston and New York: Houghton, Mifflin and Co., 1899).

38 Ralph Chaney, "Synopsis of Lectures in Paleontology 10. Outline and General Principles of the History of Life," 1947, p. 80, in Bancroft Library.

39 N. Drury to Charles Goethe, 6 January 1966, SRL/A/Goethe; see also Clark Wissler to Ruthereum, 17 December 1920, Merriam, "Memorandum of Conversations with Dr. Wissler," 7 November 1930, LC/JM/184; "Report and Recommendations of the Committee on Scientific Problems of Human Migration, presented to the Division of Anthropology and Psychology, National Research Council," 13 May 1924.

40 Quote from Goethe to Aubrey Drury, 13 October 1942. See also Goethe to R. W. Westwood, 5 October 1954, SRL/A/Goethe.

41 Goethe, *Seeking to Serve*, pp. 14, 22, 200; Charles M. Goethe, *Garden Philosopher* (Sacramento, Calif.: Keystone Press, 1955).

42 Quote from Goethe, *Seeking to Serve*, p. 163. See also Goethe to N. Drury, 7 February 1949, SRL/A/Goethe; Charles M. Goethe, *Sierran Cabin from Skyscraper* (Sacramento, Calif.: Keystone Press, 1943), pp. viii, 154—55. For financial contributions, see SRL/A/Goethe.

43 John Higham, *Strangers in the Land*, p. 150; Richard Hofstadter, *Social Darwinism in American Thought* (Boston: Beacon Press, 1955), pp. 164—69.

44 First quote from Ralph Chaney, "Synopsis of Lectures in Paleontology 10," p. 70; second quote from Goethe, *Garden Philosopher*, pp. 213, 215, 259, 309.

45 Quotes from Henry Fairfield Osborn, *Impressions of Great Naturalists* (New York and London: Charles Scribner's Sons, 1928), p. 198. See also above pp. 163, 188—97, and Henry Fairfield Osborn, *Evolution and Religion in Education: The Fundamentalist Controversy of 1922—1925* (New York: Charles Scribner's Sons, 1926).

46 SRL, *Annual Report, 1927—1928*, p. 39. See also Ray Lyman Wilbur, Speech at Dedication of Charles Felton Grove, 12 June 1927, p. 20, in SRL office; John Masefield, *The Taking of Helen and Other Prose Selections* (New York: Macmillan Company, 1924), p. 110.

47 Hermann A. Keyserling, *The Travel Diary of a Philosopher* (New York: Harcourt, Brace and Company, 1925), pp. 287—90. For correspondence between Merriam and Grant in June 1926 regarding this book, see LC/JM/82.

48 Merriam believed in eugenic principles; the Carnegie Institution, which he directed, supported eugenic research. But he refused affiliation with the American Eugenics Society and the American Genetics Society. He was well disposed toward "colored people" and the Chinese in California; see Merriam to American Genetics Society, 18 December 1926, Merriam to Eugenics Society, 30 September 1930, LC/JM/6—7; Merriam to W. M. Butler, 3 January 1934, LC/JM/29; Merriam to F. D. Frick, 2 April 1923, LC/JM/75; Merriam to Mason-McDuffie Realty Company, 29 November 1924, 9 December 1924, LC/JM/120; Merriam to Charles Merriam, 9 November 1909, B/JM/2:1; Charles Davenport to Merriam, 4 April 1930, LC/JM/51; Merriam to Wheeler, 18 May 1922, LC/JM/180.

49 John Merriam, *The Highest Uses of the Redwoods: Messages to the Council of the Save-the-Redwoods League, 1922—1941* (Berkeley: SRL, n.d.).

50 Merriam, *The Garment of God*, p. 2.

51 John Merriam, "Shelley and Men of Science," *Christian Register* (Boston) 116, no. 45 (1936): 747.

52 Crane Brinton, *Ideas and Men: The Story of Western Thought* (Englewood Cliffs, N.J.: Prentice-Hall, Inc., 1965), p. 292.

53 John Merriam, *Ultimate Values of Science*, Carnegie Institution supplementary pub. no. 15 (Washington, D.C.: Carnegie Institution, 1935), pp. 1—8.

54 Comparison made with Alfred Tennyson, "In Memoriam" (1850).

55 Stock, "John C. Merriam as Scientist and Philosopher," p. 776.

56 Merriam to Professor Albert Heim, Zurich, 17 November 1906, B/JM/1:2.

57 Quote from Merriam, *The Garment of God*, p. 33. See also Merriam to Roland Bortz, 1 April 1933, LC/JM/21.

58 John Merriam, "Science and Belief," in *A Century of Social Thought*, lectures delivered at Duke University, 1938—1939 (Durham, N.C.: Duke University Press, 1939), p. 89.

59 Quote from John Merriam, "Earth Science as the Background of History," *Published Papers*, 1:16. See also Merriam, *The Garment of God*, pp. 39—40.

60 First quote from Merriam to J. Thaliath, 13 November 1931, LC/JM/172; second quote from Burton Livingstone (secretary, American Association for the Advancement of Science) to Merriam, 4 November 1925, LC/JM/4. See also Merriam to J. M. Clark, 24 May 1923, LC/JM/44; Merriam to George Ashley, 20 August 1925, LC/JM/44.

61 Merriam, "Shelley and Men of Science," p. 748.

62 Quotes from Merriam, *The Garment of God*, p. 80, and Merriam, "Shelley and Men of Science," p. 747.

63 Quotes from Merriam, *The Garment of God*, p. 99. See also Merriam, "Conservation and Evolution in a Changing Social Program," pp. 351—70.

64 John Merriam, "The Responsibility of Federal and State Governments for Recreation," National Conference on Outdoor Recreation (69th Cong., 1st sess., Senate Document no. 117), 1926, p. 33.

65 Quote from John Merriam, "Forest Windows," *Scribner's Magazine* 83, no. 6 (June 1928): 734. See also Merriam to George Green, 25 November 1935, LC/JM/83.

66 Tennyson, "In Memoriam," 1850.

67 Morton White, *Social Thought in America: The Revolt against Formalism* (Boston: Beacon Press, 1966), pp. 203—19.

68 William F. Badé, "An Ennobling Gift," Address at Russ Pioneer Memorial Grove Dedication, 2 September 1923, in Bancroft Library; Osborn, *Evolution and Religion in Education*; Chaney, "Synopsis of Lectures in Paleontology 10"; Goethe, *Garden Philosophers*.

69 First quote from Merriam, *The Garment of God*, p. 42; second quote from Merriam, "Science and Belief," pp. 96—97.

70 Quotes from Merriam, *The Garment of God*, pp. 26—27. See also Merriam to G. Ashley, 10 and 11 April 1935, LC/JM/13.

71 Quotes from Merriam to James Breasted, 19 May 1934, LC/JM/23.

72 Quote from Merriam, "Science and Belief," p. 89. See also Merriam to H. F. Osborne, 1 June 1922, LC/JM/138; Merriam, *The Garment of God*, p. 40.

73 Quote from Merriam, *The Garment of God*, p. 67. See also review of *The Garment of God*, *New York Herald Tribune*, 28 March 1943.

74 Ibid., p. 62; John Muir, *The Mountains of California* (New York: Doubleday and Company, Anchor Books. 1961), pp. 192—93.

75 Charles Davenport, "Light Thrown by Genetics on Evolution and Development," *Scientific Monthly* 30 (April 1930): 307—14; Davenport to Merriam, 4 April 1930, LC/JM/51, written to refute statements by Merriam in *The Living Past*, p. 137. This school of thought bore much in common with the earlier work of Herbert Spencer; see Richard Hofstadter, *Social Darwinism in American Thought* (Philadelphia: University of Pennsylvania Press, 1944).

76 A. E. Wiggam, "New Decalogue of Science," *Century Magazine* 103 (March 1922): 643—50; Lothrop Stoddard, *The Revolt against Civilization* (New York: Charles Scribner's Sons, 1922).

77 Merriam to Benjamin Ide Wheeler, 18 May 1922, LC/JM/22.

78 First quote from Merriam, "Earth Science as the Background of History," 1:16; second quote from Merriam, *The Garment of God*, p. 38.

79 First quote from Report on address by Merriam before the American Association for the Advancement of Science, *Science Supplement* (1926), p. xxviii; second quote from John Merriam, "Are the Days of Creation Ended?" *Scribner's Magazine* 81, no. 6 (June 1927): 612—18.

80 Quote from Merriam, *The Garment of God*, p. 106. See also Report on address by Merriam before the American Association for the Advancement of Science, p. xxviii.

81 Quotes from Merriam to A. E. Wiggam, 15 May 1922, LC/JM/181. See also Merriam to Oscar Meinzer, 3 March 1936, LC/JM/122.

82 Merriam, *The Garment of God*, p. 2.

83 Merriam, "Are the Days of Creation Ended?" p. 616.

84 Quote from Merriam to James Angell, 13 March 1930, LC/JM/12. See also Merriam, "Are the Days of Creation Ended?" pp. 612–13.

85 Quote from Roderick Nash, *Wilderness and the American Mind* (New Haven: Yale University Press, 1967), p. 182. Aldo Leopold, *A Sand County Almanac* (New York: Oxford University Press, 1949); for Merriam's opinion of Leopold, see John Merriam, "Memorandum of conversation with Secretary Wallace," 26 December 1933, CI/JM/Memorandum of Merriam.

86 Quote from Merriam, *The Garment of God*, pp. 35–36. See also Merriam to G. Ashley, 10 April 1935, LC/JM/13.

87 Report on address by Merriam before the American Association for the Advancement of Science, p. xxviii.

88 Quote from Clarence Urmy, "Dreams in the Redwoods," in *A California Troubadour* (San Francisco: A. M. Robertson, 1912). See also Charles Keeler, "A Redwood Reverie," in *Sequoia Sonnets* (Berkeley, Calif.: Live Oak Press, 1919), p. 14.

89 Don Blanding, "From a Window in Vagabond's House," *Carmel Pine Cone*, 16 September 1928.

90 Bret Harte, "In the Carquinnez Woods," *The Works of Bret Harte*, Argonaut ed. (New York: P. F. Collier, n.d.), 2:265.

91 Quote from Don W. Richards, *The Soul of Sequoia*, First Annual Forest Play of the Sempervirens Club of California in the Redwood Park, Santa Cruz, California (San Jose, Calif.: Hillis-Murgotten Co., 1919), in University of California—Berkeley General Library. For other examples of classically inspired pagan symbolism, see Albert W. Atwood, "Redwood Dividends," *Saturday Evening Post* 197 (25 April 1925): 169; Masefield, *The Taking of Helen and Other Prose Selections*, p. 110; Archibald G. Macdonell, *A Visit to America* (London: Macmillan and Co., 1935).

92 Statement by C. I. Moore, Vice-President, Pacific Mutual Life Insurance Company, in SRL office.

93 Quote from Charles Keeler, "Evolution," in *Sequoia Sonnets* (Berkeley, Calif.: Live Oak Press, 1919), p. 75. Other references to the evolutionary past include Henry A. Kendal, *A Saga of the Redwoods and Other Writings* (Eureka, Calif.: n.p., 1942), in Bancroft Library; Henry S. Graves, "Speech at Henry S. Graves Grove Dedication," 6 September 1925, in SRL office; James Clifford Shirley, *The Redwoods of Coast and Sierra* (Berkeley: University of California Press, 1936); Masefield, *The Taking of Helen and Other Prose Selections*, p. 110; Georgia Russ Williams, "Dedication of the Humboldt Pioneer Memorial Grove," 2 September 1923, in SRL office.

94 Quote from *Napa Journal*, 9 April 1941, and SRL, *Annual Report, 1924–1925*, p. 21.
95 Quotes from Edith Daley, "In the California Redwoods," in *California Poets* (New York: Henry Harrison, 1932), p. 149, and Keeler, "Redwood Reverie," p. 14.
96 Quote from Basil Woon, *San Francisco and the Golden Empire* (New York: H. Smith and R. Haas, 1935), p. 239. For similar instances of religious imagery, see Donald Peattie, "Trees," *Reader's Digest* 32 (January 1938): 47–50; "Rev. Douglass Makes Plea for Redwoods," *Ferndale Enterprise*, 27 February 1920; Jesse Hildebrand, "California Coastal Redwood Realm," *National Geographic Magazine* 75, no. 2 (February 1939): 164–65; Dr. Aurila H. Reinhardt, Dedicatory Address, Garden Club of America Redwood Grove, 1934; George W. James, *California Romantic and Beautiful* (Boston: Page Company, 1914), p. 331; Delmar L. Thornbury, *California's Redwood Wonderland, Humboldt County* (San Francisco: Sunset Press, 1923), p. 37; Waldo Glock to Merriam, 4 September 1937, LC/JM/80; Edwin Markham, *California the Wonderful* (New York: Heart's International Library Co., 1941), p. 305.

Chapter 4: Parks

1 Minutes of the Board of Directors, SRL, 22 March 1938; Drury to Arno Cammerer, 20 May 1938, SRL/A/RNP.
2 Merriam to Arno Cammerer, 27 December 1935, LC/JM/32.
3 Robert Sterling Yard, "Historical Basis of National Park Standards," n.d., LC/JM/187.
4 Act of 1 March 1872, ch. 24, 17 Stat. 32; Act of 25 August 1916, ch. 408, 39 Stat. 535.
5 Hubert Work to Senator Duncan U. Fletcher of Florida, 14 January 1924, letter published in *National Parks Bulletin*, no. 37 (21 January 1924), p. 1.
6 John Merriam, "The Responsibility of Federal and State Governments for Recreation," *National Parks Bulletin* 7, no. 49 (1926): 5–8; Greeley to Merriam, 21 May 1924, LC/JM/149; Merriam to McDuffie, 6 October 1924, LC/JM/120; Merriam to Graves, 9 and 10 June 1926, LC/JM/83.
7 Quotes from John Merriam, "Nature's Super-Universities," Speech delivered before Commonwealth Club, 22 June 1928, reported in *Commonwealth* 4, no. 27 (3 July 1928). See also Donald C. Swain, *Wilderness Defender: Horace M. Albright and Conservation* (Chicago: University of Chicago Press, 1970), pp. 247, 253.
8 John Ise, *Our National Park Policy: A Critical History* (Baltimore: Johns Hopkins Press, 1961), pp. 443–44; Merriam to Vernon Kellogg, 25 October 1928, LC/JM/105; Yard to George Pratt, 14 November 1930, LC/JM/187; Yard to W. W. Atwood, 3 March 1931, Merriam to Atwood, 18 March 1931, 13 August 1931, LC/JM/14; Merriam, "Memorandum," 29 September 1931, LC/JM/187; William Colby, "Reminiscences," interview conducted by Corinne Gilb (Berkeley: ROHO, 1953); Duncan McDuffie, Speech about William Colby at Sierra Club Annual Meeting, 9 February 1927, in Bancroft Library.

9 Swain, *Wilderness Defender*, pp. 53, 68, 45.

10 Lane to Mather, 13 May 1918, LC/JM/149.

11 Quotes from ibid. See also Swain, *Wilderness Defender*, p. 45.

12 Quotes from U.S., National Park Service, *Annual Report of the Director to the Secretary of the Interior for the Fiscal Year Ended June 30, 1925* (Washington, D.C.: GPO, 1925), pp. 1–2. For analysis of early Park Service rhetoric and emphasis on economic considerations, see Michael Turchen, "The National Park Movement: A Study of the Impact of Temporal Change on Rhetoric" (Ph.D. diss., Purdue University, 1972), pp. 48–50.

13 Albright to Drury, 12 December 1945, A/NPS/RG79.

14 Swain, *Wilderness Defender*, p. 247.

15 First quote from Merriam to Chaney, 5 April 1926, LC/JM/41; second quote from Merriam to Charles Adams, 2 July 1938; Adams to Merriam, 26 August 1938, LC/JM/1.

16 For Merriam's descriptions of confrontations during meetings of the Committee on Educational Problems in the National Park Service during the 1920s, see "Memorandum of Conversations with Dr. Bumpus," n.d., LC/JM/27.

17 Quotes from Merriam to Drury, 19 March 1935 and 22 October 1934, B/SRL/2:10–11.

18 Newton B. Drury, "The Debt of Conservation to Dr. John C. Merriam," *American Forests* (December 1945), pp. 597, 621.

19 First quote from Harold Bryant, "Great Outdoor Universities," *Journal of Adult Education* 4 (June 1932): 305–10; for Merriam's retort, see "Memorandum Concerning HAROLD BRYANT'S article entitled 'Great Outdoor Universities,'" 21 August 1932, LC/JM/26.

20 Swain, *Wilderness Defender*, p. 247.

21 SRL, *Annual Report, 1927–1928*, p. 43; Minutes of the Council, SRL, 28 August 1930.

22 Yard's consistency is shown in a letter to Arno Cammerer (23 July 1923, A/NPS/Cammerer) in which he declared, "Secretary Work mistakenly says that 'National Parks were established primarily to afford outdoor recreational facilities' . . . and discusses education as 'a new mission.'" That the league's conception of the movement from the early 1920s was educational and scientific is apparent in the preceding chapter.

23 First and second quotes from Drury to Merriam, 29 January 1934; third quote from Drury to Merriam, 21 February 1936, LC/JM/57–58. See also Drury to Merriam, 6 June 1938, B/SRL/3:2; John Merriam, Speech delivered before National Parks Association, 1931, LC/JM/187.

24 First quote from John Merriam, *The Garment of God: Influence of Nature in Human Experience* (New York: Charles Scribner's Sons, 1943), pp. 56–59; for "Dogwood Day" quotes, see Merriam to Drury, 10 May 1937, LC/JM/56; on Easter, see Merriam to Drury, 12 June 1936, B/SRL/2:12.

25 Quotes from Merriam to Cammerer, 27 December 1935, LC/JM/32. See also Merriam to Drury, 28 January 1932, B/SRL/2:9.

26 *San Francisco Call-Bulletin*, 23 September 1936.

27 Merriam, "Notes for Reply to Cammerer's letter of January 14," 16 January 1935, LC/JM/32.

28 Drury to Merriam, 9 February 1937, LC/JM/56.

29 Merriam, "Notes for Reply to Cammerer's letter of January 14," 16 January 1935, LC/JM/32.

30 Quotes from Isaiah Bowman to Harold Bryant, 2 November 1932, LC/JM/22. See also Merriam, "Memorandum Regarding Administration of Educational Work in National Parks," CI/JM/Merriam and Associates; Merriam to Drury, 12 June 1936, B/SRL/2:12.

31 John Merriam, Speech delivered before National Parks Association, 1931, LC/JM/187.

32 Merriam to J. P. Buwalda, 29 July 1932 and 5 May 1928, LC/JM/30.

33 Merriam to the Committee on Study of Educational Problems in National Parks, 26 December 1929, LC/JM/132; Merriam to Albright, 28 February 1930, LC/JM/2; Ansel Hall to Director of National Park Service, 18 February 1930, LC/JM/131; Hall to Director, 15 January 1930, LC/JM/89; U.S., Department of the Interior, "Memorandum for the Press (P.N. 54646)," 13 June 1931, LC/JM/2.

34 "Statement by Henry S. Graves," 3 April 1923, LC/JM/83; Drury to Merriam, 4 March 1935, B/SRL/2:11; Merriam, "Memorandum Regarding Organization of National Parks," 26 February 1936, LC/JM/131; Merriam to Drury, 16 April 1937, B/SRL/3:1.

35 Merriam, "Memorandum for Conversation with Dr. Henry B. Ward," 2 April 1931, LC/JM/177; Merriam, "Memorandum Regarding National Park Standards," n.d., LC/JM/81.

36 Robert Shankland, *Steve Mather of the National Parks* (New York: Alfred A. Knopf, 1954), p. 282.

37 Quotes from Merriam, "Memorandum Regarding National Park Standards," n.d., LC/JM/81. See also Merriam, "Memorandum on Quachita and the Everglades," n.d., LC/JM/81; Robert Sterling Yard, "Historical Facts and Conditions Affecting the Making, Preservation and Use of the National Park System," 1 May 1931, SRL/A/McDuffie.

38 Roger Toll to Drury, 28 April 1932, A/NPS/RG79.

39 Merriam, "The Everglades of Florida," 1 March 1929; Merriam to Bryant, 13 March 1929, A/NPA/RG79; Merriam, "Memorandum of Conversation with John Merriam and Coe," 4 October 1929, LC/JM/45; Merriam, "Memorandum for Conversation, Dr. Henry B. Ward," n.d., LC/JM/177.

40 Ernest Davidson (landscape architect) to Thomas Vint (chief architect, National Park Service), 30 June 1937, A. E. Demaray to Drury, 19 July 1937, B/SRL/3:1; Drury to Merriam, 27 July 1937, LC/JM/56.

41 Act of 30 May 1934, ch. 371, 48 Stat. 816.

42 Merriam to David Fairchild, 25 March 1930, LC/JM/131; Merriam to H. B. Ward, 2 November 1931, LC/JM/177; Merriam, "Regarding No Federal Appropriation for Purchase of Everglades National Park," 4 January 1932, LC/JM/70; Merriam to Lorne Barclay, 12 March 1932, LC/JM/16; Merriam to W. W. Atwood, 22 February 1933, LC/JM/14.

43 Merriam, "Memorandum for Conversation with Dr. Henry B. Ward," 2 April 1931, LC/JM/177.

44 *Humboldt Times*, 5 February 1936; *Humboldt Standard*, 26 January 1939; see correspondence between Ward and SRL, 1930, LC/JM/117, and between Drury and Merriam, April and May 1936, LC/JM/56 and B/SRL/2:12.

45 John Merriam, "Memorandum Regarding Organization of National Parks," 26 February 1936, LC/JM/131; Merriam to Drury, 16 April 1937, B/SRL/3:1.

46 Drury to Merriam, 26 March 1934, LC/JM/58; Merriam, "Regarding National Park Standards," n.d., LC/JM/81.

47 Merriam, "Memorandum for Conversation with Dr. Henry B. Ward," 2 April 1931, LC/JM/177.

48 Drury to Merriam, 22 March 1938, B/SRL/3:2.

49 Quotes from "Statement by Henry S. Graves," 3 April 1923, LC/JM/83. See also Yard to Hubert Work, 17 April 1923, A/I/Work-2.

50 Cammerer to Albert Stoll, 12 December 1931, A/NPS/Cammerer Misc.

51 Minutes of the Board of Directors, American Forestry Association, 27 April 1936, 25 January 1938, association's papers held by Forest History Society, Santa Cruz, Calif.; Merriam to Drury, 25 February 1937, LC/JM/56.

52 "Statement by Henry S. Graves," 3 April 1923, LC/JM/83; Yard to Hubert Work, 17 April 1923, A/I/Work-2.

53 For the early history of this wilderness program, see William Greeley to Merriam, 21 May 1924, LC/JM/149. At first the Park Service supported the wilderness concept in national forests; see Albright to Don Colton (House Committee on Public Lands), 6 February 1929, LC/JM/3; Cammerer to Albright, 16 August 1929, A/NPS/18; Robert Y. Stuart to Merriam, 27 October 1929, LC/JM/170. For the purists' position, see Merriam to Graves, 23 June 1930, LC/JM/83.

54 Yard to Merriam, 8 January 1932, LC/JM/187.

55 Joel Hildebrand, "Sierra Club Leader and Ski Mountaineer," interview conducted by Ann and Ray Lage (San Francisco: Sierra Club, 1974), pp. 17−25; Frank A. Kittredge, "The Campaign for Kings Canyon National Park," *Sierra Club Bulletin* 45, no. 9 (December 1960): 41−43. For another example of purist opposition to such transfers, see Madison Grant, "Alaskan Bears," and "Vanname'l Land," 24 December 1931, LC/JM/82.

56 Act of 4 March 1940, ch. 40, 54 Stat. 41; Albright to Drury, 1 February 1939, B/SRL/4:10.

57 Drury to Merriam, 19 February 1939, B/SRL/3:3.

58 Quote from Merriam to Drury, 27 February 1939. See also Drury to Merriam, 19 February 1939, 20 February 1939, B/SRL/3:3.

59 Quote from Sperry to Drury, 9 February 1939. See also Arnold to Drury, Graves to Drury, Wentworth to Drury, 9−14 February 1939, B/SRL/4:10.

60 Drury to Merriam, 10 March 1939, B/SRL/3:3.

61 U.S., Department of Agriculture, Office of Information, Press Service Release, "Forest Purchase Program Expanded," 27 March 1934.

62 Emanuel Fritz, "Memorandum to Save-the-Redwoods League Committee

on Redwood National Forest," 7 December 1934, Fritz to Drury, 19 January 1935, SRL/F/RNF.

63 Graves to Fritz, 9 October 1934, 30 October 1934, 13 February 1935, SRL/F/RNF.

64 Fritz to Ovid Butler, 6 March 1935, SRL/F/RNF; Emanuel Fritz, "Memorandum for Save-the-Redwoods League Committee on National Forests"; Minutes of meeting, 11 March 1935, SRL/F/RNF; Fritz to Merriam, 11 March 1935, SRL/A/McDuffie; T. D. Woodbury (assistant regional forester) to Fritz, 12 March 1935, SRL/F/RNF.

65 *Del Norte Triplicate*, 18 May 1934, 25 May 1934, 6 September 1935; *Humboldt Times*, 20 April 1934, 22 May 1934, 15 June 1934, 18 July 1934, 26 January 1939, 19 March 1939; Resolution, Mendocino County Improvement Club, 12 June 1934.

66 T. D. Woodbury to Fritz, 30 August 1935, SRL/F/RNF; *Republican Press* (Ukiah), 11 September 1935; Fact Sheet on Southern Redwood Purchase Unit, 30 September 1936, SRL/F/RNF.

67 Emerson Knight, "Report on the Mill Creek-Rust Tract, Project IV," 22 September 1925; Knight, "Supplement to a Report for the Save the Redwoods League on the Mill Creek-Rust Tract," 16 January 1928 SRL/A/IV; SRL, *Annual Report, 1925–1926*, p. 3; Frederick Law Olmsted, *A State Park Survey of California* (Berkeley: SRL, 1927).

68 Interview with Tom Greig, conducted by Susan R. Schrepfer (San Francisco: SRL, 1969), pp. 5–10.

69 Drury to Merriam, 20 April 1927, Drury, "Summary of the Main Projects of the Save the Redwoods League," 15 September 1927, LC/JM/61; Duane D. Fischer, "The Short, Unhappy Story of the Del Norte Lumber Company," *Forest History* 2, no. 1 (April 1967): 12–25.

70 Minutes of the Council, SRL, 28 August 1930; SRL, *Annual Report, 1936–1937*.

71 Merriam to Drury, 17 April 1935, LC/JM/57.

72 A. E. Demaray to Drury, 15 December 1937, SRL/F/RNF; John S. McLaughlin, "Report on Mill Creek Forest Tract," January 1938, Drury to Graves, 11 April 1938, SRL/F/RNF; A. E. Demaray, "Memorandum for the Secretary of the Interior," 14 September 1938, A/I/12-0; Minutes of the Board of Directors, SRL, 12 January 1939.

73 Minutes of the Board of Directors, SRL, 22 March 1938.

74 Drury to Cammerer, 20 May 1938, SRL/A/RNP.

75 Drury to Merriam, 8 March 1932, 30 September 1939, LC/JM/59; Merriam, "Memorandum for Conversation with Secretary Wilbur," 18 January 1932, LC/JM/Merriam and Associates.

76 Drury to Merriam, 3 February 1938, LC/JM/56; Minutes of the Board of Directors, SRL, 22 March 1938.

77 Drury to Merriam, 13 July 1937, 27 March 1938, LC/JM/55–56.

78 Drury to Merriam, 2 November 1939, 15 November 1939, 24 November 1939, B/SRL/3:3; Minutes of the Board of Directors, SRL, 28 July 1941.

79 C. E. Rachford to Drury, 14 July 1939, "Statement by Mr. Chester Morse

for U.S. Forest Service at Supervisors Hearing in Crescent City," 2 August 1939, SRL/F/RNF; National Forest Reservation Commission to Secretary of War, transmitting Pursuant to Law, a Report of the National Forest Reservation Commission for the Year Ending, 30 July 1943, 78th Congress, 2nd sess., Senate Document no. 145.

Chapter 5: Progressive Opposition to the New Deal

1 Otis Graham, Jr., *An Encore for Reform: The Old Progressives and the New Deal* (London: Oxford University Press, 1968), pp. 24–100.

2 First quote from Drury to Merriam, 12 December 1934; second quote from Drury to Merriam, 15 December 1934, LC/JM/56–58. See also Drury to Merriam, 14 November 1934, 14 and 20 December 1934, LC/JM/56–58.

3 First quotes from Drury to Merriam, 30 December 1934; last quote from Drury to Merriam, 22 December 1934, LC/JM/56–58. See also Drury to Merriam, 10 and 26 January 1935, 13 July 1936, Merriam to Frank Merriam, 24 December 1934, 29 October 1935, LC/JM/56–58.

4 "Summary Redwood Park Lands Acquired as of May 15, 1930," SRL/A/I.

5 Quote from Drury to Merriam, 16 January 1935, LC/JM/56–59. See also Drury to Merriam, 29 March 1935, 9 and 30 September 1936, LC/JM/ 56–59.

6 Quote from *Humboldt Times*, 1 November 1936. See also Drury to Merriam, 13 and 14 November 1936, LC/JM/56.

7 Drury to Merriam, 10 October 1936, B/SRL/2:12.

8 Quotes from Drury to Merriam, 5 and 26 March 1937, LC/JM/56.

9 William Colby, "Reminiscences," interview conducted by Corinne Gilb (Berkeley: ROHO, 1953), pp. 60–68.

10 Drury to Merriam, 24 November 1939, B/SRL/3:3; William Colby to SRL, 29 June 1936, B/SRL/4:7.

11 First quote from Drury to Merriam, 12 March 1937; second quote from Drury to Merriam, 15 December 1934, LC/JM/56. See also Drury to Merriam, 9 November 1939, LC/JM/56.

12 First quote from Charles Merriam, *University Record* 14, no. 2 (April 1928): 69–70; second quote from J. D. Grant, "Twenty Rings in the Redwoods: An Informal History of the Save-the-Redwoods League," p. 92, in SRL office. See also *San Francisco Chronicle*, 12 September 1938.

13 Quote from Hubert Work to R. S. Yard, 16 October 1926, A/I/Work-2. See also Kellogg to Work, 20 October 1926, George Grinnell to Work, 22 October 1926, A/I/Work-2; Merriam to McDuffie, 27 June 1928, LC/JM/ 120; Drury to Merriam, 29 January 1934, LC/JM/58; Vernon Kellogg, *Herbert Hoover: The Man and His Work* (London: D. Appleton and Company, 1920); Merriam, speech before American Legis Association, 26 February 1933, LC/JM/9; Drury to Merriam, 18 September 1934, B/SRL/ 2:10; A. W. Atwood to Merriam, 14 May 1936, LC/JM/5; Walter Mulford, "Forestry in California," *California Journal of Development* [*Pacific Business*] 26, no. 3 (March 1936): 14–18, 29–30.

14 W. W. Campbell to Drury, 29 April 1935, SRL/A/SPL; Drury to Merriam,

18 September 1934, B/SRL/2:10; Albert W. Atwood, "How Far Should Government Go?" *Saturday Evening Post*, 18 April 1931, pp. 25, 28, 90, 95; Atwood, "Leaning on Uncle Sam," *Saturday Evening Post*, 10 January 1931, pp. 22–23, 117–18.

15 Quote from Merriam to Drury, 1 March 1935, B/SRL/2:11. See also Merriam to Drury, 16 February 1934, LC/JM/58.

16 Drury to Merriam, 18 and 26 April 1934, Merriam to Drury, 17 April 1934, B/SRL/2:10; Drury to Merriam, 25 February 1935, Merriam to Drury, 13 February 1937, LC/JM/56–57.

17 Minutes of the Council, SRL, 11 September 1931, 1 September 1932. Lawrence Merriam, "A Protection Plan for Bull Creek and Dyerville," SRL/A/I; J. D. Grant to Merriam, 28 August 1932, LC/JM/82; Merriam to Drury, 11 May 1933, B/SRL/2:9.

18 First quote from Drury to Merriam, 25 February 1934, LC/JM/58; second quote from Drury to Merriam, 6 October 1934, B/SRL/2:10. See also SRL, *Annual Report, 1932–1933*; Fritz to Drury, 6 October 1939, B/SRL/4:7.

19 J. D. Grant to Merriam, 28 April 1932, LC/JM/82.

20 *Congressional Record*, 71st Cong., 2d sess., 23 January 1930, 72, pt. 2:2256.

21 F. W. Wentworth to Drury, 21 October 1929, Cornwall to Drury, Grant to Drury, 6 February 1930, G. S. Arnold to Drury, 13 February 1930, McDuffie to H. Evison, 15 April 1930, SRL/A/SPL.

22 Merriam to Graves, 14 May 1930, LC/JM/83; Yard to Merriam, 8 October 1930, "Report of Committee on Federal Subsidy for State Parks, National Parks Association," 20 January 1931, LC/JM/187; Drury to Merriam, 8 March 1930, 22 January 1936, LC/JM/57–59; Colby to Merriam, 30 July 1935, LC/JM/82; Albright to Yard, 13 May 1930, LC/JM/2; Albright to Drury, 21 December 1931; J. L. Bossemeyer, "Proceedings of the Far West Regional Conference on State Parks," 31 August 1936, SRL/A/SPL.

23 "Report of Committee on Federal Subsidy for State Parks, National Parks Association," 20 January 1931, LC/JM/187; Merriam to Drury, 14 February 1931, LC/JM/59; Atwood, "How Far Should Government Go?" pp. 25–28; Drury to W. W. Campbell, 21 May 1935, Campbell to Drury, 29 April 1935, SRL/A/SPL.

24 Act of 23 June 1936, Ch. 735, 40 Stat. 1894.

25 Drury to Nordenholdt, 21 July 1936, SRL/A/SPL.

26 Quotes from Emerson Knight, "Memorandum for the Regional Officer, Attention of Raymond E. Hoyt, Recreational Planner, Confidential Comment on Park, Parkway and Recreation-Area Study," 5 March 1937. See also Drury to Merriam, 15 March 1937, B/SRL/3:1; Colby to Merriam, 30 July 1935, LC/JM/82; Colby to Yard, 7 May 1936, LC/JM/45.

27 First quote from Farquhar to Drury, 13 April 1938, LC/JM/55; second quote from Knight, "Memorandum for the Regional Officer," LC/JM/56. See also Drury to Merriam, 8 February 1937, LC/JM/56.

28 Quote from Merriam, speech before American Legis Association, 26 February 1933, LC/JM/9. See also Drury to Merriam, 24 November 1939, B/SRL/3:3.

29 Quote from Merriam to A. W. Atwood, 22 October 1930, LC/JM/13. See

also Grant, "Twenty Rings," p. iv; Drury to Merriam, 2 June 1934, LC/JM/57; Campbell to Drury, 29 April 1935, SRL/A/SPL.

30 Drury to Merriam, 18 September 1934, B/SRL/2:10.

31 Merriam, "Memo from Merriam to H. Ickes," 8 March 1933, LC/JM/98; Merriam to Henry Ward, 21 June 1935, LC/JM/177.

32 Merriam to C. Merriam, 11 March 1932, LC/JM/123; Drury to Merriam, 10 January 1935, 29 March 1935, LC/JM/57−58; Drury to Merriam, Merriam to Drury, 17 and 21 April 1936, B/SRL/2:12; Newton Drury, "Parks and Redwoods: 1919−1971," interview conducted by Amelia Fry and Susan R. Schrepfer (Berkeley: ROHO, 1972), pp. 188−90. Interview with George Waldner conducted by Susan R. Schrepfer, 1969, Ferndale, Calif., in SRL office.

33 Quote from Merriam, speech before American Legis Association, 26 February 1933, LC/JM/9. See also Merriam to C. Merriam, 11 March 1932, 11 July 1937, LC/JM/123; Drury to Merriam, 25 May 1933, 9 February 1937, LC/JM/56−58.

34 Minutes, Society of American Foresters, 4 June 1934, held by Forest History Society, Santa Cruz, Calif.; Merriam to Drury, 23 March 1929, B/SRL/2:5; Farquhar to Drury, 13 April 1938, LC/JM/55.

35 Quote from Merriam to Drury, 5 October 1935, B/SRL/2:11. See also Drury to Merriam, 9 March 1935, B/SRL/2:11; Drury to Merriam, 25 February 1934, LC/JM/58; Drury to Merriam, 2 March 1938, B/SRL/3:2; Merriam to J. D. Grant, 21 December 1932, LC/JM/82.

36 Quote from Board of Directors, SRL, 12 February 1939. See also J. D. Grant, "Random Notes by Mr. Grant on Redwoods," n.d., SRL/A/Grant; Drury to Merriam, 25 February 1934, 8 February 1937, LC/JM/56−58; Merriam to Drury, 1 April 1935, Drury to Merriam, 2 August 1934, 3 January 1936, B/SRL/2:9−12.

37 Quotes from Merriam to Drury, 21 March 1932, LC/JM/59. See also Merriam to Arno Cammerer, 25 June 1935, LC/JM/32; J. D. Grant, "Twenty Rings," p. iv, 92; Work to R. S. Yard, 16 October 1926, Vernon Kellogg to Work, 20 October 1925, George Grinnell to Work, 22 October 1925, A/I/Work-2; Merriam to Charles Davenport, 7 April 1930, LC/JM/56; Merriam, "Notes Made at the Meeting of the Board of Directors of the American Forestry Association," 18 December 1930, LC/JM/7.

38 Merriam, "Notes on Democracy, Equality and Indians," 14 May 1934, LC/JM/46.

39 Albert W. Atwood, "Let George Do It," *Saturday Evening Post*, 14 February 1931, pp. 23, 134−40; Atwood, "Leaning on Uncle Sam" pp. 2−23, 117−18; Drury to Merriam, 14 February 1931, Merriam to Drury, 9 March 1931, LC/JM/59; Drury to Campbell, 21 May 1935, Campbell to Drury, 29 April 1935, SRL/A/SPL.

40 Drury to Merriam, 8, 13 and 14 November 1936, 12 March 1937, LC/JM/56.

41 On Sierra Club, see Colby to Merriam, 29 June 1934, B/SRL/2:10; Colby to Harold Hopkins, 4 December 1935, LC/JM/45. There were exceptions: Ray Lyman Wilbur was a states' rightist and a booster, and Ickes was a

New Dealer and a purist, in theory if not in practice; see Ickes to Jensen, 18 March 1938, Ickes to Ross, 10 June 1942, LC/HI/222.

42 First quote from Merriam to Drury, 5 January 1938, B/SRL/3:1; second and third quotes from Merriam to Drury, 22 May 1936, B/SRL/2:12. See also Drury to Merriam, 29 December 1937, B/SRL/3:1; Merriam to Drury, 24 January 1936, B/SRL/2:12.

43 Minutes of the Executive Board, SRL, 20 August 1919.

44 Drury to Merriam, 15 and 27 March 1922, 7 November 1922, B/SRL/ 1:22; Albright to Merriam, 27 March 1922, LC/JM/3; Drury to Merriam, 20 March 1923, 31 August 1923, 12 January 1924, LC/JM/64.

45 Quote from Cammerer to Samuel Shortridge, 13 January 1923, SRL/A/ RNP. See also Greeley to William Stephens, 28 May 1921, Graves to Kent, 10 March 1923, LC/JM/83−84; *San Francisco Examiner*, 1 April 1925.

46 Merriam to Sperry, 10 February 1921, B/SRL/1:21; Barrington Moore to J. B. Payne, 4 May 1925, LC/JM/126; Council Minutes, National Conference on Outdoor Recreation, 22 January 1926; Merriam to Ray Lyman Wilbur, 7 February 1927, LC/JM/81; Merriam to W. W. Atwood, 25 September 1929, LC/JM/14.

47 U.S., National Park Service, *Annual Report of the Director to the Secretary of the Interior for the Fiscal Year Ended June 30, 1925* (Washington, D.C.: GPO, 1925), p. 6; Kent to J. D. Grant, 20 January 1925, LC/JM/63; Kent to Drury, 25 May 1926, SRL/A/RNP; Work to Yard, 25 May 1925, A/I/NPS-2; Merriam, "Memorandum of Conversation with Mr. Hoover, April 24, 1925," LC/JM/157.

48 Act of 21 August 1935, ch. 593, 40 Stat. 667; Ickes to Merriam, 15 July 1935, LC/JM/98; Merriam to Colby, 31 July 1935, LC/JM/45; Merriam to H. Marvin, 23 August 1935, LC/JM/118.

49 Merriam, "Memorandum of Conversation with Secretary Wilbur," 2 April 1929, CI/JM/Memoranda.

50 Department of the Interior, Press Release, 3 February 1936; Merriam to Campbell, 8 February 1936, LC/JM/32; Ickes to W. W. Atwood, 24 February 1936, Atwood to Merriam, 27 February 1936, Merriam to Atwood, 28 February 1936, LC/JM/13; Colby to Yard, 7 May 1936, LC/ JM/45.

51 Merriam, "Memorandum on Conference with Mr. Silcox, Mr. Show and Mr. Lawrence Merriam," 22 January 1924; Merriam, "Memorandum of Conversation with Mr. L. F. Knepp," 27 December 1938, LC/JM/ Memoranda; F. Silcox to Drury, 29 June 1936, B/SRL/4:7.

52 Quote from Merriam to Drury, 24 May 1934, LC/JM/58. See also Yard to Merriam, 8 October 1933, LC/JM/187; Minutes, AFA, 17−20 October 1934.

53 Drury to Cammerer, 23 April 1939, Cammerer to Drury, 28 June 1939, Kittredge to Drury, 28 February 1939, SRL/A/RNP.

54 Quotes from Merriam to C. Merriam, 8 and 9 March 1933, LC/JM/122. See also C. Merriam to Merriam, 23 and 26 February 1933, LC/JM/122; Merriam to Ickes, 8 March 1933, LC/JM/98.

55 Quote from Merriam to F. Delano, 28 March 1933, LC/JM/52. See also Merriam to C. Merriam, 7 April 1933, LC/JM/122; Merriam to I. Bowan,

3 June 1933, LC/JM/22; Drury to Merriam, 25 May 1933, 29 January 1934, LC/JM/58.

56 Minutes of the Council, SRL, 15 July 1939.

57 J. D. Grant, "Random Notes," SRL/A/Grant; Grant, "Twenty Rings," p. iv.

58 Newton Drury, interview conducted by Ann Lage, June 1977, San Francisco.

59 Graham, *An Encore for Reform*, pp. 24, 29, 41.

60 Joel Hildebrand, "Sierra Club Leader and Ski Mountaineer," interview conducted by Ann and Ray Lage (San Francisco: Sierra Club, 1974), pp. 17−20; Colby to Merriam, 30 July 1935, LC/JM/82.

61 Samuel P. Hays, "The Social Analysis of American Political History, 1880−1920," *Political Science Quarterly* 80 (September 1965): 388−89.

62 Drury to Merriam, 29 January 1934, LC/JM/58.

63 Quote from David R. Brower, "Environmental Activist, Publicist, and Prophet," interview conducted by Susan R. Schrepfer (Berkeley: ROHO, 1978), p. 51. See also Drury-Albright correspondence, 1943, A/NPS/ RG79.

64 Quote from Ickes to Irving Brant, 19 July 1943, LC/HI/222. See also Brant to Ickes, 7 July 1943, Drury to Ickes, 28 July 1944, LC/HI/222; Elmo Richardson, *Dams, Parks and Politics* (Lexington: University of Kentucky, 1973), pp. 42−47, 51−56, 62−67, 141.

65 Interview with Drury by Lage, June 1977.

66 *Saving the Redwoods, 1939* (Berkeley: SRL, 1939); Arthur Connick, "Memorandum," 16 June 1938, SRL/H/I.

67 U.S., House of Representatives, 79th Cong., 2d sess., *Journal*, 18 April 1946, p. 953.

68 Quote from *Del Norte Triplicate*, 26 April 1946. See also *Del Norte Triplicate*, 9 August 1946; *Humboldt Times*, 11 January 1949.

69 Olmsted to Smith, 9 and 11 August 1945, 11 December 1945, Smith to Drury, 1 December 1945; Drury to Smith, 3 April 1946, SRL/A/RNF.

70 Drury to McDuffie, 10 September 1946; "Telephone transcript of September 11, 1946, between Major Tomlinson, F. L. Olmsted of S.F., and Drury of Chicago"; Olmsted, "Memorandum for the Director, NPS," 12 September 1946, SRL/A/RNF.

71 Drury, "The California Redwoods and the Relation Thereto of the Federal Government," 9 November 1946; Drury to Rep. Lea, 25 November 1946, SRL/A/RNF.

72 Drury to Wright, 12 February 1947, SRL/A/RNF; Drury to McDuffie, 22 March 1949, SRL/A/McDuffie; U.S., House of Representatives, 81st Cong., 1st sess., *Journal*, 5 January 1949, p. 93.

73 Quotes from SRL, Council, 12 September 1946, SRL/A/RNF. See also McDuffie to Smith, 12 January 1946; Emanuel Fritz, "Why Douglas Bill Should be Defeated," 18 September 1946; McDuffie to *Del Norte Triplicate*, 14 August 1946, Drury to Humboldt Chamber of Commerce, 17 September 1946, SRL/A/RNF; *Humboldt Standard*, 8 November 1946.

Chapter 6: Evolution and Ecology

1 Vernon Kellogg, *Darwinism To-day* (New York: Henry Holt, 1908), p. 1; E. D. Cope, *The Primary Factors of Organic Evolution* (Chicago, 1896), p. 9; Thomas Eimer, *On Orthogenesis and the Importance of Natural Selection in Species Formation* (Chicago: Open Court, 1898), p. 21; Maynard Metcalf, "Adaptation through Natural Selection and Orthogenesis," *American Naturalist* 47, no. 554 (1913): 66, 69. For secondary sources, see G. S. Carter, *A Hundred Years of Evolution* (London: Sidgwick and Jackson, 1958), pp. 96–106; Sewall Wright, "The Foundation of Population Genetics," in R. Alexander Brink, *Heritage from Mendel* (Madison: The University of Wisconsin Press, 1967), p. 246.

2 Garland E. Allen, "Hugo de Vries and the Reception of the 'Mutation' Theory," *Journal of the History of Biology* 2, no. 1 (1969): 55–76; L. C. Dunn, *A Short History of Genetics* (New York: McGraw-Hill, 1965), p. 56.

3 Quote from Robert F. Griggs, "The Course of Evolution," *Journal of the Washington Academy of Sciences* 29, no. 3 (1939): 133. See also Leo S. Berg, *Nomogenesis or Evolution Determined by Law* (London: Constable & Co., 1926), pp. 377–84; Francis B. Sumner, "Is Evolution a Continuous or Discontinuous Process?" *The Scientific Monthly* 29, no. 1 (1929): 72–78. On the debate over continuous versus discontinuous variation before and after de Vries, see Ernst Mayr, "The Recent Historiography of Genetics," *Journal of the History of Biology* 6, no. 1 (1973): 146–51.

4 Stephen Jay Gould, *Ever Since Darwin, Reflections in Natural History* (New York: W.W. Norton and Company, 1977), pp. 84–85.

5 Quote from Kellogg, *Darwinism To-day*, pp. 56, 77. See also Henry Fairfield Osborn, *The Titanotheres of Ancient Wyoming, Dakota and Nebraska*, U.S. Geological Survey Monograph 55 (Washington, D.C.: G.P.O., 1929), pp. 834–43. On early doubts, see H. J. Muller, "The Darwinian and Modern Conceptions of Natural Selection," *Proceedings of the American Philosophical Society* 93, no. 6 (December 1949): 459–61.

6 Berg, *Nomogenesis*, p. 35. [In the event that only one bibliographic item by a given author appears in this chapter, subsequent references will include last names only.]

7 Harold Blum, "A Consideration of Evolution from a Thermodynamic View-point," *American Naturalist* 69, no. 723 (1935): 368–69. Richard Holman and Wilfred Robbins, *A Textbook of General Botany for Colleges and Universities* (New York: John Wiley & Sons, 1946), p. 592; William Bateson, "Evolutionary Faith and Modern Doubts," *Science* 55, no. 1412 (1922): 56–59. For secondary sources on early twentieth-century scientists' doubts that natural selection was the primary cause of progressive evolution, see Wright, "The Foundations of Population Genetics," p. 246; Mayr, "The Recent Historiography of Genetics," p. 149; Allen, pp. 55–56.

8 Henry Fairfield Osborn, "Aristogenesis, the Observed Order of Biomedical

Evolution," *Proceedings of the National Academy of Sciences* 19, no. 7 (1933): 699−703; Edward Sinnott, *The Biology of the Spirit* (New York: Viking Press, 1955), pp. 47, 131, 169; Allen, pp. 76−77; Philip G. Fothergill, *Historical Aspects of Organic Evolution* (New York: Philosophical Library, 1953), pp. 166−67; Ernst Mayr and William B. Provine, eds., *The Evolutionary Synthesis, Perspectives on the Unification of Biology* (Cambridge, Mass.: Harvard University Press, 1980).

9 First quote from David Starr Jordan and Vernon Kellogg, *Evolution and Animal Life* (New York: D. Appleton & Co., 1908), p. 563; second quote from N. I. Vavilof, "Homologous Variation," *Journal of Genetics* 12 (1922): 47−89; third quote from Kellogg, "Is There Determinate Variation?" *Science* 24 (1906): 621−28; fourth quote from A. Franklin Shull, "Weismann and Haeckle: One Hundred Years," *Science* 81, no. 2106 (1934): 448. See also John Schaffner, "The General Course of Evolution in the Plant Kingdom," *The Ohio Journal of Science* 28, no. 6 (1928): 227−28; Metcalf, pp. 67−70; Allen, pp. 77−78.

10 Henry Fairfield Osborn, "Orthogenesis as Observed from Paleontological Evidence Beginning in the Year 1889," *American Naturalist* 56, no. 643 (1922): 135−42; Fothergill, *Historical Aspects of Organic Evolution*, pp. 168, 274.

11 On incipient structures, see Osborn, *The Titanotheres of Ancient Wyoming, Dakota and Nebraska*, pp. 133−39, 813−17, 834−43; Shull pp. 448−50; Schaffner, pp. 227−28; Metcalf, pp. 67−70; Gould, *Ever Since Darwin*, pp. 103−10. On parallelism, see Charles B. Davenport, "The Form of Evolutionary Theory that Modern Genetical Research Seems to Favor," *American Naturalist* 50, no. 596 (1916): 453−58; Sumner, pp. 72−78; M. F. Guyer, "Orthogenesis and Serological Phenomena," *American Naturalist* 56, no. 643 (1922): 118−19; Schaffner, pp. 279−91.

12 Shull, pp. 447−50; Metcalf, pp. 70; Davenport, pp. 449−50; Osborn, "Orthogenesis as Observed from Paleontological Evidence," pp. 135−42.

13 John Greene, *The Death of Adam* (Ames, Ia.: The Iowa State University Press, 1959), pp. 295−335; Cynthia Eagle Russett, *Darwin in America* (San Francisco: W. H. Freeman & Co., 1976), pp. 25−43; Richard Hofstadter, *Social Darwinism in American Thought* (Boston: Beacon Press, 1955); Stow Persons, *Evolutionary Thought in America* (New Haven: Yale University Press, 1950), pp. 426−27.

14 Blum, pp. 367−68; Schaffner, pp. 279−80; Griggs, p. 133; Osborn, *The Titanotheres of Ancient Wyoming, Dakota and Nebraska*, 2:883. For the history of the law of "irreversibility," see Glenn Jepsen, Ernst Mayr, G. G. Simpson, eds., *Genetics, Paleontology, and Evolution* (Princeton: Princeton University Press, 1949), pp. 109−13; Jacques Monod, *Chance and Necessity: An Essay on the Natural Philosophy of Modern Biology* (New York: Alfred Knopf, 1971), pp. 197−99; Stephen Jay Gould, "Dollo on Dollo's Law: Irreversibility and the Status of Evolutionary Laws," *Journal of the History of Biology* 3, no. 2 (1970): 202−3.

15 Quote from Edmund W. Sinnott, *Botany* (New York: McGraw-Hill Book

Co., 1935), pp. 344–45. See also Holman and Robbins, *A Textbook of General Botany*, p. 582.

16 Davenport, pp. 449–50; Shull, p. 445; Bateson, p. 60; Mayr and Provine, *The Evolutionary Synthesis*, pp. 11–13, 18–19, 123–34.

17 L. J. Henderson, "Orthogenesis from the Standpoint of the Biochemist," *American Naturalist* 56, no. 643 (1922): 104.

18 Shull, p. 448.

19 Bashford Dean, "Evolution in a Determinate Line, as Illustrated by the Egg-Cases of Chimaeroid Fishes," *Biological Bulletin* 7 (104): 105–12; Guyer, pp. 121–33; Leo S. Berg, *Nomogenesis or Evolution Determined by Law* (Cambridge, Mass.: M.I.T. Press, 1969), p. x.

20 Shull, p. 449.

21 Henri Bergson, *Creative Evolution*, trans. Arthur Mitchel (New York: Holt, 1911); Blum, p. 354; Schaffner, p. 279; Charles Lipman, "Orthogenesis in Bacteria," *American Naturalist* 56, no. 643 (1922): 106.

22 Quote from John H. Schaffner, "Principles of Plant Taxonomy," *Ohio Journal of Science* 28, no. 6 (1928): 291. See also C. O. Whitman, "The Problem of the Origin of Species," *Proceedings of the Congress of Arts and Science* 5 (1906): 41–58.

23 Sinnott, *Botany*, pp. 344–45; Holman and Robbins, *A Textbook of General Botany*, pp. 588–98.

24 Quote from Edgar Altenburg, *How We Inherit* (New York: Henry Holt & Co., 1928), p. 120. For other critics, see Malcolm Thorpe, ed., *Organic Adaptation to Environment* (New Haven: Yale University Press, 1924), p. 129; A. P. Jacot, "The Status of the Species and Genius," *American Naturalist* 66 (1932): 346–64; P. E. Raymond, *Prehistoric Life* (Cambridge: Harvard University Press, 1939), p. 306.

25 In addition to advocates of orthogenesis otherwise cited in this chapter, see E. B. Babcock, "The Role of Factor Mutations in Evolution," *American Naturalist* 52 (1918): 116–28; O. F. Cook, "Aspects of Kinetic Evolution," *Proceedings of the Washington Academy of Science* 8 (1907): 197–203; J. M. Coulter, "A Suggested Explanation of 'Orthogenesis' in Plants," *Science* 42 (1913): 859–63; C. W. Crile, "Orthogenesis and the Power and Infirmities of Man," *Proceedings of the American Philosophical Society* 72 (1933): 245–54; A. Dendy, "Progressive Evolution and the Origin of the Species," *American Naturalist* 49 (1915): 149–82; C. Grant, "Orthogenetic Variation," *Proceedings of the Indiana Academy of Science* 46 (1937): 240–45; R. F. Griggs, "The Course of Evolution," *Journal of the Washington Academy of Science* 29, no. 3 (1939): 118–37; E. A. Hooten, *Up from the Apes* (New York: Macmillan, 1931), p. 600; F. B. Loomis, "Momentum in Evolution," *American Naturalist* 39 (1905): 839–44; R. Pearl, "Fecundity in the Domestic Fowl and the Selection Problem," *American Naturalist* 50 (1916): 89–105; Arthur H. Sturtevant, "An Interpretation of Orthogenesis," *Science* 59 (1924): 464–67; L. R. Wheeler, *Harmony of Nature* (New York: Longmans, Green and Co., 1947); C. O. Whitman, *Orthogenetic Evolution in Pigeons*, vol. 1, Carnegie

Institution of Washington Publication 257 (1919); J. C. Willis, *Age and Area: A Study in Geographical Distribution and Origin of Species* (Cambridge: Cambridge University Press, 1922), p. 215. The best-known twentieth-century American exponent in botany was John Schaffner, "Orthogenetic Series Resulting from a Simple Progressive Movement," *Ohio Journal of Science* 30 (1930): 61–79; in zoology, Maynard Metcalf, "Trends in Evolution: A Discussion of Data Bearing on Orthogenesis," *Journal of Anatomy and Physiology* 45 (1913): 1–45; in paleontology, Henry Fairfield Osborn, *Fifty-Two Years of Research, Observation and Publication, 1877–1929* (New York: Charles Scribner's Sons, 1930), pp. 64–73. For discussions of orthogenesis, see Theodosius Dobzhansky, *Genetics and the Origins of the Species* (New York: Columbia University Press, 1951), p. 100; G. G. Simpson, *The Meaning of Evolution* (New Haven: Yale University Press, 1949), p. 49; Glenn Jepsen, "Selection, 'Orthogenesis,' and the Fossil Record," *Proceedings of the American Philosophical Association* 93, no. 6 (1949): 479–500.

26 Quote from introd. by Theodosius Dobzhansky, in Berg, *Nomogenesis*, 1969, p. viii.

27 Emanuel Radl, *The History of Biological Theories*, trans. Edith Jesse Hatfield (London: H. Mildord, Oxford University Press, 1930), p. 352.

28 G. G. Simpson, *The Major Features of Evolution* (New York: Columbia University Press, 1953), pp. 134–35; Julian Huxley, *The Modern Synthesis* (London: George Allen & Unwin, 1944), pp. 38, 173.

29 Julian Huxley, *Essays of a Biologist* (New York: Alfred Knopf, 1923), pp. 8–33.

30 H. H. Newman, *Readings in Evolution, Genetics and Eugenics* (Chicago: University of Chicago Press, 1921), p. 36.

31 Jepsen, p. 496.

32 Frederick Hoffman, *The Twenties* (New York: The Free Press, 1965), pp. 275, 277.

33 Quotes from H. H. Newman, ed., *The Nature of the World and of Man* (New York: Garden City Publishing Co., 1926), pp. 98, 161, 218, 239, 348. See also Sinnott, *Botany*, pp. 344–45; Joseph Barrell, Charles Schuchert, et al., *The Evolution of Earth and Its Inhabitants* (New Haven: Yale University Press, 1918), p. 146; G. T. Patrick, *Introduction to Philosophy* (New York: 1924), p. 160. There were of course scientists who wrote of the evolutionary deterioration of modern man; see for example George A. Batisell, ed., *The Evolution of Earth and Man* (New Haven: Yale University Press, 1918), pp. 386–92.

34 Holman and Robbins, *A Textbook of General Botany*, pp. 1–2, 612.

35 Joseph LeConte, *Evolution and Its Relation to Religious Thought* (New York: D. Appleton & Co., 1889), pp. 299–307.

36 Quote from Linnie Marsh Wolfe, *Son of the Wilderness: The Life of John Muir* (New York: Alfred A. Knopf, 1951), p. 77. See also William F. Badé, *The Life and Letters of John Muir* (New York: Houghton Mifflin, 1924); Duncan McDuffie, unpublished writing, in SRL office; William F. Badé, "An Outdoor Litany," *Sierra Club Bulletin* 11, no. 3 (1922): 270;

Chester Rowell, "The Mountain and the Sea," *Sierra Club Bulletin* 11, no. 3 (1922): 261.

37 Jordan and Kellogg, *Evolution and Animal Life*, p. 468.

38 Ibid.; Kellogg, "Is There Determinate Variation?" pp. 621—28.

39 Osborn, *The Titanotheres of Ancient Wyoming, Dakota and Nebraska*, pp. 813—17; Henry Fairfield Osborn, *Men of the Old Stone Age: The Earth Speaks to Bryan* (New York: Charles Scribner's Sons, 1925); Ralph Chaney, "Plant Distribution as a Guide to Age Determination," 22 May 1936, LC/JM/39; Ralph Chaney, "Trees and History," in *Science in the University* (Berkeley: University of California Press, 1944), pp. 247—54; Willis Jepson, *Trees, Shrubs, and Flowers of the Redwood Region* (San Francisco: SRL, 1935), p. 6.

40 For Muir on "The God of the Mountains" and nature as a temple, see Edwin Way Teale, ed., *The Wilderness World of John Muir* (Boston: Houghton-Mifflin, 1954), p. 320; William Badé, "Palestine and California: A Contrast and a Warning," dedication of the Harris Whittemore Memorial Grove (1929), in SRL office.

41 Alfred Runte, "The National Park Idea: Origins and Paradox of the American Experience," *Journal of Forest History* 21, no. 2 (April 1977): 65—75.

42 Quote from Joseph LeConte, *Evolution: Its Nature, Its Evidence, and Its Relation to Religious Thought* (New York: Appleton Press, 1891), p. 79. See also LeConte, "The Theory of Evolution and Social Progress," *Monist* (July 1895), pp. 481—500.

43 Stowe Persons, *Evolutionary Thought in America* (New Haven: Yale University Press, 1950), pp. 442—43; Russett, *Darwin in America*, pp. 102—12, 147—48. On this paradox of reform and faith in progress, see William O'Neill, *The Progressive Years* (New York: Dodd, Meade & Co., 1975), pp. 93—95.

44 Merriam to Hale, 11 November 1920, Merriam to Grant, 31 January 1925, LC/JM/82—87.

45 Quotes from Albert Atwood, "Nature as Created," *Saturday Evening Post* 197 (28 February 1925): 16—17. See also Atwood, "Redwood Dividends," *Saturday Evening Post* 197 (25 April 1925): 10—11, 169—73; John Merriam, *The Garment of God: Influence of Nature in Human Experience* (New York: Charles Scribner's Sons, 1943), pp. 16—17.

46 Quote from Donald Fleming, "Roots of the New Conservation Movement," *Perspectives in American History* 6 (1972): 10. See also Holway Jones, *John Muir and the Sierra Club: The Battle for Yosemite* (San Francisco: Sierra Club, 1963), pp. 83—169.

47 Alfred Runte, "'Worthless' Lands: Our National Parks," *American West* 10 (May 1973): 4—11.

48 At a 1895 club meeting, Muir commented, "Even the soulless Southern Pacific R.R. Co., never counted on for anything good helped nobly in pushing the bill. . . ." for Yosemite National Park, *Sierra Club Bulletin* 1, no. 7 (January 1896): 275.

49 *Sierra Club Handbook*, November 1947, p. 5; Harold C. Bradley and David

R. Brower, "Roads in the National Parks," *Sierra Club Bulletin* 34, no. 6 (June 1949): 31—54; Richard Leonard, "Mountaineer, Lawyer, Environmentalist," interview conducted by Susan R. Schrepfer (Berkeley: ROHO, 1975), pp. 18—21; David R. Brower, "Environmental Activist, Publicist, and Prophet," interview conducted by Susan R. Schrepfer (Berkeley: ROHO, 1978), pp. 19—24, 53—56 [hereafter Brower, "Environmental Activist"].

50 Richard Lillard, "The Siege and Conquest of the National Parks," *American West* 5, no. 1 (January 1968): 30—31, 69.

51 Francis Farquhar, *History of the Sierra Nevada* (Berkeley: University of California Press, 1969), p. 209.

52 Minutes of the Council, SRL, 15 February 1921; SRL, *Annual Report, 1924—1925*, p. 15; Joseph D. Grant, "Twenty Rings in the Redwoods: An Informal History of the Save-the-Redwoods League," Chap. 2, pp. 2, 3, in SRL office; Donald Bruce, M. B. Pratt, and R. F. Hammatt, "Report on Investigation for Proposed Redwood National Park" (October 1920), p. 2, SRL/A/RNP. For the Sierra Club's purism, see Resolution adopted by the Board of Directors, 12 December 1936, in Sierra Club office [hereafter club abbreviated SC].

53 National Highways Association and the National Conference on Outdoor Recreation, map of United States entitled "Good Roads Everywhere," 1926.

54 Marion Clawson, *Statistics on Outdoor Recreation* (Washington, D.C.: Resources for the Future, 1958), pp. 22—23; Robert Shankland, *Steve Mather of the National Parks* (New York: Alfred Knopf, 1954), pp. 78, 102, 146—47.

55 U.S., National Park Service, *Report of the Director to the Secretary of the Interior for the Fiscal Year Ending June 30, 1925* (Washington, D.C.: GPO, 1925), pp. 1—2; National Park Service, News Release, 24 November 1939.

56 Leonard, "Mountaineer," p. 51.

57 Quote from Merriam, *The Garment of God*, p. 2; Merriam's earlier prediction from "Are the Days of Creation Ended?" *Scribner's Magazine* 81, no. 6 (June 1927): 616.

58 Teale, *The Wilderness World of John Muir*, pp. 316—17.

59 Bestor Robinson, "Thoughts on Conservation and the Sierra Club," interview conducted by Susan R. Schrepfer (San Francisco: SC, 1974). pp. 5, 49.

60 SC, Board of Directors, 31 August 1947, 4 September 1949, in Bancroft Library. Susan Schrepfer, "Perspectives on Conservation: Sierra Club Strategies in Mineral King," *Journal of Forest History* 20, no. 4 (October 1976): 176—91.

61 Brower, "Environmental Activist," p. 17.

62 Quote from David Brower, "Introduction," *Sierra Club Bulletin* 50, no. 10 (December 1965): 2. See also David Brower, "Galapagos: The Flow of Wildness," *SC Explorer* (Fall 1968): 1—8; Loren Eiseley and Eliot Porter,

Galapagos: The Flow of Wildness (London: SC, 1968); Robinson Jeffers and David Brower, *Not Man Apart: Photographs of the Big Sur Coast* (San Francisco: Sierra Club, 1964), preface.

63 Loren Eiseley, *The Invisible Pyramid: A Naturalist Analyzes the Rocket Century* (New York: Charles Scribner's Sons, 1970), pp. 1, 40, 16−17.

64 Maxine McCloskey, ed., *Wilderness: The Edge of Knowledge* (San Francisco: SC, 1970), pp. 226−27; Loren Eiseley, *The Unexpected Universe* (New York: Charles Scribner's Sons, 1964), pp. 31−33; Eiseley, "Evolutionist Looks at Modern Man," *Saturday Evening Post* 230 (April 26, 1958): 28−29.

65 Loren Eiseley, *The Night Country* (New York: Charles Scribner's Sons, 1947), p. xi.

66 Edmund Sinnott, *Botany, Principles and Problems* (New York: McGraw Hill, 1923, 1935, 1946), pp. 238, 344−45, 420−23. The 1923 and 1935 editions endorsed orthogenesis. The 1946 edition did not. See also Wright, "The Foundations of Population Genetics," p. 246.

67 Jepsen, pp. 489−90, 496; Muller, pp. 462−63.

68 Quote from Jepsen, pp. 495−96. See also Mayr and Provine, *The Evolutionary Synthesis*, p. 163.

69 G. Ledyard Stebbins, Jr., "Reality and Efficiency of Selection in Plants," *Proceedings of the American Philosophical Society* 93, no. 6 (1949): 509−12.

70 Adolph Knopf, "Measuring Geologic Time," *The Scientific Monthly* 85, no. 5 (1957): 225−36.

71 Muller, p. 460.

72 Ibid., pp. 462−64; G. G. Simpson, *The Major Features of Evolution* (New York: Columbia University Press, 1953), p. 143; Mayr and Provine, *The Evolutionary Synthesis*, p. 167.

73 Stebbins, p. 506; Muller, pp. 466−67; K. Mather and L. G. Wigan, "The Selection of Invisible Mutations," *Proceedings of the Royal Society of London* 131 (1942): 50−65; Julian Huxley, "Degeneration and Relict Adaptation," *Nature* 149, no. 3790 (20 June 1942): 687−88.

74 Julian Huxley, *Evolution: The Modern Synthesis* (London: George Allen & Unwin, 1942).

75 William B. Provine, "The Role of Mathematical Population Genetics in the Evolutionary Synthesis of the 1930s and 1940s," in William Coleman and Camille Limoges, eds., *Studies in History of Biology* (Baltimore: Johns Hopkins Press, 1978), pp. 176−77.

76 Quote from Mayr and Provine, *The Evolutionary Synthesis*, p. 40. See also pp. 15−21, 31, 37, 40, 124−34, 399; Mayr, "The Recent Historiography of Genetics," pp. 145−54. Mayr dates synthesis 1936−1947; see Mayr and Provine, *The Evolutionary Synthesis*, pp. 1, 39−43.

77 For idealized systematics, see Holman and Robbins, *A Textbook of General Botany*, pp. 338−39; on transition, see Ernst Mayr, "Specialization and Selection," *Proceedings of the American Philosophical Society* 93, no. 6 (December 1949): 515; Dobzhansky, "Mendelian Populations

and Their Evolution," pp. 576—77; Mayr and Provine, *The Evolutionary Synthesis*, pp. 21—22, 29—34, 40; Simpson, *The Major Features of Evolution*, pp. 340—41; for new taxonomy, see Storer and Usinger, p. 232.

78 Quote from William B. Provine, *The Origins of Theoretical Population Genetics* (Chicago: University of Chicago Press, 1971), pp. 4—5. In contrast to Provine, Mayr views population geneticists as "not quite so exclusively responsible for this synthesis"; see Mayr, "The Recent Historiography of Genetics," p. 152. For agreement with Provine, see Theodosius Dobzhansky, "A Review of Some Fundamental Concepts and Problems of Population Genetics," *Cold Springs Harbor Symposia on Quantitative Biology* 20 (1955), pp. 1, 13—14; Arnold W. Ravin, *The Evolution of Genetics* (New York and London: Academic Press, 1965), pp. 29—30; L. C. Dunn, ed., *Genetics in the Twentieth Century* (New York: Macmillan, 1965), p. 575. For contributions of Sergei Chetverikov, see Mark B. Adams, "Toward a Synthesis: Population Concepts in Russian Evolutionary Thought, 1925—1935," *Journal of the History of Biology* 3, no. 1 (Spring 1970): 107—30. For Wright's description of his own work, see Sewall Wright, "On the Roles of Directed and Random Changes in Gene Frequency in the Genetics of Populations," *Evolution* 2, no. 4 (1948): 279—91.

79 G. H. Hardy, Letter to Editor, *Science* 28, no. 706, N.S. (10 July 1908): 49—50.

80 Mather and Wigan, pp. 50—65; C. Stern and E. Novitski, "The Viability of Individuals Heterozygous for Recessive Lethals," *Science* 108 (1948): 538—39; Arnold W. Ravin, *The Evolution of Genetics*, pp. 29—30; Theodosius Dobzhansky, "Mendelian Populations and Their Evolution," in L. C. Dunn, ed., *Genetics in the Twentieth Century* (New York: The Macmillan Company, 1951), pp. 575.

81 Garrett Hardin, *Nature and Man's Fate* (New York: Mentor Books, 1959), p. 69.

82 Sewall Wright, "Evolution in Mendelian Populations," *Genetics* 16 (1931): 97—159; Sewall Wright, "On the Roles of Directed and Random Changes," *Evolution* 2, no. 4 (1948): 279—82; Wright, "The Foundations of Population Genetics," pp. 247—50; Muller, p. 468.

83 Sewall Wright, "Genetics and Twentieth Century Darwinism," *American Journal of Human Genetics* 12, no. 3 (1960): 369; Sewall Wright, "Population Structure in Evolution," *Proceedings of the American Philosophical Society* 93, no. 6 (1949): 475.

84 Wright, "Population Structure in Evolution," p. 477.

85 Wright, "Genetics and Twentieth Century Darwinism," p. 367.

86 Provine, "The Role of Mathematical Population Geneticists," pp. 18, 174, 189; G. G. Simpson, *Tempo and Mode in Evolution* (New York: Columbia University Press, 1944), p. 31.

87 Muller, p. 468; Simpson, *The Major Features of Evolution*, pp. 132—59; Dobzhansky, "Mendelian Populations and Their Evolution," pp. 585—87.

88 Mather and Wigan, pp. 50—65; Wright, "The Foundations of Population Genetics," pp. 248—49.

89 Provine, "The Role of Mathematical Population Genetics," pp. 179–90.
90 Simpson, *The Major Features of Evolution*, pp. 132–59; Mayr and Provine, *The Evolutionary Synthesis*, pp. 38, 153–54, 158–63.
91 Wright, "Population Structure in Evolution," p. 477.
92 Provine, "The Role of Population Genetics," p. 175.
93 Monod, *Chance and Necessity*, p. 24.
94 Muller, p. 461.
95 Provine, "The Role of Mathematical Population Genetics," p. 182; G. G. Simpson, "The Problem of Plan and Purpose in Nature," *Scientific Monthly* 64, no. 6 (1947): 481–95.
96 Quote from G. G. Simpson, *The Major Features of Evolution*, pp. 132–59. See also Hardin, *Nature and Man's Fate*, p. 226; Leo F. Koch, "Vitalistic-Mechanistic Controversy," *Scientific Monthly* 85, no. 5 (1957): 248–54. For two widely read scientists who continued to advance teleological explanations of evolution, see L. DuNoüy, *The Road to Reason* (New York: Longmans Green, 1949); Edmund Sinnott, *The Biology of the Spirit* (New York: Viking Press, 1955).
97 Quotes from Wright, "On the Roles of Directed and Random Changes," p. 279; Dobzhansky, "Medium Populations and their Evolution," p. 583; Hardin, *Nature and Man's Fate*, pp. 57–85; Simpson, *Major Features of Evolution*, pp. 135, 160, 185, 5; G. G. Simpson, Colin Pittenbrigh, and Lewis Tiffany, *Life: An Introduction to Biology* (New York: Harcourt, Brace & Co., 1957), pp. 36, 450–55.
98 Quote from Hardin, *Nature and Man's Fate*, p. 69. See also Hardin, "In Praise of Waste," *Saturday Evening Post* 232 (29 August 1959): 18–19.
99 Julian Huxley, *Evolution* (London: George Allen & Unwin, 1963), p. 466.
100 Tracy Storer and Robert Usinger, *General Zoology* (New York: McGraw-Hill, 1957), pp. 222–23.
101 Marston Bates, *The Nature of Natural History* (New York: Charles Scribner's Sons, 1950), p. 282.
102 Hardin, *Nature and Man's Fate*, pp. 69–70, 85, 243, 274, 281.
103 Jepsen, "Selection, 'Orthogenesis,' and the Fossil Record," p. 493.
104 Simpson, *The Meaning of Evolution*, p. 160.
105 Hardin, *Nature and Man's Fate*, p. v.
106 Quote from Julian Huxley, *Knowledge, Morality and Destiny* (New York: Mentor, 1957), pp. 171, 152. See also Koch, "Vitalistic-Mechanistic Controversy," p. 245.
107 Quote from Bates, *The Nature of Natural History*, p. 252. See also Bates, *The Forest and the Sea* (New York: Vintage, 1960), p. 253.
108 Quote from Huxley, *Knowledge*, p. 186. See also Simpson, Pittenbrigh, and Tiffany, *Life*, pp. 651–53.
109 Edmund Sinnott, *Botany*, pp. 678–96; Simpson, Pittenbrigh, and Tiffany, *Life*, p. 36; Storer and Usinger, *General Zoology*, p. 614; Koch, "Vitalistic-Mechanistic Controversy," pp. 245–47.
110 Paul Sears, "On Coming to Terms with Our Environment," *Sierra Club Bulletin* 44, no. 7 (October 1959): 37–40; Hugh H. Iltis, "Whose Fight is the Fight for Nature?" *Sierra Club Bulletin* 52, no. 9 (October 1967): 34–39.

111 Brower, "Environmental Activist, Publicist, and Prophet," pp. 11, 16, 147.

112 First quote from René Dubos, *So Human an Animal* (New York: Charles Scribner's Sons, 1968), p. 65; second quote from Eiseley, *The Invisible Pyramid*, pp. 1, 16–17, 40.

113 Quotes from David Brower, "Definitions for Inner Space," *Sierra Club Bulletin* 47, no. 9 (December 1962): 40; Huxley, *Knowledge*, p. 186; Bates, *The Nature of Natural History*, p. 252; Eiseley, *The Invisible Pyramid*, p. 40; Paul Ehrlich, *The Population Bomb* (New York: Ballantine Books, 1968), pp. 11, 160.

114 Citizens Committee for the Hudson Valley and Sierra Club v. John Volpe et al., U.S. Dist. Court, Southern District of N.Y., no. 69, 11 July 1969; Sierra Club v. Morton et al., 405 U.S. 727 (1972), pp. 741, 755–57; Eiseley, *The Invisible Pyramid*, pp. 41–55.

115 Schrepfer, "Perspectives on Conservation," pp. 176–91.

116 Huxley, *Evolution*, pp. 576–77.

117 Bates, *The Nature of Natural History*, p. 252.

118 Quotes from David Brower, ed., *Wilderness: America's Living Heritage* (San Francisco: SC, 1962), pp. 16, 5. See also Sears, "On Coming to Terms with Our Environment," pp. 38–40.

119 Maxine McCloskey, ed., *Wilderness: The Edge of Knowledge* (San Francisco: SC, 1970), p. 250.

120 Quotes from Lynn White, Jr., "The Historical Roots of Our Ecological Crisis," *Science* 1955 (10 March 1967): 1203–7. See also Brower, "Environmental Activist, Publicist, and Prophet," pp. 304–5.

121 Brower, "Environmental Activist, Publicist, and Prophet," pp. 11, 16, 147.

122 Albert Etter, "Jewels, Gold, and God," *Sierra Club Bulletin* 50, no. 7 (September 1965): 9–10.

123 Quote from Eiseley, *The Invisible Pyramid*, p. 25. See also Eiseley, *The Unexpected Universe*, p. 43.

124 Quote from Brower, "Environmental Activist, Publicist, and Prophet," p. 70. See also Brower, *America's Living Heritage*, p. 110; McCloskey, *Wilderness: The Edge of Knowledge*, p. 250; Sears, "On Coming to Terms with Our Environment," pp. 37–40.

125 Donald Fleming, "Roots of the New Conservation Movement," pp. 23, 37–38, 48–50, 89–90; Lewis Mumford, *The Pentagon of Power* (New York: Harcourt Brace Jovanovich, 1970), p. 286.

126 Walter Mulford, "The Redwood League," *Sierra Club Bulletin* 11, no. 3 (1922): 302.

127 Ralph Chaney, "Comment on Human Values of the Redwoods," 22 August 1941, B/SRL/4:11; SRL, Council, 31 August 1944, report by Chaney, in SRL's Minute Books.

Chapter 7: The Roots of Militancy

1 Quote from Brower to Warlow, 16 January 1959, B/HB/4. See also *Sierra Club Bulletin* 52, no. 9 (October 1967): 9–12 [hereafter *Bulletin* abbreviated *SCB*].

2 Lewis Mumford, "California and the Human Prospect," *SCB* 47, no. 9 (December 1962): 43.

3 Elmo Richardson, *Dams, Parks and Politics: Resource Development and Preservation in the Truman-Eisenhower Era* (Lexington: University of Kentucky, 1973), pp. 54–70; Roderick Nash, *Wilderness and the American Mind* (New Haven: Yale University Press, 1971), pp. 209–20.

4 Brower to McKay, 26 January 1955, SC/MB/1319; Brower to Conservation Cooperators, 23 November 1962, Eissler Papers; David R. Brower, Environmental Activist, Publicist, and Prophet," interview conducted by Susan R. Schrepfer (Berkeley: ROHO, 1978), pp. 111, 132–33. William Colby, "Walter Leroy Huber, 1883–1960," *SCB* 45, no. 9 (December 1960): 81–84.

5 Richardson, *Dams, Parks and Politics*, pp. 62–65; Richard Leonard, "Mountaineer, Lawyer, Environmentalist," interview conducted by Susan R. Schrepfer (Berkeley: ROHO, 1976), p. 115.

6 SC, Minutes of the Board of Directors, 20 November, 27 December 1955, SC/MB/1068–1318 [hereafter SC board minutes abbreviated BOD].

7 Quote from McKay to Brower, 30 November 1954, SC/MB/1319. See also SC, BOD, 22 July 1962; Brower to Nolan, 14 May 1962, SC/MB/62; "Rainbow's Day in Court," *SCB* 47, no. 9 (December 1962): 83–93; Brower, "Environmental Activist," p. 134.

8 Quote from SC, BOD, 15 October 1955, SC/MB/1068–1318. See also Bestor Robinson, "Thoughts on Conservation and the Sierra Club," interview conducted by Susan R. Schrepfer (San Francisco: SC, 1974), p. 23; Brower, "Environmental Activist," pp. 130–39.

9 Eliot Porter, *The Place No One Knew: Glen Canyon on the Colorado* (San Francisco: SC, 1963).

10 Quote from John Muir and Richard Kauffman, *Gentle Wilderness: The Sierra Nevada* (San Francisco: SC, 1953). For a typical Forest Service tour, see John Barnard to SC Members, 13 January 1955, B/AB/Wilderness.

11 For Kern Plateau controversy, 1956–62, see B/SC/1–7; on Three Sisters, 1955–56, see B/AB/Wilderness.

12 Quote from David Brower, "Logging Operations Mammoth Lakes Area," 16 February 1955, SC/MC/1319. See also Brower, "Deadman Creek Controversy," 27 June 1957, B/EW/1.

13 Quote from Baker to Brower, 29 September 1953, SC/MB/1319. For Forest Service's position, see McArdle to Albright, 7 April 1955, B/EW/1.

14 Quote from Brower to McArdle, 2 July 1954. See also Brower, "Logging Operations Mammoth Lakes Area," SC/MB/1913; Brower to Wayburn, 28 June 1956, B/EW/1; Brower, "Environmental Activist," pp. 83–87, 93.

15 Brower, "Sierra Club—Confidential Draft Only," n.d., SC/MC/1319.

16 Quote from Hildebrand, "Memo," 18 June 1956, B/EW/1. See also Hildebrand to Brower, 2 July 1956, Bradley to Wayburn, 23 June 1956, Wayburn, "Report on Inspection of Proposed Deadman Creek Recreation Area," 28 June 1956, B/EW/1.

17 Quote from SC, Press Release, 18 January 1959, B/HB/4. See also Brower to Warlow, 16 January 1959, B/HB/4.

18 Quote from SC, BOD, 4 July 1959 and 5 December 1959, SC/MB/59. See also Brower, "Environmental Activist," pp. 90–92, 208.

19 SC, BOD, 14 December 1963; Brower to Leonard, 14 January 1964, SC/MB/63–64; "Environmental Perspectives, 1979: A Videotaped Interview with Four Leading Environmentalists," conducted by Ann Lage, 5 March 1979, in Bancroft Library.

20 First quotes from Leonard, "Mountaineer," p. 351; last quote from William Devall, "The Governing of a Voluntary Organization and Democracy in the Sierra Club" (Ph.D. diss., University of Oregon, 1970), pp. 329–30.

21 Kathleen Jackson, "Sierra Club Council Resume, May 1956 to May 1958," 3 May 1958, SC/MB/ 58.

22 David Brower, "A New Decade and a Last Chance: How Bold Shall We Be?" *SCB* 45, no. 1 (January 1960): 3–4.

23 "Note, Trees, Earth, Water and Ecological Upheaval: Logging Practices and Watershed Protection in California," 54 *Cal. Law Review* (1965), pp. 1117–22; Peggy Wayburn, "The Tragedy of Bull Creek," *SCB* 45, no. 1 (January 1960): 10–11; Comments by Emanuel Fritz, *Journal of Forestry* 65, no. 5 (May 1967): 12; *Proceedings of a Symposium on Management for Park Preservation: A Case Study at Bull Creek, Humboldt Redwoods State Park*, Scotia, Calif., Sponsored by School of Forestry, University of California, Berkeley, (13–14 May 1966), pp. 50–62.

24 SRL, BOD, 9 January, 19 May 1953, 21 October 1954, 20 October 1955.

25 SC, BOD, 11 October 1960; SC, Conservation Committee, 16 September 1960; SC, BOD, Resolution, 13 October 1962, SC/MB/60-62.

26 First quote from Michael McCloskey, "The Last Battle of the Redwoods," *American West* 6, no. 5 (September 1969): 56; second quote from François Leydet, *The Last Redwoods and the Parkland of Redwood Creek* (San Francisco: SC, 1969), p. 72.

27 Quote from Philip Hyde and François Leydet, *The Last Redwoods* (San Francisco: SC, 1963), p. 69. See also SC, Conservation Committee Minutes, 15 September 1960; Sierra Club, "Redwood Crisis: What we rescue today, this hour, this very minute, is the most that can ever be saved," *Outdoor Newsletter* 2, no. 7 (6 November 1964).

28 Dewey Anderson, *An Action Program for the Redwood Forest of California* (Washington, D.C.: Public Affairs Institute Publication no. 5, 1949). Anderson proposed that the 2 million-acre redwood belt be publicly acquired with state of California funds and a federal Reconstruction Finance Corporation loan.

29 First quote from Drury to Smith, 3 November 1949; second quote from Drury to Packard, 16 February 1954, 12 April 1954, SRL/A/RNF. See also Fritz to Horning, 20 October 1949, SRL/A/RNF.

30 W. C. Lowdermilk, "A Report to the SRL on the Critical Problems in the Bull Creek Basin" (Morongo Valley, Calif: 1960); SRL, BOD, 8 September 1960; Arthur Connick to Charles De Turk, 4 November 1960, B/SC/MM.

Industrial spokesmen denied that there was a relationship between logging and the 1964 flood damage; see California Committee of American Forest Products Industries, San Francisco, "An Analysis of Logging and the 1964 California Floods," January 1965.

31 Newton Drury, "A Suggested Operating Program for the SRL," in SRL, BOD, 16 October 1959.

32 Newton Drury, "Five Year Master Plan," California Division of Beaches and Parks, 1956, in SRL office; Newton Drury, "Parks and Redwoods, 1919—71," interview conducted by Amelia Fry and Susan R. Schrepfer (Berkeley: ROHO, 1971), pp. 245—48, 270—76.

33 Lawrence Merriam to Acting Regional Chief, 14 December 1960, NRC/NPS/74.

34 Drury to Merriam, 29 January 1934, LC/JM/58.

35 SRL, BOD, 6 September 1960.

36 Drury to Grosvenor, 6 November 1963, NRC/NPS/65.

37 Quote from *SCB* 47, no. 1 (January 1962): cover, 12—13. See also Stewart Udall, "We Must Act *Now* for More National Parks," *SCB* 46, no. 3 (March 1961): 4—5.

38 Wayburn to Udall, 14 December 1965, SC/SF/RNP; Interview with Edgar Wayburn conducted by Susan R. Schrepfer, 30—31 July 1976, San Francisco (Berkeley: ROHO, in process).

39 Brower to Udall, 7 December 1961, UA/SU/190—4.

40 For club recollections of early discussions with Udall about the park, see Brower to Udall, 6 January 1966, UA/SU/190—4; Wayburn to Udall, 14 December 1965, SC/SF/RNP.

41 Grosvenor to Wirth, 26 November 1962, NRC/NPS/74; SRL, Council, 6 December 1962.

42 Wirth to National Geographic Society, 8 March 1963, Grosvenor to Wirth, 22 March 1963, Wirth to Grosvenor, 9 April 1963, Director to Western Regional Director, 3 April 1963, NRC/NPS/74.

43 Grosvenor to Wirth, 28 May 1963, NRC/NPS/74; National Geographic Society Press Release, 31 May 1963, NRC/NPS/74; SRL, Council, 14 August 1963.

44 Brown to Director, 31 July 1963, NRC/NPS/74. In 1961 the Simpson Lumber Company had begun cutting in areas the league wished to add to the northern state parks; the State Division of Beaches and Parks had no money to buy the land; see Charles De Turk to Robert Kirby, 25 May 1961, James Tryner to Wayburn, 5 June 1961, B/SC/MM. The league's need for federal help had grown further in 1962 when the California State Bond Issue failed.

45 Ibid.; Wirth to National Geographic Society, 8 March 1963, National Geographic Society Press Release, 31 May 1963, NRC/NPS/74.

46 Interview with Wayburn by author, 30—31 July 1976; Hyde and Leydet, *The Last Redwoods* (1963), p. 93.

47 Quote from Litton to Grosvenor, 21 August 1963, NRC/NPS/74. See also Wayburn to Hugo Fisher, 23 May 1963, SC/MB/63.

48 Brown to Director, 23 October 1963, NRC/NPS/74.

49 Brown to Director, 3 September 1963, NRC/NPS/74. Litton subsequently flew other federal officials over Redwood Creek; see Ed Crafts to Litton, 9 April 1965, B/SC/MM—1.

50 Howell to Assistant Director, 14 January 1964, NRC/NPS/65.

51 Turnbow to Interior, 23 September 1963, Interior to Turnbow, 6 November 1963, Luntey to Western Regional Director, 14 November 1963, NRC/ NPS/74.

52 Assistant Director, NPS, to Clausen, 31 May 1963, Luntey to Director, 15 October 1963, Diederick to Director, 21 October 1963, Acting Director to Secretary of the Interior, 24 December 1963, NRC/NPS/74; De Turk to Udall, 3 February 1964, Brown to Director, 1 May 1964, Western Regional Director to Director, 2 July 1964, Park Planner to Western Regional Director, 30 July 1964, NRC/NPS/65—66.

53 U.S. Department of Commerce to Regional and Division Engineers, 25 May 1964, NRC/NPS/66; Berry to Wayburn, 30 June 1965, B/WS/3:3; Minutes, California State Parks Commission, 16 July 1965; *Chicago Daily News*, 6 September 1965; *New York Times International Edition*, 10 January 1964; *San Francisco Chronicle*, 22 July 1964, 15 October 1964; *San Francisco Examiner*, 24 January 1964; *Sacramento Bee*, 23 January 1964; *New York Times*, 27 February 1964, 18 April 1964; *Fresno Bee*, 27 March 1964. For local position, see *Humboldt Times*, 25 January 1964; Wayburn to Governor Brown, 22 January 1964, SC/SF/RNP.

54 Howell to Swem, 14 January 1964, Brown to Director, 7 April 1964, NRC/NPS/65.

55 Stewart Udall, *The Quiet Crisis* (New York: Holt, Rinehart and Winston, 1963).

56 Quotes from Udall, Memorandum to the President, 27 May 1964, UA/SU/ 115-8. For May, see also Udall, Report to the President, 26 May 1964, UA/SU/115-7. On White House Conference in June, see Udall, Report to the President, 23 June 1964, UA/SU/115-7; Udall, Memorandum for Jack Valenti, 1 June 1964, UA/SU/115-9; Press Release, Office of the White House, 25 June 1964. For comments on meeting, see Grosvenor to Udall, 1 July 1964, UA/SU/119-1; for photograph of meeting and list of attendance, see UA/SU/119-1.

57 Paul A. Zahl, "Finding the Mt. Everest of All Living Things," *National Geographic* 126 (July 1964): 10—45; Brown to Zahl, 17 December 1963, NRC/NPS/74.

58 Grosvenor to Udall, 1 May 1964, UA/SU/155-15.

59 Quote from Weyerhaeuser to Grosvenor, 11 May 1964, NRC/NPS/65. See also Grosvenor to Udall, 1 June 1964, Weyerhaeuser to Hartzog, 26 June 1964, NRC/NPS/65; M. M. Payne, "Notes on meeting with Directors of the Arcata Lumber Company at Eureka, California, on Tuesday, April 28, 1964," and "Notes on meeting with Mr. Frank Blagen, General Manager, Georgia-Pacific Company, at Samoa, California, on April 28, 1964," UA/SU/155-15.

60 Quote from Diederick to Director, 10 September 1964, NRC/NPS/67. U.S., National Park Service, *The Redwoods: A National Opportunity for*

Conservation and Alternatives for Action (Washington, D.C.: National Park Service, 1964), pp. 42—46.

61 Quote from Drury to Hartzog, 12 January 1963, SRL/A/RNP. See also SRL, BOD, 6 September 1960; SRL, Council, 14 August 1963; SRL, BOD, 9 April 1965; SRL, spring and fall bulletins, 1966; SRL *Spring Bulletin*, 1970; Leonard, Farquhar, Menzies, Howard, Chaney, Haas, Sproul, Drury, "A Redwood National Park: Position of the SRL," 1 December 1966, SRL/A/RNP.

62 Alfred Runte develops the thesis that most early preservationists valued only the "monumental" or most spectacular in nature; see Alfred Runte, *National Parks: The American Experience* (Lincoln: University of Nebraska Press, 1979), pp. 33—47.

63 Drury to Hartzog, 12 January 1963, SRL/A/RNP.

64 Initially the club urged the Park Service to save both the Mill Creek and Redwood Creek watersheds. The club also agitated for increased state aid for Jedediah Smith State Park. For the club's position, see Wayburn to Brown, 27 March 1964, B/SC/RW; Wayburn to Siri, 28 September 1964, Wayburn to Hummel, 23 November 1964, B/WS/3:1, SC, BOD 13 March 1965; SC, Executive Committee of the BOD, 17 October 1964; SC, Conservational Committee, 21 October 1965, SC/MB/65. On Litton's role, see Brower, "Environmental Activist," pp. 159, 165. The club hired Rudolf Becking for advice on the comparative value of Mill Creek and Redwood Creek; see McCloskey to Becking, 6 April 1965, B/SC/MM-1. Club dissenters included directors Richard Leonard and Ansel Adams and honorary vice-president Francis Farquhar; see SC, BOD, 13 March 1965; Adams to Udall, 18 July 1967, Adams to SC, BOD, 18 July 1967, UA/SU/190-1.

65 Wayburn to Edward Hummel, 23 November 1964, SC/SF/RNP; Edgar Wayburn, "A Proposed National Park," *SCB* 50, no. 1 (January 1966): 8—9. Interview with Wayburn by author, 30—31 July 1976.

66 First quote from McCloskey, "The Last Battle of the Redwoods," p. 56; second quote from Brower, "Environmental Activist," p. 175.

67 Quotes from SC, BOD, 14 October 1962, 4 May 1963, SC/MB/63. See also "Environmental Perspectives, 1979," tape 2, side 1.

68 Brower to Fruge, 23 August 1963, SC/MB/63.

69 Hyde and Leydet, *The Last Redwoods* (1963), pp. 51—65.

70 Livermore, Jr., to George Marshall, 16 February 1967, B/WS/3:3; Emanuel Fritz, review of *The Last Redwoods* (1963) in *The Journal of Forestry* (September 1964), p. 23; Leonard, "Mountaineer," p. 166; Brower, "Environmental Activist," p. 161; Hyde and Leydet, *The Last Redwoods* (1963), pp. 49—50, 67—69, 74—75.

71 Ibid.

72 Brandborg to Congressman Ken Dyal, 15 February 1966, B/GM/RNP.

73 Quotes from Leydet, *The Last Redwoods* (1969), p. 21. See also Sierra Club, "From the Sierra Club, Facts about the Redwoods and the Need for a Redwood National Park," pamphlet [1968]; Peggy and Edgar Wayburn, "Conservation in 1959," *SCB* 45, no. 1 (January 1960): 12.

74 Peggy and Edgar Wayburn, "Conservation in 1959," p. 12; Leonard,

"Mountaineer," pp. 18–21; "Sierra Club Policy and Standards for National Park and Other Scenic Roads," *SCB* 45, no. 9 (December 1960): 57–69.

75 Leydet, *The Last Redwoods* (1969), p. 48.

76 Hugh H. Iltis, "Whose Fight is the Fight for Nature?" *SCB* 52, no. 9 (October 1967): 34–35.

77 Quotes from Hyde and Leydet, *The Last Redwoods* (1963), p. 120. See also Leydet, *The Last Redwoods* (1969), pp. 152, 154; Sierra Club, "A Case for Redwood Creek. The Last Opportunity for a *Real* Redwood National Park," 10-page pamphlet (January 1966).

78 Paul Sears, "On Coming to Terms with Our Environment," *SCB* 44, no. 7 (October 1959): 37–40.

79 Brower, "Environmental Activist," p. 51.

80 "Environmental Perspectives, 1979," tape 2, side 1.

81 Statement by Martin Litton before the Assembly Committee on Natural Resources, Planning and Public Works, Arcata, Calif., 24 July 1964, B/SC/MM-1; Peggy and Edgar Wayburn, "Epilogue," *SCB* 50, no. 9 (October 1967): 65.

82 Iltis, "Whose Fight is the Fight for Nature?" p. 34.

83 Quote from Sears, "On Coming to Terms with Our Environment," p. 38. See also Paul Brooks, "Wilderness in Western Culture," *SCB* 50, no. 10 (December 1965): 7.

84 *New York Times*, 7 March 1967.

85 William O. Douglas, speech before the Governor's Conference for California Beauty, 11 January 1966, B/SC/MM.

86 Quotes from Hyde and Leydet, *The Last Redwoods* (1963), pp. 69, 120. See also Leydet, *The Last Redwoods* (1969), p. 154.

87 Michael McCloskey to Wayburn, 5 February 1965, B/SC/MM.

88 First quote from Iltis, "Whose Fight is the Fight for Nature?" p. 35; second quote from Brower, "Environmental Activist," pp. 51, 67. See also Michael McCloskey, "The Wilderness Act of 1964: Its Background and Meaning," *Oregon Law Review* 45 (June 1966): 293.

89 First quote from Dave Van de Mark (Northern California representative, SC) to Sierra Club Leaders, 23 November 1970, B/SC/MM; second and third quotes from Sierra Club, "The Need for a Redwood Park: Why Redwood Creek?" 11-page pamphlet (21 June 1967), pp. 4–5. See also Sierra Club draft, "Suggested Remarks for Senators Gaylord Nelson and Lee Metcalf on Legislation to Establish a Redwood National Park," 30 October 1967, B/SC/RW; Sierra Club, *Fact Sheet no. 2*, "Perpetuation of Primeval Redwoods," August 1966, B/SC/RW; Statement by Wayburn, *Congressional Record*, 89th Cong., 2d sess. (20 September 1966); Van de Mark to Wayburn and McCloskey, 17 April 1970, B/SC/RW; Wayburn to Udall, 14 December 1965, SC/SF/RNP.

90 Sierra Club, "The Need for a Redwood National Park: Why Redwood Creek?" pp. 4–5; Sierra Club to Senator Alan Cranston, 19 May 1970, B/SC/RW; Leydet, *The Last Redwoods* (1969), pp. 137–39.

91 Quotes from Sierra Club, "The Need for a Redwood National Park: Why

Redwood Creek?" 21 June 1967, pp. 4—5. See also *SCB* 50, no. 9 (October 1967): 51, 62.

92 Edgar Wayburn, "A Proposed National Park," *SCB* 50, no. 1 (January 1966): 8—9; Statement by Edgar Wayburn, *Congressional Record*, 89th Cong., 2d sess., 20 September 1966; Michael McCloskey, "Draft Speech for Congressman Jeffrey Cohelan," 19 June 1967, B/SC/RW; News Release, Jeffrey Cohelen's Office, 27 June 1967; McCloskey to Rudolf Becking, 7 April 1965, B/SC/MM-1.

93 Wayburn, "A Proposed National Park," pp. 8—9.

94 Dave Van de Mark to Wayburn and McCloskey, 17 April 1970, B/SC/RW.

95 David R. Brower, "Definitions for Inner Space," *SCB* 47, no. 9 (December 1962); 39.

96 Leonard, "Mountaineer," pp. 244—45; Brower, "Environmental Activist," p. 164; Bruce Kilgore, "Restoring Fire to the Sequoias," *National Parks and Conservation Magazine* 44, no. 277 (October 1977): 16—22.

Chapter 8: The Redwood National Park

1 Quote from Palmer Williams, executive producer, "Bulldozed America," *CBS Reports*, 14 September 1965. For public response to 1964 report, see Diederick, Luntey to National Park Service [hereafter abbreviated NPS] Director, 5 and 29 January 1965, 13 May 1965, 8 and 10 November 1965, Bradley to LBJ, 22 December 1964, Jones to Udall, 27 November 1964, Gordon to LBJ, 5 January 1965, Lindsay to NPS, 2 February 1965, Fredine to Harrison, 17 February 1965, Brandborg to Hartzog, 26 February 1965, Audubon Society to LBJ, 19 December 1965, NRC/NPS/66—67; Raymond F. Dasmann, *The Destruction of California* (New York: Macmillan and Company, 1965).

2 McCloskey to Wayburn, 4 February 1965, B/WS/3:1; Wayburn to Udall, 18 March 1965, NRC/NPS/66; Grosvenor to Drury, 2 and 25 June 1965, Drury to Grosvenor, 7 June 1965, SRL/F/RNP.

3 Quotes from Fisher to Udall, 2 April 1965, NRC/NPS/66. See also Farr to Hartzog, 8 April 1965, NRC/NPS/66; State of California, Resources Agencies News Release, 3 April 1965; KNXT, 6 p.m. News Statement, 6 April 1965.

4 Myer to NPS Director, 13 May 1965, NRC/NPS/66.

5 Interview with Charles Daly (Daly Brothers Department Store) conducted by Susan R. Schrepfer, 16 September 1969, Eureka, Calif., pp. 8—14; Interview with George Waldner (*Ferndale Enterprise*) conducted by Susan R. Schrepfer, 17 September 1969, Ferndale, Calif., pp. 39—41, both transcripts in SRL office; *Del Norte Triplicate*, 2 September 1965; *Humboldt Times*, 17 September 1965; *Crescent City America*, 15 September 1965; see correspondence from Humboldt County Board of Supervisors, Orick School Board, Del Norte Board of Supervisors, and Eureka City Council to Department of the Interior, October and November 1964, NRC/NPS/66—67.

6 Dave James (Simpson Timber), "Redwoods and the Sierra Club," 1965,

McCabe to Udall, 5 May 1965, Benson to NPS Assistant Director, 14 July 1965, NRC/NPS/66.

7 First quote from Fritz to NPS Regional Director, Western Division, 11 February 1965, NRC/NPS/66; second quote from interview with Daly by author, September 1969. See also interview with Waldner by author, September 1969, pp. 7–12, 39–41.

8 McCloskey to Wayburn, 5 February 1965, B/WS/3:1; Fritz to NPS Regional Director, 11 February 1965, Diederick to NPS Director, 17 February 1965, 1 March 1965, NRC/NPS/66. Interview with Michael McCloskey conducted by Susan R. Schrepfer, 13 February 1981, New York, N.Y. (Berkeley: ROHO, in process).

9 Brower to McCloskey, 21 December 1964, SC/SF/RNP; SC, BOD, 13 March 1965; SC, Minutes of the Executive Committee, 21 October 1965, SC/MB/65; Interview with McCloskey by author, February 1981.

10 "More Debate of a Redwood National Park," *SCB* 50, no. 4 (April 1965): 63; Edgar Wayburn and Michael McCloskey, "Plans for a Redwood National Park," *SCB* 50, no. 5 (May 1965): 3–6; Wayburn to Valenti, 7 July 1965, LBJ/PA3/17; Michael McCloskey, "The Last Battle of the Redwoods," *American West* 6, no. 5 (September 1969): 57.

11 "A Proposed Redwood National Park," 12 pp. [1965], Stevens, Memorandum for the Record, 18 June 1965, Hartzog to Udall, 24 June 1965, Crafts to Legislative Counsel, Department of the Interior, 14 July 1965, NRC/NPS/66.

12 U.S. Department of the Interior, Redwood Meeting, 22 November 1965, NPS Testimony, transcript, pp. 16–28, NRC/NPS/66; Drury, "Memorandum on the Redwood National Park," 25 November 1965, SRL/F/RNP; James Craig, "The Redwood Pot Begins to Boil," *American Forests* (January 1966), pp. 55–57.

13 Diederick to NPS Director, 29 July 1965, 16 August 1965, 3 September 1965, Luntey to NPS Director, 12 August 1965, Udall to McCormack plus attached "Bill to Authorize the Establishment of the Redwood National Park in California and for other Purposes," [1965], NRC/NPS/66.

14 Secretary's Calendar, 22 November 1965, UA/SU/190-4.

15 For Udall's offer, see Veatty to Glasgow, 26 October 1965, Udall to Brown, 5 January 1966, NRC/NPS/41; for Brown's position, see Minutes of the California State Park Commission, 16 July 1965, Eureka; Sylvester to NPS, 19 July 1965, NRC/NPS/66. For November meeting, see Secretary's Calendar, 23 November 1965, UA/SU/121-5; Irv Sprague to Winslow Christian, 23 November 1965, UA/SU/155-15; Udall to Crafts, 26 November 1965, UA/SU/134-2.

16 Quote From Brower to Udall, 6 January 1966, UA/SU/190-4. See also McCloskey, "The Last Battle of the Redwoods," p. 58.

17 Quotes from Wayburn to Udall, 14 December 1965, UA/SU/133-1, and Litton to Crafts, 7 December 1965, B/WS/3. See also Wayburn to White House, 7 July 1965, Litton to Udall, 25 October 1965, Litton to Crafts, 5 November 1965, NRC/NPS/66–67.

18 Udall to Brower, 29 December 1965, B/EW/3:3.

19 Brower to Udall, 6 January 1966, UA/SU/190-4.

20 *New York Times, San Francisco Chronicle, Sacramento Bee, Los Angeles Times, Washington Post*, 17 December 1965; David R. Brower, "Environmental Activist, Publicist, and Prophet," interview conducted by Susan R. Schrepfer (Berkeley: ROHO, 1978), p. 163.

21 Secretary's Calendar, 17 December 1965, UA/SU/121-5; Richard M. Leonard, "Mountaineer, Lawyer, Environmentalist," interview conducted by Susan R. Schrepfer (Berkeley: ROHO, 1975) p. 170. For Udall's plans see Udall to Crafts, 26 November 1965, UA/SU/134-2.

22 Udall Memorandum to Assistant to Secretary and Legislative Counsel, 5 January 1966, Udall to Bureau of the Budget, 5 January 1966, NRC/I/41; Udall, "Weekly Report to the President," 4 January 1966, UA/SU/126-7; Crafts to Udall, 5 January 1966, UA/SU/155-6.

23 Udall to Joe Califano, 14 February 1966, UA/SU/126-9; White House, Press Release, 23 February 1966, UA/SU/129-3; Department of the Interior, Press Release, 26 February 1966, NRC/I/41.

24 Interview given by Drury to KGO, San Francisco, 24 January 1966, SRL/F/RNP; Drury to LBJ, 24 January 1966, Drury to Udall, 25 January 1966, NRC/NPS/68.

25 Quote from Wayburn to Club Members, 2 February 1966, B/WS/3. See also Wayburn to Crafts, 27 January 1966, SC/DC/R; Udall to McCloskey, 18 February 1966, NRC/I/41.

26 Edgar Wayburn, "The Redwood National Park: A Point of Crisis," *SCB* 51, no. 4 (April 1966): 15.

27 First quote from Drury, "Redwood National Park, memorandum for luncheon between representatives of the Sierra Club and the League," 3 November 1964; second quote from Drury to McCloskey, 17 December 1964. See also SRL, BOD, 6 September 1960; Drury, "Memorandum to Directors, RNP and In-Lieu Taxes," February 1965, SRL/A/RNP.

28 Northern California Timber Association [hereafter NCTA], "Statement to the National Park Service," 25 November 1964, NCTA to Hummell, 14 November 1964, LBJ/PA3/17; Drury to Grosvenor, 15 June 1965, SRL/A/RNP; *San Francisco Chronicle*, 12 November 1964; *Humboldt Standard*, 23 November 1964.

29 Quote from *San Francisco Chronicle*, 15 October 1956. See also Drury to Albright, 3 February 1965, SRL/A/RNP; U,S. Department of the Interior, Redwood Meeting, 22 November 1965, pp. 16—28, NRC/NPS/66.

30 Drury to Hartzog, 15 February 1965, SRL/A/RNP.

31 McCloskey, "The Last Battle of the Redwoods," p. 58.

32 Udall to Brower, 29 December 1965, B/EW/3:3; Reinemer (Metcalf aide) to Scotty, 4 March 1966, Metcalf/DC/R; Interview with Edgar Wayburn conducted by Susan Schrepfer, 30—31 July 1976, San Francisco (Berkeley: ROHO, in process).

33 Stevens, Memorandum for the Record, 18 June 1965, Hartzog to Udall, 24 June 1965, Crafts to Legislative Counsel, Interior, 14 July 1965, NRC/NPS/66; Irv Sprague to Winslow Christian, 23 November 1965, UA/SU/155-15.

34 Udall, Memorandum for the President, 31 August 1966, UA/SU/126-9.
35 U.S. Department of the Interior, Redwood Meeting, 22 November 1965, pp. 16−28; *San Francisco Chronicle*, 15 October 1965.
36 Joel Ray Dickinson, "The Creation of the Redwood National Park: A Case Study in the Politics of Conservation," (Ph.D. diss., University of Missouri, 1974), p. 264.
37 Memorandum to the Secretary of the Interior from Advisory Board on National Sites, Historic Sites, Buildings, and Monuments, 7 October 1965, SRL/A/RNP.
38 Edward Crafts, "Seminar on the Making of a National Redwood Park," University of California, 12 February 1970, p. 22, in Bancroft Library.
39 Interview with Maurice Fred Smith conducted by Susan R. Schrepfer, 17 November 1976, New York, N.Y.
40 Rockefeller to LBJ, 28 October 1966, LBJ/PA3/16.
41 Samuel Dana and Kenneth Pomeroy, "Redwoods and Parks," *American Forests* (May 1965), pp. 3−32; American Forestry Association to LBJ, 5 January 1966, NRC/NPS/68.
42 First quote from Udall to Rockefeller, 7 December 1964; second quote from Rockefeller to Udall, 9 December 1964, unsigned memorandum, 1 December 1964, UA/SU/155-15; third and fourth quotes from Smith to Udall, 9 December 1964, LBJ/P-M/2:16; last quote from Rockefeller to Wayburn, 9 June 1965, SC/MB/65. See also Udall to Clinton Anderson, 28 December 1964, UA/SU/155-15.
43 Rockefeller to LBJ, 20 July 1965, LBJ/PA2-3/16.
44 Peter Collier and David Horowitz, *The Rockefellers: An American Dynasty* (New York: Holt, Rinehart and Winston, 1976), pp. 394−95.
45 SRL, BOD, 6 September 1960.
46 Interview with Smith by author, November 1976.
47 Ibid.
48 Rockefeller to LBJ, 20 July 1965, LBJ/PA2-3/16.
49 Collier and Horowitz, *The Rockefellers*, p. 394.
50 Ed Crafts, "Memo for the Record," 27 April 1966, UA/SU/155-16.
51 Miller to LBJ, 18 June 1965, Ragan to Jacobsen, 16 January 1967, 17 February 1967, LBJ/PA3/17; Ragan to Udall, 19 August 1966, NRC/NPS/69.
52 Minutes of the California State Park Commission, 16 July 1965, Eureka; Sylvester to NPS, 19 July 1965, NRC/NPS/66.
53 First quote from interview with McCloskey by author, February 1981; second quote from interview with Wayburn by author, 30−31 July 1976.
54 Udall to Brooks Atkinson [April 1966], UA/SU/155-16.
55 Crafts, Seminar; Edward C. Crafts, "Forest Service Researcher and Congressional Liaison," interview conducted by Susan R. Schrepfer (Santa Cruz, Calif.: U.S. Forest Service and Forest History Society, 1972), pp. 64−72.
56 Phillip Hughes, Memo for LBJ, 17 February 1967, LBJ/EX-PA3/146.
57 Robert Kennedy to Metcalf, 18 February 1966, Metcalf/DC/R; SC, BOD, 5 May 1966, SC/MB/66; Interview with McCloskey by author, February 1981.

58 State of California, Press Release, 23 February 1966; Conservation Associates to Udall, 4 March 1966, Land Acquisitions Officer to NPS Assistant Director, 31 March 1966, Regional Director to NPS Director, 28 February 1966, NRC/NPS/68; Udall to Brown, 13 April 1966, 20 May 1966, NRC/I/41.

59 U.S., Congress, Senate, Committee on Interior and Insular Affairs, *Redwood National Park—Part I: Hearings before Subcommittee on S.2962*, 89th Cong., 2d sess., 17—18 June 1966.

60 Miller to Udall, 18 August 1966, UA/SU/155-16.

61 Quote from Udall to Miller, 19 August 1966, UA/SU/152. See also Udall to Alan Bible, 20 August 1966, White House News Conference with Tom Johnson and Stewart Udall, 1 September 1966, UA/SU/155-16; Robert McConnell, Memorandum to the Secretary, 1 September 1966, UA/SU/127-1.

62 *Los Angeles Times*, 21 August 1966.

63 Berry to Litton, 27 January 1966, B/CM/2.

64 Wayburn to Metcalf, 1 September 1966, Metcalf to Wayburn, 6 September 1966, SC/DC/R.

65 Udall to John W. McCormack, 1 September 1966, UA/SU/152; White House News Conference, 1 September 1966, UA/SU/155-16; U.S., Congress, Senate, *Congressional Record*, 89th Cong., 2d sess., 1 September 1966, S. Joint Res. 192, p. 20702.

66 Leonard, "Mountaineer," p. 190.

67 James (of Simpson) to Jackson, 8 September 1966, Metcalf/DC/R.

68 Press Release, Kuchel's Office, 5 September 1966; National Forest Products Association to Metcalf, 7 September 1966, Ragan to Jackson, 8 September 1966, Metcalf/DC/R; Western Division, National Park System to NPS Director, 9 September 1966, NRC/NPS/69; A. L. Newman, Memorandum to the President, 9 September 1966, UA/SU/126—7; Kuchel to Leonard, 15 September 1966, B/WS/3:3; Udall to Tewksburg, 20 September 1966, NRC/I/41.

69 Department of the Interior, "Redwood Moratorium Status," [January 1967], UA/SU/152.

70 Quote from Ragan to Javits, 26 February 1966. See also Miller to Howell, 28 February 1966, Ragan to Udall, 19 August 1966, NRC/NPS/68—69; Ragan to Metcalf, 8 September 1966, Metcalf/DC/R.

71 First quote from Ragan to Metcalf, 9 March 1966, Metcalf/DC/R; second quote from interview with Wayburn by author, 30—31 July 1976.

72 Crafts, Memo for the Record, 27 April 1966, UA/SU/155-16.

73 SRL, BOD, 26 May 1966, 9 April 1966.

74 McCloskey, "The Last Battle of the Redwoods," p. 60; SC, BOD, 20 May 1967, SC/MB/76.

75 Quote from Edgar Wayburn, "The Redwood National Park—A Forest of Stumps?" *SCB* 50, no. 7 (October 1965): 10—11. See also *SCB* 50, no. 4 (April 1966): 15.

76 James Cawley, "Toward an Earth National Park," *Sierra Club Explorer* (Fall 1968), p. 2; "The Redwood Issue," *SCB* 53, no. 6 (June 1968): 2.

77 McCloskey, "The Last Battle of the Redwoods," p. 59. For Wilderness

Society's position, see Leonard, "Mountaineer," pp. 180–82; for other groups, see SC, "Some of the Organizations Helping *Really* to Save the Redwoods," 5 January 1966; Wayburn to Crafts, 27 January 1966, SC/DC/R; Garden Club of America to Metcalf, 1 March 1966, Metcalf/DC/R.

78 Reuther to LBJ, 11 February 1966, LBJ/GEN Le-NR/145.

79 Quote from *New York Times*, 17 February 1967. See also *New York Times*, 27 August 1967, 6 September 1967; *Chicago Tribune*, 28 February 1966; *San Gabriel Valley Tribune*, 12 August 1967, 26 June 1968; *Sacramento Bee*, 21 May 1968, 7 July 1968; *Los Angeles Times*, 26 June 1968; *Washington Post*, 2 July 1968; *Christian Science Monitor*, 3 and 17 July 1968; *Long Beach Press-Telegram*, 5 July 1968; *Courier-Journal* (Ky.), 16 July 1968; *Denver Post*, 19 July 1968.

80 *Redwood National Park—Part I*, pp. 17–18.

81 *San Francisco Examiner*, 1 March 1966; McCloskey, "The Last Battle of the Redwoods," p. 60.

82 Udall, Weekly Report to the President, 6 December 1966, UA/SU/126-7.

83 Quote from Kuchel to Leonard, 15 September 1966. See also Leonard to Kuchel, 28 September 1966, B/WS/3:3; Interview with Wayburn by author, 30–31 July 1976.

84 Ogden, Memorandum for the Record, 10 October 1966, NRC/NPS/64.

85 W. C. Lowdermilk, "Report to SRL on Trip to Mill Creek Drainage, November 15 to 18 inclusive," 13 November 1967, SRL/A/RNP.

86 Quotes from Lawrence Merriam, "Memorandum for N. B. Drury," 8 December 1966, 8 pp. SRL/A/RNP. For collaborative testimony, see Volz to NPS Western Regional Director, 21 November 1966, NRC/NPS/69; Volz to Merriam, 3 January 1966, NRC/NPS/74.

87 Farquhar, Leonard, Howard, Menzies, Chaney, Haas, Sproul, Drury, "Redwood National Park: Position of the SRL," 1 December 1966; SRL, Press Release, 9 January 1967, SRL/A/RNP; SRL, BOD, 6 January 1967.

88 Wayburn to Crafts, 16 December 1966, NRC/NPS/69.

89 SC, BOD, 4 January 1967, SC/MB/67, B/WS/1.

90 Memorandum from Crafts to Udall, 27 December 1966, UA/SU/127-6.

91 Interior first submitted it to the Bureau of the Budget; see NPS to BOB, 20 January 1967, Harrison to Solicitor, 27 January 1967, NRC/NPS/69; Department of the Interior Press Release, 26 January 1967, UA/SU/134-8. In February Udall presented the plan at a cabinet meeting; see Udall, Memo for the White House, 28 February 1967, UA/SU/133-11.

92 Chaney to Cohelan, 30 January 1967, Chaney to Kuchel, 1 February 1967, NRC/NPS/69.

93 Brower told Udall of the SC's position; see Secretary's Calendar, 25 January 1967, UA/SU/133-1.

94 Harrison to Solicitor, 27 January 1967, NRC/NPS/69.

95 Transcript of Reagan's Press Conference, 10 January 1967.

96 Reagan to Luntley, 19 October 1966, NRC/NPS/69.

97 Udall, Weekly Report to the President, 22 November 1966, UA/SU/120-7;

Udall, Report to the President, 10 January 1967, UA/SU/133-8; U.S. Department of the Interior, "Redwood Statement," 31 March 1967, NRC/NPS/69.

98 U.S. Department of the Interior, Press Release, 31 March 1967, NRC/NPS/69; Crafts, Memo for the Record, 27 April 1966, UA/SU/155-16; *Congressional Record*, 90th Cong., 1st sess., 19 June 1967, p. 16267.

99 LBJ to Rockefeller, 24 February 1967, 7 March 1967, LBJ/LE-PA3/146.

100 Udall, Memo for Jack Valenti, 1 June 1964, UA/SU/115-9.

101 Rockefeller to LBJ, 16 April 1967, LBJ/LE-PA3/146; Hartzog to Assistant Secretary for Fish and Wildlife and Parks, 20 March 1967, UA/SU/155-16; Crafts to Udall, 24 March 1967, UA/SU/134-7.

102 Hughes to Jackson and Aspinall, 22 June 1967, NPS files, Washington, D.C.

103 U.S., Congress, Senate, Committee on Interior and Insular Affairs, *Authorizing the Establishment of the Redwood National Park in the State of California for Other Purposes: Rept. to Accompany S. 2515*, 90th Cong., 1st sess., 12 October 1967, S. Rept. 641, pp. 13−14.

104 Ed Crafts to Udall, 8 July 1967, UA/SU/155-16; Interview with Smith by author, November 1976; Susan Schrepfer, "Perspectives on Conservation: Sierra Club Strategies in Mineral King," *Journal of Forest History* 20, no. 4 (October 1976): 176−91.

105 NPS Director to NPS Division National Park System Planning and Survey, 21 March 1967, NRC/NPS/69; Anderson to Udall, 6 April 1967, NRC/I/41.

106 U.S., Congress, Senate, Committee on Interior and Insular Affairs, *Redwood National Park: Hearings before Subcommittee*, 90th Cong., 1st sess., 17−19 April 1967, pp. 65−66; Ragan to Hartzog, 17 January 1967, NRC/NPS/69.

107 *Denver Post, New York Times, Salt Lake Deseret-News, Salt Lake Tribune, San Francisco Chronicle*, 16 March 1967.

108 U.S., Congress, Senate, *Congressional Record—Appendix 113*, 90th Cong., 1st sess., 23 May 1967, p. 2544.

109 Quote from Udall to Conservation Forum of New York, 4 April 1967, B/SC/15. See also Hartzog to Burnham, 10 September 1967, B/SC/15; Udall to Curtis, 27 September 1967, Udall to Soule, 2 August 1967, Office of Vice-President to Department of the Interior, 7 August 1967, NRC/NPS/41.

110 U.S., Congress, Senate, Committee on Interior and Insular Affairs, *Authorizing the Establishment of the Redwood National Park in the State of California and for Other Purposes*, 90th Cong., 1st sess., 12 October 1967, S. Rept. 641, p. 5.

111 Ibid., pp. 4−5, 19−23.

112 U.S. Department of the Interior, Press Briefing, 3 November 1967, UA/SU/134-14; Interview with McCloskey by author, February 1981.

113 Miller to Watson, 13 October 1967, NRC/I/41.

114 NCTA, *Newsletter*, 27 October 1967; *New York Times*, 10 October 1967; *San Francisco Examiner*, 5 November 1967.

115 Quotes from Freeman to Metcalf, 20 October 1967, Metcalf/DC/R. See

also Freeman to Senate Interior Committee, 10 October 1967, NRC/I/41.

116 Quote from Jackson to Udall, 31 October 1967, NRC/I/41. See also Rockefeller to LBJ, 17 October 1967, Califano to Rockefeller, 20 November 1967, LBJ/LE-PA3/146.

117 Udall, Report to the President, 10 October 1967, UA/SU/133-8.

118 Quote from U.S. Department of the Interior, Press Briefing, 3 November 1967, UA/SU/134-14. For retraction, see U.S. Department of the Interior, Press Briefing, 17 April 1968, UA/SU/139-4.

119 Udall to Lenhoff, 9 November 1967, NRS/I/41.

121 Michael McCloskey, "House Takes up Redwood Bill," *SCB* 53, no. 6 (June 1968): 19.

122 Udall to Gubser, 11 September 1967, Bill to Solicitor, 6 October 1967, 16 October 1967, NRC/I/41; *Washington Post*, 6 September 1967.

123 SC, Press Release, 16 November 1967, 15 December 1967, SC/MB/67.

124 Quotes from *New York Times, Wall Street Journal, San Francisco Chronicle*, 18 December 1967. For club's advertisement, see *New York Times*, 18 January 1968, *Wall Street Journal*, 23 January 1968. See also Mitchell to Cohelan, 29 November 1967, SC/DC/R.

125 Pamplin to Wayburn, 22 January 1968, B/AA/1.

126 *Wall Street Journal*, 24 January 1968; SC, Press Release, 24 January 1968, B/RL/22.

127 Wayburn to Georgia-Pacific, 24 January 1968, B/WS/3:1.

128 Leonard to IRS, 17 January 1968, B/RL/22.

129 Transcript of interview with Moshowsky and Wayburn, 10 March 1968, KTVU-TV, Channel 2, San Francisco, B/Flannery/2.

130 Quote from Interior to Gubser, 21 March 1967, NRC/NPS/41. See also Reid to Myers, 11 January 1968, Udall to Cohelan, 11 January 1968, U.S. Department of the Interior, "Redwood Statement," March 1968, NRC/NPS/41.

131 Quote from *Congressional Record*, 90th Cong., 2d sess., vol. 114, pt. 1, 17 January 1968, p. 140–44. See also *New York Times*, 18 and 19 January 1968.

132 U.S., Congress, House, Committee on Interior and Insular Affairs, *Redwood National Park—Part II: Hearings before Subcommittee on H.R. 1311*, 90th Cong., 1st sess., 16–18 April 1968.

133 *Sacramento Bee*, 18 April 1968.

134 Quote from ibid. See also Ira Whitlock, Memorandum to the Secretary, 24 April 1968, UA/SU/138-13; *Sacramento Bee*, 26 April 1968; SC, BOD, 4–5 May 1968, SC/MB/68; Interview with Wayburn by author, 6–7 June 1978.

135 *Redwood National Park—Part II*, p. 201; *Sacramento Bee*, 21 May 1968; Udall to Aspinall, 11 May 1968, NRC/NPS/41.

136 U.S. Department of the Interior, Press Briefing, 17 April 1968, UA/SU/139-4; Udall to Aspinall, 11 May 1968, NRC/I/41.

137 Quote from Udall to Aspinall, 11 May 1968, NRC/I/41. See also McCloskey to Pollack, 12 June 1968, SC/DC/R.

138 *Redwood National Park—Part II*, p. 304.
139 U.S., Congress, House, Committee on Interior and Insular Affairs, *Redwood National Park—Part III: Hearings before Subcommittee on H.R. 1311*, 90th Cong., 2d sess., 20–22 May 1968, pp. 836–38.
140 Ibid., pp. 837–38, 866; Udall to Aspinall, 11 May 1968, NRC/I/41.
141 Interview with McCloskey by author, February 1981.
142 Interview with E. Louis Reed (Kuchel aide) conducted by Susan R. Schrepfer, 12 June 1978, San Francisco.
143 Weyerhaeuser to Grosvenor, 11 May 1964, NRC/NPS/65.
144 U.S., Department of Agriculture, Forest Service, "Timber Resources of Humboldt County," Bulletin DNW-26.
145 Interview with Howard Libbey conducted by Susan R. Schrepfer, 20 August 1969, San Francisco.
146 Quotes from McCloskey, "The Last Battle of the Redwoods," p. 63. See also Ira Whitlock, Memorandum to the Secretary, 28 June 1968, UA/SU/138-13.
147 U.S., Congress, House, Committee on Interior and Insular Affairs, *Authorizing the Establishment of the Redwood National Park in the State of California, and for Other Purposes*, 90th Cong., 2d sess., H. Rept. 1630, 28 June 1968, pp. 4–7.
148 Quotes from SC, Press Release, 11 July 1968, SC/DC/R. For the response of the press, see *Christian Science Monitor*, 3 and 17 July 1968; *Sacramento Bee*, 7 July 1968; *New York Times*, 14 July 1968; *Tribune*, (New Mexico), 15 July 1968; *Denver Post*, 19 July 1968; *Washington Post*, 2 July 1968.
149 Edgar Wayburn, "Of Parks and Politics," *SCB* 53, no. 1 (July 1968): 1.
150 Flannery to Brayhill, 12 July 1968, B/SC/15.
151 Interview with Wayburn by author, 6–7 June 1978; Dickinson, "The Creation of Redwood National Park," pp. 517–18; McCloskey, "The Last Battle of the Redwoods," p. 64.
152 Interview with McCloskey by author, February 1981.
153 Crafts to Tupling, 27 May 1968, SC/MB/68.
154 U.S., Congress, House, Committee of Conference, *Redwood National Park*, 90th Cong., 2d sess., 11 September 1968, H. Rept. 1890. For a complete legislative history of the park bills, see Dickinson, "The Creation of Redwood National Park."
155 Arcata, News Release, 2 July 1979, Menlo Park, Calif.
156 *Congressional Record*, 90th Cong., 2d sess., vol. 114, pt. 3, 2 September 1968, p. 8586.
157 Crafts to Udall, 10 September 1980, UA/SU/139-3.
158 Quote from McCloskey, "The Last Battle of the Redwoods," p. 55. See also SRL, *Fall Bulletin*, 1968; SC, BOD, 14–15 September 1968, SC/MB/68.
159 Report of the Commission on Private Philanthropy and Public Needs, *Giving in America: Toward a Stronger Voluntary Sector* (Washington, D.C.: Commission on Private Philanthropy and Public Needs, 1975), pp. 60–75.

160 Leonard, "Mountaineer," p. 176.
161 Ibid., p. 208; Interview with Wayburn by author, 6—7 June 1978; Interview with John B. Dewitt, (executive director, SRL) conducted by Susan R. Schrepfer, 12 March 1974, San Francisco, transcript in SRL office.
162 Interview with McCloskey by author, February 1981.
163 Ibid.
164 McCloskey, "The Last Battle of the Redwoods," p. 55.

Chapter 9: David Brower and the Sierra Club

1 Interview with Edgar Wayburn conducted by Susan R. Schrepfer, 6—7 June 1978, San Francisco (Berkeley: ROHO, in process); Richard M. Leonard, "Mountaineer, Lawyer, Environmentalist," interview conducted by Susan R. Schrepfer (Berkeley: ROHO, 1975), pp. 18—23.
2 Sierra Club membership grew at the following per year rate: 1963—7.4%, 1964—22.5%, 1965—23.5%, 1966—28.8%, 1967—31.1%, 1968—17.7%, 1969—23.1%, 1970—32.3%, 1971—23.2%, 1972—3.4%. The author designed a questionnaire distributed by the Sierra Club's History Committee that indicated that the majority of members who joined before 1940 had been young to middle-age professionals or semiprofessionals; see SC, History Committee Survey, 1972, in Bancroft Library [hereafter referred to as History Committee survey]. I do not wish to get entangled in the definitional quagmire surrounding professionalism. Amitai Etzioni uses *professionals* to mean doctors, lawyers, and college professors; and *semiprofessionals* to indicate teachers, librarians, nurses, and the like. See Amitai Etzioni, *Modern Organizations* (Englewood Cliffs, N.J.: Prentice-Hall, 1964), pp. 78—89.
3 William Devall, "The Governing of a Voluntary Organization: Oligarchy and Democracy in the Sierra Club" (Ph.D. diss., University of Oregon, 1970), pp. 182—89; Resources for the Future, "Environmental Movement Survey," 1978, Sierra Club membership survey, p. 21, in SC office [hereafter referred to as RFF Study]. Since *professional* was not defined, some of the 68 percent were no doubt semiprofessionals.
4 First quote from John Mitchell, Constance Stalling, and Ralph Nader, eds., *Ecotactics: The Sierra Handbook for Environmental Activists* (New York: Simon & Schuster, 1970), p. 5; second quote from Soucie to Brower, 19 April 1967, SC/MB/67.
5 History Committee survey; Devall, "The Governing of a Voluntary Organization," pp. 182—89; RFF Study; Joseph Harry, Richard Gale, and John Handee, "Conservation: An Upper-Middle Class Social Movement," *Journal of Leisure Research* (1969), pp. 246—54.
6 History Committee survey; RFF Study, p. 21.
7 William R. Burch, Jr., "Policy Making and Environmental Management: Some Thoughts on Processes and Research Issues," *Natural Resources Journal* 16, no. 1 (January 1976): 44.
8 RFF Study, p. 13.
9 Mitchell, Stallings, and Nader, *Ecotactics*, p. 55.

10 Robert Rienow and Leona Train Rienow, *Moment in the Sun* (New York: Ballantine Books, 1967), pp. 271—86.

11 Mitchell, Stallings, and Nader, *Ecotactics*, pp. 78, 5.

12 Arthur Schlesinger, Jr., *The Crisis of Confidence* (New York: Bantam, 1969), p. 153.

13 Ansel Adams and Nancy Newhall, *This Is the American Earth* (San Francisco: SC, 1960), p. iv.

14 Nancy and Retta Johnston, Marianne Moore, Mireille Johnston, and David Brower, *Central Park Country: A Tune within Us* (New York: SC, 1968); "Marianne Moore Preaches Gently Against War," *New York Times*, 20 June 1968, p. 47. For parallel between world peace and the peace of man at one with nature, compare Moore's "In Distrust of Merits" with her last lines in *Central Park Country* written on 20 July 1968; see also Brower's statements, SC, BOD, 3—4 May 1969, SC/MB/69.

15 First quote from David R. Brower, "Environmental Activist, Publicist, and Prophet," interview conducted by Susan R. Schrepfer (Berkeley: ROHO, 1978), pp. 32—37, 100—101. For petition, see Donald Aiken, Phillip Berry, et al. to Nixon, 14 May 1969. Friends of the Earth incorporated the petition into a pamphlet "Ecology and War," 14 May 1969; copy of telegram sending petition in office of Friends of the Earth, San Francisco. See also SC, BOD, 14 June 1970, SC/MB/70; John Constable and Matthew Meselson, "Defoliation," *SCB* 56, no. 4 (April 1971): 4—10.

16 Quote from Mitchell, Stallings, and Nader, *Ecotactics*, p. 47. See also RFF Study, p. 13.

17 First quote from Schlesinger, *The Crisis of Confidence*, ix—xii; second quote from René Dubos, *So Human an Animal* (New York: Charles Scribner's Sons, 1968), pp. 9—22; third quote from Mitchell, Stallings, and Nader, *Ecotactics*, pp. 46—47, 81—82.

18 Quote from Garrett Hardin, *Nature and Man's Fate* (New York: Mentor Books, 1959), p. 71. See also Dubos, *So Human an Animal*, p. 65. For impact of ideas, see Mitchell, Stallings, and Nader, *Ecotactics*, pp. 54, 56, 81.

19 First quote from Brower to Warlow, 16 January 1959, B/HB/4; Eiseley quote from Eliot Porter, *The Place No One Knew: Glen Canyon on the Colorado* (San Francisco: SC, 1963), p. 136.

20 Ronald Lora, *America in the 60's: Cultural Authorities in Transition* (New York: John Wiley and Sons, Inc., 1974), pp. 1—27.

21 Lewis Mumford, "California and the Human Prospect," *SCB* 47, no. 9 (December 1962): 43.

22 Roderick Nash, *Wilderness and the American Mind* (New Haven: Yale University Press, 1971), pp. 141—60.

23 David Brower, ed., *Wilderness: America's Living Heritage* (San Francisco: SC, 1962), pp. 29, 169; for other frontier references, see pp. iii, iv, 9, 13, 20—22, 27—28, 32, 51—52, 93, 122—23, 161, 187.

24 Ibid., p. iii.

25 Ibid., pp. 33, 178.

26 First quote from Loren Eiseley, *The Invisible Pyramid* (New York: Charles
     Scribner's Sons, 1970), p. 31; second quote from *SCB* 52, no. 9 (October
     1967): 25; for Mumford's quotes, see Mumford, "California and the
     Human Prospect," p. 42; for young club member's quote, see Mitchell,
     Stallings, and Nader, *Ecotactics*, p. 78; for Brower quote, see Paul
     Ehrlich, *The Population Bomb* (New York: Ballantine Books, 1968), p.
     ii. See also Brower, "Definitions for Inner Space," *SCB* 47, no. 9 (Decem-
     ber 1962): 40.

27 Raymond Cowles, *The Meaning of Wilderness to Science* (San Francisco:
     SC, 1960), p. 178; letters to editor, *SCB* 50, no. 5 (May 1965): 18; "Sierra
     Club Population Policy," *SCB* 50, no. 4 (April 1965): 2; *Monterey Peninsula
     Herald*, 15 October 1968.

28 William R. Burch, Jr. "Who Participates—A Sociological Interpretation of
     Natural Resource Decisions," *Natural Resources Journal* 16, no. 1 (January
     1976): 43–47; William Devall, "Conservation: An Upper-Middle Class
     Social Movement—A Replication," *Journal of Leisure Research* 2 (1970):
     123–26.

29 First quote from Eiseley, *The Invisible Pyramid*, pp. 22, 132; subsequent
     quote from Brower, *Wilderness*, p. 178.

30 Quote from Robert Wiebe, *The Search for Order, 1877–1920* (New York:
     Hill Wang, 1967), pp. 111–32. See also Richard Hofstadter, *The Age of
     Reform* (New York: Vintage Books, 1955), pp. 153–55, 217–20; Samuel
     Hays, *Conservation and the Gospel of Efficiency* (New York: Atheneum,
     1974), pp. 1–4.

31 Brower, "Environmental Activist," pp. 55–56, 90–92, 208.

32 Alfred Runte, "'Worthless' Lands: Our National Parks," *American West* 10
     (May 1973): 4–11.

33 Maxine McCloskey, ed., *Wilderness: The Edge of Knowledge* (San
     Francisco: SC, 1970), pp. 13–14, 250–52.

34 Leonard, "Mountaineer," pp. 18–20, 265, 339–44.

35 Quotes from Brower, "Environmental Activist," pp. 194, 88–89. See also
     Leonard, "Mountaineer," pp. 18–20, 265, 339–44; Joel Hildebrand,
     "Sierra Club Leader and Ski Mountaineer," interview conducted by Ann
     and Ray Lage (San Francisco: SC, History Committee, 1974), pp. 24–26;
     Informal interview with Fred Eissler conducted by Susan R. Schrepfer,
     5 April 1972, Santa Barbara, Calif.

36 First quotes from *Amicus Curiae* brief filed by National Environmental
     Law Society, p. 9, Sierra Club v. Morton et al., 405 US 727 (1972); last
     quote from Brower, "Environmental Activist," p. 192.

37 George Homans, *Social Behavior: Its Elementary Forms* (New York:
     Harcourt, Brace and World, Inc., 1961), p. 182.

38 RFF Study, p. 18; Burch, Jr., "Who Participates," p. 47.

39 C. Wright Mills, *White Collar* (New York: Oxford University Press, 1951),
     pp. 261–65; Jacques Barzun, *The American University* (New York:
     Harper & Row, 1968), p. 133.

40 Brower to Udall, 13 January 1961, UA/SU/190-4; Brower, "Environmental

Activist," pp. 46—49, 276; RFF Study, p. 15; Ernest Engelbert, "Political Parties and Natural Resources Policies: An Historical Evaluation, 1790—1950," *Natural Resources Journal* 1 (November 1961): 224—56.

41 Homans, *Social Behavior*, pp. 316—35.

42 Mills, *White Collar*, pp. 134—36.

43 Soucie to Brower, 19 April 1967, SC/MB/67.

44 Hildebrand, "Sierra Club Leader," p. 24—25, 31.

45 For first Brower quote, see Brower, "Environmental Activist," p. 181; for Brower's 1962 quote, see SC, BOD, 14 October 1962, SC/MB/63; for last quotes, see Brower, "Environmental Activist," pp. 181, 175, 152.

46 Commission on Private Philanthropy and Public Needs, *Giving in America: Toward a Stronger Voluntary Sector* (1975), pp. 64—70; Janet Koch, *The Role of Philanthropy in the Environmental Field: Preservation of Natural Lands and Historic Properties* (New York: Hartzog, Lader, and Richards, 1972).

47 Committee for an Active Bold Constructive Sierra Club, "Shall the Sierra Club Revert . . ." 8 pp. pamphlet [1969].

48 Leonard, "Mountaineer," pp. 107—31, 156; Hildebrand to Siri, 29 March 1965, SC/MB/65; Francis Farquhar, "Sierra Club Mountaineer and Editor," an interview conducted by Ann and Ray Lage (San Francisco: SC, History Committee, 1974), pp. 71—73; Bestor Robinson, "Thoughts on Conservation and the Sierra Club," interview conducted by Susan R. Schrepfer (San Francisco: SC, History Committee, 1974), pp. 56—57.

49 SC, BOD, 4 July 1959, 5 December 1959; SC, BOD, 14 December 1963, SC/MB/59—64; Albright, Bernays, Bradley, Crowe, Farquhar, Heimbucher, Alex Hildebrand, Joel Hildebrand, Milton Hildebrand, Robinson, Sproul to SC, BOD and Council, 28 April 1967, SC/MB/67.

50 Robinson, "Thoughts," pp. iv—v, 1—13, 38; Leonard, "Mountaineer," pp. 165—229; SRL, BOD, 26 January 1962, 7 February 1964.

51 Quote from Adams to Eissler, 5 May 1963. See also SC, BOD, 9 January 1963, SC/MB/63; William Siri, President's Report, 7—8 May 1966; SC, BOD, 10 December 1966, SC/MC/66. For Adams's support of Mill Creek plan, see Adams to SC, BOD, 18 July 1967, Adams to S. Udall, 18 July 1967, UA/SU/190-1.

52 *New York Times*, 15 December 1966; IRS District Office to SC, 16 December 1966; "Listing of What IRS Wants," n.d., SC/MB/66; Leonard, "Mountaineer," pp. 143—54; Robinson, "Thoughts," pp. 56—57; Farquhar, "Sierra Club Mountaineer and Editor," pp. 73—74; SC, BOD, 17 December 1968, SC/MB/68.

53 SC, BOD, 7 September 1963, SC/MB/63; Eissler to Siri, 7 September 1963, Siri to Fisher, 8 December 1964, Eissler Papers; Leonard, "Mountaineer," pp. 282—321; Leonard to S. Sibley (President, Pacific Gas and Electric), 4 July 1966, B/RL/1. For California Resources Agency's sanction of alternate site agreement, see Resolution, Resources Agency, 30 June 1965, signed Hugo Fisher and John Bonner, in office of Administrator, Resources building, Sacramento.

54 SC, BOD, 7–8 May 1966, SC/MB/66.

55 Quote from Litton to Sibling, 13 June 1966, SC/MB/66. See also Litton to SC, BOD, 9 September 1966, B/RL/1; *Santa Maria Times*, 14 July 1966.

56 Quote from Siri to Eissler, 22 June 1966, Eissler Papers. See also Litton to Adams, 14 July 1966, Eissler Papers; SC, BOD, 17–18 September 1966, SC/MB/66; Eissler to SC, BOD, 8 September 1966, B/RL/1.

57 First three quotes from SC, Council Minutes, 19 February 1967, SC/MB/67; for Adams's quotes, see Adams to Wayburn, 18 June 1968; for Porter's quote, see SC, BOD, 18 September 1968, SC/MB/68; for Eissler's quotes, see speech by Eissler, January 1967, Eissler Papers. See also R. Sill to Eissler and Litton, 7 February 1967, B/WS/1.

58 Quote from *Los Angeles Times*, 26 December 1966. See also Memo on 8 April 1967 vote: 11,341 to 5,225. Council and chapter votes upheld BOD decision; see SC, Council, 19 February 1967, Marshall to BOD, 6 April 1967, SC/MB/67; Adams to Freidman, 29 April 1967, Adams to Litton, 12 July 1966, Eissler Papers.

59 Albright, Bernays, Bradley, Crowe, Farquhar, Heimbucher, A. Hildebrand, J. Hildebrand, M. Hildebrand, Robinson, Sproul to SC, BOD and Council, 28 April 1967. For framing of letter, see Farquhar to Siri, 26 March 1967, "White Paper" listing charges, B/WS/3.

60 Quote from Porter to G. Marshall, 20 January 1967, B/WS/1. See also SC, BOD, 5–6 May 1967; letters received by SC office, SC/MB/67; *San Francisco Examiner*, 7 May 1967.

61 Quote from SC, BOD, 4–5 May 1968, SC/MB/68. See also SC, BOD, 16 September 1968; the act alienated Phillip Berry, see Berry to Sibling, 16 September 1968, SC/MB/68. For revolt of chapters against reversal, see resolutions and minutes of the following: SC, Council, 9 June 1968; Bay Area Chapter, 8 July 1968; John Muir Chapter, 31 July 1968; Angeles Chapter, 13 August 1968; Mother Lode Chapter, 16 August 1968; Los Padres Chapter, 22 August 1968; Loma Prieta Chapter, 5 September 1968, SC/MB/68.

62 Brower to Wayburn, 7 November 1967, Eissler Papers.

63 Minutes of Publications Committee: 21 July 1963, 14 October 1963, 21 January 1966, 4 March 1966, 20 May 1966, 9 and 30 November 1966, 28 July 1967, 5 September 1967, 19 January 1968; SC, BOD, 14 December 1968, SC/MB/63–68; Leonard, "Mountaineer," pp. 348, 363, 383–89.

64 *New York Times*, 14 January 1968.

65 First quote from SC, BOD, 16 February 1968, SC/MB/68; second quote from *Palo Alto Times*, 11 February 1969.

66 SC, BOD, 14–15 December 1967, SC/MB/67.

67 Quote from ABC, "Shall the Sierra Club Revert . . ." See also Brower to Wayburn, n.d. packet, SC/MB/69; SC *Explorer* 1, no. 4 (Fall 1968).

68 First quote from ABC, "Shall the Sierra Club Revert . . ."; second quote from Porter to Marshall, 29 January 1967, B/WS/1; final quotes from SC, BOD, 4–5 May 1968, SC/MB/68.

69 Quotes from "Two Important Letters to All Sierra Club Members from Past and Present Sierra Club Leaders," 4 pp. pamphlet, February 1969. See

also Leonard to Adams, Clark, Hearst, Sill, Wendling . . . , 23 September 1968; B/AA/1; Adams to *Monterey Peninsula Herald*, 15 October 1968, B/AA/1.

70 Quotes from Brower, "Environmental Activist," pp. 211, 219—23, 232. See also Eissler speech, January 1967, transcript in Eissler Papers.

71 First quote from SC, BOD, 9 December 1966; subsequent quotes from SC, BOD, 17 March 1968, SC/MB/66—68.

72 *Palo Alto Times*, 11 February 1969.

73 Quote from SC Council, "The Individual in a Growing Club," 6th SC Information and Education Conference, 26—27 March 1966, SC/MB/66. The Council and most of the chapters campaigned against the ABC slate; see Aubrey Wendling (Council) to Chapter Chairmen, 18 October 1968, SC/MB/68; *Mugelnoos* no. 432 (December 1968), p. 1; *Tehipite Topics* 15, no. 10 (December 1968): 1—2.

74 First quote from Robinson, "Thoughts," p. 53; second quote from Brower to Wayburn, 21 November 1967, Eissler Papers.

75 Quotes from John McPhee, *Encounters with the Archdruid* (New York: Charles Scribner's Sons, 1968), pp. 216—18. See also SC, BOD, 3—4 May 1968, SC/MB/68.

76 SC, BOD, 4—5 May 1973, SC/MB/73.

77 Leonard, "Mountaineer," pp. 430—33.

78 SC, BOD, 4—5 May 1969, SC/MB/69; 14 December 1974, SC/MB/74.

79 Mitchell, Stallings, and Nader, *Ecotactics*, p. 5.

Chapter 10: The Battle Rejoined

1 State of California, Board of Forestry, Memorandum, 10 August 1969; Wayburn to Hickel, 26 March 1969, B/SC/Flannery-6.

2 Map drawn by Martin Litton, 3 October 1968, NPS/LD/Rw.

3 Wilderness Society to Bible, 26 May 1971, Drury to Jackson, 6 May 1971, NPS/LD/Rw; Citizens for a Redwood National Park, circular, 27 May 1969, B/SC/Flannery-6.

4 Quote from Wayburn to Udall, 20 December 1968, I/P-S/Rw. See also Wayburn to Hickel, 26 March 1969, B/SC/Flannery-6.

5 Aspinall to Wayburn, 16 April 1969, B/SC/Flannery-6.

6 Wayburn to Hickel, 8 April 1969, Train to Wayburn, 5 May 1969, B/SC/ Flannery-6; Train to Cohelan, Train to Waldie, 23 May 1969, I/P-S/Rw.

7 Western Division to Director, 24 December 1968, McConnell to Western Division, 10 January 1969, I/P-S/Rw.

8 Quote from Edward Stone, Rudolph Grah, and Paul Zinke, "An Analysis of the Buffers and the Watershed Management Required to Preserve the Redwood Forest and Associated Streams in the Redwood National Park," 30 April 1969, p. 88, NPS/LD/Rw. See also Gordon Robinson, "Response to the Stone Report," 1969, SC/DC/R; F. Kilmerand and J. Longshore to Train, 15 July 1969, SC/DC/R.

9 Quotes from David Turella, Bruce Black, Nelson Murdock, "Concept Paper for Proposed 'Buffer and Watershed Management' Sec. 3 (e) Public

Law 90-545," 21 November 1969. See also W. Bowen and Joseph Rumburg to Deputy Director, 24 November 1969, NPS/LD/Rw.

10 Train to Georgia-Pacific and Arcata, 25 September 1969, Arcata to Train, 8 October 1969, I/P-S/Rw; Bowen and Rumburg to Deputy Director, 24 November 1969, NPS/LD/Rw.

11 Memoranda of Meetings of NPS and BOR with Georgia-Pacific, 23 October 1969 and 28 November 1969, I/P-S/Rw.

12 C. Bohlen to Cameron, 11 July 1972, I/P-S/Rw.

13 Joseph Morgenstern, "Oversight," *Newsweek*, May 1971.

14 Edgar Wayburn, "Redwood National Park . . . A Promise Unfulfilled," *SCB* 56, no. 6 (June 1971): 10.

15 Sierra Club to Morton, 19 September 1971, I/P-S/Rw; *SCB*, June 1973, p. p. 17.

16 Interior to Panek, 6 December 1971, I/P-S/Rw.

17 Kyl to Gude, 4 June 1973, I/P-S/Rw.

18 U.S., Department of the Interior, Office of the Assistant Secretary for Fish and Wildlife and Parks, Richard C. Curry, "Redwood National Park: Resource Management Actions Affecting Redwood Creek Corridor— Option Paper," February 1973, pp. 14−15; Curry to Reed, 19 March 1973, I/P-S/Rw.

19 Morton to OMB, 5 March 1973, OMB to Morton, 8 March 1973, I/P-S/Rw; Sierra Club v. Department of the Interior, et al., 376 F. Supp. 90 (N.D. Cal. May 13, 1974).

20 Curry to Under Secretary of the Interior, 27 March 1973, Interior to OMB, 27 March 1973, I/P-S/Rw.

21 Reed to Simpson Timber, Reed to Arcata Redwood, 10 August 1973, I/P-S/Rw.

22 Walker to Jackson, Walker to Hansen, 11 December 1973, NPS/LD/Rw.

23 F. F. Grambo to Richard Locke, 23 March 1973, Curry to Wayburn, 17 April 1973, Reed to McCloskey, 11 March 1976, I/P-S/Rw.

24 Curry, "Redwood National Park: Resource Management Actions," pp. 4−5.

25 Earth Satellite Corporation of Berkeley, Calif., "Aerial Photographic Documentation of Terrain and Vegetative Conditions in Redwood National Park and Adjoining Areas: Special Report," April 1972, p. 1, I/P-S/Rw.

26 Sierra Club v. Department of the Interior, et al., 398 F. Supp. 284 (N.D. Cal., July 16, 1975). For a legal history of the Redwood National Park battle in the 1970s, see Dale Hudson, "Sierra Club v. Department of the Interior: The Fight to Preserve the Redwood National Park," *Ecology Law Quarterly* 7, no. 3 (1979): 781−859.

27 Between 1960 and 1968 the club published twenty-eight articles on the redwoods in its *Bulletin*, four full-page newspaper advertisements, numerous pamphlets, a film, and two books; between 1970 and 1976 there were four *Bulletin* articles and no advertisements. For the opinion that publicity was not incompatible with legal action, see Michael Sherwood to Schrepfer, 9 October 1981, in author's possession.

28 For the environmentalists' earlier difficulties with standing, see "Rainbow's Day in Court," *SCB* 47, no. 9 (December 1962): 91; William O. Douglas, speech before Governor's Conference on California Beauty, 11 January 1966, pp. 5–6, B/SC/MM.

29 Scenic Hudson v. Federal Power Commission, 354 F. 2d at 616; Citizens Committee for the Hudson Valley and Sierra Club v. John Volpe, et al., No. 69 Cir. 295, 11 July 1969.

30 First quote from Sierra Club v. Morton et al., 405 US 727 (1972); second quote from Allen Talbot, *Power Along the Hudson* (New York: E. P. Dutton and Company, 1972), pp. 184–85. See also Susan Schrepfer, "Perspectives on Conservation: Sierra Club Strategies in Mineral King," *Journal of Forest History* 20, no. 4 (October 1976): 176–90.

31 Sierra Club et al. v. Morton et al., 348 F. Supp. 219 (N.D. Cal., September 12, 1972).

32 Sierra Club v. Department of the Interior, et al., 376 F. Supp. 92 (N.D. Cal., May 13, 1974); Sierra Club v. Department of the Interior, et al., 398 F. Supp. 285 (N.D. Cal., July 16, 1975).

33 NRCD v. Arcata Redwood Company, State Supreme Court, Humboldt County, June 1973 (amended May 1974): NRCD won. Arcata appealed to the State Court of Appeals in July 1973 and the decision was upheld.

34 Lindgren to Wood, 8 August 1973, Watts to Johnson, 10 August 1973, I/P-S/Rw.

35 Sierra Club v. Dept. of the Interior, et al., 398 F. Supp. 293–94 (N.D. Cal., July 16, 1975). The club offered to help Interior seek congressional funding; see McCloskey to Frizzell, 1 August 1975, B/EW/2:2.

36 Reed to Haley, 15 July, Reed to Jackson, 11 August 1975, I/P-S/Rw.

37 Nathaniel Reed, "Progress Report to U.S. District Court for the Northern District of California with Regard to the Litigation Entitled *Sierra Club v. Morton*, C-73-0163-WTS," 11 pp. (December 1975), I/P-S/Rw. The entire $92 million had not been appropriated.

38 R. Janda, M. Nolan, D. Harden, S. Colman, "Watershed Conditions in the Drainage Basin of Redwood Creek, Humboldt County, Calif., as of 1973," U.S. Geological Survey, Menlo Park, Calif., October 1975; Janda, Nolan, and Harden, "Graphic and Tabular Summaries of Water and Suspended-Sediment Discharge During Eight Periods of Synoptic Storm Sampling in the Lower Drainage Basin of Redwood Creek, Humboldt County," U.S. Geological Survey, Menlo Park, Calif., December 1975; Milton Kolipinski, Ed Helley, Luna Leopold, Steve Veirs, Gerald Witucki, and Robert Ziemer, "Status of Natural Resources in Redwood Creek Basin, Redwood National Park: A Report to the Director of the National Park Service from a Scientific Evaluation Team," 15 December 1975, NPS/LD/Rw.

39 Reed to Arcata, Simpson, Louisiana-Pacific, 1 March 1976, Arcata, Simpson, Louisiana-Pacific to Reed, 2 March 1976, Reed to McCloskey, 11 March 1976, I/P-S/Rw; "Forest Management and Redwood National Park," Hearings before a Subcommittee of the Committee on Government

Operations, House, 94th Cong., 2d sess., 18 September 1976 (Washington, D.C.: GPO, 1976), pp. 199—200 [hereafter referred to as Hearings, House Subcommittee].

40 Charles Peter Raynor, "Memorandum to Assistant Solicitor Parks and Recreation," 4 June 1976, I/P-S/Rw.

41 Ibid.; Brown to OMB, 17 February 1976, I/P-S/Rw.

42 OMB to Interior, 7 April 1976, I/P-S/Rw.

43 State of California, Division of Forestry, "Review of Redwood Harvesting," 1972.

44 Pub. Res. Code, sections 4513 (a) and 4514 (b). For description of supporters, see *Sacramento Bee*, 11 September 1973.

45 Curry to Under Secretary, 27 March 1973, I/P-S/Rw.

46 Hearings, House Subcommittee, pp. 751—54.

47 Ibid.

48 State of California, Resources Agency, "Rehabilitating the Redwood Creek Watershed," 22 August 1975.

49 Hearings, House Subcommittee, pp. 759—69; Larry E. Moss (deputy secretary for resources) to Sierra Club, 15 September 1975, SC/SF/Swatek.

50 U.S., Department of the Interior, *Report to the State of California Concerning Sedimentation Problems in the Redwood Creek Watershed, and Their Impact on Park Resources*, 10 November 1975, I/P-S/Rw.

51 State of California, "Logging Practices in the Redwood Creek Basin," Hearings before the State Board of Forestry, 17 November 1975, pp. 15—53.

52 *Los Angeles Times*, 9, 17, 20, 27 January 1976; *Eureka Times-Standard*, 29, 31 January 1976.

53 Sierra Club v. Department of the Interior, et al., 424 F. Supp. 175 (N.D., Cal., June 7, 1976).

54 Quote from ibid. For subsequent references to Judge Sweigert's words, see Hearings, House Subcommittee, p. 86; *Los Angeles Times*, 19 September 1976; "Statement of Cecil Andrus Before House Subcommittee on National Parks and Insular Affairs on H.R. 3813 and H.R. 5810," 22 April 1977, pp. 1—4, in Subcommittee office, Longworth Office Bldg., Washington, D.C.

55 *Congressional Record*, House. H.R. 10585: 91st Cong., 1st sess., 28 April 1969. H.R. 12362: 91st Cong., 1st sess., 24 June 1969. H.R. 1135: 92d Cong., 1st sess., 22 June 1971. H.R. 13001: 92d Cong., 2d sess., 7 February 1972. H.R. 1883 and H.R. 4686: 93d Cong., 1st sess., 11 January 1973 and 22 February 1973. H.R. 5193: 94th Cong., 1st sess., 19 March 1975.

56 Subcommittee on Parks and Recreation, "Oversight and Progress Analysis of the Redwood National Park, Senate," 92d Cong., 1st sess., 10 May 1971 (Washington, D.C.: GPO, 1971); Report on adjudication for 1968 lands; Interview with Edgar Wayburn conducted by Susan R. Schrepfer, 31 July 1976, San Francisco (Berkeley: ROHO, in process).

57 Hearings, House Subcommittee, pp. 1—3.

58 Ibid., pp. 210—41, 406—45. For debate on clearcutting, see *Report of the*

President's Panel on Timber and the Environment, 1973 (Washington, D.C.: GPO, 1973); U.S., Congress, Senate, *Congressional Record,* 92d Cong., 2d sess., 1 March 1972, 118, pt. 30:2986–94; *Los Angeles Times,* 20 August 1976; *Eureka Times-Standard,* 18 September 1976.

59 Hearings, House Subcommittee, p. 1.
60 Ibid., pp. 68, 210, 213–18, 235, 568; Gordon Robinson, "Response to the Stone Report on Preservation of the Redwood National Park," 1969, 19 pp., SC/DC/R.
61 Hearings, House Subcommittee, pp. 210, 213–18, 235.
62 Ibid., pp. 210, 235.
63 Ibid., pp. 406, 28–29, 536–45, 238–41, 432–45.
64 Ibid., pp. 68, 130–32, 183–85, 195–99; Drury to Jackson, 6 May 1971, NPS/LD/Rw.
65 Hearings, House Subcommittee, pp. 406, 431.
66 State of California, Divison of Forestry, "Review of Redwood Harvesting," 1972; U.S. Forest Service, Yurok Experimental Forest, "Redwood Study," 1950. Pacific Lumber was not clearcutting in the 1970s. For industry defense of clearcutting, see Hearing, House Subcommittee, pp. 195–96, 201–11, 235, 549–52; George Craig to Ryan, 22 September 1976, NPS/LD/Rw; Western Timber Association, "Clearcutting and a Quality Environment," *Newsletter* (23 April 1973), pp. 3–5; Arcata Redwood, Louisiana-Pacific, and Simpson Timber, "Enlargement of the Present Redwood National Park Does Not Make Environmental or Economic Sense," 7-page pamphlet, 1977.
67 Hearings, House Subcommittee, pp. 405, 432.
68 *Report of the President's Panel on Timber and the Environment* (Washington, D.C.: GPO, 1973), p. 23.
69 Interview with Linda Billings conducted by Susan R. Schrepfer, 4 August 1978, Washington, D.C.
70 Hearings, House Subcommittee, pp. 239, 536–37.
71 At the House Subcommittee hearing on 18 September 1976, Ryan said Arcata had labelled his hearing political while one of Arcata's employees, Mike Scanlon, was on "outside duty" campaigning for President Ford; see p. 193.
72 *New York Times,* 1 November 1976.
73 "Redwood Agreement," signed by Peter Taft (Department of Justice) and William Walsh (Arcata), Harry Merle (Louisiana-Pacific), and the president of Simpson Timber, 8 November 1976, I/P-S/Rw.
74 "Forest Management and Redwood National Park," II, Hearings before a Subcommittee of the Committee on Government Operations, House of Representatives, 95th Cong., 1st sess., 9 February 1977 (Washington, D.C.: GPO, 1977), p. 63.
75 Ibid., pp. 68, 56–57, 71.
76 Ibid., p. 44.

Chapter 11: A Second Redwood Park Act

1 Interview with Linda Billings conducted by Susan R. Schrepfer, 4 August

1978, Washington, D.C.

2 H.R. 3813: *Congressional Record*, 95th Cong., 1st sess., 22 February 1977, 123, pt. 4: 4974; U.S., Congress, House, Subcommittee of the Committee on Government Operations, *Forest Management and Redwood National Park, II: Hearing on H.R. 5810*, 95th Cong., 1st sess., 9 February 1977, pp. 481, 51.

3 Ibid., pp. 68−69; Warren, Speth, and Eddy to the President, 10 April 1977, NPS/LD/Rw.

4 "Responses of Cecil D. Andrus, Secretary of the Interior, to Question 24 posed at his confirmation hearings, 17−18 January 1977," Andrus to Jackson, 20 April 1977, R. Curry to Legislative Council, 27 May 1976, plus proposed legislation to add 48,000 acres to Redwood National Park, NPS/LD/Rw.

5 "Statement of Secretary of the Interior Cecil Andrus before House Subcommittee on National Parks and Insular Affairs on H.R. 3813 and H.R. 5810," 22 April 1977, in Subcommittee office, Longworth Office Building, Washington, D.C.

6 Billings to Pinnex, 2 April 1977, SC/DC/R.

7 Wayburn to Billings, 5 February 1977, Billings to Wayburn, McCloskey, Swatek, and Robinson, 15 February 1977, SC/DC/R.

8 Udall, Jackson, Burton, and Abourezk to Carter, 14 March 1977, NPS/LD/Rw.

9 Sierra Club, FOE, Izaak Walton League, National Audubon Society, National Wildlife Federation, SRL, and Wilderness Society to Andrus, 11 March 1977, SC/DC/R; Andrus to Simpson Timber, Louisiana-Pacific, and Arcata, 29 March 1977, I/P-S/Rw.

10 Memorandum from Billings, 15 April 1977, Billings to Pinnex, 21 April 1977, SC/DC/R.

11 Interior to Morris Udall, 31 May 1977, I/P-S/Rw.

12 *Los Angeles Times*, 23 March 1977; Department of the Interior News Release, 19 April 1977, I/P-S/Rw.

13 Quote from transcript of speech in *Forest Management and Redwood National Park, II*, p. 63. See also Arcata Redwood, Louisiana-Pacific, and Simpson Timber, "Enlargement of the Present Redwood National Park Does Not Make Environmental or Economic Sense," 7-page pamphlet, 1977; *Arcata Union*, 27 March 1977.

14 *Los Angeles Times*, 8 March 1978; *Humboldt Times-Standard*, 14 April 1977; Interviews with subcommittee personnel conducted by author, 15 August 1978, Washington, D.C.

15 U.S., Congress, House, Subcommittee on National Parks and Insular Affairs, Minutes of Hearings in Eureka, Calif., 13 April 1977, pp. 238−54, 336−45, unpublished transcript in Subcommittee office, Washington, D.C.

16 First quote from *Forest Management and Redwood National Park, II*, pp. 13, 5, 19, 30; second quote from John Amodio, "Park Relief in Sight," *Econews* 7, no. 5 (May 1977): 3.

17 Minutes of the Subcommittee on National Parks and Insular Affairs, 13 April 1977, pp. 328−35.

18 Ibid., pp. 245−46, 250−51.
19 U.S., Congress, House, Subcommittee on National Parks and Insular Affairs, Hearing in San Francisco, 14 April 1977, unpublished transcript in Subcommittee office, Washington, D.C.; *Humboldt Times-Standard*, 14−15 April 1977.
20 "Protecting Redwood National Park: First Report by the Committee on Government Operations together with Additional and Dissenting Views," House Report, 95−106, 95th Cong., 1st sess., 23 March 1977 (Washington, D.C.: GPO, 1977).
21 "Statement of Secretary of the Interior Cecil Andrus before House Subcommittee on National Parks and Insular Affairs, . . ." 22 April 1977, p. 10; "Enlargement of the Present Redwood National Park Does Not Make Environmental or Economic Sense." Local residents and the timber companies based their predictions in part upon a study by the National Resources Management Corporation of Eureka that estimated the park and other environmental pressures would reduce the annual cut by about 85 percent; see John Miles, *Humboldt County Timber Supply and Predicted Production Rates, 1965−2026*, 1 June 1977.
22 *Humboldt Times-Standard*, 17 January 1976.
23 U.S., Congress, House, Subcommittee of the Committee on Government Operations, *Forest Management and Redwood National Park, I: Hearings*, San Francisco, 94th Cong., 2d sess., 18 September 1976, p. 186; Sierra Club, "The Harsh Realities of Redwood National Park," Fact Sheet, n.d., SC/DC/R; Gordon Robinson to Paul Swatek, 13 March 1977, SC/SF/Swatek.
24 Robinson to Edwin Z'Berg, 22 July 1966, SC/MB/65−66; Robinson to Swatek, 15 May 1977, Sierra Club, "A Rebuttal to Timber Industry Misinformation" [1976], p. 2, SC/DC/R.
25 Minutes of the Subcommittee on National Parks and Insular Affairs, 14 April 1977, pp. 30−42.
26 First quote from *Forest Management and Redwood National Park, II*, pp. 37−38; subsequent quotes from Emerald Creek Committee, "Redwood National Park," August 1976, 16-page pamphlet. See also John Amodio, "Briefing Sheets," March 1977, SC/DC/R.
27 For Amodio's quote, see "Park Relief in Sight," p. 2; second quote from *Forest Management and Redwood National Park, II*, p. 63. *Eureka Times-Standard*, 25 August 1976, 14 September 1976.
28 James Linquist and Marshall Ralley, California Agricultural Experiment Station Bulletin 796, "Empirical Yield for Young-Growth Redwood," (1963), p. 1.
29 U.S., Department of Agriculture [hereafter USDA], Forest Service, "Timber Resources of Humboldt County," PNW-26 (1968); USDA, Forest Service, "Two Projections of Timber Supply in the Pacific Coast States," PNW-70 (1975); USDA, Forest Service, "A Technique and Relationship for Projections of Employment in the Pacific Coast Forest Products Industries," PNW-189 (1975); USDA, Forest Service, "Prospects for Sawtimber Output in California's North Coast, 1975−2000," PNW-195 (1977).
30 *Forest Management and Redwood National Park, I*, p. 30.

31 Returns from old growth are high; Standard and Poor's reveals that between 1970–76 redwood production accounted for 10 percent of the Arcata National Corporation's sales but 50 percent of its profits.
32 Jacob Toby and Robert Hermanson in *Monthly Review*, Federal Reserve Bank (June 1967), pp. 121–27.
33 Quote from *Humboldt Times-Standard*, 19 October 1975. See also City of Eureka, "Economic Conditions, General Plan," 1976.
34 *Los Angeles Times*, 8 March 1978.
35 *Klamity-Kourier* (Willow Creek), 20 April 1977; *Oakland Tribune*, 21 April 1977; *Humboldt Times-Standard*, 11 February 1977. For exception, see *Roseville Press-Tribune*, 30 May 1977.
36 *San Francisco Examiner*, 18 April 1977; *San Francisco Chronicle*, 2 August 1977; *San Jose News*, 18 April 1977; *Fresno Bee*, 18 April 1977, 11 October 1977; *Santa Rosa Press-Democrat*, 25 February 1977, 12 March 1978; *California Aggie*, 3 May 1977; *Sacramento Union*, 20 October 1977; *Sacramento Bee*, 24 April 1977, 4 August 1977, 9 January 1977, 24 April 1977; *Chico Enterprise-Record*, 14 August 1977; *San Bernardino Sun*, 28 May 1977. For exception, see *San Jose Mercury*, 26 May 1977.
37 *Los Angeles Times*, 22 March 1977, 8 April 1977, 7 June 1977, 8 and 31 July 1977, 3 November 1977; *Washington Post*, 15 April 1977, 3 May 1977; *Boston Globe*, 22 August 1977; *New York Times*, 22 March 1977; *Baltimore Sun*, 15 May 1977.
38 Billings to Pinnex, Beirne, Wilson, Hales, Curry, 24 May 1977, SC/DC/R; "Newspapers that have been personally contacted and background information supplied—as of October 7, 1977 on redwoods," SC/SF/Swatek.
39 Quotes from *Cleveland Plain Dealer*, 13 May 1977; *Fort Wayne Journal Gazette*, 4 August 1977; *Norfolk Pilot*, 20 May 1977; *Lincoln Star*, 21 May 1977; Ashland (Ky.) *Independent*, 2 June 1977; *Akron Beacon-Journal*, 27 November 1977. See also *Detroit Free Press*, 5 and 30 April 1977, 30 May 1977, 14 July 1977; *Courier-Journal* (Ky.), 30 April 1977) *Battle Creek Enquirer and News*, 2 June 1977; *Houston Post*, 2 August 1977; *St. Paul Pioneer Press*, 17 April 1977.
40 SRL, Press Release, 23 May 1977, 3 June 1977; SRL, *Fall Bulletin*, 1977; Andrus to Leonard, 27 June 1977, Andrus to Morris Udall, 31 May 1977, I/P-S/Rw.
41 Andrus to John Dewitt, 27 July 1977, I/P-S/Rw.
42 Richard M. Leonard, "Mountaineer, Lawyer, Environmentalist," interview conducted by Susan R. Schrepfer (Berkeley: ROHO, 1975), pp. 216–17.
43 For example, between January and April 1974, SRL purchased 250 acres along the highway in Humboldt County, 704 acres of second growth in Humboldt Redwoods State Park, 57 acres in Richardson Grove, 270 acres in Big Basin, and 37 acres in San Mateo County.
44 SRL, Press Release, 31 March 1975.
45 Interview with Howard Libbey conducted by Susan R. Schrepfer, 10 July 1968, San Francisco; Robert Wernick, "The Battle of the Redwoods," *Saturday Evening Post* (22 April 1967), pp. 91–95.

46 Moshosky to Hartzog, 22 June 1970, I/P-S/Rw.

47 Arcata National Corporation v. The United States, U.S. Circuit Court, No. 777-71, December 31, 1974. Arcata respected Skunk Cabbage Creek scenic easement from 1969 to 1975; see Murray to Train, 8 October 1969, Train to Wayburn, 5 May 1969, I/P-S/Rw.

48 SRL, *Bulletins*, 1972—76; SRL, Press Releases, 1 April 1974, 3 June 1976.

49 SRL, Press Release, 26 April 1977; Leonard to Membership, 20 May 1977, John Dewitt, "Supplemental Statement to the Subcommittee on National Parks and Insular Affairs of the Committee on Interior and Insular Affairs," 20 May 1977, Dewitt to Rob Byrd (U.S. Senate), 27 October 1977, SRL/F/RNP.

50 Dewitt to Dedrick, 10 June 1977, NPS/LD/Rw; Billings to Wayburn, 4 March 1977, SC/DC/R.

51 Leonard to CMC, 20 April 1969; Leonard, "Mountaineer," pp. 335—402.

52 Leonard, "Mountaineer," pp. 320—34.

53 Ibid., pp. 282—306; "Testimony of Frederick Eissler before the California Public Utility Commission in the Diablo Canyon Case," May 1967; SC, Board of Directors, 9—10 December 1968, SC/MC/68.

54 Leonard, "Mountaineer," pp. 165—97.

55 Ibid., pp. 409—10, 201.

56 Quote from *San Francisco Examiner*, 24 May 1977; *San Bernardino Sun*, 28 May 1977; *Ashland* (Ky.) *Independent*, 2 June 1977. See also *Michigan Enquirer and News*, 2 June 1977; *Sacramento Bee*, 9 June 1977; *Los Angeles Times*, 8 July 1977; *Detroit Free Press*, 14 July 1977; *Houston Post*, 2 August 1977; *Fort Wayne Journal Gazette*, 4 August 1977; *San Francisco Examiner*, 10 June 1977.

57 *Humboldt Times-Standard*, 12 June 1977.

58 90 Stat. 2662.

59 Dedrick to Reed, 21 March 1976, 21 April 1976, NPS/LD/Rw; *Forest Management and Redwood National Park, I*, p. 38. For state's position at height of battle, see William C. Kellop, *Economic Losses Associated with Reduction of Timber Output Due to Expansion of the Redwood National Park*, April 1977, State of California Resources Agency, Department of Forestry.

60 Department of the Interior, Press Release, 19 April 1977, I/P-S/Rw.

61 *New York Times*, 25 May 1977; Department of the Interior, Press Release, 12 July 1977, I/P-S/Rw.

62 Andrus to Morris Udall, 26 July 1977, I/P-S/Rw.

63 H.R. 8641: *Congressional Record*, 95th Cong., 1st sess., 29 July 1977, 123, pt. 20:25682; McCloskey to Billings, 14 June 1977, SC/DC/R.

64 Billings and Lau to Wayburn, McCloskey, and Swatek, 15 July 1977, SC/DC/R; S. 1976: U.S., Congress, Senate, *Congressional Record*, 95th Cong., 1st sess., 1 August 1977, 123, pt. 21:25847—48; Press Release, Office of Senator Alan Cranston, 7 September 1977; Abourezk to National Audubon Society, 12 October 1977, SC/DC/R.

65 McCloskey to Billings, 14 June 1977, Billings to McCloskey, Swatek, Wayburn, 13 October 1977, SC/DW/R. For organized labor's initial

negative response, see *Humboldt Times-Standard*, 27 June 1977.

66 Throughout the 1950s most SC and SRL leaders were Republicans. SC's position on redwoods in 1950s mirrored that of SRL; see B/HB/4.

67 Interview with Wayburn conducted by Susan R. Shrepfer, 30 July 1976, San Francisco (Berkeley: ROHO, in process); Reuther to Johnson, 11 February 1966, LBJ/Gen Le-NR/145.

68 Patrick Hefferman, "Jobs and Environment," *SCB* 60, no. 4 (April 1975): 25–29; SC, BOD, 5–6 November 1977, SC/MB/77; *Jersey Sierran*, vol. 6, no. 1 (January–February 1978): 3.

69 Billings to Hatfield, 8 March 1978, SC/DC/R.

70 Pacific Northwest Research Center, "Labor and Log Exports," pamphlet printed by International Woodworkers of America and the Association of Western Pulp and Paper Workers (Portland, Ore., n.d.).

71 Interview with Billings by author, August 1978.

72 Billings to Hayden, 27 October 1977, AFL-CIO to Billings, 9 January 1978, SC/DC/R; United Brotherhood of Carpenters to Andrus, 21 March 1978, I/P-S/Rw.

73 Tom Turner, "What About the Loggers?" *Not Man Apart* 5, no. 7 (April 1975): 8; Leonard Woodcock, "Jobs and Environment—No Conflict," *Not Man Apart* 6, no. 1 (January 1976): 1–2; David R. Brower, "Environmental Activist, Publicist, and Prophet," interview conducted by Susan R. Schrepfer (Berkeley: ROHO, 1978), p. 275. Title II endorsements included: National Audubon Society to Abourezk, 7 October 1977, American Rivers Conservation Council to Burton, 25 September 1977, Defenders of Wildlife to Burton, 14 October 1977, National Resources Defense Council to O'Neill, 14 October 1977, FOE to Burton, 12 October 1977, Environmental Defense Fund to Burton, 30 September 1977, Environmental Action to Burton, 21 March 1977, Wilderness Society to Burton, 29 September 1977, Conservation Foundation to Burton, 7 October 1977, Environmental Policy Center to Burton, 18 October 1977, SC/DC/R.

74 Billings to Abourezk, 27 October 1977, SC/DC/R.

75 Rudolf Becking, "An Analysis of the Redwood National Park in Relation to the Timber Economy of Humboldt and Del Norte Counties" (Arcata, Calif., 1975), pp. 44–45, I/P-S/Rw.

76 Quotes from Mēca Wawona, "A Labor Intensive Approach to Watershed Repair," Center for Education and Manpower Resources, Ukiah, Calif., 1977, p. 2. For club's support, see Paul Swatek, Memo to SC Accounting, 6 May 1977, SC/SF/Swatek.

77 Wawona to Swatek, 2 May 1977, SC/SF/Swatek; Billings and Lau to Wayburn, McCloskey, and Swatek, 15 July 1977, SC/DC/R. For philosophy behind labor-intensive reconstruction, see Brower, "Environmental Activist," pp. 274–76; Peggy Wayburn, "Jobs and Redwoods," *Cry California* (Winter 1978), pp. 34–39.

78 For club's position on Burton bill, see McCloskey to Billings, 14 June 1977, SC/DC/R.

79 Reed to Morris Udall, 19 January 1977, Assistant Secretary to Andrus, 19 January 1977, I/P-S/Rw.

80 Report of the Controller General, "Information on the Acquisition for the Redwood National Park," 16 August 1977, Ryan to Controller General, 20 April 1977, I/P-S/Rw; Billings to Burton, 28 February 1978, McCloskey to Billings, 14 June 1977, SC/DC/R; John Dewitt, "Supplemental Statement to the Subcommittee on National Parks and Insular Affairs," 20 May 1977, NPS/LD/Rw; Andrus to Mondale, 26 July 1977, I/P-S/Rw. For administration's position, see Andrus to Mondale, 26 July 1977, I/P-S/Rw.

81 For the administration's position, see Andrus to Carter, 22 March 1978, NPS/LD/Rw; on committee activity, see memo from Billings and Steve Lau, 1 August 1977, SC/SF/Swatek.

82 Meeds to American Plywood Association, 23 August 1977, Metcalf/ DC/R.

83 The only significant amendment made in the committee was the deletion of sections authorizing citizen suits; U.S., Congress, House, Interior and Insular Affairs Committee, 5 August 1977, *U.S. Code Congressional and Administrative News* No. 3, 95th Cong., 2d sess. (April 1978), H. Rept. 95-581 (I), pp. 797–800, 807–808.

84 Quote from ibid., pp. 814–17. See also U.S., Congress, House, Appropriations Committee, 23 September 1977, *U.S. Code Congressional and Administrative News* No. 3, 95th Cong., 2d sess. (April 1978), H. Rept. 95-581 (II), pp. 821–25.

85 U.S., Congress, Senate, Energy and Natural Resources Committee, *Redwood National Park: Report, together with Minority Views, to accompany S. 1976*, 95th Cong., 1st sess., 21 October 1977, S. Rept. 95-528, pp. 29–31.

86 *San Francisco Examiner*, 11 September 1977.

87 S. Rept. 95-528, pp. 29–31; SC, "Proposed Amendment to H.R. 3813 and S. 1976," 19 January 1978, SC/DC/R.

88 Testimony of California Labor Federation, AFL-CIO, before the Subcommittee on Parks and Recreation of the Senate Committee on Energy and Natural Resources, 7 September 1977, San Francisco.

89 *Congressional Insight*, 1, no. 42 (October 1977): 2; *Fort Wayne Journal Gazette*, 9 October 1977; *Palm Springs Desert Sun*, 7 December 1977.

90 Billings to O'Keefe, 7 October 1977, Billings to Scott, 13 December 1977, Stapke to Billings, n.d., SC/DC/R; Interview with Jay Power (legislative advocate, United Carpenters and Joiners of America) conducted by Susan R. Schrepfer, 18 July 1979, Washington, D.C.

91 Billings to McCloskey, Swatek, Wayburn, and Billings to Coan, 13 October 1977, SC/DC/R; Interview with Power conducted by author, July 1979.

92 S. Rept. 95-528. p. 8.

93 Ibid.; Meeds to Lewis, 23 August 1977, Meeds to McCoy, 31 October 1977, Dicks to Buman, 26 September 1977, Les Au Coin to Fordyce, 20 October 1977, SC/DC/R.

94 Anthony Wayne Smith, "The Scandal of the Redwoods: I," *National Parks and Conservation Magazine* (November 1976), pp. 1–3; Wayburn to McCloskey, 25 August 1977, SC, "Land Use Regulations," n.d., Lau and Billings to Meeds, 30 September 1977, Billings Memorandum, 13 October 1977, SC/DC/R. For a study of regulation, see Institute for Public Interest Representation, Georgetown University Center, to National Parks and Conservation Association, 2 September 1977; Jarvis (NPCA) to Burton, 3 October 1977, SC/DC/R.

95 Sections authorizing citizen suits were dropped; see S. Rept. 95-528, 21 October 1977, pp. 5–15. For the club's efforts to restore them, see Billings to McCloskey, 14 June 1977, McCloskey to Billings, 14 June 1977; for the club's decision that the change was insignificant, see Billings to McCloskey, Swatek, and Wayburn, 13 October 1977, SC/DW/R.

96 For companies' efforts to win concessions, see *San Francisco Examiner*, 15 January 1978; *New York Times*, 24 January 1978. On the issue of the courts, see Brotherhood of Carpenters to Andrus, 21 March 1978, I/P-S/Rw, and S. Rept. 95-528, pp. 6–7. For industry's efforts to have access roads deleted from the park and the committee's grant of continued access instead, see S. Rept. 95-528, pp. 9–10; Billings to McCloskey, Swatek, Wayburn, 13 October 1977, SC/DC/R.

97 American Rivers Council, The Conservation Foundation, Defenders of Wildlife, Dennis Bass, Environmental Defense Fund, Environmental Policy Center, FOE, Garden Club of America, Izaak Walton League, National Parks and Recreation Association, Natural Resources Defense Council, SC, Wilderness Society, and Emerald Creek Committee to Byrd, 27 October 1977, SC/DC/R.

98 U.S., Congress, Senate, Committee on Appropriations, *Redwood National Park Report to accompany S. 1976*, 95th Cong., 1st sess., 2 November 1977, S. Rept. 95-578.

99 *Sacramento Bee*, 7 October 1977; *San Francisco Chronicle*, 19 October 1977.

100 Arcata Redwood Company and Louisiana-Pacific Corporation v. State Board of Forestry, Lewis A. Moran, Director of Forestry, No. 61910. In the Superior Court of the State of California in and for the County of Humboldt, decision 13 September 1977.

101 B. Herbst to Henry Vaux, 9 January 1978, I/P-S/Rw; Vaux to Herbst, 30 January 1978, NPS/LD/Rw.

102 Dedrick to Reed, 21 April 1976, K. G. Sebelius to Brown, Jr., 30 June 1977, Huey Johnson to Sebelius, 30 August 1977, NPS/LD/Rw.

103 Vandals slashed trees in Humboldt Park; see *Humboldt Times-Standard, San Francisco Chronicle, Washington Post*, 6 and 28 January 1978.

104 U.S., Congress, Senate, *Congressional Record*, 95th Cong., 2d sess., 31 January 1978, 124, pt. 2:1562–92; Interview with Power conducted by author, July 1979; John Amodio, "Senate's Redwood Results," 31 January 1978, SC/SF/Swatek.

105 Interview with Power conducted by author, July 1979.

106 Quote from *New Yorker*, 26 February 1976, p. 76. For SC's pressure, see Wayburn to O'Neill, 19 October 1977, Billings to O'Keefe, 7 October 1977, Billings to D. Scott, 13 December 1977, Billings to Wayburn and Swatek, 1 December 1977, SC/DC/R; for pressure orchestrated by the club, see Zagata to Abourezk, 7 October 1977, Brown to Burton, 29 September 1977, Kelly to O'Neill, 8 October 1977, Grandy to Burton, 14 October 1977, Sandler to O'Neill, 14 October 1977, SC/DC/R.

107 For Burton's threat, see *Congressional Insight* 1, no. 42 (7 October 1977): 2. For adverse press coverage of labor pressure and O'Neill's action, see *San Francisco Examiner*, 11 September 1977; *Sacramento Bee*, 7 October 1977; *Fort Wayne Journal-Gazette*, 9 October 1977; *Los Angeles Times*, 13 September 1977; *Washington Post*, 19 November 1977; *Fresno* (Calif.) *Bee*, 11 October 1977; *Washington Star*, 25 November 1977; *Christian Science Monitor*, 23 November 1977.

108 Interview with Power conducted by author, July 1979.

109 Republican Les Au Coin and Democrat Meeds, from the timber industry regions of Oregon and Washington respectively, led opposition to regulation; Meeds to Lewis, 23 August 1977, Meeds to McCoy, 31 October 1977, Au Coin to Fordyce, 30 October 1977, SC/DC/R.

110 H.R. 10760: *Congressional Record*, 95th Cong., 2d sess., 9 February 1978, 124, pt. 3:2931−38. On downed timber, see Chapman to NPS 1 March 1978, NPS/LD/Rw; William Ragen to Train, 1 March 1969, Memoranda of meetings between Georgia-Pacific and Interior, 13 February 1969, 24 September 1970, I/P-S/Rw.

111 S. Rept. 95-528, pp. 29−31; *Congressional Record*, 95th Cong., 2d sess., 9 February 1978, 124, pt. 3:2931.

112 *Congressional Record*, 95th Cong., 2d sess., 9 February 1978, 124, pt. 3:2931, 2938.

113 Gordon Robinson to Wayburn, 4 March 1977, Robinson, "Statement before the Subcommittee on National Parks and Insular Affairs," 21 and 22 March 1977, 9 pp. typed, Billings to Scott, 13 December 1977, "Proposed Amendment to H.R. 3813 and S. 1976," 19 January 1978, SC, "Analysis of Proposed Amendment to H.R. 3813 and S. 1976," February 1978, SC/DC/R.

114 Quote from Amodio to Abourezk, 19 October 1977, SC/DC/R. See also SC, "Fact Sheet on National Forest Allowable Cut," [n.d.], SC/DC/R; Interview with Power conducted by author, July 1979.

115 Billings to Wayburn and Swatek, 1 December 1977, Billings to Scott, 13 December 1977, SC/DC/R.

116 Billings to Burton and Abourezk, 28 February 1978, Billings to Amodio and McCloskey, 28 February 1978, Billings to Sherwood, Amodio, Swatek, and McCloskey, 24 March 1978, SC/DC/R.

117 Udall to O'Neill, 8 February 1978, I/P-S/Rw; *Congressional Record*, 95th Cong., 2d sess., 9 February 1978, 124, pt. 4:2931−45; Interviews with Billings and Power conducted by author, August, July 1979.

118 Department of the Interior, Press Release, 21 June 1977, 12 July 1977;

Green to Andrus, 29 November 1977, Andrus to Green, 10 January 1978, I/P-S/Rw; D. Tobin, Jr. to Jefferson, 24 February 1978, Andrus to Carter, 22 March 1978, NPS/LD/Rw; *Congressional Record*, 95th Cong., 2d sess., 9 February 1978, 124, pt. 3:2945.

119 U.S., Congress, Senate, *Congressional Record*, 95th Cong., 2d sess., 28 February 1978, 124, pt. 4:4988.

120 U.S., Congress, House, Conference Committee, 8 March 1978, *U.S. Code Congressional and Administrative News* No. 3, 95th Cong., 2d sess. (April 1978), H. Rept, 95-931, pp. 826—29. The House passed H. Rept. 95-931 by a vote of 317 to 60 (with 56 not voting), see *Congressional Record*, 95th Cong., 2d sess., 8 and 14 March 1978, 124, pt. 5:6083—90, 6857—66. The Senate passed H. Rept. 95-931 by vote of 63 to 26 (with 11 not voting), see U.S., Congress, Senate, *Congressional Record*, 95th Cong., 2d sess., 21 March 1978, 124, pt. 6:7791—7801.

121 Andrus to Carter, 22 March 1978, NPS/LD/Rw.

122 Leo Rennert, "Redwood Park . . . Easy as Falling Off Log?" *Sacramento Bee*, 25 March 1978. The Senate vote went from 72—20 to 63—26. For concern caused in House by OMB position, see *Congressional Record*, 95th Cong., 2d sess., 9 February 1978, 124, p.3:2939—45.

123 Interview with Power conducted by author, July 1979.

124 The only precedents for Title II were the Regional Rail Reorganization Act of 1973 (Public Law 93-236), which the club had supported, and the Trade Expansion Act of 1962. For the redwood act as a precedent, see Billings to Hatfield, 8 March 1978, SC/DC/R.

Chapter 12: No Place to Stand

1 Quote from Alfred Runte, "'Worthless' Lands: Our National Parks," *American West* (May 1973), pp. 4—11. See also Richard Hofstadter, *The Age of Reform* (New York: Vintage Books, 1955), pp. 11—12, 302—16; Samuel P. Hays, *Conservation and the Gospel of Efficiency* (New York: Atheneum, 1974), pp. 1—4; Gabriel Kolko, *The Triumph of Conservatism* (Chicago: Quadrangle Books, 1963), pp. 1—6; John Morton Blum, *The Republican Roosevelt* (New York: Atheneum, 1965), p. 5; Arthur Link, *Woodrow Wilson and the Progressive Era* (New York: Harper & Row, 1954), p. 80.

2 Robert H. Wiebe, *The Search for Order, 1877—1920* (New York: Hill and Wang, 1967), pp. 111—32.

3 Donald Fleming, "Roots of the New Conservation Movement," *Perspectives in American History* 6 (1972): 10.

4 Sierra Club, History Committee Survey, 1972, in Bancroft Library; William Devall, "The Governing of a Voluntary Oligarchy," (Ph.D. diss., University of Oregon, 1970), p. 189; Resources for the Future, "Environmental Movement Survey," 1978, in SC office. Definitions for *professional* and *semiprofessional* taken from Amitai Etzioni, *Modern Organizations* (Englewood Cliffs, N.J.: Prentice-Hall, 1964), pp. 77—89.

5 Wiebe, *The Search for Order*, p. viii.

6 Hays, *Conservation and the Gospel of Efficiency*, pp. 143, 189—98. On

the nostalgic component of progressives in general, see Hofstadter, *The Age of Reform*, pp. 1—22.

7 Wiebe, *The Search for Order*, pp. 111—32.

8 David L. Hull, *Philosophy of Biological Science* (Englewood Cliffs, N.J.: Prentice-Hall, 1974), p. 46.

9 Fleming, "Roots of the New Conservation Movement," p. 74.

10 First quote from Garrett Hardin, *Nature and Man's Fate* (New York: Mentor Books, 1959), p. 69; second quote from Julian Huxley, *Evolution* (London: George Allen & Unwin, 1944), p. 466.

11 First quote from Leo Marx, "Reflections on the Neo-Romantic Critique of Science," *Daedalus* 107, no. 2 (Spring 1978): 61—74; second quote from John Mitchell, Ralph Nader, and Constance Stallings, eds., *Ecotactics: The Sierra Club Handbook for Activists* (New York: Pocket Books, 1970).

12 David Brower to Chester Warlow, 16 January 1959, B/HB/4.

13 Resources for the Future, "Survey," 1978.

14 Susan Flader, *Thinking Like a Mountain: Aldo Leopold and the Evolution of an Ecological Attitude toward Deer, Wolves, and Forests* (Columbia: University of Missouri Press, 1974), p. 270.

15 Alfred Runte, "The National Park Idea," *Journal of Forest History* 21, no. 2 (April 1977): 68—70.

16 Lewis Mumford, *The Pentagon of Power* (New York: Harcourt Brace and Jovanovich, 1970), p. 386; Fleming, "Roots of the New Conservation Movement," pp. 89—90.

17 Flader, *Thinking Like a Mountain*, p. 5.

18 David R. Brower, "Environmental Activist, Publicist, and Prophet," interview conducted by Susan R. Schrepfer (Berkeley: ROHO, 1978), p. 157.

19 Richard M. Leonard, "Mountaineer, Lawyer, Environmentalist," interview conducted by Susan R. Schrepfer (Berkeley: ROHO, 1975), p. 51.

20 Ibid.

21 Joel Hildebrand, "Sierra Club Leader and Ski Mountaineer," interview conducted by Ann and Ray Lage (San Francisco: SC, 1974), p. 31; U.S. Department of the Interior v. Arcata Redwood, U.S. Court of Claims, Washington, D.C., 25 July 1974, pp. 22—26, 37—38. The trial judge recognized the validity of widely disparate estimates on redwood land values and rendered a judgment midway between Arcata's demand and the government's figure.

22 C. Wright Mills, *White Collar* (New York: Oxford University Press, 1951), pp. 330—31.

BIBLIOGRAPHY OF
UNPUBLISHED SOURCES

WITHIN THE notes the locations of all primary documents have been given in the following symbols:

A/I/NPS-2: Washington, D.C., National Archives, Records of the Secretary of the Interior, National Park Service Papers—Box 2.

A/I/12-0: Washington, D.C., National Archives, Records of the Secretary of the Interior, Proposed National Parks.

A/I/Work-2: Washington, D.C., National Archives, Records of the Secretary of the Interior, Secretary Hubert Work—Box 2.

A/NPS/Cammerer: Washington, D.C., National Archives, National Park Service Papers, Arno Cammerer.

A/NPS/RG 79: Washington, D.C., National Archives, National Park Service Papers, Record Group 79.

B/AA/Box: Berkeley, University of California, Bancroft Library, Ansel Adams Papers.

B/AB/Wilderness: Berkeley, University of California, Bancroft Library, Art Blake Papers, Wilderness Files.

B/CM/Box: Berkeley, University of California, Bancroft Library, Charlotte Mauk Papers.

B/EW/Box—Folder: Berkeley, University of California, Bancroft Library, Edgar Wayburn Papers.

B/GM/RNP: Berkeley, University of California, Bancroft Library, George Marshall Papers, Redwood National Park Folders.

B/HB/Box: Berkeley, University of California, Bancroft Library, Harold Bradley Papers.

B/JM/Box—Folder: Berkeley, University of California, Bancroft Library, John Merriam Papers.

B/RL/Carton: Berkeley, University of California, Bancroft Library, Richard M. Leonard Papers.

B/SC/Box—Folder: Berkeley, University of California, Bancroft Library, Sierra Club Papers.

B/SC/Flannery—Folder: Berkeley, University of California, Bancroft Library, Sierra Club Collection, John Flannery Papers.

B/SC/MM—Folder: Berkeley, University of California, Bancroft Library, Sierra Club Collection, Michael McCloskey Papers.

B/SC/RW: Berkeley, University of California, Bancroft Library, Sierra Club Collection, Redwood Papers.

B/SPC/Box: Berkeley, University of California, Bancroft Library, State Parks Council Papers.

B/SRL/Carton: Folder: Berkeley, University of California, Bancroft Library, Save-the-Redwoods League Papers.

B/WS/Carton: Folder: Berkeley, University of California, Bancroft Library, William Siri Papers.

CI/JM/Folder: Washington, D.C., Carnegie Institution of Washington, D.C., John Merriam Papers.

I/P-S/Rw: Washington, D.C., Department of the Interior, Parks and Sites Files, Redwood Folders.

LBJ/EX-PA3/Box: Austin, Texas, Lyndon Baines Johnson Library, Legislative Files.

LBJ/Gen Le-NR/Box: Austin, Texas, Lyndon Baines Johnson Library, General Legislation Files.

LBJ/Int/I-2: Austin, Texas, Lyndon Baines Johnson Library, Administrative History, Department of the Interior.

LBJ/Int/II-Doc: Austin, Texas, Lyndon Baines Johnson Library, Administrative History, Department of the Interior.

LBJ/LE-PA3/Box: Austin, Texas, Lyndon Baines Johnson Library, Legislative Park Files.

LBJ/PA 2-3/Box: Austin, Texas, Lyndon Baines Johnson Library, National Park Service Files.

LBJ/PA3/Box: Austin, Texas, Lyndon Baines Johnson Library, National Park Service Files.

LBJ/P-M/Box—Folder: Austin, Texas, Lyndon Baines Johnson Library, Parks and Monuments.

LC/HI/Box: Washington, D.C., Library of Congress, Harold Ickes Papers.

LC/JM/Box: Washington, D.C., Library of Congress, John Merriam Papers.

Metcalf/DC/R: Washington, D.C., Sierra Club Office, Senator Lee Metcalf Papers, Redwood Files.

NGS/A/Knopf: Washington, D.C., National Geographic Society, Archives, Alfred Knopf Papers.

NGS/A/NPS: Washington, D.C., National Geographic Society, Archives, National Park Service Papers.

NPS/LD/Rw: Washington, D.C., National Park Service, Legislative Division, Redwood Files.

NRC/I/Carton: Washington, D.C., National Records Center, Department of the Interior Files.

NRC/NPS/Carton: Washington, D.C., National Records Center, National Park Service Files.

SC/DC/R: Washington, D.C., Sierra Club Office, Redwood Files.

SC/MB/Binder: San Francisco, Sierra Club Office, Minute Books.

SC/SF/RNP: San Francisco, Sierra Club Office, Redwood National Park Files.

SC/SF/Swatek: San Francisco, Sierra Club Office, Paul Swatek Papers. Swatek Papers.

SRL/A/Goethe: San Francisco, Save-the-Redwoods League Office, Archives, Charles M. Goethe Papers.

SRL/A/Grant: San Francisco, League Office, Archives, J. D. Grant and Madison Grant Papers.

SRL/A/I-IV: San Francisco, League Office, Archives, Project Files.

SRL/A/McDuffie: San Francisco, League Office, Archives, Duncan McDuffie Papers.

SRL/A/RNP or RNF: San Francisco, League Office, Archives, Redwood National Park or Redwood National Forest Papers.

SRL/A/Sperry: San Francisco, League Office, Archives, James C. Sperry Papers.

SRL/A/SPL: San Francisco, League Office, Archives, State Park Legislative Papers.

SRL/F/History: San Francisco, League Office, Files, History Folders.

SRL/F/Mather: San Francisco, League Office, Files, Stephen Mather Papers.

SRL/F/RNP or RNF: San Francisco, League Office, Files, Redwood National Park or Forest Papers.

UA/SU/Box—Folder: Tucson, University of Arizona, Special Collections, Stewart L. Udall Papers.

Additional Collections

American Forestry Association Papers, Forest History Society, Santa Cruz, California.

California Resources Agency Papers, Office of Administrator, Resources Building, Sacramento.

Ralph Chaney Papers, Bancroft Library, University of California, Berkeley.

Fred Eissler Papers, Santa Barbara, California.

Robert Underwood Johnson Papers, Bancroft Library, University of California, Berkeley.

State Park Council Papers, Bancroft Library, University of California, Berkeley.

Oral Histories

David R. Brower, "Environmental Activist, Publicist, and Prophet," interview conducted by Susan R. Schrepfer (Berkeley: University of California, Regional Oral History Office, 1978) [hereafter office abbreviated ROHO].

Ralph Chaney, "Ralph Works Chaney, Ph.D., Paleobotanist, Conservationist," interview conducted by Edna Daniels (Berkeley: ROHO, 1960).

William Colby, "Reminiscences," interview conducted by Corrine Gilb (Berkeley: ROHO, 1953).

Edward C. Crafts, "Forest Service Researcher and Congressional Liaison," interview conducted by Susan R. Schrepfer (Santa Cruz, California: U.S. Forest Service and Forest History Society, 1972).

Charles Daly (Humboldt County businessman), interview conducted by Susan R. Schrepfer (San Francisco: SRL, 1969).

John B. Dewitt (Save-the-Redwoods League executive director), interview conducted by Susan R. Schrepfer (San Francisco: SRL, 1974).

Newton Drury, "Parks and Redwoods: 1919−1971," interview conducted by Amelia Fry and Susan R. Schrepfer (Berkeley: ROHO, 1972).

Newton Drury, interview conducted by Ann Lage, 7 June 1977, San Francisco. Tape in author's possession.

Francis Farquhar, "Sierra Club Mountaineer and Editor," interview conducted by Ann and Ray Lage (San Francisco: SC, 1974).

Enoch P. French, interview conducted by Susan R. Schrepfer (San Francisco: SRL, 1969).

Tom Grieg, interview conducted by Susan R. Schrepfer (San Francisco: SRL, 1969).

Joel Hildebrand, "Sierra Club Leader and Ski Mountaineer," interview conducted by Ann and Ray Lage (San Francisco: SC, 1974).

Richard Leonard, "Mountaineer, Lawyer, Environmentalist," interview conducted by Susan R. Schrepfer (Berkeley: ROHO, 1975).

Michael McCloskey, interview conducted by Susan R. Schrepfer (Berkeley: ROHO, in process).

Bestor Robinson, "Thoughts on Conservation and the Sierra Club," interview conducted by Susan R. Schrepfer (San Francisco: SC, 1974).

George Waldner (editor, *Ferndale Enterprise*), interview conducted by Susan R. Schrepfer (San Francisco: SRL, 1969).

Edgar Wayburn, interview conducted by Susan R. Schrepfer (Berkeley: ROHO, in process).

Untaped Interviews by Author

Linda Billings (Sierra Club staff), 4 August 1978, Washington, D.C.

Fred Eissler (Sierra Club volunteer leader), 5 April 1972, Santa Barbara, California.

Howard Libbey (president, Arcata Redwood Company), 20 August 1969, San Francisco.

Jay Power (legislative advocate, United Brotherhood of Carpenters and Joiners of America), 18 July 1979, Washington, D.C.

E. Louis Reed (Thomas Kuchel's aide), 12 June 1978, San Francisco.

Maurice Fred Smith (conservation consultant to Laurance Rockefeller), 17 November 1976, New York, N.Y.

INDEX

Abourezk, James, 206, 215, 220, 222, 223, 226

Acadia National Park, 58

Adams, Ansel, 171, 178, 179, 180, 181, 183, 184, 289*n64*

Advisory Board on Educational and Inspirational Use of the National Parks, 41, 43

Advisory Board on National Parks, Historic Sites, Buildings and Monuments, 73. *See also* U. S. National Park Service, advisory boards and committees

AFL-CIO, 220. *See also* CIO

Albright, Horace, 60, 61, 89, 104; league councilor, 73; national park purposes, view of, 53, 54−55, 76; and Redwood National Park, 72, 136, 137, 160; and Sierra Club, 177, 180

American Association for the Advancement of Science, 72, 83, 98, 260*n22*

American Association of Museums, 260*n22*

American Bison Society, 4

American Forestry Association, 69, 71, 72, 73, 131, 136, 143

American Museum of Natural History, 39

American Philosophical Association, 91

American Rivers Conservation Council, 216

American Society of Naturalists, 82

American Society of Zoologists, Symposium on Orthogenesis, 84

Amodio, John, 207, 208

Anderson, Clinton, 156

Anderson, Dewey, 111

Andrus, Cecil, 205, 206, 215

Arcata National Corporation, 154, 158−59, 162, 312*n31*, 313*n77. See also* Arcata Redwood Lumber Company

Arcata Redwood Lumber Company, 108*fig10*, 120, 141, 142, 222, 309*n71*, 319*n21*; logging near Redwood National Park, 186−89 passim, 192, 194, 195, 199, 202, 204, 206, 211, 212, 214; opposes Redwood Creek site, 133, 138, 139, 146, 153−54. *See also* Arcata National Corporation

Aristogenesis. *See* Orthogenesis

Aspinall, Wayne: and Redwood National Park Act (1968), 132, 143−44, 146, 147, 151, 152, 154, 155, 156, 159, 162; and Redwood National Park enlargement, 197; and threats to Redwood National Park, 187

Atwood, Albert W., 68, 70, 71, 88

Atwood, W. W., 55

Au Coin, Les, 317*n109*

Audubon Society, 216, 239

Automobile associations, and park preservation, 12, 30

Automobiles, in parks, 88, 89

Avenue of the Giants, 74, 76, 110, 116, 122, 133, 212

Ayer, Edward E., 4*fig1*, 13, 20, 21, 41

Badé, William F., 48, 86, 87, 102

Balfour, Francis, 4

Bartlett, Dewey, 221, 222

Barzun, Jacques, 173

Bates, Marston, 98, 99, 235

Bayh, Birch, 150

Reid, Ogden, 197
Rensch, Bernhard, 92
Republican party, 73, 75, 146, 173, 219, 222, 240; in California, 20, 30−31, 32. *See also* Ford Administration; Nixon Administration
Resources for the Future, 165−66, 236
Richardson, Elmo, 104
Richardson, Friend, 31
Robinson, Bestor, 90, 105, 126, 171, 177, 178
Robinson, Gordon, 187
Rock Creek Park, 56−57
Rockefeller, John D., Jr., 74, 137, 174
Rockefeller, Laurance, 134, 136−39, 147, 148, 150, 160, 174, 239
Rockefeller Forest, 108−9, 110, 111, 136, 243. *See also* Bull Creek Flat
Rockefellers, The (Horowitz and Collier), 137
Rolph, James, 67
Romanticism, and preservation, 10, 41, 45−48, 50, 171, 231
Roosevelt, Franklin Delano, 62, 71. *See also* New Deal
Roosevelt, Theodore, 10, 12, 15, 28, 229
Runte, Alfred, 170, 229
Rush, J. A., 236
Russell, Bertrand, 85
Ryan, Leo J., 198, 199, 200, 202, 203, 205, 207
Ryan, William, 152, 155

Sacco, Sam, 207
San Mateo County, 7, 195
Santa Clara Valley, 168
Santa Cruz County, 7
Saturday Evening Post, 21, 42, 71, 88
Save-the-Redwoods League: background and motives of councilors, 13−17, 21, 25−28, 175, 184; and California state park system, 28−33, 63−64, 66−67, 243; and federal involvement in redwoods, 18, 20, 21−22, 65, 68−69, 70, 72−75, 111, 116, 211, 212−13, 287n44; funding of, 18−20, 21−22, 23, 74, 76−77, 175; lumber industry, relations with, 23, 24−25, 26, 28−29, 142; memorial grove system, 23, 76; moderate nature of, 23, 24−25, 27−28, 110−11, 216, 230, 232, 237, 239; and New Deal, 65−66, 69−72, 73−75, 77; organiza-

tional structure of 12−13, 20, 22−23, 103−4, 113; Park Service, estrangement from, 56−60, 61−62, 63−64; progressives in, 15−17, 27−28, 74−75; purists' view of parks, 52−64 passim, 76, 89; and Redwood National Park campaign (1961−68), 117, 121−22, 135−36, 137−39, 143, 144, 159; and Redwood National Park enlargement, 200, 204, 211−13, 218, 312*fig43*; and redwood preservation (1920s−1940s), 24−25, 36, 52−53, 62, 77; Sierra Club, relations with, 79, 101−2; and world view of leaders, 43, 48, 86−87, 101−2, 122. *See also* Drury, Newton; Merriam, John; Redwood National Park, conflict over site of
Saylor, John, 155, 156
Scenic Hudson case, 190−91
Scenic preservation. *See* Preservation movement
Schlesinger, Arthur, Jr., 166
Schultze, Charles L., 132
Schurz, Carl, 6
Sears, Paul, 98, 127
Sebelius, K. G., 207
Sempervirens Club, 11, 30, 51, 239
Sequoiadendron gigantea (Big Tree), 7
Sequoia National Park, 147
Sequoia sempervirens. See Redwoods
Sequoia Sonnets (Charles Keeler), 51
Shenandoah National Park, 58, 59
Sherwin, Raymond, 183
Sherwood, Michael, 203
Sierra Club, 71, 73, 75, 78, 82, 105, 111, 117, 195, 314n66; advertising program, 134, 148, 163−64, 176, 178−79, 181, 182; change and expansion, 143, 144, 163−64, 168, 184−85, 230−32, 300n2; and cultural and social milieu of 1960s, 163, 165−69, 173−74; founding and early history of, 10−11, 88, 89−90; internal schism (1960s), 106−7, 122, 177−84; and labor unions, 216, 228; litigation, 190−94, 197; membership characteristics, 10, 163−65, 171, 172−73, 216, 231, 232, 235, 300n2; militancy of, 143, 144, 163, 165−66, 170−73, 175−76, 180, 184−85, 236, 237, 240; organizational structure of, 103, 107, 124, 177−78; park philosophy of, 54, 56, 61−62, 88, 125; publications

148, 296*n9*. *See also* United States Office of Management and Budget
—Bureau of Outdoor Recreation, 188
—Bureau of the Public Roads, 147
—Bureau of Reclamation, 100, 104, 105
—Coast and Geodetic Survey, 10
—Congress: House Appropriations Committee, 219; House Conservation, Energy, and Natural Resources Subcommittee, 198—200; House Interior and Insular Affairs Committee, 132, 143—44, 151—52, 154—56, 158, 197—98, 203, 219; House National Parks and Insular Affairs Subcommittee, 197, 203, 205, 206; legislative intent, Redwood National Park Act, 187; Senate Energy and Resources Committee, 220; Senate Interior and Insular Affairs Committee, 140, 143, 144, 148, 215. *See also* Redwood National Park, legislative history of; Redwood National Park enlargement, legislative history of
—Council on Environmental Quality, 205
—Court of Claims, 159, 193, 218, 219, 224, 226, 319*n21*
—Department of Agriculture, 10, 147, 150, 171, 191. *See also* United States Forest Service
—Department of Commerce, 119
—Department of Defense, 147
—Department of the Interior, 10, 11, 77, 105, 118, 131, 147, 150, 171, 187, 206; office of the secretary, 144, 188, 194; and protection of Redwood National Park, 189, 190, 192, 193—95, 196—97, 211. *See also* Andrus, Cecil; Udall, Stewart L.; United States National Park Service
—Department of Justice, 194, 202
—Department of Transportation, 191
—Division of Forestry, 9
—Federal Power Commission, 191
—Federal Trade Commission, 153
—Forest Service, 5, 10, 11, 153, 171, 221; and clearcutting, 198, 201; and Park Service, rivalry with, 61—62; and preservationists, 60—63, 105—7, 177; and redwood national forest purchase units, 53, 62—64, 76—77, 147—48, 149—50, 152, 158
—Geological Survey, 10
—Internal Revenue Service, 179

—National Park Service, 11, 16, 59—60, 69, 116, 171, 217, 268*n53*; advisory boards and committees, 41, 43, 54, 73, 136; Coastal Redwood Survey, 117; Forest Service, rivalry with, 60—61; interpretive programs, 41—42, 55—56; preservationists, relations with, 69—70; promotes park development, 53, 54—56, 57, 89; and Redwood National Park, damage to, 187—90, 193, 195, 196, 202—3; Redwood National Park enlargement proposal, 205; redwood national park proposals (1960s), 117—21, 130, 132—33, 135, 137, 143, 146, 148; redwood park proposed (1938), 52, 72
—Office of Management and Budget, 189, 194, 195, 197, 205, 227. *See also* United States Bureau of the Budget
—States Emergency Relief Administration, 69
—Supreme Court, 19, 192—93
University of California, 5, 10, 11, 12, 14, 23, 26, 30, 43, 55, 68, 81, 83, 174, 175, 187
University of Michigan, 82
University of Munich, 5
Upper Colorado River Project, 104
Urbanization, and preservation movement, 16—17
Usinger, Robert, 97

Varian, Dorothy, 179
Veblen, Thorstein, 48, 50, 85, 87
Verkler, Jerry, 144
Vietnam War, 135, 147, 151, 161, 165—66, 231

Wall Street Journal, 151
Walsh, William, 206
Walt Disney, Inc., 191
Warren, Earl, 111
Washington Post, 143
Wawona, Mēca, 217—18
Wayburn, Edgar: efforts to protect Redwood National Park, 187, 189, 198—99; and freeways in redwoods, 119; and Redwood National Park campaign (1960s), 111, 117, 118, 122, 128, 132, 133, 134, 139, 142—55 passim, 160; and Redwood National Park enlargement, 197, 200, 205; as Sierra Club leader, 107, 163, 164*fig19*, 178, 180, 181, 183, 184

JACKET DESIGNED BY CAROLINE BECKETT
COMPOSED BY FIVE STAR PHOTO TYPESETTING, INC., NEENAH, WISCONSIN
MANUFACTURED BY THOMSON-SHORE, INC., DEXTER, MICHIGAN
TEXT AND DISPLAY LINES IN TIMES ROMAN

Library of Congress Cataloging in Publication Data
Schrepfer, Susan R.
The fight to save the redwoods.
Bibliography: pp. 321—324.
Includes index.
1. Redwood—History. 2. Forest conservation—California,
Northern—History. I. Title.
SD397.R3S37 1983   333.7′4   81-69828
ISBN 0-299-08850-2